Writing Travel
Series Editor, Jeanne Moskal

Writing Travel
Series Editor, Jeanne Moskal

The series publishes manuscripts related to the new field of travel studies, including works of original travel writing; editions of out-of-print travel books or previously unpublished travel memoirs; English translations of important travel books in other languages; theoretical and historical treatments of ways in which travel and travel writing engage such questions as religion, nationalism/cosmopolitanism, and empire; gender and sexuality; race, ethnicity, and immigration; the history of the book, print culture, and translation; biographies of significant travelers or groups of travelers (including but not limited to pilgrims, missionaries, anthropologists, tourists, explorers, immigrants); critical studies of the works of significant travelers or groups of travelers; and pedagogy of travel and travel literature and its place in curricula.

Other Books in the Series

Nellie Arnott's Writings on Angola, 1905-1913: Missionary Narratives Linking Africa and America, ed. Sarah Robbins and Ann Ellis Pullen (2010)
Au Japon: The Memoirs of a Foreign Correspondent in Japan, Korea, and China, 1892–1894, Amédée Baillot de Guerville, ed. by Daniel C. Kane (2009)
Sarah Heckford: A Lady Trader in the Transvaal, ed. by Carole G. Silver (2008)
Vienna Voices: A Traveler Listens to the City of Dreams, Jill Knight Weinberger (2006)
Eating Europe: A Meta-Nonfiction Love Story, Jon Volkmer (2006)

Maria Graham's Journal of a Voyage to Brazil

Jennifer Hayward and M. Soledad Caballero

Parlor Press
Anderson, South Carolina
www.parlorpress.com

Parlor Press LLC, Anderson, South Carolina, USA

© 2010 by Parlor Press
All rights reserved.
Printed in the United States of America

SAN: 254-8879

Library of Congress Cataloging-in-Publication Data

Callcott, Maria, Lady, 1785-1842.
  [Journal of a voyage to Brazil]
  Maria Graham's Journal of a voyage to Brazil / [edited by] Jennifer
    Hayward and M. Soledad Caballero.
      p. cm. -- (Writing travel)
  Scholarly edition.
  Includes bibliographical references and index.
  ISBN 978-1-60235-187-5 (pbk. : alk. paper) -- ISBN 978-1-60235-188-2
    (hardcover : alk. paper) -- ISBN 978-1-60235-189-9 (Adobe ebook)
  1. Brazil--Description and travel. 2. Brazil--Social life and customs--
    19th century. 3. Callcott, Maria, Lady, 1785-1842--Travel--Brazil.
    4. Graham, Maria--Diaries. 5. Women travelers--Brazil--Diaries. 6.
    British--Brazil--Diaries. I. Hayward, Jennifer, 1961- II. Caballero, M.
    Soledad, 1973- III. Title.
  F2513.C14 2010
  981'.04--dc22
                            2010030681

Cover design by David Blakesley.
Cover illustration: "Val Longo, or the Slave Market at Rio." Courtesy of the Catholic University of America, Oliveira Lima Library, Washington, D.C.

Printed on acid-free paper.

Parlor Press, LLC is an independent publisher of scholarly and trade titles in print and multimedia formats. This book is available in paper, cloth and Adobe eBook formats from Parlor Press on the World Wide Web at http://www.parlorpress.com or through online and brick-and-mortar bookstores. For submission information or to find out about Parlor Press publications, write to Parlor Press, 3015 Brackenberry Drive, Anderson, South Carolina, 29621, or e-mail editor@parlorpress.com.

Contents

Introduction *ix*
Editorial Method *lix*
Acknowledgments *lxiii*

Journal of a Voyage to Brazil *3*

Appendix I: Maps of Brazil, 1818 and 1819 *253*
Appendix II: Sketch of the History of Brazil *255*
Appendix III: The Quarterly Review *321*
Appendix IV: Maria Graham's Unpublished
   "Life of Don Pedro" *334*
Selected Bibliography *347*
Index *353*
About the Authors *359*

Illustrations

Frontispiece. Lady Maria Callcott by A. W. Callcott.   viii
Figure 1. Two young Dragon Trees.   11
Figure 2. The Green Dragon Tree of Oratava.   21
Figure 3. Part of Pernambuco, seen from Coco-nut Island, with the Reef.   33
Figure 4. View of Count Maurice's Gate at Pernambuco, with the Slave Market.   43
Figure 5. Slaves Dragging a Hogshead in the Streets of Pernambuco.   68
Figure 6. Cadeira, or Sedan Chair of Bahia.   70
Figure 7. Gamella Tree at Bahia.   74
Figure 8. Church and Convent of Sant Antonio da Barre at Bahia.   94
Figure 9. The Sugar-loaf Rock, at the Entrance to the Harbour of Rio de Janeiro.   95
Figure 10. Larangeiras.   99
Figure 11. View of Rio from the Gloria Hill.   105
Figure 12. View from Count Hoggendorp's Cottage.   107
Figure 13. The End of an Island in the Harbour of Rio de Janeiro.   135
Figure 14. Convicts carrying Water at Rio de Janeiro.   150
Figure 15. Corcovada, from Botafogo.   151
Figure 16. Palace of San Cristovaŏ.   179
Figure 17. Dona Maria de Jesus.   220
Figure 18. English Burial Ground.   237
Figure 19. Stone Cart at Rio de Janeiro.   249

Lady Maria Callcott by A. W. Callcott. Courtesy of the Government Art Collection, London, U.K.

Introduction

Jennifer Hayward and M. Soledad Caballero

EXILED FROM THE PALACE

On October 9, 1824, alone in her suite of rooms in the Imperial Palace of Brazil, the travel writer Maria Graham packed her things. Her maids, quick to notice that the fortunes of this woman they had dubbed "the second stranger" were in rapid decline, had already deserted her. That afternoon, Emperor Dom Pedro I had ordered her confined to her rooms until further notice, except when "called down to give the little Princesses an English lesson." As governess to the five-year-old Dona Maria da Gloria (the future Queen of Portugal) and her younger sisters, Graham considered herself far more than a language teacher: in her own mind at least, she was responsible for the princesses' moral as well as intellectual development. After writing the Emperor that "I should never have quitted England nor a family which is honorable even in that distinguished Country to be a mere Teacher of the English Tongue," she prepared to leave the palace.[1]

The Empress Maria Leopoldina, considered the "first stranger" in the court and Maria Graham's sole ally, heard the news and rushed to help her friend. In tears and ignoring Graham's half-horrified, half-admiring objections, "empress of Brazil and Archduchess of Austria as she was, nothing could prevent her from using her small white hands in packing books and clothes in short whatever she could find" ("Life"

---

1. Information on Graham's time in the Imperial Palace comes from Maria Graham's unpublished "Life of Don Pedro," 1835, held by the Biblioteca Nacional in Rio de Janeiro with facsimiles in the British and Bodleian Libraries (hereafter "Life"). This passage comes from a letter to Dom Pedro, which is transcribed in "Life" chapter 3 (since the manuscript does not provide reliable page numbers, none will be used here).

ch. 3). Two privileged European women, unused to servants' tasks, jumbled Maria's things into her trunks. But the Empress could not stay long; she dared not disturb the Emperor's routine. Maria finished her preparations alone, shared a scanty supper with one of Maria Leopoldina's wardrobe women (the Empress had warned Graham not to touch food given her by the servants, due to an apparently justified fear of poison), and prepared to set out into Rio de Janeiro. She had nowhere to live, and few friends, since she had recently offended most of the English community by slighting them as "incurious moneymakers" in her newly published *Journal of a Voyage to Brazil*.

Just a year earlier, Maria Graham's prospects looked much brighter, largely as a result of her own indomitable spirit. When her husband died off the coast of Chile, she defied the English community's advice and expectations by remaining, alone and unprotected, in South America. She explored its flora, fauna, and culture, contributing to and correcting existing representations of the New World by Europeans. In the wake of Alexander von Humboldt's accounts of South America beginning in 1805,[2] the continent acquired a powerful role in the European imaginary: it was constructed as a tropical sublime, teeming with raw materials ripe for European exploration and exploitation. Although shaped by this trope of the "new continent" in the European imagination, Graham also countered it, emphasizing the New World instead as a place of culture, communities, and commerce rather than highlighting only its natural wonders and landscape aesthetics. Graham made friends among Chileans and traveled through the country as much as her always precarious health permitted. But after nine months, having survived a difficult few weeks in a country rocked not only by a major earthquake but also by the threat of civil war, she fled for the comparative stability of Brazil. In Rio de Janeiro, she found herself unexpectedly honored by a prestigious offer: the Empress Maria Leopoldina asked her to accept the position of governess to their eldest child, Princess Maria da Gloria, then just four years old.

---

2. Humboldt's publication history is complex, reflecting both the cost and the lack of copyright protection in the publishing industry of the early nineteenth century; briefly, he published some 30 volumes of his travels in Paris from 1805 to 1834, but other versions appeared in German and English in the early years of the century, including an English translation, *Personal narrative of travels to the equinoctial regions of America, during the years 1799-1804*, issued by Graham's first publishers Longman, Hurst, Rees et al. in 1807.

Maria Graham, always conscious of status, accepted eagerly. Besides the obvious cachet of living in the Palace, she was not immune to England's imperial ambitions—in fact, perhaps she was all the more anxious to further those ambitions because as a Scotswoman she had never felt entirely "at home" amongst the English. She dreamed of the moral and even political influence she might wield over the developing country: "I confess that I was carried away by the notion of bringing up a person upon whose education and personal qualities the happiness of a whole Empire was to depend. I fancied what Brazil might be under a better government than any country but my own had ever enjoyed" ("Life" ch. 3).

And then suddenly, not even two months into her new position, Maria found herself ignominiously ejected from the Palace and separated from the two Marias, mother and daughter, whom she had already come to love. Despite the threat of a downpour, Palace courtiers conspired to ensure that no carriage was available to carry her trunks to her hastily arranged lodgings. The Empress had to intervene—ordering her own carriage—to spare the tubercular Graham the disgrace and danger of a long walk in the heavy rain. So her departure was as uncomfortable and undignified as hostile servants could make it. Not even the affectionate messages and packages sent by the Empress in the days after her exile could console her for the humiliation. After her return to England, Maria Graham never set foot in South America again.

What could have happened in such a short time to bring about so much mistrust and misunderstanding? The story of Maria Graham, first governess to the first Imperial family in Brazil, is both individual and archetypical, radical and representative. As an early woman traveler who scripted plots for future women to follow, reshaping the few narratives already available for the solitary British woman abroad, Maria Graham's story connected continents as she explored the limitations shaping early nineteenth century women's lives. As a Scotswoman whose own narrative became intimately entwined—in ways whose Gothic twists ultimately proved her undoing—with the domestic life of the first royal family of an independent Brazil, she exposed the complex interactions of class, race, ethnicity, and national and cultural affiliations as they shaped international relations in the imperial age.

Mary Dundas to Maria Graham: Dislocations of Identity

Maria Graham was born plain Mary Dundas near Liverpool on July 19, 1785, the daughter of George Dundas, a Scottish naval officer, and his wife Ann Thompson Dundas, an American emigrée. Her family embodied the complexities resulting from shifting constructions of national identity: both her parents crossed the Atlantic and spent considerable portions of their lives far from "home" (which, for Graham's Anglo-American mother at least, was always already a displacement from her "origins," her birthplace in England), and their lives reveal an uncomfortable familiarity with the dislocations and disturbances of the migratory class. Their daughter would continue their perambulations when, as an adult, she refashioned herself into the travel writer Maria Graham and journeyed to India, Europe and South America, writing well-received narratives about each location.

In 1793, eight-year-old Mary was sent south to a small town near Oxford, apparently due to her mother's rapidly declining health; her father arrived home from one of his frequent long absences on naval business, and announced the plan to his wife. In her descendent Rosamond Brunel Gotch's invaluable biography, which makes excellent use of family papers, an autobiographical fragment left by Graham vividly captures the child's half-baffled perception of events:

> I saw that my mother had been weeping. She took me upon her lap and said several times to my father—"I cannot, indeed I cannot bear it" [. . .] Two or three days after, I saw the tall horse, Bob [. . .] and the pony also saddled, brought to the door. I thought my mother was going to ride, but I soon found that the pony was for me, and that I was going to Liverpool, but I wondered why my mother should weep so bitterly as she did. (Gotch 14)

Her father carried little Mary off to Richmond, where she met her uncle, aunt and cousins, who pronounced her clothes "unfit to wear, and I was hurried off to a warehouse, where [. . .] I was completely metamorphosed [. . .] This was my first, but by no means my last suffering in the cause of fashion, and created in me such a dislike of dress and finery as required years to overcome" (Gotch 17). In her alien costume, the child was packed off to school. She never saw her mother again.

In 1804, eighteen years old and now known more elegantly as Maria Dundas, she accompanied her father (whom she had not seen since he left her at school) to Edinburgh to meet her extended family. In Scotland, she felt surrounded by her own kind for the first time since early childhood: whereas in England her schoolmates and her aunt and uncle in Richmond made her feel that "it was a pity I was not a boy, for then my talents might be of some use, but no good ever came to learned ladies, that they were in general extremely conceited and unfit for anything useful," in Scotland she became part of an active intellectual community (Gotch 33). Nobody seemed surprised that she enjoyed reading, discussing ideas, and debating the nature of truth; in her uncle's house she met leading intellectuals of the day, including Edinburgh University's Dugald Stewart, John Playfair, Sir John Leslie, and Dr. Thomas Hope (Gotch 75).

During her first year in Scotland she enjoyed an active social life, discussing moral philosophy in ballrooms and finding herself amusingly accused of wielding her learning to flirt with eligible young academics (Gotch 83). She must have discussed, among many other ideas, those of Adam Smith in *The Wealth of Nations* (1776) which circulated widely at the time and proved influential not only in disseminating the doctrine of free trade, but in abolitionist critiques of slavery.[3] During the following winter, confined to bed by her first attack of tuberculosis, she read widely: history, literature, philosophy. The following autumn, she was sent south again, to Richmond, for the sake of her health, but she never forgot her first taste of life among people as passionate about books and learning as she was herself.

Graham began her travels at age 23 in 1809, when she sailed with her father and older sister for Bombay, where her father had been appointed head of the naval works at the British East India Company's dockyard. En route she studied the literature, history, and languages of her destination with Lieutenant Thomas Graham, a young Scottish naval officer and third son of Robert Graham, laird of Fintry. She and Thomas married on Dec. 9, 1809, shortly after their arrival in Bom-

---

3. Graham's later writings energetically engage both topics, and her ideas are based on Smith's; for example, in discussing the importance of free trade in the face of Brazilian and Chilean protectionism, she emphasizes the advantage not only to Britain—whose merchants obviously lobbied heavily to reduce the import taxes in South America—but also to Chileans, who could develop their own economies while enjoying greater luxuries than they were yet able to manufacture for themselves.

bay; he soon had to leave her, first to join his ship, H.M.S. *Russell*, in Madras, and then in 1810 to command H.M.S. *Hecate* and later the *Eclipse*. Meanwhile she explored the country, keeping careful notes with an eye to future publication.

On returning to England in 1811, she became involved in literary work for the well-known publisher John Murray II. She also published her first book, *Journal of a Residence in India* (1812); it was well enough received to warrant a second edition, although the *Quarterly Review* commented condescendingly in an otherwise positive review that "'The Journal of a Residence in India,' by a young lady who probably went thither, like most young ladies, to procure a husband instead of information, is a literary curiosity which we are not disposed to overlook."[4]

In the wake of the Napoleonic wars, a long peace led to near-desperation among the British naval officers lingering in port towns on half-pay, trying to make ends meet while hoping that family connections could produce a commission. Graham maintained her contact with distant intellectual and social communities via long letters. She wrote publisher John Murray to discuss editing work, books, and authors of the day, especially George Gordon, Lord Byron, one of Murray's authors (when writing about Byron, Graham gushed in a way wholly uncharacteristic of her). She wrote her husband's influential kinsman Lord Lynedoch, who was able to help both Graham's brother and her husband to advance their careers. In 1812, for instance, she thanked Lynedoch for helping Thomas to obtain the post of Captain to the ship *Laurentians*; in 1813 she wrote, like a dutiful niece, to seek his approbation of her plan to join her husband in Halifax, where he had been posted:

> My intention of going to Halifax will not surprise you I am sure, and I hope you will not disapprove of it for I am very jealous of your approbation. I would not go out *with* my husband nor would I cruize with him because when a man is on public duty I think the less he is led to consider his private and domestic ties the better, but as he is likely to be some years on the American station whether peace or war and as I have no tie

---

4. "Journal of a Residence in India, by Maria Graham." *Quarterly Review* 8:16 (Dec. 1812), 406-421; 406. Graham, rightly annoyed by the dismissive comment, refuted it in a footnote to her second edition.

to this country in his absence I feel it almost as much a duty as a pleasure to be the nearest to him that I can. And then—I have so long led a wandering life that the very circumstance of change is become agreeable to me especially as I feel no inconvenience from any kind of lodging or food.[5]

But she never did follow Thomas to Nova Scotia. His ship was wrecked and Thomas returned home; by 1815 they had moved to Broughty Ferry, Scotland, apparently for economy's sake.

In letters to John Murray, she complained of isolation. Although she could see the College of St Andrews from her windows, she felt distanced from "the nearest court of *Modern* Literature." Always passionately interested in politics, too, Graham went on to lament her lack of information about revolutionary events of the day; she told Murray that "while you are listening to tales from Paris of oppressed people and King and spoiled galleries and humbled conquerors and imprisoned Emperors," in Broughty Ferry "a weekly paper at most connects us with the news of the Southern world" while local discussions "[carry] one back only to times of violence and civil war and make one expect to hear more particulars of Huntley's conspiracy, or of Mary's [Queen of Scots] weakness and Knox's hard justice." "But," she concluded on a more optimistic note:

> We have books and a garden and like all poor people plenty of occupation for our hands and even heads that we may live and not lose caste, which in this *poor proud* country where Montrose and Dundee are still in the mouths of the very people, is even more difficult than in most parts of the southern portion of the Island.—Our establishment here consists of our two selves, a sister of Graham's, two women, two dogs—, and some poultry—and our cottage is large enough to entertain a friend so that in spite of peace—and half pay we are far better off than most of our brother officers.[6]

---

5. Maria Graham, letter to Lord Lynedoch, 1813. Lynedoch papers, National Library of Scotland.

6. Maria Graham, letter to John Murray, 9 Dec. 1815. John Murray Archive, National Library of Scotland.

By 1819, Graham was out in the world again, traveling to Gibraltar, Malta, Naples, and Rome with her husband and their artist friend Charles Eastlake. While scanty evidence leaves us to guess at the purpose of this trip—perhaps Captain Graham was posted to the Mediterranean?—it resulted in Graham's *Three Months passed in the Mountains East of Rome, during the year 1819*, published in London in 1820.

In 1821, Graham's letters and other records tell us that her husband at last received command of a ship, the H.M.S. *Doris*, with orders to sail for South America to protect British interests along the coast; Graham accompanied him. She remained in Chile (much to the chagrin of the Anglo colony, which attempted to ship her back to England immediately) even after her husband died en route in 1823.

Having been offered the post of governess to the eldest child of the Emperor and Empress of Brazil in October 1823, she briefly returned to England to see her two Journals on Chile and Brazil into print and to gather teaching materials for young Maria. Remaining in England only seven months, she sailed back to Brazil in July of 1824 to take up her new post—but as we already know, she would be forced to leave the Palace just over a month later and under mysterious circumstances.[7]

By 1826, back in London, Graham continued with her literary work, compiling others' notes and journals into *Voyage of H.M.S. Blonde to the Sandwich Islands in the years 1824–1825 under Captain the Right Hon. Lord Byron, commander.* In 1827, she married Augustus Wall Callcott, who was knighted in 1837, giving her—always so conscious of rank and precedence—her own title at last: Lady Callcott. In 1831, her longstanding tuberculosis resurfaced. After breaking a

---

7. Her *Journal of a Voyage to Brazil, and Residence There* and *Journal of a Residence in Chile* (both 1824) provide among the few firsthand accounts of the independence movements in South America. Graham lived in Chile and Brazil at key historical moments and met major political figures; in Brazil she was in time to "witness the entrance of the first Brazilian guard into the Palace, while the last Portuguese guard marched out amid wild huzzas from the onlookers", while she depicts Chile in such accurate detail that Chileans consider hers one of the best early accounts of their country. Both narratives have remained in print, in good translations, in South America; historian José Miguel Barros Franco and Neville Blanc Renard have just issued a complete new translation of Graham's *Diario de una residencia en Chile* (Santiago: Larrain Vial).

In the first years of the century, the first large-scale history of Brazil was written by the Romantic poet Robert Southey, who blithely ignored the minor inconvenience of never having set foot in the country. In 1806, after a decade's research and two short visits to Portugal, he modestly announced, "On Portugal I am probably better informed than any other foreigner, and as well informed as any Portuguese" (qtd. in Bethel, "British" 6). After Independence, British mercenaries' involvement in South American naval campaigns as well as an influx of British merchants and explorers meant that British influence continued to expand.[9] In his lists of British writing about Brazil, historian Leslie Bethel includes "mineralogists, merchants, naval officers (and their wives), diplomats (and their secretaries), naturalists, clergymen and missionaries, doctors, newspaper owners and journalists, employees of railway and navigation companies, civil engineers, travellers and writers" ("British" 8; note that Maria Graham, although she is probably the best-known and most enduring of this wave of writers, is here marked off in the parenthesis reserved for "wives"). By the time Graham set foot in Brazil, British trade was well established and travelers frequented South America, publishing their experiences with the explicit goal of increasing opportunities for British abroad—and, often enough, the implicit imperialist goal of disseminating British values and political systems.

In her South American journals, Graham plotted the course of her almost three years' exploration along the edges of the continent. She accompanied her husband Thomas Graham on his assignment to take

1748), which recounts George Anson's explorations; and Commodore John Byron's *A voyage round the world in H.M.S. Dolphin* (London 1767). Captain James Cook visited Brazil in 1768, bringing with him a botanist and two artists; after the voyage, one of these, Sydney Parkinson, published a travel narrative including scientific drawings. The first woman to write about Brazil was Jemima Kindersley, who stopped in the country en route to India and published *Letters from the island of Teneriffe, Brazil, the Cape of Good Hope, and the East Indies* (London 1777) simultaneously in German and English.

9. Unlike other parts of South America, however, Chile and Argentina perhaps most notably, Neill Macaulay argues that "Brazil never became part of a British 'informal empire'. The British barred Brazilian sugar from their market, bought most of their cotton from the United States (after 1815), and drank precious little coffee" (xii). Nevertheless, the British who did establish roots in the country developed cultural institutions to support a thriving colony that managed to preserve British values while flooding the market with British manufactured goods.

the ship *Doris* to safeguard British interests along the South American coast during the turbulent years of independence. After three months in Brazil, the Grahams headed for their next posting, Chile. But Thomas Graham was already weakened by a succession of fevers and battles with gout. As they rounded Cape Horn in frigid weather, he died.

Despite offers of passage home, Graham refused to be packed onto the next ship back to England. Instead, after burying her husband, she rented herself a small house in the Chilean—not the English—part of Valparaíso, bought "my roan horse Fritz," and proceeded to ride around the country, meeting prominent Chilean families and becoming embroiled in the wars of independence. Staying with Admiral Cochrane, commander of the Chilean navy, in December 1822, she survived a massive earthquake. With "earthquake under me, civil war around me; my poor sick relation apparently dying; and my kind friend, my only friend here indeed, certainly going to leave the country," it seemed high time she follow suit, so when Cochrane offered her passage to Brazil—where he was heading to accept the position of commander of the Brazilian navy, since he seemed to have overstayed his welcome in Chile—she accepted gratefully.[10]

Her Brazil journal, then, encompasses the first three and last seven months of her time in South America. The intervening 11 months are covered in her Chile journal. In the latter, she created herself as a

---

10. Thomas Cochrane, tenth Earl of Dundonald (1775-1860), eldest son of an old but impoverished Scottish family; his heritage helps to explain Graham's admiration of him. Cochrane was elected to Parliament in 1806-07 but forced to resign following a scandal involving stock exchange fraud. In 1818, he fled Britain for South America, where he led the Chilean Navy in its war of independence from Spain; when relations with Chile's government turned sour, he became commander of the Brazilian Navy. Cochrane authored a series of apologies for his career as a mercenary: *Autobiography of a Seaman*, 2 vol. (1860–61) and *Narrative of Services in the Liberation of Chili, Peru and Brazil*, 2 vol. (1859). From all accounts, including his own, it is clear that Cochrane could be difficult. The CHLA describes him bluntly: "Arrogant, ill-tempered, cantankerous, bellicose, Cochrane was one of the most daring and successful frontline frigate captains of his day. He had been struck off the Navy List following a Stock Exchange scandal in 1814, but a few years later began a new career as a mercenary, selling his services to the highest bidder—although usually, it is true, on the side of liberty and national independence" (189). Graham, by contrast, describes him as heroic, charming, and misunderstood.

Gothic heroine and plotted her narrative along a typically Gothic arc: beginning with her initial abandonment in the country, she traced her gradually increasing independence and paralleled her own story with a gradual transformation of Lord Cochrane into a Romantic hero. By contrast, during her interrupted and often difficult months in Brazil, she found no ready-made novelistic plot to shape her experiences.

In the first half of her journal, Graham describes her first experience of South America. As a result, she emphasizes its difference from Europe, its landscape, and her superficial impressions of its people. The second half of the journal provides more authoritative perspectives on these issues, but because she first landed in the country in 1821, Graham is able to offer remarkable insight into the political developments and social transformations leading up to Independence, as we will see shortly. In these early years too, Graham is the only female traveler to have published an account of her experiences in Brazil, so she provides a unique glimpse of domestic lives.[11] By contrast with male writers, Graham offers the advantage of a gendered insider's perspective: men struggled to obtain entry into domestic spaces since custom isolated women from strangers—a custom male travelers despairingly dubbed "Moorish."

Thus Graham's precursor John Mawe (1812) and her contemporary Gilbert Mathison (1825) were rarely permitted to so much as see—much less converse with—middle- or upper-class women in houses they stayed in while travelling in the interior of Brazil; Mawe tells us for example that "The few females we occasionally saw at any formal place generally secluded themselves on our arrival and during our stay; and, when they came near us by chance, they commonly ran away in as much apparent alarm as if they had been accustomed to be frightened at the name of an Englishman" (153). Another contemporary, Alexander Caldcleugh (1825), complained in a similar vein that Brazilian society remained so closed to him that he rarely succeeded in so much as setting eyes on a woman of the middle or upper classes; ultimately he consoles himself, rather improbably, with the theory that Portuguese living in Brazil chose not to socialize due to reluctance to

---

11. Not until Ida Pfeiffer published her *Eine Frau fährt um die Welt* (Vienna, 1850), over two decades after Graham, did another woman provide her perspective on Brazil. Jemima Kindersley did focus on the colony of Brazil in a short section of her travels, which were published simultaneously in German and English in 1777, but she describes a very different country: the colony as it was before independence.

furnish their houses. John Luccock (1820) had better luck, probably because the presence of his wife and family gave him greater informal access to domestic spaces, but his perspective on the everyday life of a Brazilian household nevertheless remained oddly limited. His greatest insights involve such matters as the "corpulence" of women, which he attributes to the fact that "they were seldom seen out of doors, except when going to mass." One of his few vignettes of domestic life describes a woman surrounded by slaves as too lazy even to reach for a glass of water, instead demanding that a slave place the glass in her hand (112, 113).

Only Henry Koster (1816) approaches Graham's depth and complexity in his representation of everyday life in Brazil, probably because (as we will see shortly) his long knowledge of Portuguese language and culture and his personal introductions to Brazilians permitted him increased access and insight. Like Graham's, Koster's account is highly respected by Brazilians today for his detailed portrayal of their country in its first years. Although of an English family, he was born in Portugal (where his father's sugar firm had a branch) and he grew up with, as he expresses it, "the idiom of a foreign language [. . .] perhaps more familiar to me than that of my own" (v). Yet despite his intimacy with Brazilian culture, as a male traveler descriptions of the domestic were not part of his expected repertoire; therefore his account does not convey the level of detail that we find in Graham's journal.

Graham's first impression of Brazilian women comes one October morning in Bahia, just two days after anchoring off the city and a month after arriving in Brazil, when Miss Pennell (an English friend and the daughter of the British consul in Bahia, William Pennell) takes her on a round of visits to Brazilian ladies. The morning call was an established tradition in nineteenth century England, but Graham acknowledges, "as it is not their [Brazilians'] custom to visit or be visited in the forenoon it was hardly fair to take a stranger to see them. However, my curiosity, at least, was gratified." Her "curiosity" seems to mean desire to observe Brazilians in their "natural habitat," subject to an anthropological gaze that scarcely acknowledges the humanity of her objects of study. She expresses disgust at the disarray of their houses, lambasts their clothing, bodies, and hygiene, casts aspersions on their class status—and feels no apparent hesitation at the thought that these people might someday read her account of them.

In this early stage of her time in South America, Graham reacts in a typically colonial way to the unfamiliar mores she observes. While conscious that British clothing and habits may not be suitable in this very different climate and culture, she nonetheless clings to the notion that British styles are more "civilized" than lighter, looser dress. Louise Guenther develops an astute comparative reading of the British colony in early nineteenth century Brazil: as colonists struggled to maintain a clearly British identity predicated on difference from Brazilians, clothing became part of the signifying system distinguishing Self from Other. The British insisted on a visual contrast with their hosts, even when doing so required physical discomfort. In the orders they sent home, British merchants reflected their understanding that the clothing needed in Brazil was quite different from that appropriate for Britain; black cloth, for example, was "absurd" in a hot climate, so John Luccock "rejected several bales of fabric for being 'too gloomy for people who laugh at themselves. Let us have no drabs—we have no Quakers here. We want no dismal colours suitable for an English November [. . .] We live in a lively climate, and with people who love to laugh'" (qtd. in Guenther 18). Even while acknowledging its incongruity, however, British residents insisted upon good thick dark British wool for their own clothes. So Graham's disgust at women who wore cool, loose-fitting clothing suitable to the climate reveals the process of colonial identity-formation.

Between Graham's first and second visits to Brazil, her personal circumstances changed drastically. Oddly, this bipolar narrative structure allows a greater breadth than might otherwise be possible: Graham emphasizes the struggle for independence, contrasts with European "civilization," and ethnographic portraits of Brazilians in the first half of the narrative, and she provides a more informed exploration of domestic life and personal engagement with Brazilians in the second.

After spending nine months in Chile learning about its history and participating—to the extent a woman was able—in its Independence efforts, Graham returned to Brazil en route to England. When she landed again in Rio de Janeiro, on March 13th, 1823, Graham was newly widowed and ill with tuberculosis: altered, then, in both body and spirit. Since her husband died en route to Chile, too, she was no longer associated with the British navy and thus no longer restricted by the navy's profession of neutrality—a constraint that had clearly irked her in the first half of the journal. As a result, during the second half of the journal, Graham is able to go anywhere and socialize with whom she pleases; she seems liberated to observe the country in a more immediate and direct way.

Having now passed a year and a half in South America, Graham understood its customs and culture more fully. Moreover, without the buffer of the British naval community, her self-consciously English identity was less strongly reinforced. Perhaps as a result, while Graham's persona resembles the intrepid adventurer in the first half of her Brazil journal and a Gothic heroine in need of rescue in her Chile journal, in the second half of the Brazil journal she assumes the narrative persona that German critic Marie-Claire Hoock-Demarle has described as the "exploratrice sociale" (summarized in Pratt 160). Making a point of visiting cultural institutions including the public monuments, House of Assembly, museum, library, theatre, botanical gardens, arsenal, orphan asylum, and hospital, she also finds time to attend balls and visit country houses as well as an *enghenho* or sugar mill, where she observes the process of sugar cane production as carried out by slaves. Throughout her visits, she finds much to admire in Brazil, and she provides commentary on the country's political, cultural, and moral future. She understands clearly that she witnesses times of enormous historical importance; therefore, during her second visit she immerses herself in Brazilian history in the newly created national library, so that her narrative can more accurately convey the political changes she describes.

By the end of April she has been befriended by Dona Ana, wife of Luis José de Carvalho e Melo. Her relationship with Dona Ana and her family marks a turning point in Graham's narrative: before this close friendship with a Brazilian family, she emphasizes harsh judgment and cross-cultural comparison; after, she rejects the gleeful gossip and casual condemnation of Brazilians by the British community. With her entrée into the cultivated and educated de Campos family circle, Graham's early view that Brazilian women are unintelligent, uncultivated, and slovenly begin to change. By contrast with the "disgusting" Brazilian women of the first visit, during the second visit she describes "a very agreeable Brazilian lady [. . .] a regular Brazilian *bas-blue* in the person of Dona Maria Clara: she reads a good deal, especially philosophy and politics; she is a tolerable botanist, and draws flowers exceedingly well; besides, she is what I think it is Miss Edgeworth calls 'a fetcher and carrier of bays,'—a useful member of society, who, without harming herself or others, circulates the necessary literary news." Intellectual pursuits are paramount for Graham, particularly in women, so this is high praise indeed. Shortly thereafter, Graham notes a difference in the way she chooses to spend her time: "I have improved my acquaintance with my foreign friends; but of English I see, and wish to see, very little of any body but Mrs. May." Similarly, at a ball she avoids the few English guests to converse with "some sensible and well-bred Brazilians, so that I was scarcely aware of the lateness of the hour, when I left my younger friends dancing at midnight." And she concludes with authority, after spending time with Dona Ana's extended family, "The family attachments here are quite beautiful; they are as close and as intimate as those of clanship in Scotland."

Even as her own perspective changes as a result of increased understanding, the independent Brazil in which she landed on March 13, 1823, was likewise transformed from the Portuguese colony she had left months earlier.[12] Admiring the French and English furniture of a "neat and elegantly fitted up" house in Rio de Janeiro, "all as different as possible from the houses I saw in Bahia," she comments, "I am told that they are likewise as different from what they were here twenty years since, and can well believe it; even during the twelve months of my absence from Rio, I see a wonderful polishing has taken place, and every thing is gaining an European air." But has Brazil really changed so much in her absence—or has Graham been swept away by the political charge in the South American air as she became accustomed to a South American aesthetic? As the daughter of a North American

---

12. The *Doris* left Brazil for Chile on March 10, 1822. Graham outlines a version of Brazilian history that emphasizes Dom Pedro, and by metonymy the country itself, as a rebellious son, telling us that Pedro's father João VI of Portugal ordered his son to return "to Lisbon to begin his personal Education," but that Dom Pedro, attached as he was to Brazil where he had lived from age 11, "espoused its interests. [. . .] and for his own part, he naturally enough protested against being treated like a school boy altho' he was already a husband, and a father and had exercised the functions of a sovereign Prince" (Graham, "Life" ch. 2). In all this, Graham constructs Pedro Primero as standing metonymically for his country. The reality may have been quite different: Pedro seems to have been acting in accord with the Court of Portugal, which, seeing Brazil slipping towards independence, agreed to have Pedro remain behind and then advised him to declare himself Emperor as a strategy to retain Brazil under the control of the Braganza family.

émigrée and a Scot, she scarcely bothers to conceal her revolutionary sympathies; having seen independence in Chile firsthand, she seems dazzled by the glorious future Brazil has scripted for itself in the process of its own struggle for independence.

In the second half of her *Journal*, then, Graham begins to emphasize the unprecedented potential of this new land. She is pleased with the rulers who set the tone for the citizens, too: "nobody is more good-natured than Don Pedro." And it is not only her relationships with individuals that have changed; in her view, the country itself becomes a prototype for European nations seeking revolutionary models. Of Brazil's acquisition of the island of Maranham, for example, she notes approvingly, "the first act of the new government was to issue a proclamation to the inhabitants of the province of Maranham, congratulating them on being no longer a nation of slaves to Portugal, but a free people of the empire of Brazil." Of Brazil's new-scripted Constitution, she exults, astoundingly, that "all Christians are eligible to all offices and employments; and I only wish older countries would deign to take lessons from this new government with its noble liberality." [13]

As discussed earlier, Graham provides a richer and more detailed account of Brazilian domestic life than male travelers could do, and that is exactly what we might expect given the gendered conventions of travel writing. However, we would *not* expect another difference we see in Graham: she is more astute and more involved politically than many male writers of her time. Because of the constraints on writers, Graham is careful to provide the obligatory disclaimers before venturing into forbidden political territory, saying in her introduction (which is largely an historical summary intended to facilitate the reader's understanding of the country's present political situation) that she will not "pretend to speak of" political issues of the day with any claim to authority, since "my opportunities of information were too few; my habits as a woman and a foreigner never led me into situations where I could acquire the necessary knowledge."

Amusingly, however, within moments of landing in Pernambuco—her first port of call on her first visit to Brazil—Graham tips her

---

13. In all this praise, with its rhetoric of freedom from colonial slavery, it is important to note—particularly in light of the discussion of Graham's abolitionist discourse to follow—that Graham now no longer mentions the *actual* slaves whose condition so horrified her when she first landed in Brazil, nor the fact that they, although often Christians, were of course not eligible for all offices and employments.

hand. After telling us first that a canoe carrying two "patriot officers" (or supporters of Brazilian independence) arrived shortly after they anchored "to ascertain [. . .] if we had come, as was reported, to assist the royalists, or if we would assist them," she notes how difficult it is for the politically involved to believe "in the strict neutrality we profess." British naval personnel were strictly enjoined to neutrality, and as the wife of an officer, Graham was expected to conform to this expectation. Here, though, Graham's use of the ambiguous term "profess" implies her own disbelief in that neutrality—an implication born out in the next paragraph, when she recounts a visit, the following morning, from the Royalist Colonel Patronhe, who asks that an English ship carry official Portuguese governmental dispatches to Lisbon. Graham comments, "we felt glad that the strict rules of service prevented the captain from giving any such order to the master of the packet. It would be at once a breach of that neutrality we profess to observe, and, in my opinion, an aiding of the worst cause."

Again the "profess," which here confirms that neutrality is an official policy rather than a personal conviction—and now she cannot resist also betraying her sympathy for the patriot, or revolutionary, perspective by stating her clear opinion that the royalist is the "worst" cause. In a letter written at this time to John Murray, who by now had become a close friend, she articulates her own views still more directly: "I confess I wish our orders had been such as allowed us to take part with the *changers* for I have heard such things within 24 hours of the old regime that I am sure any change must be for the better. The packet sails tomorrow—if any fresh attack should be made tonight on Olinda or Recife I will write but I doubt it—I imagine our being here to protect the British property will awe both sides a little."[14]

Graham clearly defies the prohibition that women not meddle in politics from the first pages of her journal—and the more she learns of Brazil and Chile, the more involved she becomes in the extraordinary political ferment transforming the New World. She was a keen botanist and appreciated the scientific importance of Brazil's biodiversity—indeed, she even carried botanical specimens back to the British Museum and to William Hooker, later director of the Royal Botanic Gardens at Kew. But she found the social transformation even more

---

14. Maria Graham, letter to John Murray, 23 Sept. 1821. Murray Archive, National Library of Scotland.

fascinating, and in political terms, no topic—with the possible exception of free trade—was more loaded for British travelers than slavery.

The Historical Context of Slavery: The Anglo-Lusitanian Connection and Brazilian Independence

As we've suggested, when Graham travels to Brazil, she witnesses revolutionary changes taking place in the Portuguese colony. While these shifts predate her visit and continue after her departure, her travel narrative is a vivid account of the radical events taking place across South America as both Spanish and Portuguese colonies began agitating for independence from their European metropoles. Events in Europe, in particular the rise of Napoleon Bonaparte, markedly affected the independence movements in South America and especially in Brazil. And when Bonaparte moves across the Iberian Peninsula, Portugal's political landscape shifts dramatically and Brazil's future is irrevocably transformed.

Britain and Portugal had close political and economic relationships throughout the sixteenth and seventeenth centuries, well before Britain's involvement in Brazilian independence. Leslie Bethel notes, "Under treaties going back to the end of the fourteenth century England was also the guarantor of Portugal's independence and the territorial integrity of the Portuguese empire" (*Brazil: Empire* 3). By the eighteenth century, with the decline of Iberian power and the rise of British economic and political dominance, "the British had established factories (that is, commercial houses) in the Iberian peninsula. England had become a major carrier for the Iberian nations and virtually held Portugal as an economic colony" (Liss 8). At the end of the eighteenth century, war between France and the whole of Europe forced Portugal even further under British control, as Napoleon Bonaparte demanded Portugal declare war against Britain or risk invasion. This French threat was not as daunting to the Portuguese crown as declaring war against Britain, which could easily lose Portugal its primary colonial possession, Brazil, since British naval power could control trade routes to South America.

When Napoleon demanded that Dom João, Prince Regent of Portugal (after his mother, the queen, was declared mentally insane), "close his ports to English ships, imprison English residents in Portugal and confiscate their property, or face the consequences of a French invasion," the Prince Regent, escorted by four British warships, moved his entire royal court to Brazil in 1807 (Bethel, *Brazil: Empire* 14). The royal party that crossed the Atlantic Ocean was immense and impressive. Not only did it include the immediate royal family, but members of the government, councils of state, justices of the High Courts, not by the handful but by the thousands. According to Bethel, "between the morning of 25 November and the evening of the 27th November some 10–15000 people [. . .] embarked on the flagship *Prince Real*" and headed for Brazil (*Brazil: Empire* 15).

The transfers of the Royal Court to Rio de Janeiro signaled a significant shift for Brazil and for Portugal. "The viceregal capital since 1763, and in the late eighteenth century increasingly important economically, Rio de Janeiro overnight became the capital of a worldwide empire stretching as far as Goa and Macao" (Bethel, *Brazil: Empire* 16). Ironically, this transfer, though intended to maintain the integrity of the Portuguese empire while under French threat in Europe, signaled an unalterable shift in Brazilian history. It allowed a colony to attain a central role in the continuation of the Portuguese empire. This rise in stature was further cemented in 1815 when Dom João declared Brazil a kingdom, equal politically to Portugal. Russell-Wood notes:

> The decision to transfer the court to Brazil had been ill-received in Lisbon, although it was an inevitable expedient. Once the immediate threat of French occupation of Portugal had diminished, the continued presence of the king in Brazil merely fueled resentment already felt towards the colony by members of the Cortes in Lisbon. Recognition that the roles of the colony and the metropolis had been neatly reversed was bitter but unavoidable. The decree of December 16, 1815, whereby Brazil was raised to the status of a kingdom on a level with Portugal, did nothing to smooth the already ruffled feathers of the deputies of the Cortes. ("Preconditions and Precipitants" 35)

British ships escorted the convoy transferring the Royal Court to Brazil; this protection allowed Britain to position itself at the center of political policy and trade in South America.

In January 1808, as a favor for British assistance in the Royal Court's move across the Atlantic, Dom João opened the ports of Brazil to "friendly nations." Russell-Wood argues, "This was an event of momentous importance, transcending the arrival of the royal court and even the declaration of independence" ("Preconditions and Precipitants" 34). The desire for this trading status between Brazil and Britain had in many ways been at the center of British calculations when escorting Dom João and his entourage to Rio. With this act, not only would Britain gain access to Brazilian markets, but this would also give it greater access to South American markets, still officially closed to British trade by a weakened but wary Spain that was embroiled in its own troubles with its colonies. Though it suffered the loss of its North American colonies at the end of the eighteenth century, Britain's influence and role in South America grew as it was strategically situated to gain economic and trading ground, while also seeming to remain "neutral" in the conflicts between colonies and Iberian metropoles.

Portugal and Britain signed the Treaty of Navigation and Commerce in 1810, increasing British access to Brazilian-Portuguese trade. As Leslie Bethel explains, these trade concessions "fixed a maximum tariff of 15 per cent ad valorem on British goods, mainly cottons, woollens, linens, hardware and earthenware, imported to Brazil." Commercial concessions were not the only thing granted; British merchants were not only given "the right to reside in Brazil [and] to engage in the wholesale and retail trades," but in addition "the British government was given the right to appoint judges conservators, special magistrates responsible for dealing with the cases involving British subjects in Brazil." The treaty favored British subjects culturally and economically in Brazil; by contrast, it did little for Brazilian/Portuguese goods traded in Britain, which continued to be subject to exorbitant duties (Bethel, *Brazil: Empire* 19-21).

The opening of its ports and therefore its trade was not the only Portuguese concession given, if grudgingly, by Dom João. Even more significant for Portuguese/Brazilian and British relations was the separate Treaty of Alliance and Friendship, which dealt specifically with the question of abolition and the slave trade. Since the end of the eighteenth century, the slave trade had become a central issue, first of British domestic and then of foreign policy. Portugal, and in particular Brazil, the largest slave-holding and trading empire that remained, incited particular fervor for British abolitionists. This question of the slave trade came under the purview of the Treaty of Alliance and Friendship. Up to this point, Britain had been unable to attain many concessions from Portugal regarding the slave trade. After all, though slavery was abolished in Portugal in 1761 as was the trade of slaves beyond the Portuguese Empire, the slave trade remained intact in Brazil and territories (Bethel, *Abolition* 5). Indeed, regardless of late Enlightenment ideas about the dignity of man, Portugal's economy and empire relied on slavery, and as such, even by its more enlightened thinkers, "slavery and the slave trade [...] were indispensable for the agricultural development of Brazil, where land was plentiful and labour in short supply, and thus for the prosperity and security of Portugal and the empire as a whole" (Bethel, *Abolition* 6).

However, in its weakened state at the beginning of the nineteenth century, Portugal was, for the first time, forced to give way to British abolitionist demands, at least on paper. In Article 10 of the Treaty of Alliance and Friendship, the Portuguese government declared that it was "fully convinced of the injustice and mistaken policy of the trade in slaves," and with the assistance of Britain would undertake the "cause of humanity" of abolition by "adopting the most effective means of achieving a gradual abolition in all its domains" (qtd. in Marques 10). What gradual abolition meant, however, was far from clear since Portugal "retain[ed] the right to pursue the slave trade in areas of the African coast belonging to Portugal" (Marques 10).

From this moment, British pressure to end the slave trade in Brazil would be relentless and powerful. The transfer of the Royal Court to Brazil provided a rare occasion for increased social pressure on the slave trade. As historian Manchester notes, "the most serious friction which has ever arisen between England and Portuguese America resulted from the attempts of the British government to suppress the slave trade. From 1808 through the century until slavery was abolished in Brazil (1888), the constantly increasing pressure which the London Foreign Office brought to bear in its effort to abolish the traffic caused such an intense feeling of resentment on the part of the Brazilians that friendly relations of the two countries were seriously menaced" (159). And indeed, while Britain gained concessions from Portugal that it would, at least theoretically, restrict and ultimately abolish the slave trade, in the period between 1808 and independence the slave trade only increased. As Manchester notes, "between 1808 and 1822 the British Foreign Office restricted the Portuguese slave trade on paper, but to carry those restrictions on to the total abolition of the traffic, or even to make them effective, was beyond its power. More slaves entered Brazil in 1821 than in 1808" (185).

Nonetheless Britain actively sought to curtail the trade from Africa to Brazil. After the Treaty of Alliance and Friendship, British ships began energetically and, by official standards of the 1810 treaty, illegally restricting the trade. The Treaty of Alliance and Friendship was vague about the exact parameters of Portugal's abolition policies, allowing wide leeway for interpretation. In the years between 1810 and 1813, the British navy restricted the Portuguese slave trade north of the equator, something that had not been agreed to in the Treaty of Alliance and Friendship. British abolitionist sentiment "deliberately interpreted" the 1810 treaty "in a broader and more concrete sense, giving the Royal Navy the excuse to start policing the Portuguese slavers in transit on the Atlantic Ocean" (Marques 37). Having defeated Napoleon, British power in Europe and on the seas was unrivaled, and it planned to continue leaning on Portugal to end the slave trade. The British Royal navy, having identified four anti-slavery cruisers for the explicit purpose of curtailing the Portuguese slave trade, intervened along the West African coast (Marques 37). This cost Brazilian traders in Bahia and Pernambuco heavy losses, but did not stop British demands that Portugal curtail and ultimately end what William Wilberforce called "the infamous commerce." And though at the Congress of Vienna in 1815, Portugal agreed "to ban the slave trade north of the equator in return for a financial indemnity and reiterated its determination to bring about a gradual end to the trade," the slave trade would continue to be a source of friction between Portugal and England until Brazilian independence and throughout the nineteenth century, indeed until Brazil banished slavery and enforced it in 1888 (Bethel, *Brazil: Empire* 24).

In this context, a paradox emerged concerning the relationship between the British rise to foreign international power and its focus on abolition of the slave trade in Brazil. On the one hand, after the 1815 Treaty of Paris and with the final defeat of Napoleon, the power and influence of Britain was internationally undeniable. Britain could demand not just that Portugal diminish its slave trade north of the equator but also, Bethel argues, "the British navy was given the right to visit and search on the high seas Portuguese vessels suspected of illegal slaving north of the equator and Anglo-Portuguese mixed commissions were to be set up to adjudicate the captures and liberate the slaves"

(Bethel, *Brazil: Empire* 24). This caused a great deal of consternation to Brazilians, who were, in fact, the ones directly affected by such interference. Marquez points out that "in allowing the British navy and British judges to intervene in controlling and trying offenders, the Portuguese government gave up the chance to retain for an indefinite period the 'system of doing nothing,' which, in the suggestive words of the British charge d'affaires in Rio, had been its typical attitude to the suppression of the slave trade" (47).

On the other hand, ironically, it was the strength and power of British control of the Atlantic that drove the illegal growth of the Portuguese/Brazilian slave trade. Connected to Britain's abolitionist policies were its interests in the emerging markets of the soon-to-be independent colonies of South America. After all, it was Prince Regent Dom João's opening of Brazilian ports to "friendly nations" that allowed for the influx of British goods into South American markets in the first place. And it was not just goods and materials that entered into Brazil, but also the power of British credit. One hundred trading companies set up shop in Brazil once foreign shipping was allowed, and with them came not only cheap goods but also involvement with British financial markets. The slave trade had many components, but at its root it was a business and there was money to be made, even by nationals from the nation so radically and morally opposed to it. So while abolitionist policies demanded Portugal's compliance in attempting to end the slave trade, Marquez emphasizes the complex economic context: "On the African coast, as in America, the slave trade was an economic activity, in which settlement was made more or less long-term. Credit was therefore a key mechanism of the slaving enterprise, and it was credit which the British trading companies came prodigally to dispense, advancing merchandise to the slavers and agreeing to wait sometimes up to two years for payment" (68). We see then that British influence in South America and in particular in Brazil demanded Portugal's grudging agreement to abolition—and yet, ironically, this same British eminence created economic conditions that increased the desirability of continuing slaving even under more contained conditions. And, it must be remembered, by the 1820s Portugal was the single remaining colonial nation to have an active slave trade south of the equator.

For all its pressure, Britain did not have much of a hold on the Portuguese slave trade. Portugal continued to fuel its colonies with slave labor and British capital; its connections to the single largest abolitionist nation in Europe did little to curtail the slave trade or its role in it. This all changed when Brazil declared its independence from Portugal in 1822. Unlike Spanish colonies in the rest of South America, Brazil, even when finally declaring independence, did not forge a clear, unified identity for itself as a nation independent of Portugal. Nor did it seek to separate itself from Portugal until other options seemed utterly exhausted. As Russell-Wood argues, "For the most part Brazilians were content to accept the continuation of a monarchial form of government. The struggles between republicans and royalists which took place in Spanish South America were absent in Brazil. In fact the social tensions, regionalisms, economic disparities, and presence of a hard-core colonial administration prevented the independence movement in Brazil from being truly nationalist in spirit or revolutionary in execution" ("Preconditions and Precipitants" 35).

However, this did not mean that Brazilians wanted to return to the status of colony after having gained equal footing with Portugal. Once Bonaparte's threat was contained in Europe, the Cortes in Lisbon demanded the immediate return of the Prince Regent, Dom João, to Lisbon. In essence Portugal wanted to re-establish its central authority over Brazil and to turn back the clock since the transfer of the Royal Court to Rio de Janeiro. The early 1820s were a time of strife as the Cortes attempted to regain what it considered to be its sole and rightful place at the center of the Portuguese empire. In April of 1821, after the return of the Prince Regent to Lisbon, "the Cortes without much success, began bypassing Rio de Janeiro" and also tried "to revoke the trade agreements with Britain" (Bethel, *Brazil: Empire* 20). In particular the Cortes wanted to "direct British goods through the metropolis once more and to impose a much higher tariff" (Bethel, *Brazil: Empire* 29). The ultimate goal of the Cortes was to reassert Portuguese centrality in its empire and return the institutions established in Rio de Janeiro back to Lisbon.

Though the Prince Regent returned to Lisbon in 1821, leaving his son Dom Pedro I in power in Brazil, tensions between Portugal and its colony continued. And although Brazilians had no real interest in separating from Portugal, they had gained too much since the transfer of the Royal Court to cede any power or privileges conferred to them by the Regent, especially their more advantageous place in the world economy. Brazilians were unwilling to return to their colonial status only to feed the wealth of Portugal at their expense.

Yet few Brazilians considered independence or revolution as the viable solution. It has been argued that as late as 1822, some in the Brazilian dominant class "constantly emphasized their loyalty to the crown" and "independence, when mentioned at all, still meant autonomy within a dual monarchy and the continuation of some kind of union with Portugal" (Bethel, *Brazil: Empire* 31). Brazilians wanted to be recognized as Brazilians but not in order to disconnect themselves from their connection to Portugal. As Russell-Wood argues,

> ... there was a general determination to be Brazilians and to be recognized as such, coupled with the demand for recognition of the very quintessence of Brazilian civilization, as something sui generis, imbued with *Bresilianite*. Finally, the Brazilians wanted recognition of the special nature of Brazilian society and the particular interests of the Brazilian economy, but few saw it as a prelude to independence, or failure to gain it as a perquisite for a separatist movement. ("Preconditions and Precipitants" 35)

When Dom Pedro I declared independence from Portugal in December of 1822, emphatically stating, "Long live independence, liberty, and the separation of Brazil," it was after many attempts by delegations of Brazilians in Lisbon to strive for autonomy within the empire (qtd. in Bethel, *Brazil: Empire* 33). The actual "war" of independence was muted and hardly bloody. What Brazilians wanted was parallel autonomy within the Portuguese Empire. They saw themselves aligned to their monarch and to the Portuguese empire, but they also refused to become an outpost for enriching Portugal at the expense of their own political and economic interests. Independence was not the goal of resistance to the Lisbon Cortes's interference for Brazilians, and it was only after recognizing the futility of striving for parallel status as a possession of Portugal that Brazilians rallied behind its call.

When Maria Graham traveled to Brazil, beginning her journey in July of 1821, independence was imminent and certain parts of Brazil were already at arms against the Portuguese stronghold. These Loyalist regions were mostly located in the Northeast and North, in particular Bahia. For the most part, the perspective of her first journal in

Brazil reflects the enclosure of the ship; she visited the major ports and much of her journal offered vivid, intelligent descriptions not only of the countryside, domestic life and manners, but also her sense of the possibilities for Brazil under the corrective influence of the British. She also witnessed first hand the various permutations of the growing disaffection between the colony and the metropole. By the end of her first visit, she claimed the "cause of that independence [. . .] is now so inevitable, that the only question is whether it shall be obtained with or without bloodshed." As we've suggested, the "inevitability" of independence was not a given for most Brazilians. Though her first visit contextualized this inevitability, and though by the time of her second visit he had declared himself Constitutional Emperor and Perpetual Defender of Brazil, Dom Pedro I still needed to consolidate his authority.

When Graham returned to Brazil in March of 1823 with Lord Cochrane, Dom Pedro I asked Cochrane to assist him in defeating the Portuguese naval domination of the coastal routes. Graham's early support for Brazilian independence increased still further as a result of her enthusiasm for any cause Cochrane espoused. During her second visit, she had relatively direct access to the struggle for independence and particularly to battles fought by Lord Cochrane. In her journal she related the movements of the naval squadron, especially Cochrane's various naval victories, as well as the proclamations of the new Emperor as various developments between former colony and metropole emerged.

She also explored the potentially problematic role of slavery in the newly independent nation. When Brazil separated from Portugal, it became one of largest slave holding nations in the world. And, simultaneously, it required England's support and recognition as well as its intercession on its behalf with Portugal. As we've suggested above, the thorny issue of slavery permeated the relationship between Portugal and England prior to Brazil's declaration of independence. After independence, slavery would dominate relations between Great Britain and Brazil. Britain did not want to unsettle its ally Portugal too much by overwhelmingly supporting the cause of Brazilian independence. This became a delicate dance for British foreign minister George Canning, but in the end, Canning considered Portugal too weak to bring its wayward colony back under its control. More importantly, by this point, and because of the Royal Court's residence in Rio de Janeiro,

"Brazil was now Britain's third largest foreign market. By proffering the hand of friendship in her hour of need Britain would consolidate its political power and economic ascendancy over Brazil" (Bethel, *Brazil: Empire* 37).

That hand of friendship meant that Britain demanded not only further commercial and trade privileges, but that the question of the slave trade be at the forefront of any discussions of recognition of Brazil as an independent nation. Yet this demand placed the new ruler of Brazil, Emperor Dom Pedro I, in a difficult position, as he had relied heavily on the sectors of the Brazilian population, the Absolutists and the Patriots, who though antagonistic towards each other were equally opposed to the Loyalists, those Portuguese still loyal to the Cortes in Lisbon. And these two groups either relied heavily on slavery or chafed under the economic power of England and "had long cherished a particular grievance against the preemption of Brazilian trade and commerce by English agents who were acting under the special privileges obtained in 1810 by the treaty of commerce" (Manchester 191). In the end, and despite his tendencies towards absolutism, "between 1821 and 1824 by relying on the Brazilians, or Patriots, for support he [Dom Pedro I] succeeded in establishing authority throughout the empire. Separatist movements were suppressed, the new constitution was in force, and no foreign or soldier functionary was in Brazil" (Manchester 191).

But Britain demanded suppression of the slave trade as a central condition for recognition of Brazilian independence. Though the British needed to tread carefully in the question of recognizing Brazil even if it conceded to all its demands, the slave trade was central in any arrangement between the two nations. As Britain considered how best to achieve recognition of an independent Brazil under conditions best suited to its own economic and political interests, it had to be mindful of questions about the succession of the Portuguese crown, about its own relationship with other European nations, and in particular what its relationship to Brazil would be given its long relationship with Portugal. Of particular interest were the treaties signed in the years following the Royal Court's transferral to Rio de Janeiro. Would Brazil be beholden to honor the treaties Portugal had signed with Britain?

As we have noted, Graham left Brazil at the end of 1823 to return as governess to the Royal family the following year. When she shipped off, independence was all but assured not only on the ground and in material terms but also in political and global terms, with Britain having positioned itself as intermediary between Portugal and its once central colony. Though initially Portugal asked for British intercession, it had no interest in letting go of Brazil nor in recognizing its independence. When talks broke down between Portugal and Brazil, despite the complications of proffering recognition to Brazil, Britain decided to establish an independent relationship with Brazil, even if this ran counter to Portugal's wishes.

There were multiple reasons for such a political move, not the least of which was the growing alliance between Spain and France. As significantly, the 1810 Commerce and Trade Treaty signed between Portugal and Britain would expire and be renegotiable in the middle of 1825. If Portugal had no interest in extending its trade relationship with Britain, dealing directly with a British-recognized, independent Brazil would be necessary to ensure England economic privileges in Brazil. And for British abolitionists, the potential to negotiate directly with Brazil was another serendipitous opportunity to re-establish a Brazilian commitment to the ending of the slave trade.

When Brazil declared independence from Portugal in 1822, then, Britain saw its opportunity to insist that the newly independent nation abolish the slave trade. As Bethel notes, "just as Britain had squeezed anti-slave trade agreements, however limited in scope, from a reluctant Portugal [. . .] so Britain's pre-eminence in Europe and the world at large, [. . .] now appeared to present her with an opportunity to wring concessions from an even more reluctant Brazil" (*Abolition* 30). Canning's declaration that "no state in the New World will be recognized by Great Britain which has not frankly and completely abolished the trade in slaves" most clearly articulated Britain's position regarding the slave trade in the 1820s (qtd. in Bethel, *Abolition* 31).

In order to comply with British demands to curtail its slave trade, Brazil "issued a law in 1831 freeing all slaves arriving from outside the empire and imposing severe penalties on slave smugglers" (Viotti da Costa 130). This, however, did not curtail or even diminish the trade or the voraciousness with which Brazilians clung to it as a part of national pride and identity. In fact, the slave trade only increased in the years following this law, which, though ineffectual, remained on the books. Yet, Viotta da Costa tells us,

> Neither British cruisers not Brazilian authorities managed to put a stop to the action of the smugglers. The

> blacks they brought in, though legally free after 1831, were still sold as slaves. Plantation owners and slave traders simply defied the law, resisted British pressures, and disregarded Brazilian authorities. The slave trade continued after 1831 at an increasing rate. Between 1840 and 1850 an average of 30,000 to 40,000 blacks were smuggled into Brazil each year, under the complaisant eyes of the Brazilian authorities. (131)

Not only did this law do little to curtail the illegal selling of and trafficking in slaves, it also became a source of tensions between Britain and Brazil, as Brazilians considered British intervention in their national affairs to be a direct violation of sovereignty. This was a sticky issue, since in part the resentment and animosity of some sectors of the Brazilian population against the British concerned the continued favorable trade conditions re-established by the 1827 Anglo-Brazilian treaty. Brazilians were further goaded by the fact that British subjects living in Brazil owned slaves. These tensions intensified when the Brazilian government increased tariffs on British goods in 1842. Viotta da Costa demonstrates that tensions escalated further when, in 1845, "the British Parliament, apparently in retaliation, voted a bill known in Brazil as the Aberdeen Bill, which not only authorized the seizure of ships involved in the slave trade but stipulated that violators be considered pirates and tried in Admiralty courts" (131).

Despite British efforts, slavery remained a global issue both in Brazil and in North America for most of the nineteenth century. In Brazil, the trade grew relentlessly, with more than 50,000 slaves entering the country illegally, and sold illegally, each year until 1851. In Brazil, abolition did not emerge as an official position until the latter third of the nineteenth century, and while it is beyond the scope of this introduction to discuss Brazil and its political development beyond the years Graham travels to and writes about it, it is worth noting here that abolition sentiments in Brazil emerged as economic forces shifted both labor needs and the development of an industrial base rather than a merely agricultural one.

The Rhetoric of Abolition: Travelers' Voices

On first landing in Brazil, Graham writes to John Murray, "The Negro population is alarmingly large for the Old Portuguese. I could tell such stories of Negroes—and New slaves.—God help us that one half of mankind should be born without hearts."[15] Almost immediately after setting foot on Brazilian soil, she includes an intentionally shocking description of a slave market in her journal (to be discussed below).

By contrast with Graham's clear investment in contributing to the growing body of abolitionist discourse, in the early years of the century other British travelers in Brazil seem to intentionally avoid the topic. John Mawe, a mineralogist who had worked for the Portuguese, was the first foreigner allowed to visit Minas Gerais following the opening of the Brazilian ports to trade in 1808. Perhaps because he was given unusual permission to travel, Mawe remains carefully silent on controversial topics, concentrating instead on safer subjects like mining, geography and geology. He does describe the varying treatment of "negroes" throughout Brazil—finding that the worst treatment of "this unfortunate race of men" is in the diamond mines—but does not refer to them as slaves and certainly does not mention abolition (196).

John Luccock, who traveled as the representative of his family's Yorkshire textile industry from 1808 to 1818, virtually ignores slavery as well—which seems particularly odd given his thematic emphasis on the superiority of British morality. This avoidance apparently struck even its author as unusual, since he excuses it by saying, "It was intended in other Chapters to have described the condition of Negro Slaves, and that of the Aboriginal Inhabitants of South America, but as the number of pages swelled beyond the appointed limits, it was found necessary to throw some of the leading facts relating to these topics into other parts of the work, and to be satisfied with marking the stations of the Indian tribes upon the Maps alone" (vi). True to his word, his pages indeed "swell" with commercial facts and figures as well as with instances of Brazilian depravity, but the marginalized population—Africans and indigenous peoples—barely rate a mention. (In one of his few brief references, he asserts that slavery is not always an unpleasant condition and offers anecdotes in support of this claim.)

Since many British residents of Brazil in fact owned slaves by this time, perhaps travelers chose to ignore this central fact of Brazilian life because it disrupted their dominant narrative: that British morality would serve to enlighten and civilize ignorant Brazilians. Alexander Caldcleugh's apparent anxiety to avoid discussion of slavery parallels

---

15. Maria Graham, letter to John Murray, 23 Sept. 1821. Murray Archive, National Library of Scotland.

Luccock's, though he at least does engage the topic explicitly. He, too, asserts that "the kindness exhibited to the slaves and servants is too well known to be mentioned here" (76). His comment confirms the fact that by 1825, conventions for representing slavery were well established: tropes attempting to convey the positive aspects of slavery include descriptions of contented, thriving slaves and scenes of childlike devotion to paternalistic masters, while negative conventions include descriptions of slave markets, children torn from parents (usually mothers), and masters beating slaves. Later, in a more extensive discussion, Caldcleugh reinforces convention when assuring readers that "on quitting the warehouse the slaves leave the greatest part of their miseries behind, and without wishing it to be inferred that they lead an enviable life, nobody can affirm, on seeing them singing and dancing in the streets, that they are wretched and continually pining over their unhappy fate. In many cases they appear to do as they please, and completely rule their indolent masters" (83). Caldcleugh does occasionally qualify his apparent defense of slavery; for example, he admits that slaves sometimes "fall into the hands of a poor man, and, like a horse under similar circumstances in England, must work harder and fare worse; and occasional instances of severity are recorded, but these are rare" (83). On the whole, he paints enslaved blacks as happy, well cared for, secure—and, as the reference to the horse indicates, not quite human. He contrasts these portraits of happy slaves with images of "idle, vicious, and disorderly" free blacks, and he includes instances of inhumanity to slaves only as exceptions that prove the rule of the "benevolent institution" (86).

Gilbert Mathison, whose time in Brazil exactly coincides with Graham's first year there, offers a sharply contrasting portrait of slavery. While other travelers tend to maintain a careful silence or to condemn the institution while praising individual practitioners of it—and while, as we will see, Graham uniformly expresses outrage over slave markets and slave owning as well as pity and compassion for individual slaves—Mathison conveys disgust for the slaves themselves. Assuming an objective tone to imply that his experience is universal, he describes slaves in relentlessly negative detail: "When a traveller first lands at Rio, his attention will be naturally attracted by the appearance of the negroes. Their colour [. . .] savage and uncouth countenances [. . .] barbarous language, and noisy vociferations—the wild melody of their national airs, (if the term may be used,) [. . .] all concur in exciting surprise, horror, and disgust" (12). Mathison's portrayal of racial Others as savage and barbarous discounts any possibility of their having a national identity—a particularly interesting move when these people are inhabitants of a country in the process of declaring independence and therefore of constructing a narrative of nationhood.

To be sure, Mathison does mention that obligatory set-piece, the description of a slave market, with something of the same horror Graham describes, but he handles the scene in a very different way: by denial. He describes the markets as places where traders "deal out human beings to their customers with as much insensibility and *sang-froid* as they would British goods. No one who has suffered the pain of witnessing it can forget the scene; but to describe it and read of it would be almost as heart-sickening as the sight itself, and I shall therefore pass over the subject without further remark" (156). In his overview of slavery, Mathison slips past the topic just as rapidly:

> The general subject of slavery has of late been too often viewed, under all its bearings, *usque ad nauseam*, to require reconsideration here [. . .] Of the personal condition and happiness of the slaves, it is absurd to judge from the feelings which we ourselves would entertain if placed in a similar situation. They certainly appear to be a cheerful-minded and contented race of people, and ignorance may be termed bliss to them, in the lowest sense of the word. (153–54)

After dismissing the slaves' response to slavery, however, Mathison concludes with a statement complicating his readers' response to his apparent racism. Following the easy "ignorance is bliss," he continues, "not so, however, to the society at large, of which they form a part. Happiness, founded upon ignorance and insensibility, is at least degrading to the character of man; and whatever degrades its members, must entail degradation upon the whole body politic" (153–54).

Here, like Adam Smith (and Graham after him), Mathison suddenly acknowledges that slavery's presence in a society shapes the lives of all its members, not just its apparent victims. In understanding Mathison's perspective on slavery, we must note that he owned a plantation in Jamaica—in fact, his wealth derived from this plantation. He wrote a study of slavery in that colony, *Notices respecting Jamaica 1808–1809–1810* (London 1811), outlining his system of treating slaves with greater humanity. However, as his discussions in *Narrative of a visit to Brazil* show, he did not reject slavery itself.

By contrast with Mathison, Henry Koster's 1816 journal parallels Graham's most closely in the amount and type of scrutiny he devotes to slavery. As noted earlier, Koster's background was unique among British travel writers—he had been raised partly in Portugal, spoke the language fluently, and had friends and business connections in Brazil. In addition, while living in Brazil he bought a sugar plantation and owned slaves himself. In his journal, Koster devotes considerable space to the topic, including two chapters titled "Slavery" and "Impolicy of the Slave Trade." He included assessment of differences in slaves from different parts of Africa; slavers' treatment of family bonds; diet; work conditions; education; and religion. Even more notably, he describes individual Africans and discusses the emotional consequences of slavery, providing anecdotes demonstrating strong familial bonds and advancing unusually complex psychological interpretations. For example, describing a husband and wife facing the sale of their children "with no change of countenance," he explains, "That their parents did feel deeply the separation which they must have apprehended [. . .] I have not the slightest doubt [. . .] But whether it proceed from resignation, from despair, from fear, or from being ashamed to shew what they felt before so many strangers, there was no demonstration of feeling. Negroes may have feelings, and yet not allow the standers-by to know what they feel" (417).

In addition to breaking convention by his unusual attention to the domestic lives of slaves, Koster departs from the expected by engaging in self-reflection. If he had stayed in Brazil as planned, he muses, "I should have soon become a Brazil planter; the state in which a man who rules over slaves is placed, is not likely to make him a better creature [. . .] I should perhaps shortly have been totally unfit to become a member of any other society. Although I am fully aware of the evils which attend a feudal state of society, I liked to have dependants. I might have become so arbitrary, so much a lover of a half savage life [. . .] as to have been dissatisfied with what is rational and to be desired in this world" (334). In arguing that plantation life is akin to and can develop "savage" identities even in Englishmen, Koster complicates the system of racial classification common in his time. In his unusual awareness of the ways identity shifts according to cultural context, Koster parallels Graham.

Graham's narrative is distinguished from those of Mawe, Caldcleugh and Luccock by the sheer volume and energy of her discussions of slavery, as well as by the personal interest she takes in individual slaves. And Graham's perspective and circumstances differ from Koster's because his experience with Portugal and the Portuguese language, as well as his long residence in Brazil, gives him still greater insight. With the exception of Koster, though, no other contemporary traveler comes close to matching her length and frequency of commentary. While Mathison and Koster are as interested in slavery as Graham—and more knowledgeable given their direct experience as slave-owners—her account differs from theirs also in her deliberate use of abolitionist rhetorical strategies. We would resist labeling these strategies as gendered, because they anticipate the sentimental power wielded by Victorian writers like Charles Dickens, but we note that in Graham's time, among travel writers, the strategies she uses are more typical of woman writers.

From the first pages of her *Journal of a Voyage to Brazil,* Graham seeks to mobilize our sympathy as she dramatizes her own reaction to slavery. "We had hardly gone fifty paces into Recife," she tells us, when

> we were absolutely sickened by the first sight of a slave-market. It was the first time either the boys or I had been in a slave-country; and, however strong and poignant the feelings may be at home, when imagination pictures slavery, they are nothing compared to the staggering sight of a slave-market. It was thinly stocked, owing to the circumstances of the town; which cause most of the owners of new slaves to keep them closely shut up in the depôts. Yet about fifty young creatures, boys and girls, with all the appearance of disease and famine consequent upon scanty food and long confinement in unwholesome places, were sitting and lying about among the filthiest animals in the streets. The sight sent us home to the ship with the heart-ache and resolution, "not loud but deep," that nothing in our power should be considered too little, or too great, that can tend to abolish or to alleviate slavery.

Graham here uses the set-piece of the slave market to demonstrate the depth and power of English sensibilities, which have both aesthetic and moral dimensions. She and the two English midshipmen who accompany her onshore are "absolutely sickened," staggered, and filled with "heart-ache and resolution." It is significant, also, that in this passage Graham does not mention the adult man (a ship's officer, Dance) who escorts her; instead, she emphasizes a feminized sensibility by falsely limiting the English observers to a woman and boys, eliding the adult male who did in fact accompany the group.

Note, too, that Graham concludes the passage by emphasizing that she and the boys felt a "resolution, 'not loud but deep,' that nothing in our power should be considered too little, or too great, that can tend to abolish or to alleviate slavery." She borrows the phrase "not loud but deep" from Shakespeare (*Macbeth* V:3). Her fellow Scot, Thomas Carlyle, would use the same phrase a decade later in *The French Revolution*—a textual path that reinforces the intellectual underpinnings of Graham's abolitionist views, shaped by her apprenticeship in Edinburgh, where she absorbed Scottish Enlightenment ideals.[16]

Scenes of slave hunting and slave beating had hardened into convention by the time Graham was writing, so she occasionally breaks the mold in ways calculated to re-mobilize horror and sympathy. Because readers expect a male overseer's cruelty and may be inured to it, for example, she provides a twist on a conventional scene: "This morn-

---

16. Graham drew not only on the political context and the discursive history of the British abolitionist movement, but also on Scottish Enlightenment philosophers and political economists—particularly David Hume and Adam Smith—who contributed powerfully to the British abolitionist movement. For example, David Hume's insistence that slavery disallowed humanity by degrading masters as well as slaves becomes a central motif in Graham's critique (qtd. in Webster 486). Graham quotes Hume directly at one point, providing a rhetorical counterweight to her emphasis on the "common humanity" of slaves by emphasizing the ways slavery corrupts slaveowners as well. Throughout her accounts of slavery, too, she implicitly echoes Hume's arguments. She explicitly instructs us, "wherever slavery is established it brings a twofold curse with it. It degrades both parties." To be sure, Graham does not echo the Scottish philosophers' emphasis on the economic disadvantages of slavery; Adam Smith, for example, argued that "the experience of all ages and nations, I believe, demonstrates that the work done by slaves, though it appears to be the cheapest, is, in the end, the dearest of any," because slaves had no motivation to be productive or innovative (qtd. in Webster 482).

ing before breakfast, looking from the balcony of Mr. S.'s house, I saw a white woman, or rather fiend, beating a young negress, and twisting her arms cruelly while the poor creature screamed in agony, till our gentlemen interfered." Here, expectations are reversed: the male figures in the scene are sympathetic rather than cruel, while a woman violates conventional notions of femininity. For Graham, the woman's actions effectively defeminize and dehumanize her; she becomes "a white woman, or rather fiend"—and one who must, ironically, be stopped by British men.

If Graham focuses on slavery in Brazil, she seeks particularly to emphasize the effects on British observers rather than to communicate the lived experience of slaves themselves. Graham asserts the depth and power of British sensibilities, portrayed as rebelling "naturally" and "instinctively" against slavery and as having both aesthetic and moral dimensions. Anne Mellor analyzes gendered conventions of sensibility developed by female abolitionists like Hannah More; Graham draws heavily on this discourse when she depicts English innocence as marked by strong "distress" at scenes that degrade other human beings.[17] For example, we see conventions of sensibility shaping Graham's narration of a startling spectacle she witnesses one evening while strolling along the beach:

> I saw [a dog] drag the arm of a negro from beneath the few inches of sand, which his master had caused to be thrown over his remains [. . .] When the negro dies, his fellow-slaves lay him on a plank, carry him to the beach, where beneath high-water mark they hoe a little sand over him; but to the new negro even this mark of humanity is denied. He is tied to a pole, carried out in the evening and dropped upon the beach, where it is just possible the surf may bear him away.

---

17. As Mary Karasch has suggested, though, the anger of travelers at such scenes did effect marginal changes in the actual mechanics of the slave market in Rio de Janeiro: "eventually, the housing and auction of so many emaciated Africans [and] the appalling condition of so many new Africans gave the imperial court a bad image among foreigners. As a consequence, after 1824 the sale of new Africans was banned in port and business district areas" (36). This does not, of course, mean that sales ceased—merely that they were concealed.

And she concludes, "These things sent us home sad and spiritless, notwithstanding the agreeable scenes we had been riding among." Here, horror at the inhumanity shown to slaves even trumps the picturesque, that prime Romantic trope that ought to dominate these "agreeable scenes." Graham underlines the principle emphasized in the popular abolitionist slogan, "Am I not a man and a brother?" Her repeated emphasis on slaves as human beings, and on the shock to healthy sensibilities when their humanity is denied, works to train readers to understand slavery as a moral issue and to shape their own responses accordingly.

Graham draws on abolitionist rhetoric again in highlighting the ways slavery corrupts the slave-owner as well as the slave: both are dehumanized, a point Graham illustrates by explaining the consequences to human morality "when [slaves] were hunted on their own grounds, where all the details, disgusting and iniquitous as they are, of the seeking, capturing, and bending to the yoke, pass under the eye till the heart grows callous to the cry of the orphan, the grief of the widow, and the despair of the parent in being torn from whatever has been dear to them." And lest this be too subtle, she reinforces her argument with a maxim: "wherever slavery is established it brings a twofold curse with it. It degrades both parties even where the slaves are imported."

Of course, it is easy to condemn slavery, as Graham does. By the time of her travels to Brazil, as we saw above, Britain had abolished the slave trade (though not slavery itself). But Graham's perspective on Luso-Brazilian race relations is complicated by her own blindness to her ethnographic assumptions. Even as she virtually gloats over the evils of Brazilian slavery and highlights British moral superiority, Graham seems unconscious of her own collusion in racial and ethnic discrimination. She may follow Hume in insisting upon the common humanity of slaves and masters alike, but she echoes him also in her unexamined racism. To cite just one example, the lone black man on board her husband's ship *Doris* is given the role, in the shipboard celebration of crossing the line, of "Triton's horse." As he plays the only animal role in the festivities, this is a dehumanizing assignment. Graham notes it, however, without irony or even a trace of self-consciousness.

Once in Brazil, too, Graham conflates race and class in the way she positions native-born Portuguese creoles as "other," in dire need of the "civilizing influence" of the French and English colonists and merchants who introduced new fashions and manners even as they marketed manufactured goods. Her understanding of and engagement with race beyond British or slave populations is even more paradoxical. Born and bred in northern Britain, Graham had never been confronted with the range of colors and ethnicities that faced her in Brazil. She repeatedly notes, with renewed astonishment each time, the intermixing of races. Unable to understand why anyone would choose to "muddy" distinctions that seem essential to her, she proceeds to classify races using economic or moral criteria (and perhaps these are equivalents for this staunchly Protestant daughter of capitalism?). Quite systematically throughout her narrative, Graham categorizes blacks, mulattos, Brazilians and Portuguese according to a kind of Linnaean taxonomy that must have appealed strongly to the amateur naturalist in her.[18]

However, Graham's racial groupings differ markedly from the much more complex distinctions drawn by Brazilians themselves. Like most British visitors of her time, she perceives only five main "classes," as she calls them, in the population: Portuguese; creoles or Brazilians (by which she means white, Brazil-born Portuguese); slaves; freed slaves, whom she often calls simply "negroes"; and mulattos (oddly, given her strong interest in the native populations of Chile, Graham rarely mentions Brazil's diverse Indian population).

In one of the many contradictions in her narrative, then, even as she insists on African humanity and emphasizes environmental causes for particular character traits, Graham simultaneously undermines her arguments by implying essential differences between races. For instance, when emphasizing a Protestant work ethic as the most admirable of moral qualities, she surprisingly suggest that Brazil-born Africans and mulattos rank higher on this moral scale than either African slaves or Portuguese creoles, because they are "more active, more industrious, and more lively than either of the other classes." Graham underlines a parallel characterization of both wealthy Brazilians and their slaves as equally improvident and lazy throughout the narrative.

In her representations of individual Africans, Graham falls into further contradictions. In one striking passage, she recounts a slave's

---

18. This was a common approach to race in Brazil at the time; for example, John Mawe, who as a mineralogist had also published "The Linnæan system of conchology: describing the orders, genera, and species of shells arranged into divisions and families," turns his analytical eye on race and sets out a six-point hierarchy in his *Travels in the Interior of Brazil* in 1821.

captivity narrative and in the process reveals her own difficulties with racial taxonomy and representation. In her neighborhood, she says,

> The most amusing [inhabitants] [. . .] are certainly the negroes, who carry about the fruit and vegetables for sale [. . .] One of them has become quite a friend in the house; and after he has sold his master's fruit, earns a small gratuity for himself, by his tales, his dances, and his songs. His tribe, it seems, was at war with a neighbouring king, and he went out to fight when quite a boy, was taken prisoner, and sold. This is probably the story of many: but our friend tells it with action and emphasis, and shows his wounds, and dances his war dance, and shouts his wild song, till the savage slave becomes almost a sublime object.

In her book *Gender and Colonial Space,* Sara Mills analyzes the trope of the sublime in relation to gendered travel writing. In attempting to capture such moments, authors work to transcend the merely human and to dissolve boundaries between self and other. But Mills concludes that in travel, typically the sublime ego confronts and attempts to dominate a landscape in ways that cannot fully be achieved. The "monarch of all I survey" subject position identified by Mary Louise Pratt cannot be sustained when confronted with the sublime, for example, which forces awareness of human insignificance and impermanence. Mills argues, further, that the sublime is gendered: "The representation of experience of the sublime is crucial to a discussion of women's relation to landscape, since the sublime subject is one who locates himself or herself in a particular spatial and power framework," and women historically experience these frameworks differently than do men (84).

In the passage above, Graham attempts to share with readers a moment when a man the British perceive only as a "savage slave" exceeds the restrictions of his subject position. As a slave and an African, he is considered by Europeans to be both powerless and without history, but this man finds a voice and reclaims his past. As he performs that history for the entertainment of people very like those who captured him, the slave reinforces those power relations even as he defies them by narrating his history.

Graham resolves this dissonance by reaching for the sublime—a term she generally uses, like most of her contemporaries, to describe awe-inspiring landscapes that arouse profound emotions and exceed language. But in the process of invoking the sublime, she creates difficulties. She attempts to evade the specific geographical and colonial networks enmeshing all participants in the scene, whether British, Brazilian or African. Like most sublime moments, this one is conflicted not only for the slave, but also for the British observers: the slave becomes "our friend," but his gestures and "wild song" make him not a subject, but "*almost* a sublime *object*" (emphasis added), one to be admired and perhaps possessed by his audience.

Although fascinated, despite her horror, by the lives of slaves, Graham had competing interests as well. First, despite Britain's official position of strict neutrality, Graham clearly sided with the Brazilians in the fight for independence from Portugal and she watched the country's civil struggles with sharp interest, even as she sought to further British abolitionist policies. Second, as an amateur naturalist Graham exulted in the extraordinary geographical and biological diversity of Brazil. And third, anticipating social Darwinism by half a century, she saw Brazil as a "half-savage" society several evolutionary steps behind Europe, and she favored free trade with Britain—of all things—as the best way to "civilize" it. Combining these competing interests, Graham constructed Brazil as a primitive space with almost unlimited possibilities and she intended her published narrative to help Brazil achieve its potential. She proposed British moral and political influence, to be disseminated through increased trade, as the best means of furthering abolitionist and political goals. As she admits, "I fancied what Brazil might be [. . .] under a better government than any country but my own had ever enjoyed" ("Life" ch. 3). That "better government" clearly looks a whole lot like Britain, and it does not include traffic in human beings among its selling points.

So impressed is Graham by the potential of this new land, in fact, that she begins to script herself a key role in the Brazilian national narrative: as educator of the future Empress. Even before accepting the position of Governess to little Maria da Gloria, Graham apparently anticipated the possibilities it might afford her for influence on national character. In her *Journal,* Graham tells us, "Six months before, indeed, I had said that I was so pleased with the little Princess, that I should like to educate her." In her unpublished "Life of Don Pedro" (excerpted in the appendices to this edition), she confesses much more:

> It is strange and it is true that I never knew how or where the idea arose of making me governess to the young Princess. I was first asked whether I should like it, by the English officer commanding the English squadron of the Nation. Not believing that he was in earnest I answered without thinking, to be sure, and added what a delightful thing, to rescue that fine child from the hands of such creatures as surrounded her: to bring her up like a European Gentlewoman to teach her since she is to govern this wide country, that the People are less made for Kings, than Kings for the People [. . .] I confess that I was carried away by the notion of bringing up a person upon whose education and personal qualities the happiness of a whole Empire was to depend. ("Life" ch. 3)

When she made this statement, Graham had been inside the Palace for just a few hours, and had met "that fine child" exactly once. Nevertheless, she utterly dismisses "such creatures as surrounded [the princess]," and does not hesitate to assert the superiority of British education as well as British morality.

So Brazil is to become a warmer, sunnier Britain, and Graham is to be instrumental in shaping the narrative that will make it so. Graham's inability to see her own prejudice towards racial and ethnic Others produced a counter-reaction in Dom Pedro I's courtiers: letters between Maria Graham and the Empress Maria Leopoldina, as well as Graham's biographical and autobiographical "Life of Don Pedro," indicate that Graham was driven from court as a result of suspicion of the quick-developing friendship between these two highly-educated, independent women and mistrust of the ways they sought to transform the education (and thus the acculturation) of the Imperial Princesses.

Thus Graham learned, again and more forcibly, the dangers of female autonomy and the costs of imperial insularity. In her *Journal of a Voyage to Brazil,* Graham's formulation of progressive (European) versus regressive (creole) societies led her, as we saw above, to a critique of slavery linked not only to the moral repugnance of owning another body, but also to the moral ambiguity of the slaves themselves. Maria Graham's vivid, individualized descriptions of the ways the institution of slavery degrades both master and slave contributed to a growing—and gendered—abolitionist discourse. For readers today, her stories about Brazilian race relations help to recapture the social landscape in early nineteenth century Brazil. In addition, they enable a more accurate understanding of the complex and often contradictory web of conventions for representing slavery, race, and ethnicity in early nineteenth century Britain. Eventually, the abolitionist movement would combine with political pressure by Britain and other countries to end slavery in the New World, including the United States and Brazil—but that victory was still decades away.

Production and Reception of Graham's *Journal of a Voyage to Brazil*

Accounts of Brazil by foreign visitors have proved invaluable to Brazilians themselves. The texts these foreigners published became essential sources for nineteenth century Brazilian social history, since Brazilians (like other South Americans during this period) were too busy overthrowing colonial rule to craft detailed descriptions of their country's mores and manners. In his 1922 Masters' thesis, sociologist Gilberto Freyre explains that his attempt "to make clear to myself what the Brazil of the middle of the nineteenth century was like [. . .] was even a more difficult task than I had imagined it to be. I had to fight my way through the accounts of prejudiced, uncritical and superficial minds—through periodicals, lithogravures, manuscripts, books of travel and diaries. I turned to foreigners as the most dependable of all the social critics of the period—a period about which Brazilian writers have written either to glorify or to blame, never—I am referring to social, not political—with a fair spirit of criticism" (10). Of course, foreigners were far from objective, but they did have the advantage of seeing Brazil through new eyes; therefore they tended to record more detailed information on geographical features, architecture, flora and fauna, climate, and—most importantly—public and domestic life.

Since Freyre's time, Graham's journal has proved of particular interest for scholars and general readers alike. Not only does she offer among the few firsthand accounts of the independence movements in South America, but she also writes vividly and accessibly about everyday life in Brazil, providing a lively view of the country in the first years of its secession from Portugal.

The *Journal* was published in London in 1824. Graham's earlier travel books had been published by Longman, Hurst, Rees, Orme, Brown and Green. However, as noted above, Graham had developed a close professional and personal relationship with publisher John Murray, a fellow Scot, translating and editing books for him and exchanging long letters on literary and personal topics; Graham even stood godmother to his daughter Maria. In 1821, on board the *Doris* and about to sail for South America, Graham wrote Murray to discuss her desire to change publishers, leaving Longman, Hurst, Rees et al. for Murray:

> Now to speak a little of myself and my worthless books.—If I had thought you would have cared about the three months near Rome I should have written to you about it from Italy. But as I had been a patient of Longman's before, and as I had no reason to complain, I thought it might appear strange if I, without explanation applied to you even before my return, and something that occurred in conversation when I did return, induced me to imagine that you would not listen to me after having once been in the hands of others—otherwise I do not think you could have a doubt that I prefer very much your ways to their ways, and that independently of the interest for myself and books which I know would be best consulted by being in your hands the friendship I have felt and experienced from and for both you and Mrs Murray would have led me directly to you—[19]

Having landed in Brazil, survived widowhood, civil war, and an earthquake in Chile, and returned to Brazil en route back home, Graham wrote once more to Murray. Her quite different manner in this letter reveals both the imperious tone she could adopt when she felt wronged and her real insecurity after almost two years of being buffeted about. She opens, winningly, with accusation: "Although you appear to have forgotten me not withstanding that I tried to rouse your memory by

---

19. Maria Graham, letter to John Murray, 31 May 1821. John Murray Archive, National Library of Scotland.

three letters since we left England," she announces (only one of these three appears to have survived, which may in part excuse Murray's apparent silence). She then hints at the value and originality of her work on Brazil and Chile while angling for sympathy:

> I have a great quantity of Journal which I hope either you or some of your brethren will not be sorry to print—I have a great many drawings too and I believe some of them to be interesting enough to be able by their means to make the widow's purse a little fuller than it is other wise likely to be.—I am just recovered from a long and very dangerous illness, which has hindered me in every way—and the consequences of which are keeping me more inactive than I like. However, I have employed myself in arranging much that I had collected before and I think I have authentic materials for a more interesting account of the countries men and things I have seen than any body as yet has.
>
> There is not a shipwreck in every Canto indeed but I have Earthquakes and Civil war; Calamities enough I assure you to last a lifetime [. . .] Now think of my journals etc. I do expect something of and from them—[20]

After landing in London in 1824, busy preparing her journals for publication while gathering teaching materials for her imperial charges, Graham writes Murray again about her difficulties in negotiating her relationship to the rival publishing houses:

> Mr. Longman has just been here. He began 'Mrs Graham do you know Mr. Murray has done very wrong in taking that MS.' I told him I was sorry for that since it was my fault that I had seen Mr. Rees so indifferent about the thing especially the second part and that as it appeared to me that nothing had been done even with the first I had insisted on its being begun because my time in England was so short that I could not afford so many weeks to go over without advancing. Mr. L. said

---

20. Maria Graham, letter to John Murray, 5 Aug. 1823. John Murray Archive, National Library of Scotland.

> I was under a mistake that they did not feel indifferent and that every thing should be done as I pleased and seems to expect *you* will communicate with him about the matter. All I say is *pray* don't dispute or quarrel about *me*—I should be miserable if I thought that my impatience w^d lead to any thing of the kind—[. . .] I hope all will be well and that I shall be able to drink a glass of your wine to commemorate the peace.[21]

After all this palaver, the publishing houses apparently reached a compromise of some kind: the book was issued jointly by both publishing houses, though Longman et al. seem to have managed the printing side of the business. On April 7, 1824, for example, a Longman partner wrote to Graham, "I inclose a statement of the expences of Brazil. [. . .] The Chile shall be published the very moment I can get it ready. You will be so good as to let me know what presentation copies you will require of that volume."[22]

Both journals were well received, and both sold enough to pay Graham royalties of £300 for the Brazil journal, and £353.2.7 for the Chile journal. With respectable print runs of 750 copies each, both books were in print through 1827,[23] though Graham's planned new edition was never published. She requested a copy of her Brazil journal to be bound without the plates (to cut the expense) and carried it with her on her third voyage to the country, updating, correcting and adding information as she re-visited locations she had experienced on her first and second voyages. Since sales did not warrant a second edition, however, she never got the opportunity to make her planned corrections and additions. We have rectified this omission in the current edition, as explained in greater detail under Editorial Method.

Perhaps as a result of the care with which she crafted her narrative persona, critical response to her work grew less dismissive (though not always more positive) as she became more established as a writer. One reviewer, William Jacob, wrote at least two responses to Graham's work: one on her Chile journal (in which he casts aspersion on her accuracy in judging the population of the country and doubts her objectivity in describing Cochrane) and the other of her *Journal*

---

21. Maria Graham, letter to John Murray, Jan. 1824. John Murray Archive, National Library of Scotland.
22. Longman Archive, Reading University Library.
23. Impressions Book 8:25, Longman Archive, Reading University Library.

of a Residence in Brazil (excerpted in this edition). In reviewing the Brazil journal, he dismisses her historical summary, calling it "a hasty and ill-arranged abridgment of Mr. Southey's valuable history of that country" and adding that since she "boasts" of having read widely in the available histories, "it would have been as well to take care to be correct in her quotations." In the course of this review, we see that Jacob disapproves of Graham, a woman venturing to comment on political matters, and he would have preferred to see her produce a "small volume" on domestic matters and minor adventures. In other words, Jacob here enforces the conventions already developing for "female adventurers" who published travel books, and condemns Graham for her departure from acceptable limits for women writers.

Unsurprisingly, Graham was not amused. She wrote repeatedly to John Murray, alternating claims of indifference with demands for more information. In one letter she says, "I wrote you a note yesterday requesting you to lend me the literary gazette in which I have been attacked. I like to see what is said. I am told it is malicious—but I really cannot bring my self to care about it." After moving on to less personal matters—a list of books and Parliamentary proceedings she would like to obtain—she cannot help returning to the topic that agitates her: "I have little doubt of Messrs Longman being the instigators of the crying down of Brazil for the sake of their other friends—but I shall know better when I have seen the thing . . . They are the greatest brutes in all ways that I ever met with—I shall try to call on you tomorrow as I have a good deal to say."[24]

Back in Brazil and having clearly seen another *Quarterly Review* article, this one a review of her Chile journal in which Jacob mocks her devotion to Cochrane and presents a detailed account of his public relations war with General San Martin over their respective roles in winning Chilean independence, she takes Murray to task again. This letter opens by disparaging the politics of the *Quarterly Review,* the conservative magazine he co-founded in 1809 (with the help of Walter Scott and others) to counter Archibald Constable's more liberal *Edinburgh Review.* She opens her letter,

> Tories as your writers in your Quarterly Review generally are, I did not think that you would ever have come to such a pitch of spite for I can call it nothing else as to

---

24. Maria Graham, letter to John Murray, 28 April 1824. John Murray Archive, National Library of Scotland.

> print a long article solely for the purpose of ridiculing any people who should try to be free and of adding one more insult to a great man [Cochrane, of course] who can have no fault in your eyes but that of having been of the liberal party in politics. I send you for the private satisfaction of your author a paper of which I have only to say that as I had the review in my hands only half an hour, (You having forgotten now, as before, to perform your agreement of sending me the reviews) the reply to the calumnies against Lord Cochrane is not perhaps so full as I might make it but as the reviewer pretends to have seen San Martin's charges and Lord C's answer, he knows where to find the rest: however, I presume he rather rejoices in the evil he can do, as he may, he thinks, do evil with impunity to an absent man.—I could forgive any abuse of myself but I never can forgive injustice to my friends.

Having defended Cochrane, she then moves on to address gender dynamics in a way that is surprisingly direct for her time and for her personality (clearly she was so angry that she was not self-censoring the way she generally did):

> It is quite evident the reviewer has not read *me*. That however no *woman* need be surprised at till we have been dead fifty or a hundred years. Men never find out that we are entitled to think or speak our minds—and then the only chance we have is, if we have been profligate mistresses to coarse princes—then indeed there is a chance of having our characters whitewashed and our talents admired *in the Quarterly Review.*[25]

Despite her awareness of the gender constraints governing the production and reception of her travel writing, Graham retains a strong sense of the value of her unique perspective on South American independence. Rather than adapting Gothic conventions by casting herself as an imperiled heroine abandoned in a far and dangerous land, as she can be argued to do in her Chile journal, in writing on Brazil Graham downplays her own role. Instead, she plots the narrative around the

---

25. Maria Graham, letter to John Murray, 19 Dec. 1824. John Murray Archive, National Library of Scotland.

birth of the independent constitutional monarchy of Brazil, as aided by the naval acumen and political example of Britain.

And this may explain why she chose to return to Brazil, ignoring the warnings of friends. Fellow author Maria Edgeworth wrote Graham before she sailed, warning of the dire consequences that might follow this third "jaunt":

> I hope you have reason to believe that this intended jaunt back to the Brazils will agree with you. Be pleased to remember a truth and a truism which enthusiastic geniuses are apt to forget while they are in the heat of racing after some favourite flying colour of Hope's rainbow [. . .] What boots it that you train in the way she should go the future Empress of the Brazils, if you lose your own health and with it (no help for it) your happiness, in the operation.
>
> Look once,- look twice,- look three times, before you leap and before you trust yourself to a new Court in a new world. Dame d'honneur sounds well—and Gouvernante des enfans [sic] de Brazil, very grand: but be clear before you take the weight of labour and responsibility that is to hang upon this title, that there is a solid well-secured remuneration balancing the weight on the other side. You open hearted people never think of these mercenary considerations till it is too late for redress, and then you may, in vain, cry your eyes out or ball [sic] your lungs out or scribble your pen to the stump (even your pen has a stump, I suppose). ("Life" ch. 3)

Graham's imperial ambitions may also help to explain why, after her expulsion from the Palace in 1824, she is devastated not only by the loss of health and the failed payment that Edgeworth predicted with uncanny accuracy, but haunted by her failure to reform the education of the infanta Maria da Gloria and her sisters. Graham seems to have assumed that Brazilians shared her perspective on the triumphant plot she had envisioned for the country, a story that would culminate in the Anglicization of Brazil. How then could she comprehend that her attempts to "civilize" the little Brazilian Princesses were not only unwelcome but unwarranted?

Editorial Method

This edition is reprinted from Graham's first edition of 1824. Although a second edition was never issued (Graham returned to Brazil in 1824), she did request a copy of the published journal to be bound without illustrations, and she carried this with her on her second journey to Brazil, where she hand-annotated the bound journal, making corrections, updates, and emendations intended to be incorporated into a second edition. This annotated edition is held by the Oliveira Lima Library, Catholic University of America, Washington, D.C. Her planned corrections and additions have never been published. The current edition is, then, unique; it incorporates the author's own notes and changes that have hitherto been unavailable to scholars unable to visit the Oliveira Lima Library. (For full details of our editorial method in handling these changes, please see below.)

All editorial decisions have been made with the goal of providing a readable, authoritative, and authentically nineteenth-century text. To that end we have adopted the policies outlined here throughout the edition, in the journal itself as well as the appendices. To produce a more readable and consistent text, we silently corrected typographical errors (including those noted by Graham in her corrections to the first edition) and regularized some spellings, choosing in all cases the most likely spelling of the time as determined by Graham's own preference coupled with the record of usage given by the *Oxford English Dictionary*. We have also regularized Graham's introductions to each journal entry, choosing her most frequently used form (italics, followed by a period and an em-dash). In the interests of producing a text that reflects its original production context, however, we have chosen to preserve Graham's outdated spellings and some irregularities; for example, she preferred "every thing" in lieu of "everything," "crape" over "crêpe," and "trowsers" to "trousers," and like her contemporaries, she used punctuation, capitalization and abbreviations creatively.

As was typical of her era and nationality, Graham had difficulty with South American languages, often spelling Spanish and Portuguese words inaccurately and using accent marks only as the spirit moved her; she found Portuguese vowels, endings, and certain consonants particularly challenging (transcribing Beberibe incorrectly as "Bibiriba"; Curado as "Curada"; Labatut as "Lebatu"; and, more dramatically, Pico do Papagaio as the almost unrecognizable "Beco do Perroquito" and Cuaxindiba as "Guazindiba"). We have regularized spellings to the correct form, if she used it; thus we have changed her few instances of "Boto Fogo" to the correct (and more frequently used) Botafogo. Other than regularizing her spelling, however, we reproduce foreign-language quotations exactly as she gave them, although at times we provide corrected versions in the notes. For the same reason, we will preserve her obsolete place-names, if they were characteristic of her time and consistent in the text. Corrected spellings of all Brazilian place-names, individual names, and quotations can be found in the notes to Américo Jacobina Lacombe's Portuguese translation (Maria Graham, *Diário de uma viagem ao Brasil*. São Paulo: Editora da Universidade de São Paulo, 1990).

This edition contains two sets of footnotes: Graham's original footnotes as well as our editorial annotations. In the latter, we identify Graham's many quotations and provide more information on both important and lesser-known individuals (we were unable to identify a few individuals, and we welcome information from readers). To distinguish between the two types of annotation, Graham's notes will be marked with symbols similar to those she used in the original text (*, †, etcetera), while editors' notes will be marked with superscript numbers.

The most interesting part of our editorial process came in locating, transcribing, and inserting Graham's own planned changes into her journal. These take a variety of forms: handwritten pages interleaved into the journal itself, cards and other documents pasted into the journal, notes scribbled in the margins, deletions and insertions into the original text, and occasional illegible signs and symbols. In working with these materials, our goal throughout was to preserve the readability of the journal as originally published, while honoring Graham's clear wish to make corrections, changes, and additions as she discovered new information or reflected on changes she witnessed during her third visit to Brazil in 1824. To achieve this goal, we have incorporated three types of additions.

First, Graham's minor editing changes have been silently made (deleting or adding one word to a sentence, deleting or adding punctuation, etcetera) and her corrections to typographical or spelling errors have been silently added (correcting Lebatu to Labatut, for example).

Second, more significant editing changes (addition of a phrase or name, clarification of meaning, etcetera) appear within square brackets to indicate added material without unduly disrupting the flow of the original text. Likewise, we have selectively incorporated her longer additions, which are often parenthetical in nature, within brackets when they simply expand upon the original journal.

Third, many of her additions—especially those in the first pages of the journal—do not simply expand upon the original journal but offer updated information on the places she visited on her first and second trips in 1821 and 1823. Since these additions are written from the perspective of her third trip in 1824, during which she keeps this interleaved journal, they could puzzle the reader if incorporated too seamlessly within the original text. To avoid confusion, we have enclosed this type of material within square brackets *and* occasionally moved its location

As a rule, we have inserted Graham's interleaved additions into the journal text on the pages she indicated. Occasionally, however, we have inserted her additions at a slightly different point in the journal text; for example, she interleaved a lengthy update on the state of relations between patriots and royalists in 1824 into the section of the text describing her landing in Pernambuco; we have moved it several pages later, immediately following her discussion of the state of relations between patriots and royalists in 1821. Similarly, she interleaved a letter giving prices for goods imported duty-free to Peru between pages where that subject did not occur; we inserted the letter after a passage discussing import and export duties in Bahia.

At times Graham has left blanks in her additional text, as if she intended to add information later; we have indicated these omissions by {blank}. At other times she simply switches the order of clauses within a sentence; in these cases, we have bracketed the entire sentence to mark its difference from the original text, although all information was included in the original.

In inserting Graham's handwritten annotations, we have chosen to regularize, correct or edit her original notes lightly. Beyond correcting obvious typographical errors, we have punctuated her notes to make them more readable, and we have written out abbreviated phrases. Because she writes in the lightly punctuated, informal style characteristic of the period (and of her own letters, rather than her more formal published journals), we have preserved this characteristic style while also allowing her handwritten annotations to be easily read.

We have selectively included the hand annotations as follows: we include all Graham's factual corrections, changes to language, corrections of typographical errors, etcetera. We inserted all those additions that seem to be made from firsthand knowledge. We have not included illegible additions, for obvious reasons; we also chose to omit several additions to her introductory material on Brazilian history, since (as Lacombe notes) Graham's information on this subject is neither reliable nor useful to contemporary historians.

Occasionally we comment on or clarify changes; {editors' remarks appear within curly brackets}, as do any words of which we are not certain and the word {illegible} as a placeholder within an otherwise legible sentence.

When we consider it of interest, we have included material she added, then crossed through; we indicate the insertions with square brackets followed by {Graham added this paragraph in her annotations, then deleted it}. Graham also deleted several passages from her original journal; while we have retained that material (invariably she chose to delete material of a more personal nature, exactly the type of passage contemporary readers find most interesting), we have noted her wishes by enclosing the relevant passage within square brackets followed by {Graham deleted this material}.

Graham does include interleaved documents, sometimes of considerable historical interest: Brazilian newspaper editorials, a list of ships' passengers (including the Andrada brothers); various proclamations; etcetera. Due to the difficulties and expense of reproduction, we have not included these materials, but they are available for consultation at the Oliveira Lima Library.

Acknowledgments

Soledad Caballero has been honored with amazing colleagues and institutional support that have been instrumental to the completion of this edition. I'd like to thank the Academic Support Committee at Allegheny College for funding summer research, the Woodring Fund of the Department of English at Allegheny College for funds used in replicating sketches and plates, the Department of English at Allegheny College for allowing me work-study students at the proofing stages, and in particular my sincere thanks to Jessica McGrady for her careful attention in reading and proofing the manuscript, and the National Endowment for the Humanities Fund for covering final editing costs. I was also fortunate to participate in two interdisciplinary writing-groups at Allegheny, and I thank my colleagues for their time and comments in the early stages of my thinking about Maria Graham. Finally I'd like to thank the Tufts University Department of English, the Tufts Graduate Student Travel Fund, and the Office of the Dean of the College at Allegheny College for conference funds that initially allowed me to meet Jennifer Hayward in 1998 at a conference in Albuquerque and for the funds that have continued to give me the opportunity to meet with her regularly at various conference venues to work on this project and develop ideas for future collaborative work.

An edition of this nature is a labor of love, not just for editors but also for those forced to contend with and still love them in private life. There are many people who belong in this list of supporters and advocates: in particular, my parents Carlos Enrique Caballero and especially Macarena Caballero Sánchez for instilling in me a love of reading; my sisters, Montserrat and Javiera Caballero, whose generous spirits make taking time off from work overly tempting; my fiercest, most receptive and cunning reader and critic, Sean Desilets; and my partner Richard Heppner, whose patience, passion, and brilliance make play of work. I owe to him the spaces of blissful calm amidst opaque, gossamer filled nights. I dedicate this book to Natalia because she's too young to know its flaws and too beautiful to care about them.

Jennifer Hayward's research for this edition was funded by several grants: the National Endowment for the Humanities summer stipend enabled three months' research in London and Edinburgh; the Huntington Library and British Academy funded additional archival work in London and Edinburgh; and the Bibliographic Society of America supported two research trips to the Oliveira Lima Library at the Catholic University of America in Washington, D.C., to transcribe Maria Graham's own planned changes to her published journal for inclusion in this edition. I am sincerely grateful for the support of these institutions. While at the Oliveira Lima Library, too, the editors benefited immensely from curator Maria Angela Leal's expertise as well as her generous spirit, and we extend our heartfelt thanks.

Over the years, the College of Wooster's generous support for faculty research from the Luce Fund, the Faculty Development Fund, and the sabbatical leave program has enabled travel to Chile, London, Oxford, Edinburgh, and even Nether Wallop in search of Graham's letters, manuscripts, and other sources; most recently, a year's research leave in 2006–07 provided time for completing research and writing.

I am grateful to the staff of the Bodleian Library, the British Library, the Biblioteca Nacional in Santiago, Chile, and the Biblioteca Nacional in Rio de Janeiro, Brazil; particular thanks go to Olive Geddes and the staff of the National Library of Scotland. To Michael Bott of the Reading University Library, Robert Jones of the Government Art Collection, Steve Bulman, and Peter and Bonnie Havholm: thank you so much for your timely and generous assistance. Kathie Clyde has helped with this edition in ways too numerous to count; thank you. From its early stages, research assistants Keli Horton, Dia Mason, Susan Tipton, and Ainsley Whitehead have contributed to this edition with generosity, creativity, and humor. I have been enormously grateful for the wisdom and enthusiasm of fellow Graham aficionados, including Carl Thompson, José Miguel Barros Franco and Regina Akel. And finally, thank you to my amazing family—John, Judith, Robert, Donna, Suzanne, Anna, Sam and especially Patrick, Nicolas and Gabriela, for your travelling spirit, openness to new experience, and especially for surviving the final months of a book yet again.

We thank the Trustees of the National Library of Scotland for permission to quote from letters in the John Murray Archive; the Oliveira

Acknowledgments

Lima Library for reproduction of and permission to use Graham's illustrations as well as 19th century maps of Brazil; and the Government Art Collection of the United Kingdom for permission to reproduce A. W. Callcott's portrait of Lady Callcott.

And finally, heartfelt thanks go to our editors, David Blakesley, Jeanne Moskal, and Rebecca Longster, for their support of this project, for their knowledge, and their patience in seeing the book through to its final stages. Any errors that remain are, of course, entirely our own.

Journal of a Voyage to Brazil

Journal of a Voyage to Brazil

{The following handwritten pages were interleaved before Graham's *Journal* and apparently intended to serve as a prologue to her planned second edition.}

[*July 1824.*—

I have carried this copy of my journal to be interleaved for a double purpose—it may serve to correct the work, to make useful alterations, and at the same time I shall use it *as* a journal of this my second voyage to Brazil.

—In pursuance of my engagement with the Empress Maria Leopoldina at the end of six months passed agreeably in England with my friends I left London on the 23rd of June to proceed to Brazil. And first I went to Richmond where my uncle, my aunt, and their children Isabella, William, and Fullerton were. My uncle Sir David Dundas is one of the most remarkable men I know both in character and intellect,—His education was simple, being that of the high school of Edinburgh during the period when Johnson said truly that in Scotland every man got a mouthful of Learning but no man got his belly full—and in Edinburgh he also studied the rudiments of his profession and at an early age he came to Richmond to reside with his uncle Sir William Robertson, surgeon, who was then apothecary to His Majesty's household at Kew.—A decided taste for Literature which my uncle early felt was much improved by his marriage with his cousin Miss Isabella Robertson, a woman of admirable understanding and elegant taste. Her mother, Miss Berry, was the intimate companion and friend of Thomson. She was also nearly related to the Miss Berrys whom Horace Walpole has celebrated. About the time of my Uncle's marriage a great intimacy subsisted between him and the family of Israel Wilkes, brother of John Wilkes—and the noble and manly mind of that unfortunate man and the useful and elegant pursuits of his family were doubtless of importance in forming that taste for reading in

3

my Uncle, which has been his consolation in many and severe family misfortunes.

The cultivated mind, polished manners, and professional skill of my uncle introduced him to the favour of many eminent men—The great Lord Mansfield—Sir Charles Stewart—Lord Bates and many of both Court and Camp. But the man he loved most and who shewed the strongest attachment to him was His Majesty George III., notwithstanding that his principles in politics conformed with those of the most liberal Whigs.

He was first personally noticed by the king on occasion of His Majesty's illness in 1788—when his conduct was such as that after His Majesty's recovery he said that Dundas was the only man who during his calamity seemed to remember that he was a king and a gentleman—shortly afterwards my uncle being confined to his room by the consequences of a fall from his horse His Majesty called and sat an hour with him, as he condescendingly said to whom the many visits he had paid to him {sic}. On the breaking out of the French revolution my uncle's Whig principles induced him to express very warmly his hopes that that event would better the condition of mankind. This was represented to the King by the late Lord M then {illegible} secretary D— who suggested that a man with such views was highly dangerous in a situation of trust about His Majesty's person—the King asked—Do you employ him yourself?—Yes—"then *you* are the imprudent person, for if he poisoned you Harry he might be my minister, but if he poisoned *me* he could never be king"—and this affectionate confidence so honorable to both continued to the end of the king's life.

On the death of Sir Caesar Hawkins, my uncle became sergeant surgeon and he has been very instrumental in the establishment of the college of surgeons of which he has been very frequently master, and his Hunterian lecture delivered there is one of the most sensible and elegant ever composed. But Sir David's goodness of heart is after all the most valuable and admirable of his qualities and in his profession and among his relations he has had ample room to exercise it. In this last quality his children equal him—but none can come near him in either talents or acquirements. He is a wonderfully handsome man—and his countenance one of the finest I ever beheld—His bust by Chantry conveys a good idea of him. These three days spent with him are perhaps the last on which we may meet in this world, and this thought has drawn me to dwell a little on his character.

From Richmond I went on Saturday with my dear brother Ralph to Bedfont where I spent nearly two days with my own sister, the wife of D. Jones vicar of Bedfont. They have four lovely children—mismanaged but very promising. On Monday I proceeded to Salisbury where Mrs. May's carriage met me, and I went to her house of Nole that I might see the children of Mr. William May of Rio de Janeiro and report their looks to him and his wife and tell how his mother and family do—all domestic friends are doubly dear at a distance. The little Mays are charming children and seem in the way to be admirably educated by their Uncle and Aunt, Mr. and Mrs. Powel. On Wednesday I proceeded to {Marley} lodge to see my husband's sister, the Honorable Mrs. Brodrich and her family. We met and parted affectionately. On leaving her on Saturday I first saw Dr. Miller at Exeter—and then proceeded to Plymouth where I staid till Wednesday with the Countess and the Lady Elizabeth Grey—and the five youngest sons of that admirable family. I saw Sir Alexander and Lady Cochrane each day and like them much more than ever, especially Sir Alexander. *He* seems to think I have done good to Lord Cochrane.—and if it be not undone by indiscreet friends will render his coming home easier and pleasanter. God grant it may be so.

Here ends the prologue to your new journal—]

Preface

Although the *Journal of a Voyage to Brazil*, and of a residence of many months in that country, was not written without a view to publication at some time; yet many unforeseen circumstances forced the writer to pause before she committed it to press, and to cancel many pages recording both public and private occurrences.

Perhaps there is even yet too much of a personal nature, but what is said is at least honest; and if the writer should suffer personally by candour, the suffering will be cheerfully borne.

As to public events, all that can be new in the Journal is the bringing together facts which have reached Europe one by one, and recording the impression produced on the spot by those occurrences which might be viewed in a very different light elsewhere. Some have, no doubt, been distorted by the interested channels through which they have reached the public; some by the ignorance of the reporters; and most by the party spirit which has viewed either with enthusiasm or malignity the acquisition of freedom in any quarter of the globe. [*Quarterly Review* of August 1824. Art.: Chile and Peru is an instance.]

The writer does not pretend to perfect impartiality, for in some cases impartiality is no virtue; but knowing that no human good can be attained without a mixture of evil, she trusts that a fair picture of both has been given, although it has cost some pain in the writing.

Of the natives of the country, or of those engaged in its service, what is said, whether of those still employed or of those no longer in the empire, was written under the impression of the moment; and the writer's confidence in the good sense and justice of the Brazilian government and people is such, that she leaves the passages as they stood at the moment of writing.

The events of the last three years in Brazil have been so important, that it was thought best not to interrupt the account of them, by continuing what may be called the writer's personal narrative after she reached Chile; therefore the two visits to Brazil are printed together, along with an Introduction containing a sketch of the history of the country previous to the first visit, and a notice of the public events of the year of her absence, to connect it with the second.

The Journal of a visit to Chile will form the subject of a separate volume.

[The forts and castles of Valdivia, defended by the Spanish regiment of Cantabria, were captured by Lord Cochrane on the afternoon of the 4th of February 1820—with the Marines of the O'Higgins and a detachment of 200 men of the First battalion of Chile. At the period of the storming, the O'Higgins was 20 leagues in the offing with 7 feet water in her hold, having struck on the Island of Quinquina some few days previous.

The force proceeded from the frigate in the Schooner Montezuma, entered the harbour under Spanish colors, and disembarked just below the Aguada Inglis, in the face of a discharge of Grape from 3 long 32 pounders that commanded the beach. This battery standing on a projecting part of the cliff—and accessible only on one side, where it was defended by high palisades, was carried in gallant style by the O'Higgins' Marines; from this post they pursued the Spaniards through a narrow pathway in the woods, from battery to battery, till they reached the Corral, at the distance of 5 miles and just at dark entered this, the principal fortress, close at the heels of the flying enemy.

The following morning the O'Higgins entered the harbour, and the batteries on the northern side after firing a few shots, struck their flags, the enemy retreating into the Country.

{On verso of this account, Graham includes a hand-drawn map of Valdivia harbour, including sounding depths, indicating that her information here comes from one of her naval sources.}]

It was thought essential that the narratives concerning Spanish and Portuguese America should be kept quite separate; the countries themselves being as different in climate and productions, as the inhabitants are in manners, society, institutions, and government.

Nothing can be more interesting than the actual situation of the whole of South America. While Europe was engaged in the great revolutionary war, that country was silently advancing towards the point at which longer subjection to a foreign dominion became impossible. Circumstances, not laws, had opened the ports of the South Atlantic and the Pacific. Individuals, not nations, had lent their aid to the patriots of the New World: and more warlike instruments and ammunition had gone silently from the warehouses of the merchant to arm the natives against their foreign tyrants, than had ever issued from the arsenals of the greatest nations. But, for a period, Brazil did not openly join in the struggle for independence. The Royal Family of Portugal took refuge there; and converted it, by that step, from a colony into the seat of government, from a state of slavery to one of sovereignty. Therefore, while the court continued to reside at Rio de Janeiro, the Brazilians had no inducement to break with the mother country. But it was very different when the King returned to Lisbon, and the Cortes, forgetting the change of men's minds produced by circumstances, endeavoured to force Brazil back to the abject state from which she had arisen. Then arose the struggle, some part of which it was the fortune of the writer to witness; and concerning which she was able to collect some facts which may serve as materials for future history. She trusts that if the *whole truth* is not to be found in her pages, that there will be *nothing but the truth*.

It is with no small anxiety that the Journal is sent into the world, in the hope that it may tend to excite interest for the country by making it better known. Perhaps the writer has over-rated her powers, in attempting to record the progress of so important an event as the emancipation of such an empire from the thraldom of the mother country. The lighter part of her task, namely, the description of the country, its inhabitants, and the manners of the different classes, both of natives and foreigners, should have been fuller; but that want of health, and sometimes want of spirits, prevented her from making use of all the means that might have been within her reach of acquiring knowledge. She trusts, however, that there is no misrepresentation of importance; and that the Journal, the writing of which has to her beguiled many a lonely and many a sorrowful hour, will not give a moment's pain to any human creature.

[I wish to know if Lord Cochrane had a vote in the plans for invading Peru on his first arrival—
Was it his plan upon which he sailed first to Callao?
Why was the San Antonio an object worth cruizing for before Callao was to be attacked?
When Lord Cochrane went in with the boats and five ships how happened the rest of the *Chile*?
Squadron not to join?
What were the cabals of Zentano against his Lordship.
Whence and how came Rodriguez to be minister?
What promises did San Martin make previous to leaving Valparaiso.
I want information from the time of Lord Cochrane's arrival to his hoisting his flag in Chile.
I want the characters of Cienfuegos, Fuentesilla, Perez—Alcalds—Rosas—and to know what share the bishop had and how he acted at first.
Who and whence is Monte Agudo.
How was Lord Cochrane received after Valdivias.]

JOURNAL

At about six o'clock in the evening of the 31st of July, 1821, after having saluted His Majesty, George IV., who at that moment went on board the Royal George yacht, to proceed to Dublin,—we sailed in the Doris, a 42 gun frigate, for South America. After touching at Plymouth, and revisiting all the wonders of the break-water and new watering place, we sailed afresh, but when off Ushant, were driven back to Falmouth by a heavy gale of wind. There we remained till the 11th of August, when, with colours half-mast high, on account of the death of Queen Caroline, we finally left the channel, and on the 18th about noon came in sight of Porto Santo.

[On the *16th of July 1824* I embarked in the Rinaldo 16 gun brig packet commanded by Lieutenant John Moore R.N. at Falmouth for Brazil—it was about 3 h. P.M. when we got under weigh with a fresh fair breeze.

On the 14th a singular occurrence took place in the harbour the tide which had been running out as usual suddenly returned and rose 23 inches, and then as suddenly retired. On the 15th I happened to be in Truro and there W.W. Tweedy asked if we had experienced any thing singular at Falmouth for that at Truro the ebbing tide had suddenly returned and they had five feet water at the bridge when it should have been nearly out.

July 23rd.—The first word I heard this morning was the voice of William Moore at daybreak saying there it is—the It is Porto Santo—by the time I was dressed we had left it out of sight and were between Madeira and the Desertas. At 1/2 past 9 A.M. we lost our breeze and were long drawing off the land with the easterly current.]

We passed it on the side where the town founded by Don Henry of Portugal, on the first discovery of the island, is situated, and regretted much that it was too late in the day to go in very near it. The land is high and rocky, but near the town there is a good deal of verdure, and higher up on the land, extensive woods; a considerable quantity of wine is made there, which, being a little manufactured at Funchal, passes for true Madeira. As usual in Portuguese colonial towns, the church and convent are very conspicuous. When we passed Porto Santo, and the Desertas, and anchored in Funchal roads, I was disappointed at the calmness of my own feelings, looking at these distant islands with as little emotion as if I had passed a headland in the channel.

[*24th. {1824.*—} I landed at Funchal (the mail went ashore in the boat last night) and spent a very pleasant day with N. Wardrope's family who came down from the mountain to meet me—Although the Island is now Loyal of the King's side the advantages gained by the Constitutional revolution have not been lost. Houses are building, lands clearing. There is a beautiful and neat new market place well arranged and clean—but the chapel of St. Sebastian is not a stone higher than when I was here three years ago. The present Governor is Don Manoel de Portugal formerly governor of the province of Minos Geraes. He has had some trouble to keep the island quiet as the people are always ready to bear a part in every popular commotion in the mother country. I am sorry to say that tranquility has been preserved at the price of arbitrary imprisonment and other harsh proceedings. Within the three years various parties have had the ascendancy here and each in its turn has wreaked its vengeance on its enemies, but the victims of one were not always released by another so that the castle of the peak is still the abode of many of different views and interests. The corn harvest is over here—but the valley of Sta. Cruz was green with cane and maize as we passed—Grapes are here and there ripe enough for eating but the vintage is fully a month later. The chestnut woods are in high beauty. When the wind blows from the eastward it has all the effect of the Sirocco—it curls the leaves and bindings of books, etc.—cracks wood and singularly affects the Human frame. The west wind however cures the ill almost instantaneously. I made some sketches and came on board at 6 o'clock. The difference I perceive in the Wardropes is that they are kinder than on any former occasion. Thermometer 75° ON board.—Since we left Falmouth the range 70 to 75.]

Well do I remember, when I first saw Funchal twelve years ago, the joyous eagerness with which I feasted my eyes upon the first foreign country I had ever approached, the curiosity to see every stone and tree of the new land, which kept my spirits in a kind of happy fever.

> Sweet Memory, wafted by thy gentle gale,
> Oft up the stream of time I turn my sail,
> To view the fairy haunts of long lost hours,
> Blest with far greener shades, far fresher flow'rs.[26]

Now I look on them tamely, or at best only as parts of the lovely landscape, which, just at sunset, the time we anchored, was particularly beautiful. Surely the few years added to my age have not done this? May I not rather hope, that having seen lands whose monuments are all history, and whose associations are all poetry, I have a higher taste, and more discriminating eye? One object never palls—that ocean where the Almighty "Glasses himself in tempests," or over which the gentle wings of peace seem to brood. The feeling that there was a change, however, either in the scene or in me, was so strong, that I ran to my cabin and sought out a sketch I had made in 1809. I compared it with the town. Every point of the hill, every house was the same, and again Nossa Senhora da Monte, with her brilliant white towers shining

---

26. Samuel Rogers (1763-1855), *Pleasures of Memory*, Part II.

Figure 1. Two young Dragon Trees; that with a single head is twenty years old, and had not when I saw it, been tapped for the Dragon's blood. The other is about a century old, and the bark is disfigured by the incision made in it to procure the gum. Courtesy of The Catholic University of America, Oliveira Lima Library, Washington, D.C.

from on high through the evening cloud, seemed to sanctify the scene, while a few rough voices from the shore and the neighbouring ships chaunted the Ave Maria.

Early in the morning of the 19th, we took a large party of the midshipmen on shore to enjoy the young pleasure of walking on a foreign land. To them it was new to see the palm, the cypress, and the yucca, together with the maize, banana, and sugar-cane, surrounded by vineyards, while the pine and chestnut clothe the hills. We mounted the boys on mules, and rode up to the little parish church, generally mistaken for a convent, called Nossa Senhora da Monte. My maid and I went in a bad sort of palankeen, though convenient for these roads, which are the worst I have seen; however, the view made up for the difficulty of getting to it. The sea with the Desertas bounded the prospect: below us lay the roadstead and shipping, the town and gardens, and the hill clothed with vineyards and trees of every climate, which deck the ashy tufa, or compact basalt of which the whole island seems to be composed. Purchas, who like Bowles, believes the story of the discovery of Madeira by the Englishman Masham and his dying mistress, says, that shortly after that event, the woods having taken fire burned so fiercely, that the inhabitants were forced out to sea to escape from the flames.[27] The woods, however, are again pretty thick, and some inferior mahogany among it is used for furniture. The pine is too soft for most purposes. In the gardens we found a large blue hydrangea very common: the fuschia is the usual hedge. Mixed with that splendid shrub, aloes, prickly pear, euphorbia, and cactus, serve for the coarser fences; and these strange vegetables, together with innumerable lizards and insects, tell us we are nearing the tropics.

We spent a very happy day at the hospitable country house of Mr. Wardrope, and our cavalcade to the town at night was delightful. The boys, mounted as before, together with several gentlemen who had joined us at Mr. W.'s, enjoyed the novelty of riding home by torch-light; and as we wound down the hill, the voices of the muleteers answering each other, or encouraging their beasts with a kind of rude song, completed the scene. The evening was fine, and the star-light lovely: we embarked in two shore boats at the custom-house gate, and, after being duly hailed by the guard-boat, a strange machine mounting one old rusty 6 lb. carronade, we reached the ship in very good time.

20th.—We walked a good deal about the town, and entered the cathedral with some feelings of reverence, for a part of it at least was built by Don Henry of Portugal, who founded and endowed the college adjoining. The interior of the church is in some parts gaudy, and there is a silver rail of some value. The ceiling is of cedar, richly carved, and reminds me of some of the old churches at Venice, which present a style half Gothic half Saracenic. Near the church a public garden has lately been formed, and some curious exotic trees placed there with great success. [*24th July 1824*—. The trees in the public garden are wonderfully grown; on one side of the square which it forms is the theater, on the other the infirmary—at the end is the Chafariz or public fountain—near it the Palace and the Friary.]

In rambling about the town, we naturally enquired for the chapel of skulls, the ugliness of which had shocked us when here formerly,

27. Samuel Purchas (1577-1626) compiled travel writing, continuing the work begun by Richard Hakluyt in *Hakluytus Posthumus or Purchas his Pilgrimes; Contayning a History of the World, in Sea Voyages and Lande Travells, by Englishmen and Others* (1625).

and were not sorry to find that that hideous monument of bad taste is falling fast to ruin. [The power of superstition is diminishing. The convents are falling to decay and no one thinks of restoring or repairing them. Santa Clara is in a sad state.] I cannot imagine how such fantastic horrors can ever have been sanctified, but so it is; and the Indian fakir who fastens a real skull round his neck, the Roman pilgrim who hangs a model of one to his rosary, and the friar who decks his oratory with a thousand of them are one and all acted upon either by the same real superstition, or spiritual vanity, craving to distinguish itself even by disgusting peculiarities.

Of late years superstition has been used as an instrument of no small power in revolutions of every kind. Even here it has played its part. A small chapel, dedicated to St. Sebastian, had been removed by the Portuguese government in order to erect a market-place, where all articles of daily consumption were to be sold, a small tax being levied on the holders of stands. This innovation was of course disagreeable to the people, and on the night of the revolution, in November last, some of their leading orators accused the market-place of having, by rudely thrusting out St. Sebastian, occasioned the failure of the vineyards, and threatened the ruin of the island. The market-place was instantly devoted; it was down in a few seconds, and a chapel to St. Sebastian begun. Men, women, and children worked all night, and the walls were raised to at least two-thirds of the intended height; but day brought weariness, and perhaps the morning breeze chilled the fever of enthusiasm. The voluntary labourers worked no more, and no subscription adequate to the hire of workmen to complete it has yet been raised: so that the new St. Sebastian's stands roofless, and the officiating priest performs his masses with no other canopy than the heavens.

Other and better consequences have, however, arisen from the revolution of November. The grievances of the inhabitants of Madeira were severe. The sons of the best families were seized arbitrarily, and sent to serve in the armies of Europe or Brazil: scarcely any article, however necessary, or however coarse, was permitted to be manufactured; the very torches, made of twisted grass and resin, so necessary for travelling these mountain roads after sunset, were all sent from Lisbon, and every species of cultivation, but that of the grape, discountenanced. Thus situated, every class joined heart and hand in the revolution: deputies were sent to the Cortes; petitions respecting the state of agriculture, manufactures, and commerce, were presented; and many, perhaps most, of the grievances were redressed, or at least much lightened.

Till the year 1821, there had never been a printing-press in Madeira; but the promoters of the revolution sent to England for one, which is now set up in Funchal; and on the 2d of July, 1821, the first newspaper, under the name of PATRIOTA FUNCHALENSE, appeared. It contained a well written patriotic preface; and the first article is a declaration of the rights of citizens, and of the pretensions of the Portuguese nation, its religion, government, and royal family, as adopted by the Cortes for the basis of the constitution to be formed for its government. The paper has continued to be published twice a week: it contains a few political addresses and discourses; all foreign intelligence; some tolerable papers on distilling, agriculture, manufactures, and similar topics; some humourous pieces in prose and verse; poems *on several occasions;* and, at the end of the month, a table of the receipts and expenditures of government. Among the advertisements I observe one informing the public where *leeches* may be bought at about two shillings and sixpence a piece. [The newspaper much fallen off under the royalists.]

I thought it curious to observe this first dawning of literature and politics in this little island. There are certainly enough anglicisms in the paper, to point out the probable country of some of the writers; and there are, as might be looked for, some traces of the residence of British troops in the colony; but on the whole, the paper is creditable to the editors, and likely to be useful to the island. I hear the articles on the making of wines and brandies very highly spoken of. Madeira, lying in the finest climate in the world, beautiful and fertile, and easy of access to foreigners, ought not to be a mere half civilised colony.

23d.—We sailed yesterday from Funchal, and soon lost sight of the

> Filha do oceano
> Do undoso campo flor, gentil MADEIRA.[28]

At night, I sat a long time on the deck, listening to the sea songs with which the crew beguile the evening watch. Though the humourous songs were applauded sufficiently, yet the plaintive and pathetic seemed

---

28. António Dinis da Cruz e Silva (1731-1799), Portuguese poet; these lines open his *Ode XLII A João Fernandes Cieira, Restaurador da Capitania de Pernambuco.*

the favourites; and the chorus to the Death of Wolfe was swelled by many voices. Oh, who shall say that fame is not a real good! It is twice blessed—it blesses him who earns, and those who give, to parody the words of Shakespeare. Here, on the wide ocean, far from the land of Wolfe's birth, and that of his gallant death, his story was raising and swelling the hearts of rough men, and exciting love of country and of glory by the very sound of his name.[29] Well may he be called a benefactor to his country who, by increasing the list of patriotic sailors' songs, has fostered those feelings and energies which have placed Britain's "home upon the mountain wave, and her march upon the deep."

The charms of night in a southern climate have been dwelt upon by travelled poets (for I call Madame de Stael's writings poetry[30]), and even travelled prose writers; but Lord Byron alone has sketched with knowledge and with love, the moonlight scenery of a frigate in full sail. The life of a seaman is the essence of poetry; change, new situations, danger, transitions from almost deathlike calm to the maddest combinations of horror—every romantic feeling called forth, and every power of heart and intellect exercised. Man, weak as he is, baffling the elements, and again seeing that miracle of his invention, the tall ship he sails in, tossed to and fro, like the lightest feather from the sea-bird's wing—while he can do nothing but resign himself to the will of Him who alone can stay the proud waves, and on whom heart, intellect, and feeling, all depend!

25th.—Nothing can be finer than the approach to Teneriffe,* especially on such a day as this; the peak now appearing through the floating clouds, and now entirely veiled by them. As we drew near the coast, the bay or rather roadstead of Oratava, surrounded by a singular

---

* The Chinerfe of the Guanches.

29. Major General James Wolfe (1727-1759), British general in the French and Indian War; his defeat of the French established British rule in Canada. Graham is probably referring to Thomas Paine's song "The Death of Wolfe, on the Plains of Abraham" (1759).

30. Anne-Louise Germaine Necker, Baronne de Staël-Holstein (1766-1817) received an enlightened education by her mother and became a renowned conversationalist, writer, and traveler, hosting famous salons and writing novels, plays, essays, history, and memoirs. A highly influential figure for Romantic women writers, Madame de Staël addressed central questions of the woman writer, the woman artist, and the woman's intellect independent of male influence. Graham may refer here to *Corinne*, a novel set in Italy (*ODNB* 52:36-38).

mixture of rocks, and woods, and scattered towns, started forth at once from beneath the mists, which seemed to separate it from the peak, whose cold blue colour formed a strong contrast to the glowing red and yellow which autumn had already spread on the lower grounds.

We anchored in forty fathoms water with our chain-cable, as the bottom is very rocky, excepting where a pretty wide river, which, though now dry, rolls a considerable body of water to the sea in the rainy season, has deposited a bed of black mud. There are many rocks in the bay, with from one to three fathoms water, and within them from nine to ten. The swell constantly setting in is very great, and renders the anchorage uncomfortable. [*1824—27th July.*—We landed the mail here having stood on and off all night not being able to make the port last night. I wrote a note to N. Galway, that being the only communication I could have with the shore.]

26th.—I went ashore with Mr. Dance, the second lieutenant, and two of the young midshipmen, for the purpose of riding to the Villa di Oratava, which is situated where the ancient Guanche capital stood. We landed at the Puerto di Oratava, several miles from the villa: it is defended by some small batteries, at one of which is the very difficult landing-place, sheltered by a low reef of rocks that runs far out, and occasions a heavy surf. I took my own saddle ashore: and being mounted on a fine mule, we all began our journey towards the hill. The road is rough, but has evidently once been made with some pains, and paved with blocks of porous lava; but the winter rains have long ago destroyed it, and it does not seem to be any body's business to put it in repair.

The first quarter of a mile on either hand presented a scene so black and stony, that I was surprised to learn that we had been passing through corn land; the harvest was over, and the stubble burned on the ground. The produce here is scanty; but being so near the port, it repays the labour and expense of cultivation. We saw the botanical garden so much praised by Humboldt;[31] but it is in sad disorder,

---

31. Alexander von Humboldt's *Personal narrative of travels to the equinoctial regions of America, during the years 1799-1804* (with Aimé Bonpland) was, by the time of Graham's journey, the standard work on South and Central America. With characteristic independence, Graham takes a few digs at the man she calls "the Baron Humboldt" in writing to her friend and editor John Murray: "Well he is a wonderful traveller and wonderfully gifted and gratified – but his eyes are too fine and philosophical for me. I saw many things at [Teneriffe] and in [Oratava] that he has thought beneath him and strained

having been for some time entirely neglected. However, the very establishment of such a thing brings in new plants, and perhaps naturalises them. Here, the sago-palm, platanus, and tamarind, as well as the flowers and vegetables of the north of Europe, flourish so well as to promise to add permanently to the riches of this rich island. As we ascended towards the villa the prospect improved; the vineyards appeared in greatest beauty, every other crop still standing in the luxuriant valleys, the rocky cliffs of the mountains clothed with wood, and every thing glowing with life. Wheat, barley, a few oats, maize, potatoes, and caravansas, all grow freely here. The food of the common people consists chiefly of Polenta, or maize flour, used nearly as the Scotch peasants use their oatmeal, in cakes, brose, or porridge, which last is suffered to grow cold, and then most commonly cut in slices and toasted. After the maize, potatoes are the favourite food, together with salt fish. The potatoe is always in season, being planted every month, and consequently producing a monthly crop. The fishery employs from forty-five to fifty vessels of from seventy to ninety tons' burden, from the island of Teneriffe alone; the fish are taken on the coast of Africa, and salted here.

To a stranger the sight of the long walls of black porous lava, built terracewise to support the vegetable mould, is very striking; but the walls cannot be called ugly, while the clustering vine and broad-spreading gourd, climb and find support on them: these, however, soon disappeared, and were replaced by field and garden enclosures. After a pleasant but hot ride, we arrived at the villa about noon, and went to the house of Señor Don Antonio de Monteverde, who accompanied us to M. Franqui's garden, to see one of the wonders of the island, the famous Dragon Tree. Humboldt has celebrated this tree in its vigour; it is now a noble ruin. In July, 1819, one half of its enormous crown fell: the wound is plaistered up, the date of the misfortune marked on it, and as much care is taken of the venerable vegetable as will ensure it for at least another century. I sat down to make a sketch of it; and while I was drawing, learned from Mr. Galway the following history of the family of its owner, [which a little skill in language and a little adorning with sentiment might convert into a modern novel.{Graham deleted this clause}]—About the year 1760, the Marquis Franqui, upon some disgust, made over his estates in trust to his brother, and emigrated to

---

my eyes after many another that has I presumed changed places since he was there" (written from Pernambuco, Sept. 23, 1821).

France, where he remained until 1810, regularly receiving the proceeds from his estates in Teneriffe. Meantime, during the early period of the revolution, he married; and his only child, a daughter, was born. This marriage, however, was only a civil contract, such being then the law of France, and with a woman divorced from another, who was still living. But neither the validity of the union nor the legitimacy of the child was ever questioned; and the Marquis Franqui returning to his native country, brought with him his daughter, introducing and treating her as his heiress. She appeared to be received as such by his family; and at his death he appointed trustworthy guardians to her and her estates, one of whom is her husband's father. No sooner, however, was the Marquis dead, than his brother claimed his property, alleging that the church had never sanctioned the Marquis's marriage, and that the daughter consequently, as an illegitimate child, could have no claim on his estates. He therefore commenced a lawsuit against her and her guardians, and the suit is still pending. Meantime the court receives the rents; the garden, the chief ornament of the town, is running wild, and the house is deserted.

The dragon tree is the slowest of growth among vegetables; it seems also to be slowest in decay. In the 15th century, that of Oratava had attained the height and size which it boasted till 1819. It may have been in its prime for centuries before; and scarcely less than a thousand years must have elapsed, before it attained its full size. Excepting the dragon trees at Madeira, the only many-headed palm I had seen before was that at Mazagong in Bombay. It is crowned, however, with a leaf like that of the palmetto; but the tufts of the dragon tree resemble the yucca in growth. The palm tree at Mazagong, like the adansonia in Salsette, is reported to have been carried thither by a pilgrim from Africa, probably from Upper Egypt, where late travellers mention this palm.

On our return from the garden to Don Antonio's house, we were most kindly received by his wife and daughter, the latter of whom played a long and difficult piece of music most excellently. It was, however, English, in compliment to us, though we should have preferred some of her own national airs. After the music, we were conducted to a table spread in the gallery that surrounds the open court in the middle of the house, and covered with fruits, sweetmeats, and wines, which were pressed upon us most hospitably; till finding it time to return, the ladies both embraced me, and we began our journey down the hill, having first looked into the churches, which are spacious and handsome, a good deal in the style of those of Madeira, but finer.

As we rode along, we observed a large Dominican convent, the only one now on the island. The recent law passed by the Spanish Cortes for the suppression of religious houses, has been strictly enforced here. No more than one convent of each denomination is allowed to subsist, and great checks are put on the profession of new members. As to the revolution here, the inhabitants had known from authentic though not official authority of what had taken place in the mother country, three weeks before they received any notification from either court or Cortes. When notice did arrive, the magistrates assembled the people, read their orders, and took their oaths to support the Cortes; the people shouted, and made a bonfire: next day the forms of law and justice were declared to be changed, the tribunals proceeded accordingly, and all was over and quiet.

The Canary Islands boast of two bishoprics, both of which are now vacant, yet have not one newspaper. The only printing press has been so long in disuse that there is nobody who can work it in the country. I could not learn that there are any manufactures in Teneriffe; if there are, I conclude they must be in the neighbourhood of Laguna or Santa Cruz. Oratava appears to be the district of corn and wine.

We returned to the port by a longer road than that by which we left it. In the hedges, the boys, with no small delight, gathered fine ripe black-berries, which were growing among prickly pear and other tropical plants. The fields, vineyards, and orchards we had seen from the former road we now passed through; and as it was a *fiesta,* we saw the peasants in their best attire, and their little mud huts cleanly swept and garnished. They seem gentle and lively, not much darker than the natives of the south of Europe; and if there be a mixture of Guanche blood, it is said to be traced in the high cheek-bones, narrow chins, and slender hands and feet which in a few districts seem to indicate a different race of men. I regret that I had not time to see more of the people and the country; but not being travellers from curiosity, and belonging to a service that may not swerve from the strictest obedience, we dared not even think of a farther excursion.

Half-way down the hill, we entered a ravine, the dry bed of a winter torrent, where there were rue, lavender, prickly pear, hypericum, and spurge; but not a blade of grass had survived the summer's drought. We passed a heap of black ashes, which anywhere but at the base of the peak would be called a respectable mountain. It has not been cold long enough to be disguised by vegetation; and though on one side the vine is beginning to clothe its rugged surface, yet the greater part is frightfully barren. Shortly after we passed it, we arrived at Mr. Galway's garden-house, and found his lady, a Spaniard of Irish extraction, ready to receive us. As I had seen in some old Scotch houses, the best bed-chamber served as drawing-room; but the dressing-room is apart, and from the front there is an opening to a pleasant terrace, commanding a charming view. Our dinner was a mixture of English and Spanish cookery and customs: the Spanish part consisted of part of a Darter, a very fine fish, white, but resembling a salmon in taste, with sauce made of small lobsters, oil, vinegar, garlic, and pimento; some excellent stews, and mixtures of vegetables and quails roasted in vine leaves; the rest were all English; and the wines, the growth of the island, and ices* were delicious. Neither the pine-apple nor water-melon grow in Teneriffe, but abundance of the latter are brought from Grand Canary. All the common garden fruits of Europe flourish here; but too little attention is paid to horticulture. This island, or at least the part I have seen, evidently belongs to a state that has once been great; but is now too poor or too weak to foster its foreign possessions. Some fine houses begun are in an unfinished state, and appear to have been so for years; others, though falling, are neither rebuilt nor repaired; and the only things like present prosperity, are the neat English country-houses.

It was sunset before we reached the boats that were to convey us to the ship; and we had some difficulty both in getting off and in going alongside of the frigate, owing to the great swell. The night, however, was fine, and the scene enlivened by the lights in the fishing boats, which, like those in the Mediterranean, are used to attract the fish. On shore, the lights of the ports and villa, and the fires of the charcoal burners shining from amidst the dark hanging forests of pine, and those of the limekilns in the direction of Laguna, appeared like a brilliant illumination; and there being not a cloud, the outline of the peak was well defined on the deep blue of the nocturnal sky.

27th August.—To-day, some of our new friends, both Spanish and English, came on board; but the swell was so great, that only one escaped sea-sickness. Mrs. Galway was fearful of suffering, so did not come, but she sent me some of the beads found in the sepulchres of the

---

* The ice is procured from a large cavern near the cone of the peak; it is almost full of the finest ice all the year round.

Figure 2. The Green Dragon Tree of Oratava, of which Humboldt has given so interesting an account. He saw it in all its greatness; I drew it after it had lost half its top. Courtesy of The Catholic University of America, Oliveira Lima Library, Washington, D.C.

Guanches: they are of hard baked clay. Mr. Humboldt, whose imagination was naturally full of South America, has conjectured that they might have been used for the same purpose as the Peruvian quipos, but they are inconveniently large for that use. They are not unlike the beads Belzoni found in the mummy pits in Egypt, and they closely resemble some of the many kinds of beads with which the Bramins have counted their mantras time immemorial.[32] The Oriental custom of dropping a bead for every prayer having been adopted by the Christians of the west, and still continuing in Roman Catholic countries, appears, on that account, too common to deserve the notice of a philosophical traveller; and therefore the Guanche shepherds, or goatherd kings, are rather supposed, like the polished Peruvians, to have recorded the annals of their reigns with clay beads, than allowed to tell them with their orisons, like the Bramins of the Ganges, the shepherds

---

32. Giovanni Battista Belzoni (1778-1823), archaeologist, excavated sites in Egypt and elsewhere.

of Mesopotamia, or the anchorets of Palestine and Egypt, because the modern monk does the same. The Guanche mummies are now of very rare occurrence. During the early times of the Spanish government of the island, their sepulchres were carefully concealed by the natives; now, intermarriage with their conquerors, and consequent change of religion and habits, have rendered them careless of them, and they are, generally speaking, really forgotten, and only discovered accidentally in planting a new vineyard, or ploughing a new field.

28th.—This morning left the "still vext" bay of Oratava, and before sunset saw Palma and Gomera. [*27th July 1824.*—We passed close to Gomera i.e. its northern and western parts. Its port is at the southeast point. The side we saw appeared totally inaccessible, and I should have fancied it not habitable but for one little valley which though very precipitous had in it a number of palm trees; and I think vines or some such green crop spreading on the rocks. A few houses were scattered there and we saw three men at the foot of the rocks apparently gathering shell fish.] The Canary Islands, supposed to be the Fortunate Islands of the ancients, were discovered accidentally in 1405. Betancour, a Frenchman, took possession of them for Spain; but the natives were brave, and it cost both the Spaniards and Portuguese, who possessed them by turns, much blood and treasure to conquer the country and exterminate the people, for their wars ended in nothing less. Purchas complains that he could not obtain the reading of some travels by an Englishman who had visited the Peak; the good pilgrim's curiosity had been strongly excited by the particulars he had learnt from books, and the journals of some of his friends who had travelled, which he has carefully related: they are such as to make me regret that he has not recorded more, and that I cannot see more. We brought with us from Oratava one of the finest goats I ever saw; I presume she was a descendant of the original flock which the supreme deity of the Guanches created to be the property of the kings alone: she is brown, with very long twisted horns, a very remarkable white beard, and the largest udder I ever saw.

29th.—Passed the island of Hierro or Ferro, the old first meridian; which honour, I presume, it enjoyed from having been considered as the most western land in the world until the discovery of America. We were very close to it, and all agreed that we never saw so hard-looking and inaccessible a place. We saw some fine woods, a few scattered houses, and one village perched upon a hill, at least 1500 feet above us. The Peak of Teneriffe still visible above the clouds.

Sept. 1st.—The flying-fish are become very numerous, and whole fleets of medusæ have passed us; some we have picked up, besides a very beautiful purple sea-snail. This fish has four horns, like a snail, the shell is very beautifully tinted with purple, and there is a spongy substance attached to the fish which I thought assisted it to swim: it is larger in bulk than the whole fish. One of them gave out fully a quarter of an ounce of purple fluid from the lower part of the fish. A fine yellow locust and a swallow flew on board; and as we believe ourselves to be four hundred miles from the nearest land, Cape Blanco, we cannot enough admire the structure of the wings that have borne them so far.

[*29th July 1824.*— Lat.24°N Long.19°21 W flying fish came on board.

August 1st—We came in sight of Sant. Antonio, the western island of the groupe of the Cape de Verde. The morning was so hazy that although the land is computed to be 7400 ft. high we did not discover it till close to it. I have seen many of the rocky and arid looking islands of the ocean but never one whose appearance was so inhospitable as this. The rocks are piled high one over the other and their hard summits stand up like the pinnacles of some ruined Gothic castle. The whole island seems rent with mighty chasms whose perpendicular sides carry the eye upwards from the shore to the topmost heights without a break—no tree or shrub grows here with the exception of a few in one little valley where the declivity is more gentle. On the side of one of the mountains, I observed a smoke which disappeared for a few minutes and then appeared again—bye and bye on approaching nearer I perceived with the glass that the rocky earth round it was blackened and numbers of stones lay confusedly in its neighborhood. The column of smoke burst out periodically and ascended in a special column nearly to the top of the ridge and then entirely dispersed. Generally three jets succeeded each within the space of ten minutes and then there was a cessation for at least ten minutes more and so it continued while I watched it for four hours. As we approached nearer to the shore, part of the rocks appeared as if they had been the sides of vast caverns which had burst. The substance of such rocks as were near enough to see fairly seemed to me to be very hard lava—and they stood like walls out of the sea. Only one valley had a green field and a few trees in it and a cottage or two with a path down to the sea. Short burnt grass covered some of the ledges of this rocky land. Here and there bare patches of very white sand were visible. Although we had a fine breeze the Thermometer stood at 75°.

6th August.— Lat.9°-9' N.Long.25°-17'-W.—Ther at 80—We sunk a bottle with a line of 40 fas—the water that came up in it sunk the mercury to 75°—while a bucket of water taken up alongside raised it to 82°.

8th.—Lat.6°-36' no casting made alternate hot calms and hotter rains for 48 hours.]

Our school for the ship's boys is now fairly established, and does Mr. Hyslop, our school-master, great credit;[33] that for the midshipmen is going on very well, being kept in the fore-cabin under the captain's eye. The boys have his presence, not only as a check to idleness or noise, but as an encouragement to industry. He is most anxious to make them fit to be officers and seamen in their profession, and good men and gentlemen both at sea and on shore. Happily they are all promising; but if G—should disappoint us, I never will believe in youthful talent, industry, or goodness more. Our days pass swiftly, because busily. The regular business of the ship, the school, astronomical observations, study of history and modern languages, and nothing permitted to pass without observation, fill our time completely.

Lord Bacon says, "It is a strange thing that in sea voyages, where there is nothing to be seen but sky and sea, men should make diaries; but in land travel, wherein so much is to be observed, for the most part they omit it, as if chance were fitter to be registered than observation."[34] However, for once, his lordship has only seen, or perhaps only spoken, in part. Sea and sky must be observed before we can know the laws by which their great changes or chances are regulated. Observations on the works of man, as cities, courts, etc. may be omit-

---

33. Probably James Hyslop, "a schoolmaster who was establishing himself as a minor Scots poet" (Vale, *Frigate* 50).

34. Sir Francis Bacon (1561-1626), English philosopher and essayist whose *Essays, Civil and Moral* are great favorites of Graham's; she cites them repeatedly in both the Brazil and the Chile journals. Here she quotes from Bacon's *Essay XVIII, Of Travel*, where the traveler is advised, "Let him not stay long in one city or town; more or less as the place deserveth, but not long; nay, when he stayeth in one city or town, let him change his lodging from one end and part of the town to another." Graham's subsequent quotation from Bacon comes from the same essay.

ted, for we know their authors, and can have recourse to them, their motives, and their history, whenever we please; but the great operations of nature are so above us, that we must humbly mark them, and endeavour to make their history a part of our experience, in order that we pass safely through their vicissitudes. Hence it is, that the commonest details of the early navigators, their sunrise and sunset, their daily portionings of food and water, are read with a deeper interest than the liveliest tour through civilised countries and populous cities; that Byron's passage through Chiloe continues to excite the most profound sympathy; while Moore's lively view of society and manners in France or Italy, are now seldom or languidly read.[35] The uncertainty, the mystery of nature, keep up a perpetual curiosity; but I suspect that if we knew the progress and dependance of her operations, as well as we do those of an architect or bricklayer, the history of the building of a theatre or a dwelling-house might vie in interest with that of a sea voyage.

The books we intend our boys to read are,—history, particularly that of *Greece, Rome, England,* and *France;* an outline of general history, voyages, and discoveries; some poetry, and general literature, in French and English; Delolme, with the concluding chapter of Blackstone on the history of the law and the constitution of England; and afterwards the first volume of Blackstone, Bacon's Essays, and Paley.[36] We have only three years to work in; and as the *business* of their life is to learn their profession, including mathematics, algebra, nautical astronomy, theory and practice of seamanship, and duty as officers, with all the *technicalities* belonging to it,—this is all we dare propose.

---

35. Frances Moore Brooke (1788/9-1881) published society novels under the pseudonym "Madame Panache"; one of her best-known works, *Historical Life of Joanna of Sicily*, was published the same year as Graham's South American journals.

36. Graham plans a traditional course of study for her "boys" the midshipmen. Jean Louis De Lolme or Delolme (1740–1806), who practiced law in Geneva, was forced into exile as a result of his criticism of the Swiss legal system. While in England he studied the constitutional system and published his highly influential *Constitution de l'Angleterre* (1771; *The Constitution of England*). William Blackstone (1723–1780), English jurist, published his *Commentaries on the Laws of England* (1765–1769). William Paley (1743-1805), theologian, wrote philosophical and theological works including *Principles of Moral and Political Philosophy* (1785) and *A View of Evidences of Christianity* (1794). For Bacon, see note 34.

5th.—We have begun to look forward to that festival of the seamen, the crossing the line. I know not whence the custom is derived, but the Arabs observe it with ceremonies not very unlike those practised by our own sailors. To-day a letter, containing a sketch of the intended festival, with thanks for permission to keep it, was sent into the cabin. I shall copy it with its answer. I find that some captains have begun to give money at the next port, instead of permitting this day of misrule. Perhaps they may be right, and perhaps in time it may be forgotten; but will it be better that it should be so? It is the sailors' only festival; and I like a festival: it gives the heart room to play. The head in one class, and the limbs in another, work every day, and in diverse, if not opposite directions; but on a festival, the hearts of all beat the same way: yet I would not have them too often, for

> If every day were playing holiday,
> To sport would be as tedious as to work;

the converse of the proverb, "All work and no play, makes Jack a dull boy." But to our letters.

> The Sons of Neptune, of His Majesty's ship Doris, commanded by Captain T. G., return their most grateful thanks for his kind condescension for granting them the favour that has been allowed to them from time immemorial, in crossing the Equinoctial, on our Old Father Neptune's dominions, when we hope the characters will meet your Honour's approbation, which will appear in the margin.

Thomas Clark, quarter-master,	—Neptune.
J. Ware, forecastle,	—Amphitrite.
W. Knight,	—Amphitrite's Son.
W. Sullivan, 2d captain main-top,	—Triton.
C. Brisbane (negro),	—Triton's Horse.
J. Thompson, gunner's mate,	—High Sheriff.
J. White, forecastle,	—Sub Sheriff.
W. Sinclair, captain forecastle,	—Barber.
J. Smith, J. Forster, Michael Jaque,	—Barber's Mates.
J. Gaggin,	—Clerk.
W. Bird, captain fore-top,	—Chief Constable.

Nine assistants.	
J. Duncan, boatswain's mate,	—Coachman.
J. Clark,	—Postilion.
J. Leath,	—Footman.
J. Speed,	—Painter.
W. Lundy,	—Bottle-holder.
W. Williamson,	—Satan.
J. Williams,	—Judge Advocate.
Eight Sea-horses.	

So we have given you as good a relation as possibly our weak abilities afford us; and, honoured Captain, believe us when we say, we wish you every happiness this life can afford, and your honoured lady entirely included, and believe us yours, etc. etc. etc.

BRITTON'S SONS.

Answer.

I received your letter with the list of characters that are to appear in Father Neptune's train on our crossing the line, of which I completely approve. I have to thank you for your kind wishes both for Mrs. G— and myself, and to assure you, that the greatest pleasure I can feel in the command of this ship, will be in promoting the happiness and comfort of the whole of Britain's sons on board the Doris.

Believe me your sincere friend,
THOS. G—,
H. M. S. Doris, at Sea, Sept. 5th, 1821.
To Britain's Sons, H. M. S. Doris.

It would be worth while to enquire into the origin of the merrymaking on crossing the line. As the Arabs, an astronomical people, have it, it has probably some reference to their now-forgotten worship of the heavenly bodies. Like us, they set on fire some combustible matter or other, and let it float away, but they add some food to it, as if there had once been a sacrifice accompanying the festival. Such, at least, I have been assured by several gentleman well acquainted with the Arab traders in the Eastern sea, is their practice.

18th.—We have done nothing but sail on with very variable weather, for the last thirteen days.

> From world to world our steady course we keep,
> Swift as the winds along the waters sweep,
> Mid the mute nations of the purple deep.[37]

One night we observed that luminous appearance of the sea so often described, but it was not so brilliant as I remember to have seen it near the same latitude. The next morning we found the temperature of the sea, at the surface, two degrees higher than that of the atmosphere. Last night at 8 P. M. we crossed the line: to-day, accordingly, our Saturnalian festival took place.

About six o'clock P. M. yesterday, the officer of the watch was informed that there was a boat with lights alongside, and begged to shorten sail. The captain immediately went on deck, and Neptune hailed from the fore part of the rigging, "What ship?" "Doris." "Who commands?" "Captain T. G." "Where from?" "Whitehall." "Where bound?" "A man of war's cruize." Upon which Triton mounted upon a sea-horse, admirably represented, appeared as bearer of a letter containing the names of all who had not yet crossed the line, and who were consequently to be initiated into the mysteries of the Water God. Triton having thus executed his commission, rode off, and was seen no more till 8 o'clock this morning, when Neptune being announced, the captain went on deck to receive him.

First came Triton mounted as before, then a company of sea-gods or constables dressed in oakum and swabs, but having their arms and shoulders bare, excepting the paint which bedaubed them. Neptune with trident and crown, Amphitrite by his side, and their son at their feet, appeared in a car drawn by eight sea-horses, and driven by a sea god: the train followed in the persons of the lawyers, barbers, and painters. The whole pageant was well dressed, and going in procession, fully as picturesque as any antique triumphal or religious ceremony; the fine forms of some of the actors struck me exceedingly. I never saw marble more beautiful than some of the backs and shoulders displayed; and the singular clothing to imitate fishes instead of legs, and seaweed skirts, which they had all adopted, carried one back for centuries, to the time when all this was religion.

After the progress round the decks, a conference with the captain, and a libation in the form of a glass of brandy, to which the god and

---

37. Samuel Rogers (1763-1855), *The Voyage of Columbus, Canto II.*

goddess vied with each other in devotion, the merriment began. Mock-shaving, or a fine paid, was necessary to admit the new comers to the good graces of their watery father; and while he was superintending the business, all the rest of the ship's company, officers and all, proceeded to duck each other unmercifully. None but women escaped, and that only by staying in my cabin. The officer of the watch, sentries, quarter-masters, and such as are absolutely necessary to look after the ship, are of course held sacred; so that some order is still preserved. It seemed really that "madness ruled the hour;" but at the appointed moment, half past eleven, all ceased: by noon, every body was at his duty, the decks were dried, and the ship restored to her wonted good order. The whole of our gunroom officers dine with us, and we flatter ourselves that we shall end the day as happily as we have begun it.*

20th.—The long tiresome calms, and the beautiful moonlight nights near the equator, have been talked of, and written of, till we know all about them. Mention but passing the line, and you conjure up a wide, apparently interminable, glassy dull sea: sails flapping, a solitary bird sinking with heat, or a shark rising lazily to catch a bait; or, at best, a calm warm night, with a soft moonlight silvering over the *treacherous* deep, and rendering the beholders, who ought to be lovers if they are not, insensible of the rocks that may lurk below.—But ours was not the *beau ideal* of crossing the line: we had fresh breezes in the day, and thunder and lightning at night; saw few tropic birds, and those very vigorous, and fish more nimble than sharks, or even sun-fish, of which, however, we met a due proportion. I had once been in a tropical calm, and I really, after trying them both, prefer the breezes and thunder-storms. The other night we had one, such as Milton talks of:

* Frezier, who crossed the line, March 5th, 1712, says,

> When it was no longer to be doubted that we were to the southward of the line, the foolish ceremony practised by all nations was not omitted.
>
> The persons to be so served are seized by the wrists, to ropes stretched fore and aft on the second deck for the officers, and before the mast for the sailors; and after much mummery and monkey tricks, they are let loose, to be led after one another to the main mast, where they are made to swear on a sea chart that they will do by others as is done by them, according to the laws and statutes of navigation: then they pay to save being wetted, but always in vain, for the captains themselves are not quite spared."

Jaques le Maire, the first who sailed round Cape Horn, mentions in his Journal, 8th July, 1615, baptizing the sailors when he arrived at the *Barrels*.—Has this any thing in common with the ceremony of crossing the line?

> Either tropic now
> 'Gan thunder, and both ends of heav'n: the clouds
> From many a horrid rift abortive poured
> Fierce rain with lightning mixt, water with fire
> In ruin reconciled; nor slept the winds
> Within their stoney caves, but rush'd abroad
> From the four hinges of the world, and fell
> On the vext wilderness.[38]

I never see a thunder-storm at sea, but it reminds me of the vision of Ezekiel:

> The sapphire blaze,
> Where angels tremble while they gaze.[39]

It is awful and grand every where: fearful in the plain, sublime among the mountains; but here, on the ocean, with nothing to intercept its bolt, the horrible is superadded, and he must be more or less than man that does not at least take thought during its continuance.

Friday, September 21st.—At length we are in sight of the coast of Brazil, which here is low and green, about two degrees to the northward of the point first discovered by Vincente Pinzon, in 1500.* The weather is very squally, and there is a heavy swell: we are anchored about eight miles from Olinda, the capital of Pernambuco, in fifteen fathoms water, but though we have fired more than one gun for a pilot, none seems to be coming off.

[*August 18th, 1824.*—On making the land near Pernambuco saw a Man of War—Soon made her out to be the Pedro Primeiro.—A midshipman (young Da Costa) came on board.—I sent a message to Lord Cochrane. Soon after Captain Grenfell boarded us, and then I went with him towards the Pedro Primeiro—Saw the Admiral leave the ship as it proved for the purpose of calling on me. I returned and dined—and had pleasant and satisfactory conversation with Lord Cochrane—see papers—The Empress has another child whether male or female I don't know—mail landed.]

* Cabral first took possession of the country which he called *that of the Holy Cross*, for the crown of Portugal; Amerigo Vespucci 1504, called it Brazil, on account of the wood.

---

38. John Milton (1608-1674), *Paradise Regained, Book IV.*
39. Thomas Gray (1716-1771), *The Progress of Poesy: A Pindaric Ode*; Gray here references Ezekiel 1:20, 26, and 28.

Pernambuco, September 22, 1821.—At nine o'clock the commodore of this place, whose office is a combination of port-admiral and commissioner, came on board with the harbour-master, and the ship was guided by the latter to the anchorage, which is about three miles from the town, in eight fathoms water. The roadstead is quite open, and we find here a very heavy swell. It is not wonderful that our guns were neither answered nor noticed last night. Mr. Dance, having been sent on shore with official letters to the governor and the acting English consul, found the place in a state of siege, and brought back with him Colonel Patronhe, the governor's aide-de-camp, who gave us the following account of the present state of Pernambuco:

Besides the disposition to revolution, which we were aware had long existed in every part of Brazil, there was, also, a jealousy between the Portuguese and Brazilians, which recent events had increased in no small degree. On the 29th of August, about 600 men of the militia and other native forces had taken possession of the Villa of Goyana, one of the principal places in this captaincy, and had forcibly entered the town-house, where they had declared the government of Luis do Rego to be at an end. They proceeded to elect a temporary provisional government for Goyana, to act until the capital of the province should be in a condition to establish a constitutional junta; and in order to accelerate that event, they had collected forces of every kind, and among them several companies of the Caçadores who had deserted from Luis do Rego; with the troops, such as they are, they had marched towards Pernambuco, and last night they had attacked the two main points of Olinda, to the north, in four different places, and Affogados to the south. They were, however, repulsed by the royal troops, under the governor, with the loss of fourteen killed and thirty-five prisoners, while the royalists had two killed, and seven wounded. This morning the alarm of the town's people was increased by finding several armed men concealed in the belfreys of the churches, whither also they had conveyed several stands of arms. Luis do Rego is a soldier, and attached to the royal cause. He served long with the English army in Portugal and Spain, and, if I mistake not, distinguished himself at the siege of St. Sebastian's. He is rather a severe man, and, especially among the soldiers, more feared than loved.—Great part of the regiment of Caçadores has left him to join the patriots, and formed the most efficient corps in the attack last night. The towns-people have been formed into a militia, tolerably armed and trained. The town is pretty well supplied with mandioc flour, jerked beef, and salt fish; but the besiegers prevent all fresh provisions from coming in. All shops are shut, and all food scarce and dear. Most people who have property of value, in plate or jewels, have packed it up, and lodged it in the houses of the English merchants. Many persons with their wives and families have left their homes in the outskirts of the town, and have taken refuge with the English. The latter, who, for the most part, sleep, at least, in country houses in the neighbourhood, called sitios, have left them, and remain altogether at their counting-houses in the port: every thing, in short, is alarm and uncertainty.

23d.—The night passed quietly, and so indeed did the day. Many messages have passed between us and the land, but I could not go on shore: we have excellent oranges, and tolerable vegetables from the town, and have been quite enough amused in observing the curious little boats, canoes, catamarans and jangadas, that have been sailing, and paddling, and rowing round the ship. The jangada resembles nothing I have ever seen before; six or eight logs are made fast together by two transverse beams; at one end there is a raised seat, on which a man places himself to steer, for they are furnished with a sort of rudder; sometimes the seat is large enough to admit of two sitters, another bench at the foot of a mast, immense for the size of the raft, holds clothes and provisions, or an upright pole is fixed in one of the logs, to which these things are suspended, and a large triangular sail of cotton cloth completes the jangada, in which the hardy Brazilian sailor ventures to sea, the waves constantly washing over it, and carries cargoes of cotton or other goods, or, in case of necessity, letters and despatches, hundreds of miles in safety.

About three o'clock a large canoe with two patriot officers came along side, to ascertain if we were really English; if we had come, as was reported, to assist the royalists, or if we would assist them: so apt are men, under the influence of strong feeling themselves, to doubt of perfect indifference in others, that I question much whether they believed in the strict neutrality we profess. They left us, however, without betraying any particular anxiety, and made a very circuitous passage home, in order to avoid the Recife cruizer, which was looking out for straggling boats or vessels of any description belonging to the patriots.

Monday, the 24th.—Col. Patronhe arrived early this morning, to request that the English packet might put into Lisbon with the Government despatches. We felt glad that the strict rules of service prevented the captain from giving any such order to the master of the packet. It would be at once a breach of that neutrality we profess to observe, and, in my opinion, an aiding of the worst cause. The colonel, adverting to the town being in a state of siege, and the uncertainty of the next attack as to time and place, advised me strongly to stay altogether on board; but I had never seen a town in a state of siege, and therefore resolved to go ashore. Accordingly, Mr. Dance, being the only officer on board who speaks either Portuguese or French, was commissioned to accompany me; and I took two midshipmen, Grey and Langford, also to call on Madame do Rego.

The name of Pernambuco, which is that of the captainship, is now generally applied to the capital, which consists of two parts; 1st, the city of Olinda, which was founded by the Portuguese, under Duarte Coelho Pedreiro, about 1530 or 1540, and, as its name implies, on a beautiful spot, where moderate, but abrupt hills, a fine river, and thick wood, combine to charm the eye; but the approach to it by sea must always have been difficult, if not dangerous[40]: and, 2nd, the town of Recife de Pernambuco, or the Reef of Pernambuco, built by the Dutch, under Maurice of Nassau, and by them called Maurice Town.[41] It is a singular spot, well fitted for trade; it is situated upon several sand banks, divided by salt water creeks and the mouth of two fresh water rivers, connected by three bridges, and divided into as many parts;

Figure 3. Part of Pernambuco, seen from Coco-nut Island, with the Reef. Courtesy of The Catholic University of America, Oliveira Lima Library, Washington, D.C.

---

40. Duarte Coelho Pereira, first donatário of Pernambuco, captain or governor of his territory in the Portuguese system of land grants; he founded the city of Olinda in about 1535.
41. John Maurice of Nassau (1604-1679), Dutch colonial governor during the seventeenth century (1636-1644).

Recife, properly so called, where are the castles of defence, and the dock-yard, and the traders; Sant Antonio, where are the government house, the two principal churches, one for the white and one for the black population; and Boa Vista, where the richer merchants, or more idle inhabitants, live among their gardens, and where convents, churches, and the bishop's palace, give an air of importance to the very neat town around them.

[{*1824.*—} The old bridge of Maurice is now entirely changed.— It had when I was last here rows of shops on either hand that paid a percentage to government—So when the bridge was known to be in a dangerous state and the engineer reported it so and that it would be necessary to remove the shops, the treasurer refused to permit it on account of the loss of rents. So they quarreled and remonstrated till one day a carriage driving along the bridge broke under it and let down shops, goods and all into the water, and so it is a decent wooden bridge. I see a few new private houses building, particularly one at the end of Boa Vista bridge by Antonio Coelho, a Mulatto who a few years since possessed two negroes and one horse to carry himself and wife to the interior—and is now one of the richest planters in the country. There are plans afloat for beginning to make potash for which nothing can be fitter than the underwood of the virgin forests of this country, and its quantity would be admirable.]

All this I knew before I landed, and thought I was pretty well prepared for Pernambuco. But no previous knowledge could do away the wonder with which one must enter that very extraordinary port. From the ship, which is anchored three miles from the town, we see that vessels lie within a reef on which the sea is perpetually breaking, but till I was actually within that reef, I had not the least idea of the nature of the harbour: the swell going ashore would have seemed tremendous, had we not been prepared for it, and made our passage of three miles a very long one. We approached the sandy beach between Recife and Olinda so nearly, that I thought we were going to land there; when coming abreast of a tower on a rock, where the sea was breaking violently, we turned short round, and found ourselves within a marvellous natural break-water, heard the surf dashing without, and saw the spray, but we ourselves were sailing along smoothly and calmly, as if in a mill-pond. The rock of which the reef is formed, is said to be coral; but it is so coated with barnacle and limpet above barnacle and limpet, that I can see nothing but the remainder of these shells for many feet down, and as deep into the rock as our hammers will break. It extends from a good way to the northward of Paraiba to Olinda, where it sinks under water, and then rises abruptly at Recife, and runs on to Cape St. Augustine, where it is interrupted by the bold granite head, that shoots through it into the ocean: it then reappears, and continues, interruptedly, towards the south. The breadth of the harbour here between the reef and the mainland varies from a few fathoms to three quarters of a mile; the water is deep close to the rock, and there the vessels often moor. There is a bar at the entrance of the harbour, over which there is, in ordinary tides, sixteen feet water, so that ships of considerable burden lie here.* His Majesty's brig Alacrity lay some time within the reef; and two feet more water on the bar, would have enabled the Doris to have entered, though, as far as I have seen, there would be no room to turn about if she wished to go out again. The reef is certainly one of the wonders of the world; it is scarcely sixteen feet broad at top. It slopes off more rapidly than the Plymouth break-water, to a great depth on the outside, and is perpendicular within, to many fathoms. Here and there, a few inequalities at the top must formerly have annoyed the harbour in high tides or strong winds, but Count Maurice remedied this, by laying huge blocks of granite into the faulty places, and has thus rendered the top level, and the harbour safe at all times. The Count had intended to build warehouses along the reef, but his removal from the government prevented his doing so. A small fort near the entrance defends it, and indeed always must, so narrow and sudden is the passage. Near it, a light-house is in a fair way of being soon finished, at the very extremity of the reef, and these are the only two buildings on this extraordinary line of rock. We rowed up the harbour among vessels of all nations, with the town on one side, and the reef on the other, until we came to one of the wide creeks, over which the Dutch built a fine stone bridge, now in decay. We were a good deal struck with the beauty of the scene; the buildings are pretty large, and white; the land low and sandy, spotted with bright green tufts of grass, and adorned with palm-trees. A few years ago a violent flood nearly destroyed the greater part of the centre of the bridge, yet the arches still serve to support light wooden galleries on each side of it, and the houses and gateways are still standing at either end. We landed pretty near the bridge, and were received by Colonel Patronhe, who apologised for

* In 1816, under the governor, Monte Negro, the harbour was cleared and deepened, and particularly the bar.

the governor, who could not come to receive us, as he was in the council room.* The colonel conducted us to the government house, a very handsome building, with a square in front, and a tower, and we entered what had evidently been a splendid hall. The gilding and painting still remained on some parts of the ceiling and walls; but now it is occupied by horses standing ready saddled; soldiers armed, and ready to mount at a moment's warning; every thing on the alert; guns in front with lighted matches by them, and an air of bustle and importance among the soldiers, that excites a sort of sympathetic curiosity as to their possible and immediate destination. On going up stairs we found almost as much confusion: for the governor has hitherto lived in the very out-skirts of the town, and has but just come to the house in Sant Antonio, which was formerly the Jesuits' college, partly to be in the centre of business, and partly to secure his family, in case of accident, as the besiegers' out-posts are very near his former residence. I found Madame do Rego an agreeable, rather pretty woman, and speaking English like a native: for this she accounted, by informing me that her mother, the Viscondeça do Rio Seco, was an Irish woman.[42] Nothing could be kinder and more flattering than her manner, and that of General do Rego's two daughters, whose air and manner are those of really well-bred women, and one of them is very handsome. After sitting some little time, refreshments were brought in, and shortly after, the governor himself appeared; a fine military-looking man. He appeared ill, being still suffering from the effects of a wound he received some months ago, while walking through the town with a friend. It has since been ascertained, that the instigator of the crime was a certain Ouvidor (judge) whom he had displaced shortly after he assumed the government. The assassin fired twice; Luis do Rego received several shots and slugs in his body, but the most severe wound

* The council or junta of provisional government consisted of ten members, of which Luiz do Rego was the head; they were drawing up an address to the inhabitants of Recife, assuring them of safety and protection; exulting in the advantage gained in the night, and asserting that there were plenty of provisions within the town; and encouraging them in the name of the king and Cortes, to defend the city against the insurgents, who were of course branded with the names of enemies to the king and country.

---

42. Luís do Rêgo was captain-general of Pernambuco during this siege and Royalist leader against the Patriots. Madame do Rêgo's mother, the Viscondessa do Rio Seco, was born D. Maria Carlota Miliard and was indeed Irish (Lacombe 220).

was in his left arm. His friend's life was for some time despaired of, but both are now nearly well. At the time the crime was committed, the perpetrator was seized more than once by some of the bye-standers; but as often, a baker's basket was pushed in between him and whoever seized him; he threw away his pistols and escaped.*

Having paid our visit, we proceeded to walk about the town. The streets are paved partly with blueish pebbles from the beach, partly with red or grey granite. The houses are three or four stories high, built of a whitish stone, and all are white-washed, with door-posts and window-frames of brown stone. The ground floor consists of shops, or lodging for the negroes, and stables: the floor above is generally appropriated to counting-houses and ware-rooms; and the dwelling-house still higher, the kitchen being universally at the top, by which means the lower part of the house is kept cool. I was surprised to find it so possible to walk out without inconvenience from the heat, so near the equator; but the constant sea-breeze, which sets in here every day at ten o'clock, preserves a temperature, under which it is at all times possible to take exercise. The hot time of day is from eight, when the land breeze fails, to ten. As we were to pass the stone bridge on our way back to the boat, which was ordered to meet us at the point of Recife, because the receding tide would have left it dry in the creek where we landed; we left it on one hand, and walked through Sant Antonio towards Boa Vista. When we came to the wooden bridge, 350 paces long, connecting it with Sant Antonio, we found that it had been cut through the middle, and is only now passable by means of two planks easily withdrawn, in case the besiegers should get possession of Boa Vista. Nothing can be prettier of its kind than the fresh green landscape, with its broad river winding through it, which is seen on each hand from the bridge, and the white buildings of the treasury and mint, the convents, and private houses, most of which have gardens. The verdure is delightful to an English eye; and I doubt not that the flat meadows, and slowly-flowing water, were particularly attractive

* Luiz do Rego was not the first governor of Pernambuco who had been shot at. In 1710, when Sebastian de Castro, in conformity to his orders from Lisbon, had erected a pillar, and declared Recife a town, San Antonio da Recife, the Olindrians shot him on his walk to Boa Vista, in four places. The Ouvidor was one of the conspirators. The bishop had a share in this unchristian action. The object of the people of Olinda and of the assassin's party was, to confine Recife to its own parish, extending only to the Affogados on one side, and Fort Brun on the other.

to the Dutch founders of Recife. We walked back by the stone bridge, 280 paces long, as we intended; in vain did we look for shops; not one was open, the shopkeepers being all on military duty. They form the militia, and, as many of them are from Europe, and as they all expect to be plundered should the country Brazilians take the town by force, they are most zealous in their attendance as soldiers.

At each end of every street we found a light gun, and at the heads of the bridges two, with lighted matches by them, and at each post we were challenged by the guard. At the end of the stone bridge, at the ponte dos tres pontes,* next to Recife, the guards are more numerous and strict. In this quarter, the chief riches of the place are lodged, and that is the point most easily defended. It is very nearly surrounded with water, the houses are high, strongly built, and close together, the streets being very narrow, and the strong gateways at each end of the bridge might secure time to demolish it entirely, and thus render that part of the town secure, except by the sand bank communicating with Olinda, and that is guarded by two considerable forts.

We had hardly gone fifty paces into Recife, when we were absolutely sickened by the first sight of a slave-market. It was the first time either the boys or I had been in a slave-country; and, however strong and poignant the feelings may be at home, when imagination pictures slavery, they are nothing compared to the staggering sight of a slave-market. It was thinly stocked, owing to the circumstances of the town; which cause most of the owners of new slaves to keep them closely shut up in the depôts. Yet about fifty young creatures, boys and girls, with all the appearance of disease and famine consequent upon scanty food and long confinement in unwholesome places, were sitting and lying about among the filthiest animals in the streets. The sight sent us home to the ship with the heart-ache and resolution, "not loud but deep," that nothing in our power should be considered too little, or too great, that can tend to abolish or to alleviate slavery,

27th.—I went on shore to-day to spend a few days with Miss S., the only English lady in the town. She is now living in her brother's town-house, where the office and warehouses are, because the country-house is within reach of the patriots. I do long to walk or ride out to the tempting green hills beyond the town; but as that cannot be, I must content myself with what is within the lines. To-day, as we were coming in from Boa Vista, we met a family of Certanejos, who had

* A little fort which defends the entrance to Recife.

brought provisions into the town some days ago, returning home to the Certam, or wild country of the interior. These Certanejos are a hardy, active set of men, mostly agriculturists. They bring corn and pulse, bacon and sweetmeats, to the sea-coast, hides and tallow also at times. But the sugar, cotton, and coffee, which form the staple exports of Pernambuco, require the warmer, richer lands, nearer the coast. Cotton is, however, brought from the Certam, but it is a precarious crop, depending entirely on the quantity of rain in the season; and it sometimes does not rain in the Certam for two years. The party we met formed a very picturesque groupe, the men clad in leather from head to foot, of which their light jerkin and close pantaloons are fitted as closely as the clothing on the Egina marbles, and have something of the same effect: the small round hat is in the form of Mercury's petasus; and the shoes and gaiters of the greater number are excellently adapted to defend the legs and feet in riding through the thickets. The colour of all this is a fine tan brown. I was vexed that the woman of the party wore a dress evidently of French fashion: it spoiled the unity of the groupe. She was mounted behind the principal man, on one of the small active horses of the country; several sumpter horses followed, laden with household goods and other things in exchange for their provisions: cloths, both woollen and cotton, coarse crockery, and other manufactured articles, especially knives, are what they chiefly take in barter; though I saw some furniture, with pretensions to elegance, among the stuff of the family I met. After the horses came a groupe of men, some walking and keeping pace with the amble of the beasts; others riding and carrying the children; the procession being closed by a very stout good-looking man, smoking as he went along, and distinguished by a pair of green baize trowsers.

In the evening we rode out; whether it was because we had been so many weeks on board ship, and without horse-exercise, or because of the peculiar sweetness and freshness of evening after the sultry tropical day we had just passed, I know not, but I never enjoyed an hour in the open air so much. We rode out of the town by some pretty country-houses, called *sitios,* to one of the outposts at Mondego, which was formerly the governor's residence. The tamarind, the silk-cotton tree,* and the palm, shaded us, and a thousand elegant shrubs adorned the garden walls. It is impossible to describe the fresh delicious feel of such an evening, giving repose and health after the fiery day. We were very

---

* Bombex pentandrium. *Jaquin.*

sorry when obliged to return home; but the sun was gone, there was no moon, and we were afraid that the guards at the various posts of defence might stop us. As we came back, we were challenged at every station; but the words, *amigos ingresos* were our passport, and we got to Recife just as the evening hymn was singing, harshly and unmusically enough, by the negroes and mulattoes in the streets; but yet every thing that unites men in one common sentiment is interesting. The church doors were open, the altars illuminated, and the very slave felt that he was addressing the same Deity, by the same privilege with his master. It is an evening I can never forget.

28th.—This morning before breakfast, looking from the balcony of Mr. S.'s house, I saw a white woman, or rather fiend, beating a young negress, and twisting her arms cruelly while the poor creature screamed in agony, till our gentlemen interfered. Good God! that such a traffic, such a practice as that of slavery, should exist. Near the house there are two or three depôts of slaves, all young; in one, I saw an infant of about two years old, for sale. Provisions are now so scarce that no bit of animal food ever seasons the paste of mandioc flour, which is the sustenance of slaves: and even of this, these poor children, by their projecting bones and hollow cheeks, show that they seldom get a sufficiency. Now, money also is so scarce, that a purchaser is not easily found, and one pang is added to slavery: the unavailing wish of finding a master! Scores of these poor creatures are seen at different corners of the streets, in all the listlessness of despair—and if an infant attempts to crawl from among them, in search of infantile amusement, a look of pity is all the sympathy he excites. Are the patriots wrong? They have put arms into the hands of the *new* negroes, while the recollection of their own country, and of the slave-ship, and of the slave-market, is fresh in their memory.

I walked to-day to the market-place, where there is but little;—beef scarce and dear, no mutton, a little poultry, and a few pigs, disgusting, because they feed in the streets where every thing is thrown, and where they and the dogs are the only scavengers. The blockade is so strict, that even the vegetables from the gentlemen's private gardens, two miles from the out-posts, are detained. No milk is to be had, bread of American flour is at least twice as dear as in England, and the cakes of mandioc baked with cocoa-nut juice, too dear for the common people to afford a sufficiency even of them. Fire-wood is extravagantly high, charcoal scarce. The negroes keep the markets: a few on their own account, more on that of their masters. The dress of the free negroes is like that of the creole Portuguese; a linen jacket and trowsers, or on days of ceremony one of cloth, and a straw hat, furnish forth either a black or a white gentleman. The women, in-doors, wear a kind of frock which leaves the bosom much exposed. When they walk out they wear either a cloak or mantle; this cloak is often of the gayest colours; shoes also, which are the mark of freedom, are to be seen of every hue, but black. Gold chains for the neck and arms, and gold ear-rings, with a flower in the hair, complete a Pernambucan woman's dress. The new negroes, men and women, have nothing but a cloth round their loins. When they are bought, it is usual to give the women a shift and petticoat, and the men at least trowsers, but this is very often omitted.

Yesterday the motley head-dresses of the Portuguese inhabitants were seen to great advantage, in a sally through the streets, made by a kind of supplementary militia to enforce the closing of all shop-doors, and the shutting up of all slaves, on an alarm that the enemy was attacking the town to the southward. The officer leading the party was indeed dressed *en militaire,* with a drawn sword in one hand, and a pistol in the other. Then followed a company that Falstaff would hardly have enlisted, armed in a suitable manner, with such caps and hats as became the variety of trades to which the wearers belonged, the rear being brought up by a most singular figure, with a small drum-shaped black cap on the very top of a stiff pale head, a long oil-skin cloak, and in his left hand a huge Toledo ready drawn, which he carried upright.[43] The militia are better dressed, and are now employed in regular turn of duty with the royal troops, who are going over to the patriots daily.

Calling at the palace this forenoon, we learned that a hundred Indians are expected in the town, by way of assistance to the garrison. They wear their aboriginal dress, and are armed with slings, bows, and arrows. We are told their ideas of government consist in believing that implicit obedience is due both to king and priests. Brandy is the bribe for which they will do any thing; a dram of that liquor and a hand-

---

43. Although Sir John Falstaff is a character in four Shakespeare plays, here Graham must refer to *Henry IV, Part I*, where Falstaff presses a ragged bunch into service to gain money for drink:

FALSTAFF: If I be not ashamed of my soldiers, I am a soused gurnet. I have misused the king's press damnably [. . .] A mad fellow met me on the way and told me I had unloaded all the gibbets and pressed the dead bodies. No eye hath seen such scarecrows. I'll not march through Coventry with them, that's flat. (IV:ii)

ful of mandioc flour being all the food they require when they come down to the port.

This evening, as there are no horses to be hired here, we borrowed some from our English and French friends, and rode to Olinda by the long sandy isthmus, which connects it with Recife. This is the isthmus fortified with a palisade, by Sir John Lancaster, during his stay at Recife, which he plundered.* The beach is defended by two castles, sufficiently strong when their situation is considered; on one side a furious surf breaking at their base, on the other a deep estuary and flat ground beyond, so that they cannot be commanded. The sand is partially covered by shrubs; one is very splendid with thick leaves and purple bell-shaped flowers; many are like those of the eastern world; many are quite new to me. I was surprised at the extreme beauty of Olinda, or rather of its remains, for it is now in a melancholy state of ruin. All the richer inhabitants have long settled in the lower town. The revenues of the bishopric being now claimed by the crown, and the monasteries suppressed for the most part, even the factitious splendour caused by the ecclesiastical courts and inhabitants is no more. The very college where the youths received some sort of education, however imperfect, is nearly ruined,† and there is scarcely a house of any size standing.

Olinda is placed on a few small hills, whose sides are in some directions broken down, so as to present the most abrupt and picturesque rock-scenery. These are embosomed in dark woods that seem coeval with the land itself: tufts of slender palms, here and there the broad head of an ancient mango, or the gigantic arms of the wide spreading silk-cotton tree, rise from out the rest in the near ground, and break the line of forest: amidst these, the convents, the cathedral, the bishop's palace, and the churches of noble, though not elegant architecture, are placed in stations which a Claude or a Poussin might have chosen for them; some stand on the steep sides of rocks, some on lawns that slope gently to the sea-shore: their colour is grey or pale yellow, with reddish tiles, except here and there where a dome is adorned with porcelain tiles of white and blue.[44] Just as we reached the highest point

---

* See the Introduction.
† This was the Jesuits' college founded under the administration of the admirable father Nobrega, and his companion De Gram. Here at eighteen years old the celebrated Viera read lectures on rhetoric, and composed those commentaries on some of the classics, which were unfortunately lost in the course of the civil wars.

---

44. Claude Lorrain (1600-1682), French landscape artist; Nicolas Poussin (1594-1665), French painter and founder of the French Classical Style.

Figure 4. View of Count Maurice's Gate at Pernambuco, with the Slave Market. Courtesy of The Catholic University of America, Oliveira Lima Library, Washington, D.C.

of the town, looking across the woody basin round which the hills are grouped, the smoke from one of the outposts caught our sight. The soldiers were standing or lying around, and their arms piled by them: they were just shadowed by tall trees behind, between whose trunks the scattered rays of the setting sun shed such a partial light as Salvator Rosa himself would not have disdained. These same soldiers, however, circumscribed our ride: we had intended to return by the inland road, but were not allowed to pass into it, as part, at least, lies without the posts, therefore we were obliged to return by the way we came.

At the spot where the present guard is placed, and where indeed a strong guard is peculiarly necessary, the river Bibiriba falls into the æstuary, which was formerly the port of Olinda. A dam is built across with flood-gates which are occasionally opened; and on the dam there is a very pretty open arcade, where the neighbouring inhabitants were accustomed in peaceable times to go in the evening, and eat, drink, and dance. It is from this dam that all the good water used in Recife is daily conveyed in water-canoes, which come under the dam called the Varadouro, and are filled from twenty-three pipes, led so as to fill the canoes at once, without farther trouble. We saw seven-and-twenty of these little boats laden, paddle down the creek with the tide towards the town. A single oar used rather as rudder than paddle guides the tank to the middle of the stream, where it floats to its destination.

The sun was low, long before we reached even the first of the two castles on our way back to the fort. The dogs had already begun their work of abomination. I saw one drag the arm of a negro from beneath the few inches of sand, which his master had caused to be thrown over his remains. It is on this beach that the measure of the insults dealt to the poor negroes is filled. When the negro dies, his fellow-slaves lay him on a plank, carry him to the beach, where beneath high-water mark they hoe a little sand over him; but to the new negro even this mark of humanity is denied. He is tied to a pole, carried out in the evening and dropped upon the beach, where it is just possible the surf may bear him away. These things sent us home sad and spiritless, notwithstanding the agreeable scenes we had been riding among.

29th.—The feast of St. Michael's has drawn out the Portuguese gentlewomen, of whom we had not yet seen one walking in the streets. The favourite dress seems to be black, with white shoes and white or coloured ribbons and flowers in the hair, with a mantle of lace or gauze, either black or white. We have seen a few priests too for the first time. I think the edict desiring them to keep within their convent walls, is in consequence of their being among the fomentors of the spirit of independence. The appropriation of so much of the church revenue by the court of Lisbon is of course unpopular among the clergy of the country; and it is not difficult for them to represent, what indeed is truth, to the people, that the drawing of so much treasure from the country to support Lisbon, which can neither govern nor protect them now, is a rational ground of complaint. It is said, that the morals of the clergy here are most depraved. This is probably true. Men cut off by vows like those of the Roman clergy, from the active charities of social life, have only the resources of science and literature against their passions and vices. But here the very names of literature and science are almost unknown. The college and library of Olinda are in decay. There is not one bookseller in Pernambuco, and the population of its different parishes amounts to 70,000 souls! A tolerably well written newspaper, of which I have not been able to procure the first number, was set up in March, under the title of "Aurora Pernambucana," with the following motto from Camoens[45]:

---

45. Luís Vaz de Camões (c. 1524/25-1580), Portuguese poet whose epic *Os Lusíadas* (1572, *The Lusiads*), recounting Vasco da Gama's voyage from Por-

> Depois da procellosa tempestade,
> Nocturna sombra e sibilante vento,
> Tras a manha serena e claridade,
> Esperança de porto e salvamiente:

alluding to the arrival of the news of the revolution in Portugal, on the 26th of that month, and the swearing of the governor, magistrates, etc. to adhere to the constitution as established by the Cortes. I am sorry to say that this only paper has been discontinued for the two last months, the editor having, as it seems, become a secretary of government, and having no longer time to superintend the press.*

30th.—Last night the patriot troops attacked the line of defence at Olinda for four hours, but I do not believe there was any loss on either side. This morning a Portuguese frigate, the Don Pedro, with troops from Bahia, arrived. The reinforcement of *350* men, partly European, partly Bahian, has put the inhabitants, from the governor downwards, into the highest spirits; so that for once we see Pernambuco active, and cheerful, and alive. Men and women are out in their gayest habits, and the military are running and riding in all directions, not a little pleased to have some to relieve them in their constant watch and ward.

Among other things which I learned by looking on, while the elders of families were engaged in the streets with the new-comers, was that the young Pernambucans are as dexterous in the use of signs as the Turkish lovers themselves, and that often a courtship is carried on in this way, and a marriage settled, without the parties having ever heard each other's voices. However, the general mode is for parents to settle their children's nuptials, without consulting any thing but pecuniary convenience.

This day several of the officers and midshipmen of the Doris accompanied us to dine at the governor's, at half-past four o'clock.

---

* Not only has this paper been continued since, but others are now published in Recife.

---

tugal to India in 1502, is foundational to Portuguese nationalism. These lines, which open Canto IV, have been translated to English in this way: "After the dark hours of tempest,/Blank night, and the screaming wind,/ Morning dawns serene and clear/With hopes of reaching harbour safely" (Camões *The Lusíads*, trans. Landeg White. Oxford and New York: Oxford University Press, 1997).

Our welcome was most cordial. His excellency took one end of the table, and an aide-de-camp the other: I was seated between M. and Madame do Rego. He seemed happy to talk of his old English friends of the Peninsula, with many of whom I am acquainted; and she had a thousand enquiries to make about England, whither she is very anxious to go. They apologised for having so little plate, but their handsome services were packed up in an English store-house, together with her excellency's jewels and other precious things. The cookery was a mixture of Portuguese and French. After the soup, a dish was handed round of boiled lean beef, slices of fat salt pork, and sausages, and with this dish, rice boiled with oil and sweet herbs. Roast beef was presented, in compliment to the English, very little roasted. Salads, and fish of various kinds, were dressed in a peculiar manner; poultry and other things in the French fashion.

The dessert was served on another table. Besides our European dessert of fruit, cakes, and wine, all the puddings, pies, and tarts, formed part of it. It was decorated with flowers, and there was a profusion of sugar-plums of every kind. The company rose from the dining table, and adjourned to the other, which Madame do Rego told me should have been spread in a separate apartment; but they have so recently taken possession of their house, that they have not one yet fitted up for the purpose. The governor and his guests proposed many toasts alternately—The King of England, the King of Portugal, the navy of England, the King of France,* Luis do Rego, and the captaincy of Pernambuco, etc.—When we all rose at once from table; some of the company went on board ship, but most adjourned to the drawing-room, a comfortable apartment, furnished with blue satin damask, where we were joined by the French naval officers of His Most Christian Majesty's ship Sappho, and several ladies and gentlemen of the city. We had some excellent music. Madame do Rego has an admirable voice, and there were several good singers and players on the piano. It was a more pleasant, polished evening than I had expected to pass in Pernambuco, especially now in a state of siege.

Wednesday, 3d October.—I went on board on Monday, and, provokingly enough, the patriots chose that very night to make an attack upon the out-post of the Affogados, so I did not see the governor, at the head of his troops, march out to meet them; nor did I hear the national hymn sung by the regiments as they filed along on their return

---

* Mr. Lamé, the very pleasing and gentlemanlike French consul, was present.

from a successful sally.* Yesterday, nothing occurred worth noting; we had the consul and British merchants on board to dinner, and the day passed as such days usually do.

Having learned that the patriots have refused to allow the linen belonging to the ship, which had been sent to the country to be washed, to return to the town, it was determined that we should send to their head-quarters, and remonstrate against this very inconvenient mode of annoying the port. I obtained leave to accompany the messengers, and accordingly we all went on shore immediately after breakfast. Our first business was to procure passports, and to learn the countersigns; after which Capt. Graham, with Col. Cottar, the governor's principal aide-de-camp, rode with us to the out-posts, where we left them, with an intention of returning to dine at Mr. Stewart's, to meet Luis do Rego's family. Our party consisted of M. Caumont, to act as interpreter, Mr. Dance, bearing the letter, my cousin Mr. Glennie as my

---

* Since writing my Journal, I have seen the official account of this attack on the Villa of the Affagados. It was a well planned expedition; but the raw troops were easily driven out of the villa of which they had already possessed themselves, by throwing a bridge over a branch of the Capabaribe, by the veteran soldiers of Do Rego.

The same morning, i.e. that of the 1st of October, the provisional junta of Pernambuco had addressed that of the patriots of Goyana, offering peace, saying, that as their avowed object was the dismissal of L. do Rego, he was ready to withdraw himself; that he had twice offered the council of Recife to do so, and had besides sent to the Cortes to beg they would appoint a successor, and allow him to retire; that his motive for this was the desire of peace, and of procuring the tranquillity of the province, so disturbed by these civil broils. They tell the patriots also, that the Don Pedro is arrived, and assure them that the troops brought by the frigate shall be employed only in the defence of Recife. They also intimate, that they are sure of assistance from the French and English frigates then there, such assistance having been offered, on the ground of the English and French property in the place. Now I know that no such assistance was offered by the English frigate. It was asked; but a strict neutrality had been enjoined by the government, all interference was refused, and no more was offered than *personal* protection to either English, French, or Portuguese; and of course protection for English property being the purpose for which the frigate was there, was understood by all parties.

cavalier, and myself.[46] It was the first time we had had an opportunity of passing the lines, and we felt like school-boys who had stolen beyond bounds, and well we might; the scenery was fresh and lovely, and the day as fine as possible.

Pernambuco is not a walled town, but broad rapid rivers and æstuaries surround it, and it is only approachable by the roads and causeways; the banks thrown up across these, for present defence, are such as might stop the Brazilian cavalry for a few minutes, or afford cover for musketry; but their best defence is the swamp at the mouth of the Capabaribe, which is flooded at high water, and which extends nearly to the Bibiriba. At the edge of the swamp there is a wooden palisade, where we left the last post of the royalists, and took leave of our friends, who had accompanied us so far. After riding across the marsh, which by the by is very fit for rice ground, and is surrounded by cocoa-nut and tamarind trees, we came to the main stream of the Capabaribe, a deep, broad, and very rapid river; its sides are steep, and the water beautifully clear:* its banks are studded with country-houses, and adorned with groves and gardens, for the present abandoned by their owners, who have taken refuge in Recife.

The hedges on each side of the road are woven of palm-leaves, and where not quite new, are covered with all splendid creeping plants; the common and winged passion-flower, white, blue, and yellow clematis, jasmine, china-rose, and many others, both gay and sweet. The ditches, too, were full of colour, but we rode too fast to stay to collect plants; and I could only promise myself, at some future time, to gather one that appeared like a bog bean, but its colour bright purple.

About two miles from Do Rego's last outpost, we came to the first post of the patriots, at a country-house on a rising ground, where arms piled at the door, and a sort of ragged guard, consisting of a merry-looking negro with a fowling-piece, a Brazilian with a blunderbuss,

---

* The Capabaribe has a course of about fifty leagues, but is only navigable to about six miles from the sea, on account of rapids and falls in the upper part; it has two mouths, one at Recife, and the other at Os Affogados.—*Chor. Brazil.*

---

46. William Glennie (1797-1856), Maria Graham's cousin, had served in Algiers and was appointed to the Doris as an Admiralty midshipman in 1821 and invalided out in 1822, most likely due to the family disease, consumption. He was promoted to lieutenant on the Samarang and survived until his late fifties—just a couple of years longer than his cousin Maria (Vale, *Frigate* 46, 156).

and two or three of doubtful colour with sticks, swords, pistols, etc., told us an officer was to be found. After a few minutes parley, we found he was not authorised to receive our letter, so we rode on under the direction of the old Brazilian with his blunderbuss, who, being on foot, threatened to shoot us if we attempted to ride faster than he walked. The slow pace at which we advanced gave us leisure to remark the beauties of a Brazilian spring. Gay plants, with birds still gayer hovering over them, sweet smelling flowers, and ripe oranges and citrons, formed a beautiful fore-ground to the very fine forest-trees that cover the plains, and clothe the sides of the low hills in the neighbourhood of Pernambuco. Here and there a little space is cleared for the growth of mandioc, which at this season is perfectly green: the wooden huts of the cultivators are generally on the road-side, and, for the most part, each has its little grove of mango and orange trees. At one of these little homesteads, we found a pretty large guard-house, established where four roads meet, and there our foot guide left us, and a gentlemanlike young officer, of the Brazilian Caçadores, rode with us, and entertained us by calling Luis do Rego a tyrant, and attributing the siege of Pernambuco entirely to the governor's obstinacy, in not joining the people of the province in throwing off the dominion of his master. Round the guard-house a number of negro girls, with broad flat baskets on their heads, were selling fruit and cold water: they had decked their woolly hair, and the edges of their baskets, with garlands of the scarlet althæa; their light blue or white cloaks were thrown gracefully across their dusky shoulders, and white jackets, so that it was such a picture as the early Spaniards might have drawn of their Eldorado.

After riding a few miles, we came suddenly to the foot of an abrupt hill, on whose sides there were scattered groups of the most magnificent trees I ever beheld. There we were met by a small military party, which, after a parley with our guide, rather ordered, than invited us to ride up. In a few seconds, we came to a steep yellow sandstone bank, shaded on one side by tall trees, and open on the other to a lake surrounded by woody hills, on the most distant of which, the white buildings of Olinda sparkled like snow. On the top of the bank, and in the act of descending, was a group of forty horsemen, one of the foremost of whom bore a white banner; several were dressed in splendid military habits, others in the plain costume of the landed proprietors. These were deputies from Paraiba on their way to propose terms to Luis do Rego; they had just left the head-quarters of the besieging army, where the provisional government of Goyana is stationed, and were accompanied by a guard of honour: after exchanging civilities, part of the guard turned back with us, and the deputies went on their way. Having reached the top of the hill, we found about a hundred men, tolerably well armed, but strangely dressed, awaiting us; and there we were detained till our guide rode forward to ask leave to bring us to head-quarters. I was sorry I had no means of sketching any part of the beautiful landscape, which, besides the striking features I have mentioned before, now displayed a broad river, over which there is a white stone bridge of several arches; at one end, a large house, more like a palace, with its arches and corridors, and the encampment of the army and the horse picquets, and, in short, a bustle and animation that seldom happen to adorn so fine a scene. Our guide soon returned with eighteen or twenty mounted soldiers, whose appearance was rather wild than military: the guard presented arms as we parted from them, and we soon cantered down the hill towards the main body of the troops. Not above two hundred had the arms or accoutrements of soldiers; but there were dresses and weapons of every kind, leather, cloth, and linen; short jackets and long Scotch plaids, and every tint of colour in their faces, from the sallow European to the ebony African. Military honours were paid us by these ragged regiments, and we were conducted to the palace square, where Mr. Dance and Mr. Caumont dismounted, and I determined to await the issue of their conference, with my cousin in the court.

This, however, was not permitted. In a few minutes, a smart little man, speaking, tolerable French, came and told me the *government* desired my company. I suspected a mistake of the word government for governor, and endeavoured to decline the honour; but no denial could be taken, and the little man, who told me he was secretary to government, accordingly assisted me to dismount, and showed me the way to the palace. The hall was filled with men and horses, like a barrack stable, excepting a corner which served as an hospital for those wounded in the late skirmishes, the groans of the latter mingling uncouthly with the soldiers' cheerful noisy voices. The stairs were so crowded, that we got up with difficulty, and then I found that I was indeed to be confronted with the whole strength of the provisional government. At the end of a long dirty room, that had once been handsome, as the form of the windows and carving of the panels on which there were traces of colour and gilding, indicated, there was an old black hair sofa, on the centre of which I was placed, with Mr. Dance on one side, and Mr. Glennie on the other; by Mr. Dance sat the little secretary, and next to him our interpreter, in old-fashioned high-backed chairs; the rest of the furniture of the room consisted of nine seats of different sizes and forms, placed in a semicircle fronting the sofa, and on each of these sat one of the members of the junta of the provisional government, who act the part of senators or generals, as the occasion may require. To each of these I was introduced; the names of Albuquerque, Cavalcante, and Broderod, struck me, but I heard imperfectly, and forget most of them: some wore handsome military coats, others the humbler dress of farmers. They politely told me they would not read the letter while I was waiting below, but as soon as we were seated, the secretary read it aloud. Instead of taking any notice of its contents, the secretary began a long discourse, setting forth the injustice of the Portuguese governor and government towards Brazil in general, and the Pernambucans in particular; that in order to resist that injustice, they had formed the present respectable government, pointing to the junta, without intending the least detriment to the rights of the king. That surely they could not be called rebels, as they marched under the royal flag of Portugal; but Luis do Rego might be reasonably stigmatised as such, for he had fired on that banner. He then went off into a long harangue upon the general principles of government; but as I understood little of the language, much of it was lost upon me, as well as on my companions; but I have no doubt that it served to impress the respectable junta with a higher idea of their secretary's understanding and eloquence: altogether, the speech reminded me of some of the best written of the Carbonari addresses of Italy; and there was something in the air, manner, and scene, not unlike what one imagines of the Barraca meetings of those ill-guided, misused people.* We then talked a great deal in French to the secretary, who repeated every word to the respectable junta, and at length got him to attend to a proposal for releasing our linen, and another for supplying the ship with fresh provisions. We had been paying forty dollars per bullock in the town; they agreed that their price should not exceed ten,

* I regret exceedingly that I was then so ignorant of the language. I have since learned that there were many causes of particular grievance in this province. I do not mean to speak disrespectfully of the popular meetings of Brazil; they had all in view the best objects, national independence and civil liberty under reformed laws. The first object has been secured to them by their constitutional emperor, the last is growing up under his government; time only can perfect it. Happy would it have been for Italy, if its popular meetings had possessed the mild character of those of Brazil, and still happier, had they found in their prince a defender and protector.

if we sent boats to the Rio Doce, or Paratije* for them. This is the mouth of a small stream on the northside of Olinda. And I must not omit to mention, that they offered to allow us to take off fresh provisions for our English or French friends in the town.

The junta was extremely anxious to learn if there was a probability of England's acknowledging the independence of Brazil, or if she took part at all in the struggle; and many were the questions, and very variously were they shaped, which the secretary addressed to us on that head. They are of course violent in their language concerning Luis do Rego, in proportion as he has done his military duty, in keeping them at bay with his handful of men: and like all oppositions they can afford to reason upon general principles, because they have not to feel the hindrances of action, and the jarring of private interests in the disposal and fulfilment of office.

I was sitting opposite to one of the windows of the council-room, and had been remarking for some time, that the sun was getting very low, and, therefore, rose to go, having received a note from the secretary, ordering the officers at their advanced posts to offer no hindrance to the passing of any thing belonging to His British Majesty's frigate, Doris. But we were not suffered to depart without a hearty invitation to sup and spend the night: and a stirrup-cup (a huge glass) was brought, and a bottle of wine, with about half as much water, poured into it; it was then handed to me to begin, and all fourteen received it in turn. By this time the guard was drawn out, the band played the national hymn, to which we all listened bare-headed, and so we mounted among those wild-looking men, in that strange, yet lovely landscape, just as the evening mist began to veil the lower land, and the bright red evening sun to gild the topmost branches of the forest.

Our journey home was much more rapid than our journey out. The evening was cool, and the horses eager to return; but we did not reach Mr. S.'s till two hours after sunset, when we found that, after the party had waited till six o'clock, Captain Graham had insisted on their dining.[47] The governor was uneasy, and offered to send a party

---

* At Rio Doce, Brito Freire and Pedro Jaques landed to assist Vieyra in the recovery of Pernambuco. See the Introduction.

---

47. Thomas Graham (~1780-1822), third son to Robert Graham, the 12th Laird of Fintry; Graham met him when he was sent out to join H.M.S. *Russell* in India on the ship in which Maria, her father Captain George Dundas, and her sister were travelling. Thomas was promoted to captain in 1811.

of Caçadores in search, as he kindly said, of me,—but this, of course, was refused; the captain assuring his excellency, that if the patriots detained his lieutenant, he would take him back with his own men, and that as to me, while I was with my two companions, he had not the least fear concerning me. We were accompanied by the same officer, who had been our companion on the latter part of the ride to head-quarters, back almost to the town lines; and when we told this to the governor, he was sorry we did not know his name, that in case he should ever have it in his power to show him kindness, he might do so. A pleasant chat on the adventures of our ride, a hearty supper, and a little concert closed the day, which, upon the whole, was to me a most agreeable one.

[*19th.* {*August, 1824.*—}] The Admiral came on board the packet to breakfast with me and remained till 1/2 past 11 o'clock—Nothing can be kinder; more as he used to be at Quintero. I went ashore in the afternoon and dined at Admiral Stewart's country house—after which I went to call on the Republican President Manoel Carvalho Paes d'Andrade who speaks good English and appears to be a remarkable man. I carried him a parcel of Lord Cochrane's proclamations, and I endeavored to persuade him that the number and strength of the Imperial forces were such as that nothing could be hoped from a persisting in his present plans but defeat and misery and a waste of human life, which I was sure he and every good man must desire to avoid. I told him that notwithstanding the prejudgement pronounced against him and his partisans and the proclamos put out by the army, I was sure that if he trusted to the Admiral and at once surrendered to him, their safety and escape might be depended on—I then took leave of him and promised to call next morning.—

At Lord Stewart's in the country I found my pleasant friend his sister looking better than formerly and very happy in her little sitio. A curious instance of the sagacity of birds occurred to me here.—The great blue Macaw Jack knew me instantly and put out his hand to perch on my arm.—and I should say that Arica came to me on board the Pedro and kissed my feet and was very happy. It appears that since I was here three years ago there has been scarcely a day's peace. On the departure of Luis do Rego, Gervasio Pires Ferrei (fine house near the Solidad) was elected president—but shortly afterward popular feeling obliged him to escape to Rio de Janeiro and the party elected Alfonso de Albuquerque Maranhaõ, and Morgado de Cabo (from whom the party of the morgadistas take name) was a member of his council. Albuquerque was dismissed and Morgado became Pro President and parties became very strong and violent, but Pedroso the Governor at arms obliged them both to leave the town. Meantime that republican spirit which has always distinguished the Pernambucans was daily acquiring strength. The Province complained that it had done and suffered much in the cause of independence. That it had been the first to enable Bahia to resist and expel the Pes do Chumbo and yet that all its revenues were drained away to the capital, its own public works neglected, its officers either kept waiting at the court or dismissed with rudeness and the promises of amendment in all departments broken. In this strait, Manoel Carvalho Paes de Andrade became president of the Council of Government. For a long time his proclamas and other public papers only called on the Emperor to dismiss all the European Portuguese from his councils and favour and to frame a liberal constitution by the assistance of his Constituent assembly. But the dismissal of that assembly in an arbitrary manner wrought upon the feeling of the parties to a degree that put them completely off their guard and broke all decency towards the Emperor. He and his power were defied and the neighboring provinces called on to assist in asserting their rights as men and citizens. Filgueras a chief in Ceara (who cooperated with Lord Cochrane in driving the Europeans from Maranhaô) is marching to their assistance. Paraiba is said to be intimidated by a republican force from Goyana and even Piauhy is disposed to join. Meantime skirmishes between the troops to the southward and the Imperialists have taken place in which the Pernambucans are said to have been uniformly victorious and strew a few little flags and standards; but they mourn the loss of Pitanga the bravest and best commander they had. Meantime the Imperial Government had blockaded the port by means of ships under Captain Taylor and there was considerable distress owing to the want of Farinha, which was the more scarce this year as there was an extraordinary flood of the Capiberibe which had destroyed a great many of the Mandioc grounds. But I am sorry to say that great indignation was excited among the people by the conduct of Captain T in a night attack in the harbour passing under the name of the Doris, then lying there the next day; several persons were killed.

The Emperor is considered as playing into his father's hands and that therefore he is a Portuguese in principle, so several peaceable Portuguese shopkeepers were shot and if any one in alarm ran in the street he was suspected and pursued with small chance of escape. The Doris's boats were attacked on coming for marketing and all their fruit etc. seized, the people being totally unwilling to believe that the English did not assist the Imperialists.—Such I think was the sum and substance of all the political conversation at the Consul's and elsewhere from the English. For the state of the foreign society it is perhaps better as to women, i.e. they have *Mrs. Parkinson*!!! the English Consul's wife, and Mrs. Bennet the American Consuless—Mrs. Pelly and Miss Stewart make up the tale but the Do Regos are a loss to society—and so is Caumont.—The rest vulgarians and now there is less intercourse than ever with the Portuguese. Since the bursting of the Bank and natural drainage of the marsh between Olinda and Recife, a plan that had been formed by the Junta of 1822 for converting that space into rice ground might easily be carried into effect but the evil state of the government prevents it.]

Thursday, 4th.—Received Madame do Rego, one of her daughters, Miss S., and several gentlemen, on board. Most of the party were sea-sick, from the rolling of the ship, caused by the heavy swell at the anchorage. They were, however, highly charmed with their visit, particularly with the fireworks with which we saluted the ladies, who had never been on board a British frigate before, on their departure.

Friday, 5th.—According to the agreement made with the patriot officers, on Wednesday, one launch and the second cutter went to Rio Doce to receive bullocks and other provisions. The officers and men were most kindly received, and returned with many presents of fresh stock and vegetables, which the patriots forced upon them. A military band attended them on landing, and conducted them to the place of meeting with the chiefs.

Messrs. Biddle and Glennie, being on shore surveying, near Cabo de Sant Augustin,* were detained as prisoners for a few hours, by a patriot detachment; but, as it appeared to be only for the purpose of obtaining money, and done by some subaltern, no notice was taken of it.

[*20th.*—Rose at six o'clock and after a pleasant stroll in the garden and orchard breakfasted early and went to town with Mr. Stewart. We drove through a considerable extent of country—and then I called

---

* The easternmost land of South America. It has two little harbours, for small vessels, each of which is defended by a small fort, and has a celebrated chapel to our Lady of Nazareth.

again on Carvalho hoping that my representations might still spare the effusion of blood. He received me most politely—had sent for his daughter to meet me and fruit and wine was set on the table—He gave me some maps and plans—shewed me the position of the troops, told me what in a month he hoped to realize {inserts 7 characters, possibly in code}!! I looked at some of his troops, boys of 10 years old and white headed negroes. He told me that he and his party would never yield on less terms that this: that the constituent assembly consisting of the very *same* members should be reassembled, that they should meet at any place but Rio and must be out of the reach of the imperial troops, that he was resolved to make Brazil free, or die on the field of glory. I took the liberty of remonstrating of shewing how unwise the assembly had been and asserted the right of the Sovereign to resolve it under the circumstances of its declaring itself permanent etc.—and our discourse ran to great length on abstract politics—I then came back on the old ground talked of the *personal* danger and responsibility etc. etc. He was sensible of the whole—and deeply impressed with the honorable character of the Admiral—if he found the cause lost, he would put himself in *his* power and feel safe and then he presented me to his daughters. I thought there was tenderness and feeling in the manner of his doing so. I grieved to leave him without effecting what I hoped. Alas that men will be careless of blood! I left Carvalho with a painful feeling and not the less for seeing him obliged to put up with the society of Zankee Rogers, a wretch who began by insulting me in the persons of the Emperor and Empress and Cochrane!!!! I brought away with me gazettes and proclamations of all kinds.

On coming on board I found Lord T not yet arrived but he was not long in coming—He dined and staid till four o'clock. I gave him my papers and told him all I had seen—Also that each night since he has been here (he anchored just after we did) they have beat to arms in the town supposing him likely to attack them.—etc. etc. He is surely the best of men!—as one little trait of kind feeling he has got poor Reeves as his servant and is very good to him.]

Saturday, 6th.—The frigate got under weigh to take a cruize, and if possible find a quieter anchorage. Mr. Dance with a party went for more provisions, to Rio Doce. The surf at the landing place was so high, that they were obliged to get into canoes, and leave the boats grappled at some distance from the beach. A guard of honour and military band attended them, as on the former day, and they were, moreover, pressed to dine with the commander of the post, which they gladly did. The dining-room was a long hut, built of wood and plaited palm leaves. In the centre, was a long table spread with a clean and very handsome cloth. The few chairs the place afforded were appropriated to the strangers, and the rest of the company stood during the meal. To the strangers, also, were given the spoons and forks, but the want of them did not appear to incommode the Brazilians. To each person a small basin of good beef broth, *bien dorée,* was served, and for the rest every man put his hand in the dish. Two principal messes occupied the centre of the table, one, a platter, containing a quantity of mandioc flour, raw; and the other a pile of fish, dressed with oil, garlic, and pimento. Each person began by stirring a quantity of the flour into his broth, till it acquired the consistence of brose, and then helping himself to the fish, which was cut up in convenient pieces, dipped it into the brose, and eat it with his fingers. Around the two principal dishes, were others of a most savoury nature,—eels fried with sweet herbs, shellfish stewed with wine and pimento, and others of the same kind. Into these also each man put his hand indiscriminately, and dipping his morsel into his basin, set our officers the example of eating that substitute for wheaten bread, and of swallowing, without regard to neatness or order, all manner of messes, mixed together, and touched by all hands. After dinner, a slave handed round a silver basin, with water and towels, after which a number of toasts were given, and the entertainment concluded with vivas, when the guard and band attended the officers to the boats, where the bullocks were ready to embark, and slaves to carry the English through the surf to the canoes, which conveyed them to the boats. On their return, I saw for the first time, the pitanga, a berry of which an excellent preserve is made; it grows upon a beautiful shrub, scarcely to be distinguished, either in flower or leaf, from the broad-leaved myrtle; the berry is as large as a filbert, and divided and coloured like the large red love-apple. Mr. Dance brought me, also, a beautiful green paroquet, the tamest, loveliest thing, with his emerald coat, and sparkling eye, I ever saw.*

Sunday, 7th.—We continued to cruize opposite to Olinda and Recife, and alarmed some of our friends on shore, by sailing round the English bank, a thing hitherto believed impossible, for so large a ship.

* All the parrot tribe in Brazil is beautiful: but neither parrots nor parroquets talk well. However, no slave ship comes from Africa without a grey parrot or two; so that in the towns they are almost as numerous as the native birds, and much more noisy, for they talk incessantly.

Monday, 8th.—We find to-day, on anchoring, that terms have been entered into with the patriots, by which their deputies are to be in the council, and take an equal share in the administration, and on the other hand they are to withdraw the investing troops, and leave Luis do Rego at the head of the military department, until the arrival of the next despatches from Lisbon. These pacific measures were brought about by the Paraiban deputies whom we met on Wednesday.

Tuesday, 9th.—Mr. Dance, Mr. Glennie, and I, were deputed to take charge of a large party of midshipmen, who had not been able before to take a run on shore, to spend the day on Cocoa-nut Island, which lies a good way up the harbour, and within the reef of Pernambuco. As we sailed along the rock, we observed that it is covered with echini, polypii, barnacles, limpets, and crusted with white bivalves less than oysters or cockles, yet containing a fish not unlike the latter in appearance, and the former in flavour. We had not exactly calculated the effect of the tide so far up the harbour as Cocoa-nut Island, consequently we got aground in the outer channel, at a considerable distance from the shore. The sailors pushed me over one flat bank in the gig, and then carried me to the beach; the midshipmen waded, and the officers and boats with the crews, went in search of a deeper passage, where they might approach with our provisions. Meantime the boys and I had full leisure to examine the island. It is perfectly flat and covered with white sand; the shore scattered with fragments of shells and coral. As its name imports, it is one grove of cocoa-nut trees, excepting where the present occupant has cleared space for a market-garden and fishponds. These last are very extensive; and as they secure a supply of fish at times when the rough seas of the outer roads prevent the canoes from going out, they have answered extremely well to the speculator. The garden produces European as well as Brazilian vegetables, in great perfection: Fruit-trees also thrive very well.* In the cuts for the fishponds I observed below the sand, a rich black earth, full of decayed vegetables, which probably renders this apparently sandy land, so fertile. The ponds were half covered with the white water-lily, and some other aquatic plants of the country. The whole island abounds in gay shrubs and gaudy flowers,† where the humming-bird, here called the

* All the orange and lemon tribe, papaws, cashew nuts, melons and gourds, pomegranates, guavas, etc.

† The Madagascar perriwinkle is the most common, many parasitic plants, and almost all the papilionaceous and the bell-shaped creepers: the passion flowers also are common.

beja flor or kiss-flower, with his sapphire wings and ruby crest, hovers continually, and the painted butterflies vie with him and his flowers in tints and beauty. The very reptiles are beautiful here. The snake and the lizard are singularly so, at least in colour. We found a very large rough caterpillar, each hair or prickle of which is divided into five or six branches; the rings of its body are scarlet, yellow, and brown; and the country people believe that it hurts the udders of cows, and prevents their giving milk, if it does not actually suck them. They are therefore very unpopular here, because the whole island that is not garden-ground is pasture, and supplies a great deal of the milk for the market of Recife.

While we were endeavouring to forget our hunger by examining the island, and drinking cocoa-nut juice, and wondering at many an ordinary thing, though new to young untravelled eyes, and such were those of most of the party, our boats were taking a circuitous track, and at length at ten o'clock landed our provisions, when we made a hearty breakfast, sitting on a sail spread under the palm shade. The elder boys with their guns, then accompanied Mr. Dance and the captain of a merchant vessel, who volunteered to act as Cicerone, to shoot; and the younger ones staid with me to collect flowers, gather vegetables, and with the assistance of the boats' crews, to superintend the preparations for dinner. At four o'clock the sportsmen returned, bringing red-crested woodpeckers, finches of various hues, humming-birds, black and yellow pies, and others of gay plumage and delicate shape, quite new to us all. A merrier party certainly never met, but the best of the expedition was to come. The tide was now favourable; and we determined to do a spirited thing, and instead of going all the way down the harbour, which would have kept us out beyond the time allowed us, we ran through a passage in the reef called Mother Cary's passage, because few things but the birds think of swimming there. The merchant-boat went first, our gig next, and as I sat in the stern of the large boat that was to follow, it was beautiful, but something fearful, to see them dash through that boiling surf between the rocks and rise over the wave secure beyond it, nor, was the sensation less mixed when we followed. There is at all times something triumphant in the sensation of sailing over the waters; but when they are roughened by storms, or rendered fearful by rocks or shoals, the triumph approaches to the sublime, and in it there is a secret dread, though not of ocean, and a raising of the soul to him who made the ocean, and gave man mind to master it. I am not ashamed to own, that as I looked round on my young charge, when Mr. Dance whispered "sit still and say nothing," and then stepping to the bow of the boat called aloud to the helmsman, "steady!" I had a moment, though but a moment, of exquisite anxiety. But we were through in an instant, and soon alongside of the frigate, where we were praised for doing what few had done before, and having shown the possibility of doing that safely, which at some future time it might be of importance to know could be done at all.

Wednesday, 10th.—We went on shore early for the first time since the armistice. The guns are removed from the streets and a few of the shops are re-opened; the negroes are no longer confined within doors, and the priests have reappeared; their broad hats and ample cloaks give them an importance among the crowd, which now is busy and active, and seemingly intent on redeeming the time lost to trade by the siege. I was struck by the great preponderance of the black population. By the last census, the population of Pernambuco, including Olinda was seventy thousand, of which not above one third are white: the rest are mulatto or negro. The mulattoes are, generally speaking, more active, more industrious, and more lively than either of the other classes. They have amassed great fortunes, in many instances, and are far from being backward in promoting the cause of independence in Brazil. Few even of the free negroes have become very rich. A free negro, when his shop or garden has repaid his care, by clothing him and his wife each in a handsome black dress, with necklace and armlets for the lady, and knee and shoe buckles of gold, to set off his own silk stockings, seldom toils much more, but is quite contented with daily food. Many, of all colours, when they can afford to purchase a negro, sit down exempt from further care. They make the negro work for them, or beg for them, and so as they may eat their bread in quiet, care little how it is obtained.

The European Portuguese are extremely anxious to avoid intermarriage with born Brazilians, and prefer giving their daughters and fortunes to the meanest clerk of European birth, rather than to the richest and most meritorious Brazilian. They have become aware of the prodigious inconvenience, if not evil, they have brought on themselves by the importation of Africans, and now no doubt, look forward with dread to the event of a revolution, which will free their slaves from their authority, and, by declaring them all men alike, will authorise them to resent the injuries they have so long and patiently borne.

Thursday, 11th.—As every thing seems quietly settled between the royalist and patriot chiefs, we are preparing to take leave of Pernambuco, and it is not without regret, for we have been kindly treated by the Portuguese, and hospitably received by our own countrymen. We went on shore to provide necessaries and comforts for our farther voyage. Among the latter I bought some excellent sweetmeats,* which are made in the interior, and brought to market in neat little wooden kegs, each containing six or eight pounds. It is astonishing to see the weight brought from two and three hundred miles' distance, by the small and slight but very swift horses of the country. The baggage horses are not shod any more than those for riding: the latter are almost universally trained to a kind of running pace, easy in itself, but not very agreeable at first, to those accustomed to English horses. To-day I saw and tasted the jerked beef, *charqui,* of Spanish South America. It appears, when hanging in bales at the shop-doors, like bundles of thick ragged leather. It is prepared by cutting the flesh in wide strips, clean off the bones, slightly salting, pressing, and drying in the air. In this state it might well have served for saddle-cloths to the Buccaneers, as tradition says they dressed their meat under their saddles. However that may be, the beef is good. Here the common mode of using it is to cut it in small squares, and boil it in the mandioc pottage, which is the principal food of the poorer inhabitants and the slaves.

After I had ended my marketing, I went to call on a Portuguese family, and as it was the first private Portuguese house I had been in, I was curious to notice the difference between it and the English houses here. The building and general disposition of the apartments are the same, and the drawing-room only differed in being better furnished, and with every article English, even to a handsome piano of Broadwood's; but the dining-room was completely foreign; the floor was covered with painted cloth, and the walls hung round with English prints and Chinese pictures, without distinction of subject or size. At one end of the room was a long table, covered with a glass case, enclosing a large piece of religious wax-work; the whole *præsepia,* ministering angels, three kings, and all, with moss, artificial flowers, shells and beads, smothered in gauze and tiffany, bespangled with gold and silver, San Antonio and St. Christopher being in attendance on the right and left; the rest of the furniture consisted of ordinary chairs

* The convents are, generally speaking, the places where the more delicate preserves are made. Those I bought were of Guava, cashew apple, citron, and lime. The cashew particularly good. They go by the general name of *Doce.*

and tables, and a kind of beaufet or sideboard: from the ceiling, nine bird-cages were hanging, each with its little inhabitant; canaries, grey finches with a note almost as fine, and the beautiful widow-bird, were the favourites. In larger cages in a passage room, there were more parrots and paroquets than I should have thought agreeable in one house; but they are well-bred birds, and seldom scream all together. We were no sooner seated in the dining-room, than biscuit, cake, wine, and liqueurs, were handed round, the latter in diminutive tumblers; a glass of water was then offered to each, and we were pressed to taste it, as being the very best in Recife; it proceeds from a spring in the garden of the convent of Jerusalem, two miles from town, and the only conduit from that spring leads to the garden of a sister convent here. From the lady, I learned, that the porous jars for cooling water, that we find here, are all made in the neighbourhood of Bahia, there being no manufactory here, except a few coarse cottons for clothing for the slaves. The air and manners of the family we visited, though neither English nor French, were perfectly well bred, and the dress pretty much that of civilised Europe, only that the men wore cotton jackets instead of cloth coats, and were without neck-cloths; when they go out of doors, however, they dress like Englishmen.

Returning from our visit, we met a monk, carried out to be buried by several of his brethren, with candle, book, and bell, and all the solemnities which human feeling has invented to solace its own fears and griefs, under the pretence of honouring the dead, and to which the Romish church has in such cases as these, added all her pageantry. I could not help contrasting it with the burials on the beach of Olinda, and smiling at the vanities that attach themselves even to corruption. "But man, vain man, plays such fantastic tricks before high heaven, as make the angels weep." [48]

But our horses were awaiting us, and we left our indignation and our pity for the follies of some, and the miseries of others, to enjoy, for the first time since the posts were free, the country air. When we went to Bibiriba, soldiers stopped us to question at every turn; piles of arms, and horses ready accoutred at the door of every considerable residence, showed that military posts had taken place of the pleasures of the country-houses, and accounted for the solitariness of the roads. Now

---

48. Graham condenses Isabella's speech in Shakespeare's *Measure for Measure* (II.ii): "Man, proud man, drest in a little brief authority, most ignorant of what he's most assur'd, glassy essence, like an angry ape, plays such fantastic tricks before high heaven, as make the angels weep."

the scene is changed—the paths are crowded with negroes, young and old, in their picturesque, though gaudy dresses, with baskets of fruit, fish, and other provisions, on their heads; little carts, of which we had not before seen one, begin to appear, and the fine oxen which draw them from no bad contrast to the half-starved bullocks of the town. 'Twas a cool evening, and the sun was just low enough to gild the edges of the palms and other tall trees, which shot up with their deep black shadows into the thin pure light, making an effect, that even Titian's landscape pencil has not reached.[49] Our ride extended to Mr. S.'s country-house, which is, I believe, on the same plan with all the others hereabouts, and which I can only compare to an Oriental bungalow; one story very commodiously laid out, a veranda surrounding it, and standing in the midst of a little paddock, part of which is garden ground, and part pasture, generally hedged with limes and roses, and shaded with fruit trees, is the general description of the country sitios about Pernambuco; the difference arising from the taste of the inhabitant, or the situation of the ground, being allowed for. The low rent of these pleasant little gardens is surprising; but it arises in great measure from the indolence and consequent poverty of the holders of original grants of land here: as long as their negroes and estates maintained them, they paid no attention to the particular parts that, being near the town, might have been at all times productive. Now, that sugar and cotton are no longer in such demand, nearly half the fazendas or factories are ruined, and such is become the indolent temper of the people, that rather than seek to redeem their estates, they will take the smallest annuity for a portion. On our way to the sitio, we stopped at a kind of public-house or venda; it is like an English huckster's, and contains a little of every thing, cloth and candles, fruit and lard, wine and pimento, which are retailed at no very extravagant profit to the poor; the draught wine is really good, being port of excellent quality, without the quantity of brandy which the English market requires. By the time we repassed it on our way home, many a negro was spending his day's savings, and becoming as happy as wine could make him; and man a traveller was regaling himself with bread, garlic, and salt, and preparing to spread his mat, and lie down in the open air for the night. Night within the tropics is always a gayer and more peopled

---

49. Pieve di Cadore Titian (1488/1490-1576), Italian Renaissance painter renowned for his use of color and his religious and mythological subjects as well as landscapes.

time than with us; the heat of the day detains many within doors all day, and evening and night become the favourite hours for walking. As we returned through Boa Vista we passed many groups enjoying like ourselves the pleasant air, and gazing idly on the reflections of the white houses and waving trees in the water; while the fire flies flitting from bush to bush, seemed like fragments of stars come down to adorn the moonlight.

Friday, 12th.—The Prince Royal of Portugal's birth-day. There is a levee at the palace. The company bow first to the governor, then to the Prince's picture, which is placed in the middle of the audience-room, to receive its due honours; and then the *beja mano,* or kiss hands, takes place. The forts and ships saluted; we of course did the same; and the people all dressed and went to mass, as on a holiday. One thing contributed, however, in no small degree to the enjoyment of the day. The troops, which lately arrived from Bahia, re-embarked in order to return. Their whole behaviour had been disorderly, and their drunkenness and riot, during the ten days they were here, had quite disgusted the people; while the disposition they manifested to join the patriots, had rendered them but suspicious auxiliaries to the governor.

Saturday, 13th.—I took leave of my amiable friends at the palace. Madame do Rego gave me several specimens of amethyst, and the stone called minha nove (like aqua marine), and also a fine piece of gold ore of the province. She told me that Luis do Rego had sent home many fine minerals from the captaincy, and also some fossils. She described some enormous bones, which may have belonged to the elephant or the mammoth, found at no great distance from Recife in digging a well, and, as far as I could understand, in such soil as I had observed lay under the sand in Cocoa-nut Island.* [Probably the Megatherium, a gigantic sloth of which bones have also been found at Buenos Ayres.]

A great dinner was given to-day, by the merchants, to the captain and officers. The governor, and other persons of dignity in the town, met them; I am told it was a very handsome dinner, that there was plenty of every kind of wine, and that nothing could exceed the friendly politeness of the governor and his party. I had remained at Mr. S.'s, where most of the company visited me after tea; and then we took

* The Sugar-loaf Hill, in the ridge of Priaca, about eight leagues N.E. of the villa of Penedo, has a lake on its western declivity, where enormous bones have been found; and on the north side there is a fearful cavern.—*Chor. Brazil.*

leave of Pernambuco, where we had received much kindness, and had at least the enjoyment of novelty. The scene at our embarking was very pretty. Our friends went with us to the jetty, and our boats lying in the clear moonshine beneath it, with sailors going up and down preparing for us, the harbour and the shipping doubled by the clear reflection in the still water, heightened and set off the sparkling of the breakers that dashed against the outer fort and light-house. Through these we soon made our way and reached the ship, where I have once more taken possession of my cabin, and put it in order for sea.

We leave Pernambuco, with a firm persuasion that this part of Brazil at least will never again tamely submit to Portugal. Where the firmness and conduct of Do Rego have failed to hold the captaincy in obedience, it will be in vain for other governors to attempt it, particularly so long as the state of the mother country is such as that she can neither fight with nor for her colonies; and while she considers them only as taxable parts of her states, that are bound to support her in her weakness.*

Sunday, Oct. 14th.—We got under weigh after breakfast, and soon lost sight of Pernambuco. All Sunday, Monday, and Tuesday, we coasted along within sight of the shores of Brazil. They are hilly and very woody, the green of the sloping banks being often interrupted by bright white patches, which seem to be of sand. In the evening of Tuesday the 16th, we anchored in the bay of All Saints, opposite to the town of St. Salvador, commonly called Bahia. It was quite dark before we got in, so that we lost the first entrance-view of that magnificent harbour; but the scattered lights show us the great extent and high situation of the town.

[*Wednesday, 25th August 1824.*—Anchored about 1/2 a mile from the shore off the arsenal of St. Salvadors. The French frigate Magisienne being in the Doris's old berth and decked in honour of St. Louis' day. The Maria de Gloria lying here with her prize the Constituiçaõ o morte taken from Carvalho's party. I find the people here expecting impossible things from Cochrane that he was to land the troops

---

* We left Pernambuco on the 14th Oct. 1821. Before Nov. 18th of the same year, the Cortes of Lisbon had recalled Luiz do Rego and all the European troops; had repented of that recal, and had countermanded it, and sent reinforcements. But by the time they arrived, the captain-general had embarked on board a French ship for Europe; and the junta, after provisioning the ships with the troops, forbid them to land, and sent them towards Rio Janeiro.

at Grande and in one night end the business at Recife—perhaps he might by sacrificing all neutrals (who could not leave the harbour before the 25th). In the first place they were landed at Massaiaõ—Deane boarded the packet and began blustering.—I made him quiet. I slept at the Nicholson's and saw a good deal of Dundas and something of Joares enough to know him for a Taylorist. It is according to him to be an article with England in any treaty that he shall be reinstated! The little man is of course considered by England as a deserter and claimed—so he retires on full pay—but is looking forward to the admiral's place.—*No!!* The suburbs of the town have suffered in beauty by the siege last year—because of the loss of several magnificent trees. But there are still enough left to make it one of the woodiest cities in the world—a great deal of ground has been cleared, but it is chiefly cultivated for Capim. Some successful attempts have been made to grow potatoes and onions—and I should think it would be wise to bring the cultivation of Mandioc also nearer the town in case of another siege.

I called on the president Viana and was received very politely by him.

Thursday 28th.— Went with Mr. Moore and Mr. Mather to the convent of the Soledad to purchase flowers for the Miss King—they were not very good nor cheap—doces-idem. The Superior Maria Joachim has been in the convent from her infancy. She calls herself sixty I should have said forty, very comely, and with a sweet countenance. There are now but 37 nuns (Ursulines)—the complement is 60. They suffer from poverty; the school they kept for the better classes of young women in reading, writing, sewing, and the dottrina is no longer attended. After being at the Soledad we went through the corn and vegetable market all is now cheap and good and plentiful. Tasted the Negro mess of vegetable stewed with Dendy oil and should have thought it excellent with salt.

In the evening the Padre Marcos Antonio de Souza secretary to Government—called on me and sat half an hour very politely and thanked me for the letters from Pernambuco. We embarked about 10 o'clock at the arsenal.

Friday 27th.—Left Bahia.—and brought two Swiss passengers Meuron and de Costere.]

Wednesday, 17th.—This morning, at day-break, my eyes opened on one of the finest scenes they ever beheld. A city, magnificent in appearance from the sea, is placed along the ridge and on the declivity of a very high and steep hill: the richest vegetation breaks through the white houses at intervals, and beyond the city, reaches along to the outer point of land on which the picturesque church and convent of Sant Antonio da Barre is placed. Here and there the bright red soil shows itself in harmony with the tiling of the houses. The *tracery* of forts, the bustle of shipping, hills melting in the distance, and the very form of the bay, with its promontories and islands, altogether finish this charming picture; then the fresh sea-breeze gives spirit to enjoy it, notwithstanding its tropical climate.

Early in the day we moved our anchorage closer in-shore; and then, on the invitation of Mr. Pennell, the British consul, we went ashore to spend the day with him. We landed at the arsenal, or rather dock-yard, where there is nothing of the neatness observable in such establishments at home. The first object we saw, however, was a fine 58-gun frigate on the stocks, the model of which I hear connoisseurs praise as beautiful. There is nothing besides the new ship, and some handsome pieces of old brass cannon, worth looking at. Every thing is visibly either suspended or on the decline, and there will probably be no improvement, until the political state of Brazil is a little more settled. We find things here, though not quite so unquiet as at Pernambuco, yet tending the same way.

The street into which we proceeded through the arsenal gate, forms, at this place, the breadth of the whole lower town of Bahia, and is, without any exception, the filthiest place I ever was in. It is extremely narrow, yet all the working artificers bring their benches, and tools into the street: in the interstices between them, along the walls, are fruit-sellers, venders of sausages, black-puddings, fried fish, oil and sugar cakes, negroes plaiting hats or mats, caderas, (a kind of sedan chair,) with their bearers, dogs, pigs, and poultry, without partition or distinction; and as the gutter runs in the middle of the street, every thing is thrown there from the different stalls, as well as from the windows; and there the animals live and feed! In this street are the warehouses and counting-houses of the merchants, both native and foreign. The buildings are high, but neither so handsome nor so airy as those of Pernambuco.

Figure 5. Slaves Dragging a Hogshead in the Streets of Pernambuco. Courtesy of The Catholic University of America, Oliveira Lima Library, Washington, D.C.

It was raining when we landed; therefore, as the streets leading out of the filthy lower town do not admit of the use of wheeled carriages, on account of the steepness of the ascent, we hired caderas, and found them, if not comfortable, at least commodious. They consist of a cane arm-chair, with a foot-board and a canopy covered with leather; curtains, generally of moreen, with gilt bordering and lined with cotton or linen, are contrived to draw round, or open at pleasure; and the whole is slung by the top to a single pole, by which two negroes carry it at a quick pace upon their shoulders, changing occasionally from right to left.*

As we ascended from the street, every step brought us in sight of some beautiful scene, generally terminated by the bay and shipping. There is something in the landscape here peculiarly agreeable. The verdure, the wood, the steep banks, and gently sloping lawns, generally opening to the sea or the lake behind the town, have a freshness and amenity that I scarcely remember seeing before. We saw but little of the upper city, but that little was handsome, in our way to the consul's. His house, like those of all the British merchants, is a little way out of town, and is in the suburb Vittoria, which occupies the greater part of a long narrow ridge extending from the town towards Sant Antonio: between it and the town is Fort Pedro, built, I think, originally of mud, by the Dutch. It was faced with stone, on the recovery of Bahia from the Dutch, about the beginning of the last century. We found the Consul and his daughter ready to receive us at their very pleasant garden-house, which literally overhangs the bay,—flowers and fruits mingle their sweets even down to the water's edge,—while

* When Frezier travelled, a cotton hammock with a canopy was used.

Seaborn gales their gelid wings expand,
To winnow fragrance round the smiling land.[50]

Eager to seize the opportunity of walking out after our voyage, we accepted Miss Pennell's kind offer, to show us some of the surrounding country before dinner, and accompanied her, as far as the church dedicated to N. S. da Graça. It was the first offering of piety, I believe, to Christian worship by a native Brazilian.

When the famous Caramuru was wrecked, together with the Donatory Coutinho, on Itaparica, Coutinho was put to death; but, Caramuru, being beloved by the natives, was spared, and he returned to his old settlement of Villa Velha.[51] His wife, Catherine Paraguaza, who had accompanied him to France, saw an apparition in the camp of the Indians, and believing it to be a real European female, Caramuru followed in the direction his wife pointed out: he discovered, accordingly, in one of the huts, an image of N. S. da Graça; and according to the directions his wife had received from the vision, built and dedicated the church, and bestowed it, and a house by it, on the Benedictines. It was at first of mud, but soon after was built of stone.

Thursday, 18th.—We rode out before breakfast, through landscape so fine, that I wished for a poet or a painter at every step. Sometimes we went through thick wild wood into bushy hollows; then emerged on clear lawns, sprinkled with palm trees, through which country-houses, farms, and gardens were seen; and from every eminence, the bay, the sea, or the lake, formed part of the scene. Here and there the huge gamela tree* stands like a tower, adorned, besides its own leaves, with numberless parasite plants, from the stiff cactus, to the

---

* The gamela, like the banyan, easily takes root in other trees, and its branches meet together in the same manner. It is the tree of which the canoes of Brazil are made, and serves besides for troughs of various kinds.

---

50. Oliver Goldsmith (1730-1774), *The Traveller*.
51. Diogo Álvares Correia (1475?-1557), Portuguese sailor shipwrecked in Bahia on the Brazil coast sometime around 1510 at the beginning of Portuguese colonization of Brazil, lived with the Tupinambá Indians, who named him Caramurú; he had half-Tupinambá children and served as an intermediary between Indians and Portuguese during the early years of colonization. His story has been retold in countless versions, both literary and historical, but in all cases Caramurú is associated with myths of Brazilian origins and provides a means of narrating the relationships between Portuguese colonists and indigenous peoples (Tenenbaum I: 549; Amado passim).

swinging air plant;† and the frequent tower of church and monastery soften and improve the features of the country.

Mr. Pennell has most kindly given our young men a general invitation to his house; and accordingly, to-day several of them dined with him, and we had a party in the evening, when some of the ladies played quadrilles, while others danced.

Friday, 19th.—I accompanied Miss Pennell in a tour of visits to her Portuguese friends. As it is not their custom to visit or be visited in the forenoon, it was hardly fair to take a stranger to see them. However, my curiosity, at least, was gratified. In the first place, the houses, for the most part, are disgustingly dirty: the lower story usually consists of cells for the slaves, stabling etc.; the staircases are narrow and dark; and, at more than one house, we waited in a passage while the servants ran to open the doors and windows of the sitting-rooms, and to call their mistresses, who were enjoying their undress in their own apartments. When they appeared, I could scarcely believe that one half were gentlewomen. As they wear neither stay nor bodice, the figure becomes almost indecently slovenly, after very early youth; and this is the more disgusting, as they are very thinly clad, wear no neck-handkerchiefs,

Figure 6. Cadeira, or Sedan Chair of Bahia. Courtesy of The Catholic University of America, Oliveira Lima Library, Washington, D.C.

† Air-plant or Tillandsia, of which there are several sorts. The Tillandsia Lingulata is the largest, and agrees with Jaquin's plate; the others are different from those described by him, and are much more beautiful.

and scarcely any sleeves. Then, in this hot climate, it is unpleasant to see dark cottons and stuffs, without any white linen, near the skin. Hair black, ill combed, and dishevelled, or knotted unbecomingly, or still worse, *en papillote,* and the whole person having an unwashed appearance. When at any of the houses the bustle of opening the cob-webbed windows, and assembling the family was over, in two or three instances, the servants had to remove dishes of sugar, mandioc, and other provisions, which had been left in the best rooms to dry. There is usually a sofa at each end of the room, and to the right and left a long file of chairs, which look as if they never could be moved out of their place. Between the two sets of seats is a space, which, I am told, is often used for dancing; and, in every house, I saw either a guitar or piano, and generally both. Prints and pictures, the latter the worst daubs I ever saw, decorate the walls pretty generally; and there are, besides, crucifixes and other things of the kind. Some houses, however, are more neatly arranged; one, I think belonging to a captain of the navy, was papered, the floors laid with mat, and the tables ornamented with pretty porcelain, Indian and French: the lady too was neatly dressed in a French wrapper. Another house belonging to one of the judges was also clean, and of a more stately appearance than the rest, though the inhabitant was neither richer nor of higher rank. Glass chandeliers were suspended from the roof; handsome mirrors were intermixed with the prints and pictures. A good deal of handsome china was displayed round the room; but the jars, as well as the chairs and tables, seemed to form an inseparable part of the walls. We were every where invited, after sitting a few moments on the sofa, to go to the balconies of the windows and enjoy the view and the breeze, or at least amuse ourselves with what was passing in the street. And yet they did not lack conversation: the principal topic, however, was praise of the beauty of Bahia; dress, children, and diseases, I think, made up the rest; and, to say the truth, their manner of talking on the latter subject is as disgusting as their dress, that is, in a morning: I am told they are different after dinner. They marry very early, and soon lose their bloom. I did not see one tolerably pretty woman to-day. But then who is there that can bear so total a disguise as filth and untidiness spread over a woman?

Saturday, 20th.—As the charts of this coast hitherto published are very incorrect, the captain asked permission from government to sound and survey the bay: it is refused on the ground of policy; as if it could be policy to keep hidden rocks and shoals, for one's own as well as other people's ships.

I walked through the greater part of the town. The lower part extends much farther than I could see the day I landed; it contains a few churches, one of which, belonging to the monastery of *A concepçaô*, is very handsome, but the smell within is disgusting; the flooring is laid in squares with stone, and within each square there is a panelling of wood of about nine feet by six; under each panel is a vault, into which the dead are thrown naked, until they reach a certain number, when with a little quick-lime thrown in, the wood is fastened down, and then another square is opened, and so on in rotation. From that church, passing the arsenal gate, we went along the low street, and found it widen considerably at three quarters of a mile beyond: there are the markets, which seem to be admirably supplied, especially with fish. There also is the slave market, a sight I have not yet learned to see without shame and indignation:* beyond are a set of arcades, where goldsmiths, jewellers, and haberdashers display their small wares, and there are the best-looking shops; but there is a want of neatness, of that art of making things look well, that invites a buyer in England and France. One bookseller's shop, where books are extravagantly dear, exists in the low town, and one other in the ascent to the upper.

The upper town is most beautifully situated on the ridge between the sea and the fresh water lake, and from its height, and the great slope of most of the streets, it is incomparably cleaner than the port. The cathedral dedicated to St. Salvador is a handsome building, and stands on one side of a square, where the palace, prison, and other public buildings are placed. The finest of these, the Jesuits' college, the marble columns of which came from Europe ready cut, is now converted into a barrack. The most useful is the hospital of Nossa Sen-

---

* Frezier says of Bahia,

> Who would believe it? there are shops full of those poor wretches, who are exposed there stark naked and bought like cattle, over whom the buyers have the same power; so that upon slight disgust they may kill them, almost without fear of punishment, or at least treat them as cruelly as they please. I know not how such barbarity can be reconciled to the maxims of religion, which makes them members of the same body with the whites, when they have been baptized, and raises them to the dignity of the sons of God—*all sons of the Most High.*
>
> I here make this comparison, because the Portuguese are Christians who make a great outward show of religion.—*Voyage to the South Sea.*

hora da Misericordia,* founded by Juan de Matinhos, whose statue in white marble, with a wig like Sir Cloudesley Shovel's in Westminster Abbey, stands at the first landing-place, and is the ugliest piece of carving I ever saw.

This hospital, besides its use as a refuge for the sick, of whom there are generally about 120, maintains 50 young girls of decent parentage, to whom a suitable education is given, and a dowry of 200 crowns bestowed on them when they marry.* The building of the Misericordia is a fair specimen of the style of the convents, public buildings, and more noble houses,—rather handsome than elegant. It surrounds a large area, subdivided into smaller courts; the staircase is of marble, inlaid with coloured stucco, and the sides are lined with tiles of porcelain, so as to form arabesques, often of very pretty design. This is both a cool and a cleanly lining to a wall, particularly for an hospital. The principal rooms are also decorated in the same manner; and many of the fronts and cupolas of the churches are covered with similar tiles, the effect of which is often exceedingly agreeable, when seen among the trees and plainer buildings of the city. The chapel belonging to the hospital is handsome, a little gaudy, however. The ceiling is respectably painted, and was probably the work of an amateur monk of the seventeenth century. The treatment of the sick is humane, and they are well provided with food and other necessaries; but the medical practice, though much improved of late years, is not the most enlightened.

There is a great deal of jealousy of foreigners in the present government, hence I was not able to enter many of the public buildings. The government treasury was one I was desirous to see, but there were objections. The treasury here was formerly considered as subordinate to that of Rio de Janeiro, and accordingly paid a portion of its receipts to bills drawn monthly by the treasurer in the capital, upon this, and those of the other provinces. But since the revolution of the 10th of February, the provisional government has taken upon itself to refuse payment, on the grounds that it is entirely independent of Rio, until the pleasure of the Cortes at Lisbon shall be known. The revenue is

* Part of the funds for supporting this and other hospitals is derived from lotteries. See advertisements in the different Bahia newspapers.

† João de Matos Aguiar, commonly called Joaõ de Matinhos, from his diminutive size, was the founder of this Recolhimento. He bequeathed 800,000 crusadoes for the retired women, 400,000 for the patients, one to each on leaving the hospital, and 400,000, dowry to 38 girls every year, at the period of the foundation, 1716.

derived from direct taxes on land and provisions, excise upon exports and imports, and harbour dues. Land is subject to a tax of one-tenth of the whole of its produce, and since the revolution, church lands are under the same law, and the clergy are paid by the government.

The taxes on provisions are annually farmed out to the highest bidder: they are imposed on beef, fresh fish, farinha, and vegetables. Each parish has its separate farmer, who pays the amount of his contract into the treasury, and then makes the most he can of his dues.

The import and export duties are paid at the custom-house, between which and the treasury a monthly settlement takes place.

[Extract of a Letter from Lima *February 19, 1825*.—

The following articles of *Good* quality will now command the price annexed to each onboard-ship free of duties, say Butter 2 1/2 rs./lb., Lard 2 1/2 rs./lb., Sperm Candles 3 1/2 rs./lb., Cider $5 1/2 box, Yellow Soap $15 gl., Tallow $13 gl., Tea Gunpowder $1 1/2 lb., White Wax $90 gl.,—Quick silver $55,—{illegible}—Claret Wine $10 doz., Champaign $24,—Brandy Cognac $1 1/4 gl., German Linens 25% advance over Invoice cost. American cottons 50% advance, at present plenty—Superfine Broadcloths; 3/4 crape shawls; Silk do; Ladies Silk Hakfs;—and Cordage much enquired for and wanted command good

Figure 7. Gamella Tree at Bahia. Courtesy of The Catholic University of America, Oliveira Lima Library, Washington, D.C.

prices.{Graham added this paragraph in her annotations, then deleted it.}]

The port dues for foreign ships are 2000 reals per day, a trifle for the light-house, and rather heavy charges for entering, clearing, etc. Portuguese and Brazilian ships pay no anchorage, but are subject to a tonnage.

We ended our perambulation of the town, by going to the opera at night. The theatre* is placed on the highest part of the city, and the platform before it commands the finest view imaginable. It is a handsome building, and very commodious, both to spectators and actors. Within it is very large and well laid out, but dirty and in great want of fresh painting. The actors are very bad as such, and little better as singers; but the orchestra is very tolerable. The piece was a very ill-acted tragedy, founded on Voltaire's Mahomed.[52] During the representation, the Portuguese ladies and gentlemen seemed determined to forget the stage altogether, and to laugh, eat sweetmeats, and drink coffee, as if at home. When the musicians, however, began to play the overture to the ballet, every eye and voice was directed to the stage, and a loud call for the national hymn followed, and not till it had been played again and again, was the ballet suffered to proceed. During the bustle occasioned by this, a captain in the army was arrested and hurried out of the pit; some say for picking pockets, others for using intemperate language on politics, when the national hymn was called for. Meantime one of the midshipmen of our party had his sword stolen, adroitly enough, from the corner of the box, yet we perceived nobody enter; so that we conclude a gentleman in regimentals in the next box thought it would suit him, and so buckled it on to go home with.

The police here is in a wretched state. The use of the dagger is so frequent, that the secret murders generally average two hundred yearly, between the upper and lower towns. To this evil the darkness and

---

* It was begun by the Conde da Ponte, and finished by the Conde dos Arcos after the arrival of the king in Brazil. It was opened May 13th, 1812.

52. Voltaire (1684-1788), pseudonym for François-Marie Arouet, French writer and philosopher. Through wit and satire, he critiqued tyranny, bigotry and religious oppression; his ideas contributed not only to the French Revolution, but also to independence movements throughout the Americas. He spent two years in exile in England, where he found much to admire in the British political system and British literature. Graham refers to his 1742 play *Mahomet*, in which Mohammed, the Prophet of Islam, is portrayed as an imposter.

steepness of the streets mainly contribute, by furnishing almost a certainty of escape. The nominal *intendente da policia* is also the supreme judge in criminal cases. No law, however, has as yet determined the limits or scope, either of his power, or that of the lieutenant-colonel of police, who calls upon a few soldiers from any of the garrisons whenever he has to act, and who appoints military patroles also from among the soldiers on duty. It often happens that persons accused before this formidable officer are seized and imprisoned for years, without ever being brought to a trial; a malicious information, whether true or false, subjects a man's private house to be broken open by the colonel and his gang; and if the master escapes imprisonment it is well, though the house scarcely ever escapes pillage. In cases of riot and quarrels in the street, the colonel generally orders the soldiers to fall on with canes, and beat people into their senses. Such being the state of the police, it is, perhaps, more wonderful that murders are so few, than that they are so many. Where there is little or no public justice, private revenge will take its place.

Sunday, 21st.—We went to the English chapel, and were well pleased with the decent manner in which the service was performed. The Rev. Robert Synge is chaplain, a man of cheerful convivial manners, yet exceedingly attentive both as chaplain, and as guardian of his poorer countrymen. The chapel and clergymen are supported by the contribution fund, as are also the hospital for English sailors and others, and its surgeon, Mr. Dundas: both the hospital and chapel are under the same roof.[53] I was surprised, perhaps unreasonably, to hear Mr. Synge pray for "Don John of Portugal, Sovereign of these realms, by whose gracious permission we are enabled to meet and worship God according to our conscience," or words to that effect. We were not so polite in Rome, I remember, as to pray for His Holiness, though it would have been but reasonable.

Returning from chapel, we saw great part of the troops drawn up in inspecting order, on the little green between *Buenos Ayres* (the name of the hospital) and Fort Pedro. Every Portuguese is, it seems, by birth a soldier; and nothing exempts a man from military duty, but his holding a place under government. There are six corps of militia in the city of Bahia: 1st, one company of mounted gentlemen, forming the government guard of honour; 2d, one squadron of flying artillery; 3d and

---

53. It is interesting that Maria Dundas Graham, usually so proud of her family connections, does not mention a family connection to this surgeon.

4th, two regiments of whites, almost all tradespeople; 5th, one regiment of mulattoes; and 6th, one of free blacks, amounting altogether to 4000 men, well armed and equipped; but the black regiment is unquestionably the best trained, and most serviceable, as a light infantry corps. The regiments of country militia, as those of Cachoeira, Piaja, etc. are much stronger, and with those of the city, amount to about 15,000 men. The officers are chosen from among the most respectable families, and with the exception of the majors and adjutants, who are of the line, receive no pay.

The troops of the capital are generally reviewed or inspected on Sundays, and sometimes the regular Portuguese are reviewed with them. There is always something gay and inspiriting in martial sounds and martial sights; and the fine weather, gay landscape, and above all, the idea that in a day or two, nay, this very night, these same soldiers might be called into action, did not render the scene less interesting. The native artillery have long garrisoned some of the forts. It appears that the royal troops of Portugal have claimed some superiority, and above all, have demanded their guns and ammunition; and so there is a dispute, in which the royalists and independents take part, and every day hostilities are expected; but both parties seem so willing to be peaceable, that I trust the matter will end without bloodshed.

Monday 22d.—This evening there was a large party, both Portuguese and English, at the consul's. In the well-dressed women I saw to-night, I had great difficulty in recognising the slatterns of the other morning. The senhoras were all dressed after the French fashion: corset, fichu, garniture, all was proper, and even elegant, and there was a great display of jewels. Our English ladies, though quite of the second rate of even colonial gentility, however, bore away the prize of beauty and grace; for after all, the clothes, however elegant, that are not worn habitually, can only embarrass and cramp the native movements; and, as Mademoiselle Clairon remarks, "she who would *act* a gentlewoman in public, must *be* one in private life."[54]

The Portuguese men have all a mean look; none appear to have any education beyond counting-house forms, and their whole time is, I believe, spent between trade and gambling: in the latter, the la-

---

54. Claire Josèphe Hippolyte Legris de Latude (1723-1803), French actress of the eighteenth century, used Madamoiselle Clairon as her stage name; she was renowned for being as independent as Graham herself. Graham may have read her *Mémoires d'Hyppolite Clairon, et réflexions sur l'art dramatique*, published in Paris in 1799.

dies partake largely after they are married. Before that happy period, when there is no evening dance, they surround the card tables, and with eager eyes follow the game, and long for the time when they too may mingle in it. I scarcely wonder at this propensity. Without education, and consequently without the resources of mind, and in a climate where exercise out of doors is all but impossible, a stimulus must be had; and gambling, from the sage to the savage, has always been resorted to, to quicken the current of life. On the present occasion, we feared the young people would have been disappointed of their dance, because the fiddlers, after waiting some time, went away, as they alleged, because they had not their tea early enough; however, some of the ladies volunteered to play the piano, and the ball lasted till past midnight.

Tuesday, 23d.—I rode with Mr. Dance and Mr. Ricken along the banks of the lake, decidedly the most beautiful scenery in this beautiful country; and then through wild groves, where all the splendours of Brazilian animal and vegetable life were displayed. The gaudy plumage of the birds, the brilliant hues of the insects, the size, and shape, and colour, and fragrance, of the flowers and shrubs, seen mostly for the first time, enchanted us, and rendered our little journey to the great pepper gardens, whither we were going, delightful. Every hedge is at this season gay with coffee blossom, but it is too early in the year for the pepper or the cotton to be in beauty. It is not many years since Francisco da Cunha and Menezes sent the pepper plant from Goa for these gardens, which were afterwards enlarged by him, when he became governor of Bahia. Plants were sent from hence to Pernambuco, which have succeeded in the botanical garden.

From the pepper gardens we rode on to a convent at the farther extremity of the town, and overlooking both the bays, above and below the peninsula of Bon fin, or N. S. da Monserrat. It is called the Soledad, and the nuns are famous for their delicate sweetmeats, and for the manufacture of artificial flowers, formed of the feathers of the many-coloured birds of their country. I admired the white water-lily most, though the pomegranate flower, the carnation, and the rose are imitated with the greatest exactness. The price of all these things is exorbitant; but the convents having lost much of their property since the revolution, the nuns are fain to make up by the produce of this petty industry, for the privations imposed on them by the reduction of their rents.

Wednesday, October 24th.—Mr. Pennell, his daughter, and a few other friends, joined us in an expedition to Itaparica,* a large island that forms the western side of the Bay of All Saints. A shoal runs off from it a long way to sea, and there are reefs of coral rocks on different parts of its coast. The distance from the city to the nearest landing place on the island is five miles and a half, which our boats' crews rowed in less than two hours. We put in between two ledges of rock, to a little jetty, belonging to the fazenda or factory of Aseoli, or Filisberti, both of whom were partners in Jerome Buonaparte's commercial establishment here. There is no town on Itaparica; but there is a villa, or village, with a fort on the Punto de Itaparica, which commands the passage between it and the mainland, and also the mouth of the river, on which stands Nazareth da Farinha, so called from the abundance of that article which it produces. There are also a great many fazendas, which, with their establishment of slaves and cattle, may be considered as so many hamlets. Each sugar farm, or ingenho, as the fazendas are oftener called here, has its little community of slaves around it; and in their huts something like the blessings of freedom are enjoyed, in the family ties and charities they are not forbidden to enjoy. I went into several of the huts, and found them cleaner and more comfortable than I expected; each contains four or five rooms, and each room appeared to hold a family. These out-of-door slaves, belonging to the great ingenhos, in general are better off than the slaves of masters whose condition is nearer to their own, because, "The more the master is removed from us, in place and rank, the greater the liberty we enjoy; the less our actions are inspected and controlled; and the fainter that cruel comparison becomes betwixt our own subjection, and the freedom, or even dominion of another."[55] But, at best, the comforts of slaves must be precarious. Here it is not uncommon to give a slave his freedom, when he is too old or too infirm to work; that is, to turn him out of doors to beg or starve. A few days ago, as a party of gentlemen

* *Itapa* is the Indian name: the Portuguese termination, Rica, indicates the fertility of the island. On this island Francesco Pereira Coutinho, the first donatory, was killed by the savages. He had founded his city near the watering place called Villa Velha, by what is now the fort of Gamboa, and not far from the habitation of the adventurer Caramura. The first Christian settlement formed here was in 1561, when the Jesuits founded an Aldea, and collected and humanised some of the natives.

55. David Hume (1711-1776), *Political Discourses*, "Discourses of the Populousness of Ancient Nations" (1752).

were returning from a *pic-nic*, they found a poor negro woman lying in a dying state, by the side of the road. The English gentlemen applied to their Portuguese companions to speak to her, and comfort her, as thinking she would understand them better; but they said, "Oh, 'tis only a black: let us ride on," and so they did without further notice. The poor creature, who was a dismissed slave, was carried to the English hospital, where she died in two days. Her diseases were age and hunger.* The slaves I saw here working, in the distillery, appear thin, and I should say over-worked; but, I am told, that it is only in the distilling months that they appear so, and that at other seasons they are as fat and cheerful as those in the city, which is saying a great deal. They have a little church and burying-ground here, and as they see their little lot the lot of all, are more contented than I thought a slave could be.

Sugar is the principal product of Itaparica; but the greater part of the poultry, vegetables, and fruit, consumed in Bahia, are also from the island, and lime is made here in considerable quantities from the madrepores and corals found on the beach. This island used to furnish the neighbourhood with horses. When the English fleet and army stopped here, on the way to the Cape of Good Hope, the horses for the cavalry regiments were procured here. However, there is nothing remarkable in Itaparica but its fertility; the landscape is the same in character with that of Bahia, though in humbler style; but it is fresh and green, and pleasing. After dining in a palm-grove, and walking about till we were tired, we re-embarked to return; but the tide was unfavourable; we drifted among the rocks, where Coutinho, the first founder of the colony of Bahia, was wrecked and afterwards murdered by the natives, and we were in consequence four hours in returning home.

26th, 27th, 28th.— passed in pleasant enough intercourse with our countrymen, though neither of us were well enough to go much on shore, therefore our friends came to us. There are eighteen English

---

* "The custom of exposing old, useless, or sick slaves, in an island of the Tyber, there to starve, seems to have been pretty common in Rome; and whoever recovered, after being so exposed, had his liberty given him, by an edict of the Emperor Claudius; where it was likewise forbid to *kill any slave, merely for old age or sickness*."—"We may imagine what others would practise, when it was the professed maxim of the elder Cato, to sell his superannuated slaves for any price, rather than maintain a useless burden."—"Discourses of the Populousness of Ancient Nations."

mercantile houses established at Bahia, two French, and two German. The English trade is principally carried on with Liverpool, which supplies manufactured goods and salt, in exchange for sugars, rums, tobaccos, cottons, very little coffee, and molasses. Lately, sugars have been shipped, on English account, for Hamburgh to a great extent, and I believe part of the returns are in German or Prussian woollen-cloths. The province of Bahia, by its neglect of manufactures, is quite dependent on commerce. But the distance from the sea of the province of Minas Geraes, has induced the inhabitants to weave not only enough coarse cotton cloths for home consumption, but even to become an article of trade with the other captaincies.

In the province of Esperitu Santo, cotton sail-cloth is made; but the chief trade of this place is *slaving*. This year no less than seventy-six slave-ships have sailed, without reckoning the smugglers in that line.

Sunday 28th.—Mr. Pennell had kindly fixed to-day for giving us a party in the country, and accordingly some of our young people were to go and assist in putting up tents, etc.; but a miscalculation of tide and time, and a mistake as to the practicability of landing on part of the beach beyond the light-house, occasioned a variety of adventures and accidents, without which I have always heard no fête champêtre could be perfect. However that may be, our party was a pleasant one. Instead of the tents, we made use of a country-house called the Roça, where beauty of situation, and neatness in itself and garden, made up for whatever we might have thought romantic in the tents, had they been erected. It is the fashion to pave the courts of the country-houses here with dark pebbles, and to form in the pavement a sort of mosaic with milk-white shells. The gardens are laid out in alleys, something in the oriental taste. The millions of ants, which often in the course of a single night leave the best-clothed orange tree bare both of leaves and flowers, render it necessary to surround each tree with a little stucco wall, or rather canal, in which there is water, till they are strong enough to recover if attacked by the ants. In the garden at Roça, every shrub of value, either for fruit or beauty, was so fenced, and there were seats, and water channels, and porcelain flower-pots, that made me almost think myself in the East. But there is a newness in every thing here, a want of interest on account of what has been, that is most sensibly felt. At most, we can only go back to the naked savage who devoured his prisoner, and adorned himself with bones and feathers here. In the East, imagination is at liberty to expatiate on past grandeur, wisdom, and politeness. Monuments of art and of science meet us at every step: *here,* every thing, nature herself, wears an air of newness, and the Europeans, so evidently foreign to the climate, and their African slaves, repugnant to every wholesome feeling, show too plainly that they are intruders, ever to be in harmony with the scene. However, Roça is beautiful, and all those grave thoughts did not prevent us from delighting in the fair prospect of

> Hill and valley, fountain and fresh shade;[56]

nor enjoying the scent of oleander, jasmine, tuberose, and rose, although they are adopted, not native children of the soil.

Of the Portuguese society here I know so very little, that it would be presumptuous to give an opinion of it. I have met with two or three well-informed men of the world, and some lively conversable women; but none of either sex that at all reminded me of the well-educated men and women of Europe. Here the state of general education is so low, that more than common talent and desire of knowledge is requisite to attain any; therefore the clever men are acute, and sometimes a little vain, feeling themselves so much above their fellow-citizens, and the portion of book-learning is small. Of those who read on political subjects, most are disciples of Voltaire, and they outgo his doctrines on politics, and equal his indecency as to religion; hence to sober people who have seen through the European revolutions, their discourses are sometimes disgusting. The Portuguese seldom dine with each other; when they do, it is on some great occasion, to justify a splendid feast: they meet every evening either at the play, or in private houses, and in the last case gamble very deeply. The English society is just such as one may expect. A few merchants, not of the first order, whose thoughts are engrossed by sugars and cottons, to the utter exclusion of all public matters that do not bear directly on their private trade, and of all matters of general science or information. Not one knew the name of the plants around his own door; not one is acquainted with the country ten miles beyond St. Salvador's; not one could tell me even the situation of the fine red clay, of which the only manufacture [here], pottery,

---

56. From Scottish phrenologist George Combe's (1788-1858) *Lectures on Phrenology* (1819); in context, the quotation reads, "But the individual in whom Ideality is large will in rapture say, that these objects, and the lofty mountain, the deep glen, the roaring cataract, and all the varied loveliness of the hill and dale, fountain and fresh shade, afford to him the banquet of the mind."

is made: in short, I was completely out of patience with these incurious money-makers. I was perhaps unjust to my countrymen: I dare say there are many who *could* have told me these things, but I am sure none *did* tell me, and equally sure that I asked information of all I met with. But a woman is not, I believe, considered as privileged to know any thing by these commercial personages. The English are, however, hospitable and sociable among each other. They often dine together: the ladies love music and dancing, and some of the men gamble as much as the Portuguese. Upon the whole, society is at a low, very low scale here among the English. Good eating and good drinking they contrive to have, for the flesh, fish, and fowl are good; fruits and vegetables various and excellent, and bread of the finest. Their slaves, for the English are all served by slaves, indeed, eat a sort of porridge of mandioc meal with small squares of jerked beef stirred into it, or, as their greatest luxury, stewed caravansas; and this is likewise the principal food of the lower classes even of the free inhabitants. In the fruit season, pumpkins, jackfruit, cocoa-nut, and melons, nearly take place of the mandioc. The huts of the poor are formed of upright poles, with branches of trees wattled between, and covered and lined either with cocoa-leaf mats, or clay; the roofs are also thatched. The better houses are built either of a fine blue stone, quarried on the beach of Victoria, or of brick. They are all white-washed: where the floor is not laid with wood, a fine red brick, six to nine inches square, and three in thickness, is used, and they are roofed with round red tiles. The houses are generally of one story high, with a room or two above by way of a look-out house. Under the house is generally a sort of cellar, in which the slaves live; and really I have sometimes wondered that human beings could exist in such.

Friday, 2d November.—Several of our people having yielded to the temptations of some worthless persons in the town, who induce sailors to desert in order that they themselves may profit by the premium given for the discovery of deserters, and having consequently swam on shore, the frigate has been moved up the harbour as far as Bom Fim, and it is intended to take her up still higher. I am glad of the opportunity of seeing more of this beautiful bay, and shall endeavour to land on the IIha do Medo, or the point of Itaparica, where the first adventurers from Europe underwent hardship that appear hardly credible in our modern days. We also wish to examine the harbour within the funil or passage between the two islands, and into which the river or creek of Nazareth, which supplies Bahia with great part of the mandioc flour consumed there, runs.

Saturday, 3d November.—Our plan of proceeding farther up the harbour is suspended for the present. The disputes between the European Portuguese and the Brazilians in the city, seem to be about to come to a crisis. Early this morning, we learned that troops were assembling from all quarters, and that therefore it was advisable, for the protection of the British property and the persons of the merchants, that the ship should return to her station opposite to the town. The first provisional junta has lost several of its members, two of them being gone as delegates to Lisbon, and others being absent on account of ill health or disgust. The party opposing this junta talk loudly of independence, and wish at least one-half of the members of the provisional government to be native Brazilians. They also complain bitterly, that instead of redressing the evils they before endured, the junta has increased them by several arbitrary acts; and assert that one of the members who has a great grazing estate, has procured a monopoly, by which no man can supply the market with beef without his permission, so that the city is ill supplied. Such a ground of complaint will always excite popular indignation, and it appears now to be at its height. There has already been some skirmishing, in which, however, I hear there have been only three men killed. The Brazilian artillery occupies Fort San Pedro; the governor, and the wreck of the junta, have the town and the palace. The governor, indeed, has arrested several, I think seventeen persons, in an arbitrary manner; among these, two of my acquaintance, Colonel Salvador* and Mr. Soares, and have put them, some on board the Don Pedro, some on board transports in the bay, for the purpose of transporting them to Lisbon. Some of these persons are not permitted to have any communication with their families; others, more favoured, are allowed to carry them with them. These are not the means to conciliate. We have sent on shore to offer shelter to the ladies, and Captain Graham has agreed upon certain signals with the consul, in case of increased danger to his family.

Sunday, November 4th.—On looking out at daylight this morning, we saw artillery planted, and troops drawn up on the platform opposite to the opera-house. I went on shore to see if Miss Pennell, her sister, or any of our other friends would come on board; but they naturally

---

* Colonel Salvador, though born in Portugal, has all his property and connections in Brazil; he served with credit in the peninsula. Mr. Soares, a Brazilian, had been long in England.

prefer staying to the last with their fathers and husbands. Notwithstanding the warlike movements of these last two days, it appears most likely that the chiefs of the opposite parties will agree to await the decision of the Cortes at Lisbon, with respect to their grievances, and at least a temporary peace will succeed to this little disturbance.

It appears, however, next to impossible that things should remain as they are. The extreme inconvenience of having the supreme courts of justice so far distant as Lisbon must be more and more felt as the country increases in population and riches. The deputies to the Cortes are too far removed from their constituents to be guided in their deliberations or votes by them; and the establishment of so many juntas of government, each only accountable to the Cortes, must be a cause of internal disorder, if not of civil war, at no distant time.

Monday 5th.—A day of heavy tropical rain, which has forced both parties on shore to house their guns, and to desist for the present from all farther hostility. The governor, however continues his arbitrary arrestations. It is curious how ancient authority awes men; for surely it is the accustomed obedience to the name of the king, and the dread of the name of rebellion, that prevents the Brazilians, armed as they are, from resisting these things.

Tuesday, November 6th.—The Morgiana, Captain Finlaison, came in from Rio de Janeiro.[57] She belongs to the African station, and came to Brazil about some prize business connected with the slave trade. Captain Finlaison tells me tales that make my blood run cold, of horrors committed in the French slave ships especially. Of young negresses, headed up in casks and thrown overboard, when the ships are chased. Of others, stowed in boxes when a ship was searched, with a bare chance of surviving their confinement. But where the trade is once admitted, no wonder the heart becomes callous to the individual sufferings of the slaves. The other day I took up some old Bahia newspapers, numbers of the Idade d'Ouro, and I find in the list of ships entered during three months of this year,

	Alive.	**Dead.**
1 slave ship from Moyanbique, 25th March, with	313	180
1 do.——6th March	378	61

---

57. Captain John Finlayson of the Royal Navy's ship Morgiana; Finlayson led the patrol intended to halt slave trafficking between Brazil and West Africa (Vale, *Frigate* 69).

1 do.——30th May	293	10
1 do.——29th June from Molendo	357	102
1 do.——26th June	233	21
	1574	374

So that of the cargoes of these five ships reckoned thus accidentally, more than one in five had died on the passage!

It seems the English ships of war on the African coast are allowed to hire free blacks to make up their complements when deficient. There are several now onboard the Morgiana, two of whom are petty officers, and they are found most useful hands. They are paid and victualled like our own seamen.*

Thursday, November 8.—We went on board Morgiana to call on Mrs. Macgregor, a lively intelligent Spaniard, who with her husband, Colonel Macgregor, is a passenger. She joined me in visits on shore, where the only news is, that the governor continues to arrest all persons suspected of favouring independence.

November 9.—The Brazilians who occupy the forts of San Pedro and Santa Maria, had threatened to fire on the Don Pedro, if she attempted to get under weigh with the state prisoners on board. Nevertheless during the night she bent her sails, and sailed early this morning, carrying, it is said, twenty-eight gentlemen, who have been taken up without any ostensible reason. They are understood to have spoken in favour of the independence of Brazil. Several of our officers went on shore to dine with the gentlemen of the English club, who meet once a month, to eat a very good dinner, and drink an immoderate quantity of wine for the honour of their country.

Tuesday, November 13.—We have had, for ten days past, some of the heaviest showers I remember to have seen, and in going to and from the ship, we have generally been wet through; nevertheless some of our friends ventured on board to-day to dine with us, among the rest Colonel and Mrs. Macgregor; they were a little late, owing to a skirmish between the Portuguese and Brazilians, that occurred close to their house, just as they were setting off. Apparently it had not been premeditated, for the parties were fighting with sticks and stones, as well as swords and

---

* The negroes of the *Cru* nation come to Sierra Leone from a great distance, and hire themselves out for any kind of labour, for six, eight, or ten months, sometimes for a year or two. They have then earned enough to go home and live like idle gentlemen, for at least twice that time, and then return to work. When their engagements on board men of war are fulfilled, they receive regular discharges and certificates.

fire-arms. The combatants would not allow any officer in Portuguese regimentals to pass, so that Colonel Macgregor was obliged to go back and change his dress before he could come. All this appears to proceed more from a want of police than any other cause.

16th.—Several of our young people and I myself have begun to feel the bad effects of exposing ourselves too much to the sun and the rain. Yesterday I was so unwell as to put on a blister for cough and pain in my side, and several of the others have slight degrees of fever. But generally speaking, the ship's company has been remarkably healthy.

Friday, 16th.—Captain Graham taken suddenly and alarmingly ill. Towards evening he became better, and was able to attend to a most painful business. Last night a man belonging to the Morgiana was killed, and the corporal of marines belonging to the ship severely wounded, on shore. It appears that neither of these men had so much as seen the murderer before. He had been drinking in the inner room of a venda with some sailors, and having quarrelled with one of them, he fancied the rest were going to seize him, when he drew his knife to intimidate them, and rushed furiously out of the room. The young man who was killed was standing at the outer door, waiting for one of his companions who was within, and the murderer seeing him there, imagined he also wished to stop him, and therefore stabbed him to the heart. Our corporal, who was passing by, saw the deed, and of course attempted to seize him, and in the attempt received a severe wound. It is said, I know not with what truth, that Captain Finlaison is so hated here, on account of his activity against the slave trade, that none of his people are safe, and the death of the unfortunate man is attributed to that cause; but it appears to have been the result of a drunken quarrel. The town, however, appears to be in a sad disorderly state: besides our two men, a Brazilian officer was dangerously wounded in the dark, and three Brazilian soldiers and their corporal were found murdered last night. Captain Graham had sent one of his officers to act for him on the occasion, and to apply through the British consul to the police magistrate, Francisco Jose Perreira, for redress.* He himself is sensibly worse since he

* Mr. Pennell accordingly wrote to Mr. Perreira, stating the circumstance and also that the prisoner was taken. The magistrate assured him that he had laid his communication before the provisional government, and that the punishment directed by law should be inflicted, and the greatest sorrow was expressed by the junta for the accident. Colonel Madera, commanding the active military police, also assured Mr.—the lieutenant of the Doris, on his honour, that the assassin should be brought to trial. But it was not done while we remained in Brazil, and it is probable not at all. The political state of Bahia shortly afterwards would scarcely leave leisure for such a matter.

exerted himself to attend to this painful business. The disorders of this climate are sadly enfeebling; they attack both mind and body, producing a painful sensitiveness to the slightest incident.

November 18th.—Our invalids have been sadly disturbed by the rockets which have been fired, ever since sunrise, from the church of our Lady of Conception,* whose feast is on the 8th of December. But the three Sundays previous to it the church and convent are adorned, sermons are preached, rockets are fired, contributions are made, and the shipping in the harbour fire salvoes at sunrise, at noon, and at sunset. The annual expense of rockets, and other fireworks, is enormous. Those used in Brazil all come from the East Indies and China. Sometimes, when manufactured goods are unsaleable here, the merchant ships them on board a Portuguese East Indiaman, and gets in return fireworks, which never fail to pay well. I have seen a set of cut-glass sent to Calcutta for the purpose, or a girandole, too handsome for Brazilian purchasers.

Yesterday the ship's pinnace, which had been absent five days with the master, my cousin Glennie, and young Grey, returned. They had gone to examine the river of Cachoeira, and came back highly delighted with their trip, though they had some very bad weather; however, with tarpaulines, cloaks, and a blanket or two, which I insisted on their taking, they managed so well as to have returned in good health.

Cachoeira, about fifty miles from Bahia, is a good town, where there is one English merchant resident. It is populous† and busy; for it is the place where the produce, chiefly cotton and tobacco, of a very considerable district, is collected, in order to be shipped for Bahia. It is divided into two unequal parts, by the river Paraguazu. Its parish church is dedicated to our Lady of the Rosary. It has two convents, four chapels, an hospital, a fountain, and three stone bridges over the small rivers Pitanga and Caquende, on which there are very extensive sugar-works. There are wharfs on both sides of the river. The streets are well paved, and the houses built of stone, and tiled: the country is flat, but agreeable. The river is not navigable more than two miles above the town; it there narrows and becomes interrupted by rocks and rapids, and there is a wooden bridge across it. About five miles from Cachoeira, there is an insulated conical hill, called that of Conception, whence there often proceed noises like explosions. These nois-

* In 1804 it contained 1088 hearths.

† One of the two parishes of the lower town.

es are considered in this country as indicative of the existence of metals. Near this place a piece of native copper was found, weighing upwards of fifty-two arobas. It is now in the museum of Lisbon.

Our exploring party landed on several of the islands, on their way up the river, and were every where received with great hospitality, and delighted with the beauty and fertility of the country.

22d.—At length all the invalids, excepting myself, are better; but, with another blister on, I can do little but write, or look from the cabin windows; and when I do look, I am sure to see something disagreeable. This very moment, there is a slave ship discharging her cargo, and the slaves are singing as they go ashore. They have left the ship, and they see they will be on the dry land; and so, at the command of their keeper, they are singing one of their country songs, in a strange land. Poor wretches! could they foresee the slave-market, and the separations of friends and relations that will take place there, and the march up the country, and the labour of the mines, and the sugar-works, their singing would be a wailing cry. But that "blindness to the future kindly given," allows them a few hours of sad enjoyment. This is the principal slave port in Brazil; and the negroes appear to me to be of a finer, stronger race, than any I have ever seen. One of the provisional junta of government is the greatest slave merchant here. Yet, I am happy to say, the Bahia press has lately actually printed a pamphlet against the slave trade. Within the last year, seventy-six ships have sailed from this port for the coast of Africa; and it is well known that many of them will slave to the northward of the line, in spite of all treaties to the contrary: but the system of false papers is so cunningly and generally carried on, that detection is far from easy; and the difficulties that lie in the way of condemning any slave ship, render it a matter of hazard to detain them. An owner, however, is well satisfied, if one cargo in three arrives safe; and eight or nine successful voyages make a fortune. Many Brazilian Portuguese have no occupation whatever: they lay out a sum of money in slaves; which slaves are ordered out every day, and must bring in a certain sum each night; and these are the boatmen, chairmen, porters, and weavers of mats and hats that are to be hired in the streets and markets, and who thus support their masters.

24th.—Yesterday the Morgiana sailed for Pernambuco, whence she will return to the coast of Africa. To—day the Antigone French frigate, commanded by Captain Villeneuve, nephew to the admiral of that name who was at Trafalgar, came in. Whenever France and England are not at war, the French and English certainly seek each other, and like each other more than any other two nations: and yet they seem like two great heads of parties, and the other nations take the French and English sides, as if there were no cause of opposition but theirs. Others may account for the fact, I am satisfied that it is so; and that whenever we meet a Frenchman in time of peace, in a distant country, it is something akin to the pleasure of seeing a countryman; and it is particularly the case with French naval men. Frequent intercourse of any kind, even that of war, begets a similarity of habits, manners, and ideas; so I suppose we have grown alike by fighting, and are all the more likely to fight again.

There is a report, but I believe not well founded, that placards are stuck up about the city threatening that all Europeans, especially Portuguese, who do not leave the place before the 24th of December, shall be massacred. I listen to these things, because reports, even when false, indicate something of the spirit of the times.

December 8th.—This place is now so quiet that the merchants feel quite safe, and therefore we are leaving Bahia. I have taken leave of many hospitable persons who have shown us much attention; but my health is so indifferent, that but for the sake of that civility which I felt due to them, I should not have gone ashore again: however, it is all done, and we are in the act of getting under weigh.

9th.—As we sailed out of the bay, we amused ourselves with conjecturing the possible situation of Robinson Crusoe's plantation in the bay of All Saints.[58] Those who had been at Cachoeira chose that it should be in that direction; while such as had been confined to the neighbourhood of the city pitched on different sitios, all or any of which might have answered the purpose. There is a charm in Defoe's works that one hardly finds, excepting in the Pilgrim's Progress. The language is so homely, that one is not aware of the poetical cast of the thoughts; and both together form such a reality, that the parable and the romance alike remain fixed on the mind like truth. And what is truth? Surely not the mere outward acts of vulgar life; but rather the

---

58. During her travels, Graham visited both factual and fictional locations important to Daniel DeFoe's (1660?-1731) novel *Robinson Crusoe* (1719): Crusoe has a plantation in Brazil, while Alexander Selkirk, one inspiration for Crusoe, was shipwrecked in the Juan Fernandez islands off the coast of Chile. DeFoe's combination of spiritual allegory and poetic imagination leads to Graham's meditations on one of her favorite topics: the distinction between historical fact and literary truth.

moral and intellectual perceptions by which our judgment, and actions, and motives, are directed. Then, are the wanderings of Christiana and Mercy, and the sufferings of the shipwrecked mariner, true in the right sense of the word truth? True as the lofty creations of Milton, and the embodied visions of Michael Angelo; because they have their basis and their home in the heart, and soul, and understanding of man.

But we are once more upon the ocean, and our young people are again observing the stars, and measuring the distances of the planets. I grieve that one of the most promising of them is now an inmate in my cabin, in a very delicate state of health.

12th.—Yesterday we found soundings, which indicated the neighbourhood of the Abrolhos, and lay-to all night, that we might ascertain the exact position of those dangerous shoals; which, at the distance of three leagues, bearing N. W. by W., appeared like one long rugged island to the westward, and two smaller very low to the east.

The banks extend very far out to the eastward. There is a deep passage between them and the mainland. With a little attention, a most profitable fishery might be established here.

Rio de Janeiro, Saturday, December 15th, 1821.—Nothing that I have ever seen is comparable in beauty to this bay. Naples, the Firth of Forth, Bombay harbour, and Trincomalee, each of which I thought perfect in their beauty, all must yield to this, which surpasses each in its different way. Lofty mountains, rocks of clustered columns, luxuriant wood, bright flowery islands, green banks, all mixed with white buildings; each little eminence crowned with its church or fort; ships at anchor or in motion; and innumerable boats flitting about in such a delicious climate,—combine to render Rio de Janeiro the most enchanting scene that imagination can conceive. We anchored first close to a small island, called Villegagnon, about two miles from the entrance of the harbour. That island, however small, was the site of the first colony founded by the Frenchman Villegagnon, under the patronage of Coligny, whom he betrayed.[59] The admiral had intended it as a refuge for the persecuted Huguenots; but when Villegagnon had, by his means, formed the settlement, he began to persecute them also:

---

59. Gaspard II de Coligny (1519-1572), Admiral of France and leader of the Huguenots during the French Wars of Religion; as Graham implies, he supported sending French Huguenots to Brazil to escape religious persecution under the Reformation. He was killed, by order of Charles IX at the instigation of Catherine de Médicis, in the massacre of St. Bartholomew's Day in 1572.

the colony fell into decay, and became an easy conquest to Mem de Sa, the Portuguese captain-general of Brazil.*

We moved from this station to one more commodious nearer the town, and higher up the harbour, towards the afternoon, which soon became so rainy, that I gave up all hopes of getting ashore. I was really disappointed to find that my excellent friend, the Hon. Capt. S. had left the station with his frigate before we arrived; I had, however, the pleasure of receiving a kind letter from him, and he had left me a copy of the great Spanish dictionary. Nobody that has always lived at home, can tell the value of a kindness like this in a foreign land.

[*4th Sept 1824.*— I returned to Rio after 11 months absence.]

Sunday, 16th.—I had the pleasure of seeing on board Mr. W. May, who has long been a resident in Brazil, and with whom I had spent many happy hours in early life. The pleasure such meetings give is of the purest and wholesomest nature. It quiets the passions by its own tranquillity; and, in recalling all the innocent and amiable feelings of youth, makes us almost forget those harsher emotions which intercourse with the world, and the operation of interest, passion, or suffering have raised.

Monday, 17th.—By the assistance of some friends ashore, we have procured a comfortable house in one of the suburbs of Rio, called the Catete, from the name of a little river which runs through it into the sea. To this house I have brought my poor suffering midshipman, Langford; and trust that free air, moderate exercise, and a milk diet, will restore him. We have been visited by several persons, who all appear hospitable and kind, particularly the acting consul-general, Col. Cunningham, and his lady.

December 18th.—I have begun house-keeping onshore. We find vegetables and poultry very good, but not cheap; fruit is very good and cheap; butcher's meat cheap, but very bad: there is a monopolist butcher, and no person may even kill an animal for his own use without permission paid for from that person; consequently, as there is no competition, he supplies the market as he pleases.† The beef is so bad, that it can hardly be used even for soup meat, three days out of four; and that supplied to the ships is at least as bad: mutton is scarce and bad: pork very good and fine; it is fed principally on mandioc and maize,

---

* See the Introduction.

† This was no longer the case at my second visit to Rio, and every thing eatable was much improved.

near the town; that from a distance has the advantage of sugar cane. Fish is not so plentiful as it ought to be, considering the abundance that there is on the whole coast, but it is extremely good; oysters, prawns, and crabs are as good as in any part of the world. The wheaten bread used in Rio is chiefly made of American flour, and is, generally speaking, exceedingly good. Neither the captaincy of Rio, nor those to the north, produce wheat; but in the high lands of St. Paul's, and the Minas Geraes, and in the southern provinces, a good deal is cultivated, and with great success. The great article of food here is the mandioc meal, or farinha; it is made into thin broad cakes as a delicacy, but the usual mode of eating it is dry: when at the tables of the rich, it is used with every dish of which they eat, as we take bread; with the poor, it has every form—porridge, brose, bread; and no meal is complete without it: next to mandioc, the feijoam or dry kidney-bean, dressed in every possible way, but most frequently stewed with a small bit of pork, garlic, salt, and pimento, is the favourite food; and for dainties, from the noble to the slave, sweetmeats of every description, from the most delicate preserves and candies to the coarsest preparations of treacle, are swallowed wholesale.

We have hired a horse for our invalid, and I have borrowed one for myself. These animals are rather pretty at Rio, but far from strong; they are fed on maize and capim, or Guinea grass, which was introduced of late years into Brazil, and thrives prodigiously: it is cultivated by planting the joints; the stem and leaves are as large as those of barley; it grows sometimes to the height of six or seven feet, and the flower is a large loose pannicle. The quantity necessary for each horse per day costs about eightpence, and his maize as much more. The common horses here sell for from twenty to one hundred dollars; the fine Buenos Ayres horses fetch a much higher price. Mules are generally used for carriages, being much hardier, and more capable of bearing the summer heat.

December 19th.—I walked by the side of Langford's horse up one of the little valleys at the foot of the Corcovado: it is called the Laranjeiros, from the numerous orange trees which grow on each side of the little stream that beautifies and fertilises it. Just at the entrance to that valley, a little green plain stretches itself on either hand, through which the rivulet runs over its stony bed, and affords a tempting spot to groups of washerwomen of all hues, though the greater number are black; and they add not a little to the picturesque effect of the scene:

Figure 8. Church and Convent of Sant Antonio da Barre at Bahia, as seen from Roça. Courtesy of The Catholic University of America, Oliveira Lima Library, Washington, D.C.

they generally wear a red or white handkerchief round the head; and a full-plaited mantle tied over one shoulder, and passed under the opposite arm, with a full petticoat, is a favourite dress. Some wrap a long cloth round them, like the Hindoos; and some wear an ugly European frock, with a most ungraceful sort of bib tied before them. Round the washerwoman's plain, hedges of acacia and mimosa fence the gardens of plantains, oranges, and other fruits which surround every villa; and beyond these, the coffee plantations extend far up the mountain, whose picturesque head closes the scene. The country-houses here are neither large nor magnificent; but they are decorated with verandas, and have often a handsome flight of steps up to the dwelling-house of the master, beneath which are either store-houses, or the habitations of the slaves: they have all a gateway, large and handsome, whatever the house may be; and that gateway generally leads to at least one walk where every kind of flower is cultivated. Brazil is particularly rich in splendid creeping flowers and shrubs; and these are mingled with the orange and lemon blossoms, and the jasmine and rose from the East, till the whole is one thicket of beauty and fragrance. I scarcely know whether my invalid or myself enjoyed the morning most. A few more such, and I should think all sickness must disappear.

December 20th.—Spent in paying and receiving visits in the neighbourhood. The houses are built a good deal like those of the south of Europe: there is generally a court, on one side of which is the dwelling-house, and the others are formed by the offices and garden. Sometimes the garden is immediately close to the house, and in the suburbs this is generally the case. In town, very few houses have the luxury of a garden at all. These gardens are rather like oriental flower-plots, but they assimilate well with the climate. The flowers of the parterres of Europe grow by the side of the gayer plants and shrubs of the country, shaded by the orange, banana, bread-fruit (now nearly naturalised here,) and the palms, between straight alleys of limes, over whose heads the African melia waves its lilac blossoms; and on the raised water channels, china vases are placed, filled with aloes and tuberoses, and here and there a statue intermixed. In these gardens there are oc-

Figure 9. The Sugar-loaf Rock, at the Entrance to the Harbour of Rio de Janeiro. Courtesy of The Catholic University of America, Oliveira Lima Library, Washington, D.C.

casionally fountains and seats under the trees, forming places of no undelightful rest in this hot climate.

Friday, December 21st.—Mr. Hayne, one of the commissioners of the slave trade commission, and his sister, having proposed a party to see the botanic gardens, we set off soon after daylight; and drove to their house on the bay of Botafogo, perhaps the most beautiful spot in the neighbourhood of Rio, rich as it is in natural beauty; and its beauty is increased by the numerous and pretty country-houses which now surround it. These have all grown up since the arrival of the court from Lisbon; before that time, this lovely spot was only inhabited by a few fishermen and gipsies, with, it might be, a villa or two on the sloping banks by the fruit gardens. Beyond the bay, we drove through a beautiful lane to the Lake of Rodrigo de Freitas: it is nearly circular, and about five miles in circumference; it is surrounded by mountains and forests, except where a short sandy bar affords an occasional outlet to the sea, when the lake rises so high as to threaten inconvenience to the surrounding plantations. It is impossible to conceive any thing richer than the vegetation down to the very water's edge around the lake.

We were to breakfast at the gardens, but as the weather is now hot, we resolved first to walk round them. They are laid out in convenient squares, the alleys being planted on either side with a very quick-growing nut tree, brought from Bencoolen originally, now naturalised here. The nut is as good as the filbert, and larger than the walnut, and yields abundance of oil; the leaf is about the size, and not unlike the shape, of that of the sycamore. The timber also is useful. The quick growth of this tree is unexampled among timber trees, and its height and beauty distinguish it from all others. The hedges between the compartments are of a shrub which I should have taken for myrtle, but that the leaves though firm are not fragrant. This garden was destined by the King for the cultivation of the oriental spices and fruits, and above all, of the tea plant, which he obtained, together with several families accustomed to its culture, from China. Nothing can be more thriving than the whole of the plants. The cinnamon, camphor, nutmeg, and clove, grow as well as in their native soil. The bread-fruit produces its fruit in perfection, and such of the oriental fruits as have been brought here ripen as well as in India. I particularly remarked the jumbo malacca, from India, and the longona (*Euphoria Longona*), a dark kind of lechee from China. I was disappointed to find no collection of the indigenous plants. However, so much has been done as to give reasonable hopes of farther improvement, when the political state of the country shall be quiet enough to permit attention to these things.

The stream that waters the garden flows through a lovely valley, where the royal powder-mills are situated; but being fearful of too much exertion for Langford we put off visiting them to another day, and returned to the garden gate to breakfast. His Majesty John VI. built a small house there, with three or four rooms, to accommodate the royal party, when they visited the gardens.[60] Our breakfast was prepared in the veranda of that house, from whence we had a charming view of the lake, with the mountains and woods,—the ocean, with three little islands that lie off the lake; and in the foreground a small chapel* and village, at the extremity of a little smooth green plain.

After waiting with our agreeable and well-informed friends till the sea-breeze set in, we returned part of the way along the lake, and then ascended to the parsonage of Nossa Senhora da Cabeça, where we were joined by several other persons who had come to dine there with us. The Padre Manoel Gomez received us very kindly, and our pic-nic was spread in the ample veranda of his parsonage. Behind the veranda three small rooms served for sleeping-room, kitchen, and pantry. Half a dozen small cottages in the field behind contain the healthy-looking negroes who are employed in his coffee-grounds, and a swarm of children of every shade, between black and white. On a little eminence in the midst of these stands the chapel of Our Lady, which is the parish church of a large district. It is exceedingly small; but serves as the place where the sacraments are administered, and the licences granted for marriages, burials, and christenings. The owners of estates have generally private chapels, where daily mass is performed for the benefit of their own people; so that the parish church is only applied to on the above-mentioned occasions. About a stone's throw behind the chapel, a clear rivulet runs rapidly down the mountain, leaping from rock to rock, in a thousand little cascades, and forming, here and there, delightful baths. Nor is it without its inhabitants, which increase the simple luxuries of the Padre's table. He tells me the crawfish in his stream are better than any in the neighbourhood; the water itself is pure, light, and delicate.

* Dedicated to St. John Baptist. I am not sure whether this or N. S. da Cabeça is the mother church; the same clergyman officiates in both.

---

60. For an account of John VI (Dom João) in Brazil, see authors' Introduction.

At length all our friends had assembled, and we returned to the veranda to dine. To judge by the materials of the feast, so blended were the productions of every climate that we could scarcely have pronounced in what part of the world we were, had not the profusion of bananas and plantains, compared with the small quantity of apples and peaches, reminded us of it. As is usual on such occasions, the oldest inhabitants of Brazil praised most what came from afar; while *we* all gave the preference to the productions of the country.

I was soon drawn away from the table by the beauty of the prospect, which I endeavoured to sketch. The coffee plantations are the only cultivated grounds hereabouts; and they are so thickly set with orange trees, lemons, and other tall shrubs, that they form in appearance rather a variety in the woods, than that mixture of cultivated with wild ground, which might be looked for so near a large city, where we expect to see the labour of man encroaching in some degree on the wild beauties of nature. But here vegetation is so luxuriant, that even the pruned and grafted tree springs up like the native of the forest. As every body was determined to be pleased, we all felt sorry when it was time to separate; but Burns has made all the reflections one can make on breaking up a pleasant party—

> Pleasures are like poppies spread,—
> You seize the flower, the bloom is shed;
> Or like the snow-falls in the river,—
> A moment white, then lost for ever;
> Or like the rainbow's fleeting form,
> Evanishing amid the storm;
> Or like the borealis race,
> That flit ere you can point their place.
> No man can tether time or tide:
> The hour approaches,—we must ride.[61]

And so we did.—We walked down to the foot of the hill, and each took his or her several conveyance; Colonel and Mrs. Cunningham their comfortable English chariot, Mr. and Miss Hayne their pretty curricle, and I my Rio caleche or *sege,*—a commodious but ugly carriage, very heavy, but well enough adapted to the rough roads between the garden and the town. The gentlemen all rode, and most of us carried home something. Fruit and flowers attracted some; Langford got

---

61. Robert Burns (1759-1796), *Tam o' Shanter* (1790).

a number of diamond beetles, and a magnificent butterfly, and I a most inadequate sketch of the scene from the Padre's house.

December 27th.—Since the jaunt to the botanical gardens, some of our invalids have been gaining ground: others who were well have become invalids, and I have done nothing but ride about or talk with them, and look at the beautiful views of the neighbourhood, and get a little better acquainted with the inhabitants; of whom the most amusing, so far as I have yet seen, are certainly the negroes, who carry about the fruit and vegetables for sale. The midshipmen have made friends with some of them. One of them has become quite a friend in the house; and after he has sold his master's fruit, earns a small gratuity for himself, by his tales, his dances, and his songs. His tribe, it seems, was at war with a neighbouring king, and he went out to fight when quite a boy, was taken prisoner, and sold. This is probably the story of many: but our friend tells it with action and emphasis, and shows his wounds, and dances his war dance, and shouts his wild song, till the savage slave becomes almost a sublime object. I have been for an

Figure 10. Larangeiras. Courtesy of The Catholic University of America, Oliveira Lima Library, Washington, D.C.

hour to-night at a very different scene, a ball given by Mr. B—, a respectable English merchant. The Portuguese and Brazilian ladies are decidedly superior in appearance to those of Bahia; they look of higher caste: perhaps the residence of the court for so many years has polished them.

I cannot say the men partake of the advantage; but I cannot yet speak Portuguese well enough to dare to pronounce what either men or women really are. As to the English, what can I say? They are very like all one sees at home, in their rank of life; and the ladies, very good persons doubtless, would require Miss Austin's pen to make them interesting.[62] However, as they appear to make no pretensions to any thing but what they are, to me they are good-humoured, hospitable, and therefore pleasing.

Monday, 31st Dec. 1822.—I went to town for the first time; our road lay through the suburb of the Catete for about half a mile. Some handsome houses are situated on either hand, and the spaces between are filled with shops, and small houses inhabited by the families of the shopkeepers in town. We then came to the hill called the Gloria, from the name of the church dedicated to N. S. da Gloria, on the eminence immediately overlooking the sea. The hill is green, and wooded and studded with country-houses. It is nearly insulated; and the road passes between it and another still higher, just where a most copious stream issues from an aqueduct (built, I think, by the Conde de Lavradio), and brings health and refreshment to this part of the town from the neighbouring mountains. Farther on, after passing the beach of the Gloria, we turned to the left, and entered the new part of that town through the arches of the great aqueduct built in 1718 by the viceroy Albuquerque.[63] This supplies four copious fountains. The largest is the Carioca,* near the convent of Sant Antonio; it has twelve mouths, and is most picturesque in itself: it is constantly surrounded by slaves, with

---

* The nickname of the inhabitants of Rio is Carioca, from this fountain.

62. In her Chile journal, Graham also uses Jane Austen (1775-1817) as a touchstone of English middle-class character types when she compares merchants' wives to "specimens of such people as one meets no where else but among the Brangtons, in Madame D'Arblay's Cecilia, or the Mrs. Eltons of Miss Austin's admirable novels" (*Journal of a Residence in Chile*, Hayward).

63. Pedro Antonio de Noronha Albuquerque e Sousa (1661-1731) was the first Viceroy of Brazil, 1714-1718; however, Lacombe tells us this aqueduct was in fact begun by Aires de Saldanha e Albuquerque, Governor of Rio de Janeiro (1719-1725), and completed under Viceroy Gomes Freire de Andrada (204).

their water-barrels, and by animals drinking. Just beyond are troughs of granite, where a crowd of washerwomen are constantly employed; and over against these, benches are placed, on which there are constantly seated new negroes for sale. The fountain of the Marecas is opposite to the public gardens, and near the new barracks; and, besides the spouts for water for the inhabitants, there are two troughs always full for the animals. The third is a very handsome one, in the palace square; and the fourth, called the Mouro, I did not see. The aqueduct is of brick, and is supported on two ranges of arches across the valley between two of the five hills of the city. The public buildings at Rio have nothing very remarkable about them. Even the churches present no architectural beauty, and owe the good effect they have in the general view to their size and situation. There are seven parish churches, and numerous chapels dependent on each. The first and eldest parish is that of St. Sebastian; the church dedicated to whom is the royal chapel, the only one I saw to-day. It is handsome within, richly gilt, and the pictures on the ceiling are far from contemptible; but I cannot praise that of the altar-piece, where Our Lady is covering with her cloak the Queen Dona Maria, and all the royal family, on their arrival in Brazil. The choir is served in a manner that would not disgrace Italy. I attended at vespers, and have seldom been more gratified with the music of the evening service. This the chapel owes to the residence of the royal family, whose passion and talent for music are hereditary. Adjoining to this chapel is the church and convent of the Carmelites, which forms part of the palace; and within which is the royal library of 70,000 volumes, where on all days, except holidays, the public are admitted to study from nine till one o'clock in the forenoon, and from four o'clock till sunset. This part of the palace occupies one side of a handsome square: the palace itself fills up another; a third has private houses, built uniformly with the palace, besides the fish-market; and the fourth is open to the sea. The water-edge is faced with a handsome granite pier and steps, the blocks of which are bolted with copper. In the centre of the pier there is a fountain, supplied from the aqueduct of Albuquerque; and altogether the appearance of the palace square is extremely handsome. We went thence into a street behind it, and saw the front of the senate-house, which is connected with the palace, and the cemetery of the Carmelite church, which is a prettier thing than church-yards usually are. In the centre of a small quadrangle there is a cross, and by it a young cypress tree: all around there are flowers, and sweet herbs, and porcelain vases, containing roses and aloes placed on little pedestals and on a broad low wall that surrounds the square. I looked at first in vain for graves; at length I observed on these low walls, and on the higher ones in the outer circle, indications of arches, each being numbered. These are the places for the dead, who are walled up there with quick-lime; and, at a certain period, the bones and ashes are removed to make room for others. At the time of removal, if the dead has a friend who wishes it, the remains are collected in urns or other receptacles, and placed in a building appropriated for them, or where the friend pleases; otherwise they go to the common receptacle, and perish totally by the addition of more quick-lime. This is, I doubt not, the wholesomest way of disposing of the dead; and, even to the sense, is better than the horrid burials at Bahia, where they must infect the air. But there seems to me so little feeling in thus getting rid at once of the remains of that which has once been dear to us, that I went away in disgust.

The city of Rio is more like an European city than either Bahia or Pernambuco; the houses are three or four stories high, with projecting roofs, and tolerably handsome. The streets are narrow, few being wider than that of the Corso at Rome, to which one or two bear a resemblance in their general air, and especially on days of festivals, when the windows and balconies are decorated with crimson, yellow, or green damask hangings. There are two very handsome squares, besides that of the palace. One, formerly the Roça, is now that of the Constituçaõ, to which the theatre, some handsome barracks and fine houses, behind which the hills and mountains tower up on two sides, give a very noble appearance. The other, the Campo de Santa Anna, is exceedingly extensive,* but unfinished. Two of the principal streets run across it, from the sea-side to the extremity of the new town, nearly a league, and new and wide streets are stretching out in every direction. But I was too tired with going about in the heat of the day to do more than take a cursory view of these things, and could not even persuade myself to look at the new fountain which is supplied by a new aqueduct.

There is in the city an air of bustle and activity quite agreeable to our European eyes; yet the Portuguese all take their siesta after dinner. The negroes, whether free blacks or slaves, look cheerful and happy at their labour. There is such a demand for them, that they find full employment, and of course good pay, and remind one here as little as possible of their sad condition, unless, indeed, one passes the street of

---

* It is 1713 feet square.

the Vallongo; then the slave-trade comes in all its horrors before one's eyes. On either hand are magazines of new slaves, called here *peices;* and there the wretched creatures are subject to all the miseries of a new negro's life, scanty diet, brutal examination, and the lash.

Tuesday, January 1st, 1823.—I went to pay a second visit to an illustrious exile, Count Hogendorp, one of the Emperor Napoleon's generals: my first had been accidental.[64] One morning last week, riding with two of our young midshipmen, we came to a pleasant-looking cottage, high on the side of the Corcovado, and at the door we saw a very striking figure, to whom I instantly apologised for intruding on his grounds, saying that we were strangers, and had come there accidentally. He instantly, with a manner that showed him to be no common person, welcomed us; asked our names, and on being told them, said he had heard of us; and, but for his infirmities, would have called on us. He insisted on our dismounting, as a shower was coming on, and taking shelter with him. By this time I perceived it was Count Hogendorp, and asked him if I had guessed rightly. He answered, yes; and added a few words, signifying that his master's servants, even in exile, carried that with them which distinguished them from other men.

The Count is the wreck of a once handsome man: he has not lost his martial air: he is tall, but not too thin; his grey eyes sparkle with intelligence, and his pure and forcible language is still conveyed in a clear well-toned voice, though a little the worse for age. He ushered us into a spacious veranda, where he passes most of the day, and which is furnished with sofas, chairs, and tables: he then ordered his servant to bring breakfast; we had coffee, milk, and fresh butter, all the produce of his own farm; and, as we sat, we saw the showers passing by and under us across the valley, which leads the eye to the bay below. The General entered frankly into conversation, and during breakfast, and while the shower lasted, spoke almost incessantly of his imperial master. Early in life the Count had entered the army, a soldier of fortune, under Frederick of Prussia.[65] On his return to his native country, Holland, he was employed by the States, successively, as governor of the

---

64. Dirk van Hogendorp (1761-1822), official of the Dutch East India Company and soldier, worked for the Dutch government until Napoleon conquered the Netherlands in 1810, when he joined Napoleon's army.

65. Frederick II of Prussia (1712-1786; ruled 1740-1786). The Count may have fought for Prussia in the Seven Years' War against France, among other countries (1756 -1763), which would make his subsequent service under Napoleon ironic.

eastern part of Java, and as envoy to one of the German courts. During his residence in Java, he had visited many of the English settlements on the mainland of India, and had learned English, which he spoke well.

On the annexation of Holland to France, he entered the French service with the rank of full colonel. He was always a great favourite with Napoleon, to whom his honesty and disinterestedness in money matters seem to have been valuable, in proportion as these qualities were scarce among his followers. The Count's affection for him is excessive, I should have said unaccountable, had he not shown me a letter written to him by the emperor's own hand, on the death of his child, in which, besides much general kindness, there is even a touch of tenderness I had not looked for. During the disastrous expedition to Russia, Hogendorp was entrusted with the government of Poland, and kept his court at Wilna. His last public service was performed in the defence of Hamburgh, where he was lieutenant governor. He would fain have attended the emperor into exile; but that not being allowed, he came hither, where, with the greatest economy, and, I believe, some assistance from the prince, who has great respect for him, he lives chiefly on the produce of his little farm.

Most of these particulars I learnt from himself, while resting and sheltered from the rain, which lasted nearly an hour. He then showed me his house, which is small indeed, consisting of only three rooms, besides the veranda; his study, where a few books, two or three casts from antique bas reliefs, and some maps and prints, indicate the retirement of a gentleman; his bedroom, the walls of which, with a capricious taste, are painted black, and on that sombre ground, skeletons of the natural size, in every attitude of glee, remind one of Holbein's Dance of Death;[66] and a third room occupied by barrels of orange wine, and jars of liqueur made of the grumaxama, at least as agreeable as cherry brandy which it resembles, the produce of his farm; and the sale of which, together with his coffee, helps out his slender income.

The General, as he loves to be called, led us round his garden, and displayed with even fondness, his fruits and his flowers, extolled the climate, and only blamed the people, for the neglect and want of industry, which wastes half the advantages God has given them. On returning to the house, he introduced to me his old Prussian servant, who has seen

---

66. Hans Holbein the Younger (1497/98-1543), German artist and draftsman best known for the woodcut series Graham mentions, his "Dance of Death" (1538), and also for his startlingly realistic portraits of King Henry VIII.

Figure 11. View of Rio from the Gloria Hill. Courtesy of The Catholic University of America, Oliveira Lima Library, Washington, D.C.

many a campaign with him, and his negroes, whom he freed on purchasing them: he has induced the woman to wear a nose jewel, after the fashion of Java, which he seems to remember with particular pleasure. I was sorry to leave the count, but was afraid some alarm might be felt at home concerning us, and therefore bade him adieu.

This evening I paid him another visit, and found him resting after dinner in his veranda. We had a good deal of conversation concerning the state of this country, from which, with prudence, every thing good may be hoped; and then the Count told me he was engaged in writing his memoirs, of which he showed me a part, telling me he meant to publish them in England. I have no doubt they will be written with fidelity, and will furnish an interesting chapter in the history of Napoleon. I was sorry to see the old gentleman suffering a good deal; and his age and infirmities seem to threaten a speedy termination to his active life.*

* Count Hogendorp died while I was in Chile. Napoleon had left him by his will five thousand pounds sterling, but the old man did not live to know this proof of the recollection of his old master. As he approached his end, the Emperor Don Pedro sent to him such assistance, and paid him such attention as his state required or admitted of, and had given orders concerning his funeral; but it was found at his death that he was a protestant, and one of the protestant consuls therefore caused him to be properly interred in the

January 8th, 1823.—The only variety in my quiet life since the first, was afforded by a large and pleasant party at Miss Hayne's. There I saw abundance of jewels on the heads and necks of the elderly Portuguese ladies, and a good deal of beauty, and some grace, among the younger ones, whom I begin to understand pretty well. We had some good music, and there was a great deal of dancing and not a little card-playing.

To-day we left the house on shore, and are again at home on board the Doris, with all our invalids much better. Having settled every body comfortably, I went ashore to the opera, as it is the benefit night of a favourite musician, Rosquellas, whose name is known on both sides of the Atlantic.[67] The theatre is very handsome; in size and proportion, some of our officers think it as large as the Haymarket, but I differ from them. It was opened on the 12th of October, 1813, the Prince Don Pedro's birth-day. The boxes are commodious, and I hear, that the unseen part of the theatre is comfortable for the actors, dressers, etc.; but the machinery and decorations are deficient. The evening's amusements consisted of a very stupid Portuguese comedy, relieved between the acts by scenes from an opera of Rossini's by Rosquellas, after which, he wasted a great deal of fine playing on some very ugly music.[68]

Wednesday, January 9th.—To-day is expected to be a day of much importance to the future fate of Brazil. But I must go back to the arrival of a message from the Cortes at Lisbon, intimating to the Prince their pleasure, that he should forthwith repair to Europe, and begin his education, and proceed to travel incognito through Spain, France, and England. This message excited the most lively indignation not only in His Royal Highness, but in the Brazilians from one end of the kingdom to the other. The Prince is willing to obey the orders of his father and the Cortes, at the same time he cannot but feel as a man the want of decency of the message, and being thus bid to go home; and

---

[* cont] English burial-ground. On undressing him after death, his body was found to be tattooed like those of the natives of the eastern islands. I never saw the count after the 1st of January.

67. Pablo Mariano Rosquellas (1784-1859), Spanish musician who traveled across Europe and beyond. During Dom Pedro's reign in Brazil, Rosquellas organized theatre performances and concerts for the Royal Court.

68. Gioachino Antonio Rossini (1792-1868), composer known for comic operas, including *The Barber of Seville* (1816) and *Cinderella* (1817), as well as for dramatic operas like *William Tell* (1829).

Figure 12. View from Count Hoggendorp's Cottage. Courtesy of The Catholic University of America, Oliveira Lima Library, Washington, D.C.

especially forbidden to carry any guards with him, as it should seem, lest they might have contracted too much attachment for his person. The Brazilians regard this step as preliminary to removing from this country the courts of justice, which have for fourteen years been held here, and so removing causes to Lisbon, by which means, Brazil would be again reduced to the condition of a dependent colony instead of enjoying equal rights and privileges with the mother country, a degradation they are by no means inclined to submit to.

The feelings of the people are sufficiently shown, in the address sent to the Prince, a few days ago, (24th of December,) from St. Paul's; as follows:—

SIR,

We had already written to Your Royal Highness, before we received the extraordinary gazette of the 11th instant, by the last courier: and we had hardly fixed our eyes on the first decree of the Cortes concerning the organization of the governments of the provinces of Brazil, when a noble indignation fired our hearts: because we saw impressed on it a system of anarchy and slavery. But the second, in conformity to which Your Royal Highness is to go back to Portugal, in order to travel *incognito* only through Spain, France, and England, inspired us with horror.

They aim at no less than disuniting us, weakening us, and in short, leaving us like miserable orphans, tearing from the bosom of the great family of Brazil the only common father who remained to us, after they had deprived Brazil of the beneficent founder of the kingdom, Your Royal Highness's august sire. They deceive themselves; we trust in God, who is the avenger of injustice; He will give us courage, and wisdom.

If by the 21st article of the basis of the constitution, which we approve and swear to because it is founded on universal and public right, the deputies of Portugal were bound to agree that the constitution made at Lisbon could then be obligatory on the Portuguese resident in that kingdom; and, that, as for those in the other three parts of the world, it should only be binding when their legitimate representatives should have declared such to be their will: How dare those deputies of Portugal, without waiting for those of Brazil, legislate concerning the most sacred interest of each province, and of the entire kingdom? How dare they split it into detached portions, each insulated, and without leaving a common centre of strength and union? How dare they rob Your Royal Highness of the lieutenancy, granted by Your Royal Highness's august father, the King? How dare they deprive Brazil of the privy council, the board of conscience, the court of exchequer, the board of commerce, the court of requests, and so many other recent establishments, which promised such future advantage? Where now shall the wretched people resort in behalf of their civil and judicial interests? Must they now again, after being for twelve years accustomed to judgment at hand, go and suffer, like petty colonists, the delays and chicanery of the tribunals of Lisbon, across two thousand leagues of ocean, where the sighs of the oppressed lose all life and all hope? Who would credit it, after so many bland, but deceitful expressions of reciprocal equality and future happiness!!!

In the session of the 6th of August last, the deputy of the Cortes, Pereira do Carmo, said, (and he spoke the truth,) that the constitution was the social compact, in which, were expressed and declared the conditions on which a nation might wish to constitute itself a body politic: and that the end of that constitution, is the general good of each individual, who is to enter into that social compact. How then dares a mere fraction of the great Portuguese nation, without waiting for the conclusion of this solemn national compact, attack the general good of the principal part of the same, and such is the vast and rich kingdom of Brazil; dividing it into miserable fragments, and, in a word, attempting to tear from its bosom the representative of the executive power, and to annihilate by a stroke of the pen, all the tribunals and establishments necessary to its existence and future prosperity? This unheard-of despotism, this horrible political perjury, was certainly not merited by the good and generous Brazil. But the enemies of order in the Cortes of Lisbon deceive themselves if they imagine that they can thus, by vain words and hollow professions, delude the good sense of the worthy Portuguese of both worlds.

Your Royal Highness will observe that, if the kingdom of Ireland, which makes part of the United Kingdom of Great Britain, besides that it is infinitely small compared to the vast kingdom of Brazil, and is separated from England but by a narrow arm of the sea, which is passed in a few hours, yet possesses a governor-general or viceroy, who represents the executive power of the King of the United Kingdom, how can it enter the head of any one who is not either profoundly ignorant, or rashly inconsiderate, to pretend, that the vast kingdom of Brazil, should remain without a centre of activity, and without a representative of the executive power: and equally without a power to direct our troops, so as that they may operate with celerity and effect, to defend the state against any unforeseen attack of external enemies, or against internal disorders and factions, which might threaten public safety, or the reciprocal union of the provinces!

Yes, august Sir! It is impossible that the inhabitants of Brazil, who are honest, and who pride themselves on being men, particularly the Paulistas, should ever consent to such absurdity and such despotism. Yes, august Sir, Your Royal Highness must remain in Brazil, whatever may be the projects of the constituent Cortes, not only for the sake of our general good, but even for the sake of the future prosperity and independence of Portugal itself. If Your Royal Highness, which is not to be believed, were to obey the absurd and indecent decree of the 29th of September, besides losing, in the world, the dignity of a man and of a prince, by becoming the slave of a small number of factious men, you would also have to answer before heaven for the rivers of blood which would assuredly inundate Brazil on account of your absence: because its inhabitants, like raging tigers, would surely remember the supine sloth in which the ancient despotism kept them buried, and in which a new constitutional Machiavelism aims even now to retain them.

We therefore entreat Your Royal Highness with the greatest fervour, tenderness, and respect to delay your return to Europe, where they wish to make you travel as a pupil surrounded by tutors and spies: We entreat you to confide boldly in the love and fidelity of your Brazilians, and especially of your Paulistas, who are all ready to shed the last drop of their blood, and to sacrifice their fortunes, rather than lose the adored Prince in whom they have placed their well-founded hopes of national happiness and honour. Let Your Royal Highness wait at least for the deputies named by this province, and for the magistracy of this capital, who will as soon as possible present to Your Highness our ardent desires and firm resolutions; and deign to receive them, and to listen to them, with the affection and attention, which your Paulistas deserve from you.

May God preserve Your Royal Highness's august person many years.

From the Government House of St. Paul's, 24th Dec. 1821.

John Carlos Augusto de Oeyenhausen, President.
Jose Bonifacio de Andrada e Silva, V. President.
Martim Francisco de Andrada, Secretary.
Lazaro Jose Gonçalves, Secretary.
Miguel José de Oliveria Pinto, Secretary.
Manoel Rodrigues Jordaen.
Francisco Ignacio de Souza Guimaies.
Joao Ferreira de Oleveira Bueno.
Antonio Leite Pereira de Gama Lobo.
Daniel Pedro Muller.
Andre da Silva Gomes.
Francisco de Paulo e Oliveira.
Antonio Maria Quartini.*

This letter to the Prince expresses the sentiments of all the southern part of Brazil, and to a certain degree those of the northern captaincies also. The latter are certainly as averse as the former to the removal of the courts of justice to Lisbon, but they would prefer a more northern city for the capital; while here, there is a wish among a considerable number of persons to remove the capital to St. Paul's, on account of its safety, and its neighbourhood to the mines, where the greatest proportion of the riches, industry, and population of Brazil is situated. His Royal Highness has not yet expressed his determination. The officers of the Lisbon troops talk loudly of his being obliged to do his duty, and

* The Prince answered this on the 4th of January, by assuring the Paulistas that he had transmitted the letter to Lisbon, and that His Royal Highness hoped from the wisdom of the Cortes that they would take measures for the good and prosperity of Brazil.

obey the mandate of the Cortes. The Brazilians are earnest in their hopes that he may stay, and there are even some that look forward to his declaring openly for the independence of this country. Whatever his resolution may be, it is feared that there will be much disturbance, if not a civil war. Our English merchants are calling meetings, I believe for the purpose of requesting this ship to remain, at least until one of equal force shall arrive, fearing that their persons and property will not be safe, and every body looks a little anxious.

10th.—Yesterday there was a meeting of the camara of Rio; and after a short consultation the members went in procession, accompanied by a great concourse of people, to the Prince, with a strong remonstrance against his leaving the country, and an earnest entreaty that he would remain among his faithful people. His Royal Highness received them graciously, and replied, that since it appeared to be the wish of all, and for the good of all, he would remain. This declaration was received with shouts of enthusiasm, which were answered by the discharge of artillery, and every mark of public rejoicing.

The day as usual, on any occasion of public interest, was ended at the opera, but I unfortunately could not get ashore; however some of the officers went. The house was illuminated. The Prince and Princess appeared in full dress in the king's box, which is in the centre of the house. They were received with enthusiasm by the people, the national hymn was sung, and between the acts of the play the people called on several of their favourite orators to address the Prince and people, on the event of the day. This call was obeyed by several speakers, and some of their addresses were printed and handed about the theatre; the best, or at least the most applauded, was the following by Bernardo Carvalho.

> It is now only necessary to exhort you to UNION and TRANQUILLITY!!!* Expressions truly sublime, and which contain the whole philosophy of politics. Without UNION you cannot be strong, without strength you cannot command TRANQUILLITY. Portuguese! Citizens! You have a Prince who speaks to you with kindness of your own work; who invites you to rally with him round the constitution; who recommends to you that moral force which embraces justice and is

* Referring to a speech of the Prince on determining to stay in Brazil.

identified with reason, and which can alone accomplish the great work we have begun. To-day you burst the bonds which threatened you with suffocation. To-day you assume the true attitude of free men. But yet all is not done. Intrigue and discord, muttering furies, perhaps even now meditate fresh plans, and still endeavour to sow division, and to overthrow the trophies you have just raised to glory and to national honour. The same enthusiasm, ill directed, might produce the greatest crimes. Fellow citizens! Union and Tranquillity. The giddiness of party is unworthy of free men. Fulfil your duties. Yield to the gentle exhortation of your august Prince; . . . . . . but in return say to him 'Sire! Energy and Vigilance. Energy to promote good,—Vigilance to prevent evil. The whole world has now its eyes fixed on you. The steps you are about to take, may place you in the temple of memory, or confound you among the number of weak princes, unworthy of the distinctions which adorn them. Perhaps you may influence the destinies of the whole world. Perhaps even Europe, anxiously and on tip-toe, reposes her hope upon you! PRINCE! ENERGY and VIGILANCE. Glory is not incompatible with youth, and the hero of the 26th February may become the hero of the 9th January. Unite yourself with a people which loves you, which offers you fortune, life, every thing. Prince! how sweet is it to behold the cordial expansion of the feeling of free men! but how distressing to witness the withering in the bud of hopes so justly founded! Banish, Sire, for ever from Brazil, multiform flattery, hypocrisy of double face, discord with her viperous tongue. Listen to truth, submit to reason, attend to justice. Be your attributes frankness and loyalty. Let the constitution be the pole-star to direct you: without it there can be no happiness for you nor for us. Seek not to reign over slaves, who kiss the chains of ignominy. Rule over free hearts. So shall you be the image of the divinity among us; —so will you fulfil our hopes. ENERGY and VILIGANCE, and we will follow your precept, UNION and TRANQUILLITY.

A priest, one of the favourites of the people, was called on to speak repeatedly. The national hymn* was sung again and again, and the Prince and Princess, who were observed to be chiefly surrounded by Brazilian officers, were again loudly cheered. And every thing in the city, which was brilliantly illuminated, went off in the utmost harmony.

Nothing can be more beautiful of the kind than such an illumination seen from the ship. The numerous forts at the entrance to the harbour, on the islands, and in the town, have each their walls traced in light, so they are like fairy fire-castles; and the scattered lights of the city and villages, connect them by a hundred little brilliant chains.

To-day our friends the merchants are under fresh alarm, and have made a formal request to the captain to stay. With that petty spirit which passes for *diplomatic,* the deputy-consul and merchants, instead of saying what they are afraid of, only say, "Sir, we are afraid, circumstances make us so, and we hope you will stay till," etc. etc.; as much as to say, "You are answerable for evil, if it happens," although they are too much afraid of committing themselves to say why. I do not trouble myself now about their official reports,which I perceive are large sheets of paper, and large seals, without one word that might not be published on every church wall, for their milk and water tenor, but which I consider as absurd and mischievous, because they tend to excite distrust and alarm where no danger is. The truth is now, that there might be some cause of fear, if they would openly express it. The language of the Portuguese officers is most violent. They talk of carrying the Prince by main force to Lisbon, and so making him obey the Cortes in spite of the Brazilians; and both parties are so violent, that they will probably fight. In that fight there will doubtless be danger to foreign property; but why not say so? why not say such is the case? However, the wisest of the sons of men in modern times,† has long ago set in the second place those who could not afford to be open and candid in matters of business; so *I* may leave them alone. {Graham apparently intended to increase the impact of this passage, writing in the margin, "To be strengthened."}

* Composed by the Prince.

† Bacon, *Essay on Dissimulation and Simulation.*

11th.—I went ashore last night to the opera, as it was again a gala night, and hoped to have witnessed the reception of the Prince and Princess. The Viscondeça do Rio Seco kindly invited me to her box, which was close to theirs; but, after waiting some time, notice arrived that the Prince was so busy writing to Lisbon, that he could not come. The double guard was withdrawn, and the play went on. I had, however, the pleasure of seeing the theatre illuminated, of hearing their national hymn, and of seeing the ladies better dressed than I had yet had occasion to do.

There is a great deal of uneasiness to-day. The Portuguese commander-in-chief of the troops, General Avilez,[69] has demanded and received his discharge. It is said, perhaps untruly, that his remonstrance to the Prince against his remaining here has been ungentlemanlike and indecent. I hear the troops will not consent to his removal, and they are particularly incensed that the choice of a successor should fall on General Curado, a Brazilian, who, it is said, will be called from St. Paul's to succeed Avilez. He is a veteran, who has commanded with distinction in all the campaigns on the southern frontier, and his actions are better known among his countrymen than those distant battles in Europe, on which the Portuguese officers of every rank are apt to pride themselves here, however slight the share they had in them, to the annoyance of the Brazilians.

12th.—Yesterday the military commission for the government of the army here was broke up, and Curado appointed commander-in-chief, and minister of war. The Portuguese General Avilez made his appearance at the barracks of the European soldiers to take leave of them; they were under arms to receive him, and vowed not to part with him, or to obey another commander, and were with difficulty reduced to such order as to promise tolerable tranquillity for the day at least. It is said, that as it had been understood that they had expressed some jealousy, because the guard of honour at the opera-house had been for the two last evenings composed of Brazilians, the Prince sent to the Portuguese barracks for the guard of last night, but that they refused to go; saying, that as His Royal Highness was so partial to

---

69. General Jorge de Avilez Zuzarte de Souza Tavares, the Portuguese general in charge of the Rio garrison, attempted to subdue Dom Pedro and the Brazilian militia; instead, he was ultimately forced by Dom Pedro to return, with his troops, to Lisbon in February 1822 (Vale, *Independence* 6).

the Brazilians, he had better continue to be guarded by them. I am not sure this is true, but from the circumstances of the day it is not improbable.

The opera-house was again brilliantly lighted. The Prince and Princess were there, and had been received as well as on the ninth, when, at about eleven o'clock, the Prince was called out of his box, and informed that bodies of from twenty to thirty of the Portuguese soldiers were parading the streets, breaking windows and insulting passengers in their way from barrack to barrack, where every thing wore the appearance of determined mutiny. At the same time, a report of these circumstances having reached the house, the spectators began to rise for the purpose of going home; when the Prince, having given such orders as were necessary, returned to the box, and going with the Princess, then near her confinement, to the front, he addressed the people, assured them that there was nothing serious, that he had already given orders to send the riotous soldiers, who had been quarrelling with the blacks, back to their barracks, and entreated them not to leave the theatre and increase the tumult, by their presence in the street, but remain till the end of the piece, as he meant to do, when he had no doubt all would be quiet. The coolness and presence of mind of the Prince, no doubt, preserved the city from much confusion and misery. By the time the opera was over the streets were sufficiently clear to permit every one to go home in safety.

Meantime the Portuguese troops, to the number of seven hundred, had marched up to the Castle-hill, commanding the principal streets in the town, and had taken with them four pieces of artillery, and threatened to sack the town. The field-pieces belonging to the Brazilians, which had remained in the town after the 26th of February, had been sent to the usual station of the artillery, at the botanical gardens, no longer ago than last week, so they entertained no fear of artillery. But they were disappointed in their expectation of being joined by that part of the Portuguese force which was stationed at San Cristovaõ. This amounted to about 500 men,* who said the King had left them to attend on the person of the Prince, and they had nothing to do with any thing else; a declaration that was looked on with suspicion by the Brazilians.

While the Portuguese were taking up their new and threatening position, the Brazilians were not idle. Every horse and mule in the

* I am not sure of the correctness of these numbers, but I believe I am nearly right.

town was pressed, and expresses despatched to all the militia regiments, and other Brazilian troops, as well as to the head-quarters of the artillery. The Prince was most active; so that by four o'clock this morning (12th), he found himself at the head of a body of four thousand men, in the Campo de Santa Anna, not only ready, but eager for action; and though deficient in discipline, formidable from their numbers and determination.

The Portuguese had by no means expected such promptness and decision; they had besides not taken provision to the hill, and they were convinced that it would be an easy matter to starve them, by means of the immense superiority of numbers in the Campo. They therefore prepared to obey an order which the Prince communicated to them early in the day, to remove from the city to Praya Grande, on the other side of the harbour, only conditioning to carry their arms with them. His Royal Highness wished to have put them instantly on board of transports, to be conveyed to Lisbon, but the port admiral reported that there was neither shipping nor provision ready for the purpose; and therefore they are to be quartered at Praya Grande, until such shall be provided.

I went ashore with an officer as early as I could, chiefly for the purpose of seeing the troops in the Campo de Santa Anna. In consequence, however, of the press of horses and mules, it was some time before I could get a chaise to convey me there, and it was much too hot to walk. At length, however, I procured one, and determined to call on the Viscondeça of Rio Seco in my way, to offer her refuge in the frigate. We found her in a Brazilian dishabille, and looking harassed and anxious. She had remained in the theatre as long as the Prince last night, and had then hurried home to provide for the safety of her family and her jewels: her family she had despatched to her estate in the country; for the jewels, she had them all packed in small parcels, intending to escape with them herself in disguise to us, in case of a serious attack on the city; and she had left a quantity of valuable plate exposed in different parts of the house to occupy the soldiers on their first entrance. Every thing, however, looks better now; and we assured her we had seen the first part of one of the Lisbon regiments ready to embark as we landed. We promised her, that on her making a signal from her house, or sending a message, she should have protection. She appears very apprehensive of evil from the liberation of the prisoners by the Brazilians during the night, and says, that there are some fears that the Portuguese will seize the forts on the other side, and hold them till the arrival of the reinforcements daily expected from Lisbon. This would, indeed, be disastrous; but I believe the apprehension to be ill founded.

Having comforted my good friend as well as I could, we went on to the Campo, and found the Brazilians housed for the most part in some unfinished buildings. The men, though slight, looked healthy, active, and full of spirit; their horses were the best I have seen in the country; and, it might be fancy, but they gave me the idea of men resolute in their purpose, and determined to guard their rights and their homes.

The scene in the Campo presented all manner of varieties. Within the enclosure where the artillery was placed, all was gravity and business-like attention: the soldiers on the alert, and the officers in groups, canvassing the events of the preceding night, and the circumstances of the day; and here and there, both within and without the circle, an orator was stationed with his group of auditors around him, listening to his political discussions, or patriotic harangues. In the open part of the Campo were straggling soldiers, or whole companies, escaped from the heated crowd of the enclosure: horses, mules, and asses, many of all lying down from sheer fatigue. In all directions, negroes were coming, laden with capim or maize for the horses, or bearing on their heads cool drink and sweetmeats for the men. In one corner, a group of soldiers, exhausted with travel and watching, lay asleep; in another, a circle of black boys were gambling: in short, all ways of beguiling the time while waiting for a great event might be seen; from those who silently and patiently expected the hour, in solemn dread of what the event might be, to those who, merely longing for action, filled up the interval with what might make it pass most lightly. I was well pleased with the view I had of the people in the Campo, and still better as the day wore away, for I staid sometime, to feel assured that all was to pass without bloodshed, beyond the two or three persons killed accidentally during the night.

On our return to the ship, we were stopped for some time in the palace square, by a great concourse of people assembled to witness the entrance of the first Brazilian guard into the palace, while the last Portuguese guard marched out, amid the loud huzzas of the people; and on reaching the stairs, where we were to embark, we found the last of one regiment, and the first of another, about to sail for the Praya Grande, so that the city may sleep in security to-night.

The inhabitants generally, but especially the foreign merchants, are well pleased to see the Lisbon troops dismissed; for they have long been most tyrannically brutal to strangers, to negroes, and not unfrequently to Brazilians; and, for many weeks past, their arrogance has been disgusting to both prince and people.*

The appearance of the city is melancholy enough: the shops are shut up, guards are parading the streets, and every body looks anxious. The shopkeepers are all employed as militia: they are walking about with bands and belts of raw hides over their ordinary clothes, but their arms and ammunition were all in good order, and excepting these and the English, I saw nobody at all out of doors.

13th.—Every thing seems quiet to-day. From the ship we see the rest of the troops going over to the Praya Grande. Yet there is necessarily a great deal of anxiety among all classes of persons. Some persons have sent some of their valuables on board the frigate, for safety; and a message, I do not know on what authority, arrived to know if the Prince and Princess, and family, could be received and protected on board.— The answer, of course, is, that though the ship must observe the strictest neutrality between the parties, yet that we are ready at once to receive and protect the Princess and children, and also, whenever he has reason to apprehend personal danger, the Prince himself. My cabin is therefore ready. I hope they will not be forced to come afloat. The more they can trust to the Brazilians the better for them, and for the cause of that independence which is now so inevitable, that the only question is whether it shall be obtained with or without bloodshed.

We have determined to have a ball on board, the day after tomorrow, that the people may get acquainted with us,—and then if any thing occurs to render it advisable to take refuge with us, they will know who they are to come amongst.

14th.—The shops are open, and business going on as usual to-day. The Prince is granting discharges to both officers and men of the Portuguese regiments, who wish to remain in Brazil instead of returning to Europe. This is stigmatised by the Portuguese as *licensing desertion,* from the army of the King and Cortes; whatever they may call it, I am convinced that the measure tends to the present tranquillity of the capital. The Princess and children are gone to Santa Cruz, a country

---

* The heavy step of the Portuguese infantry has earned for them the nickname of *Pedechumbo,* or leaden foot; now applied to all partisans of Portugal.

estate, formerly belonging to the Jesuits, now to the crown, fourteen leagues on the road towards St. Paul's.*

15th.—Our ball went off very well: we had more foreigners than English; and as there was excellent music from the opera-orchestra, and a great deal of dancing, the young people enjoyed it much. I should have done so also, but that Captain Graham was suffering with the gout so severely, that I could have wished to put off the dance. I had commissioned the Viscondeça do Rio Seco and some other ladies to bring their Portuguese friends, which they did, and we had a number of pretty and agreeable women, and several gentlemanlike men, in addition to our English friends.

A dance on ship-board is always agreeable and picturesque: there is something in the very contrast afforded by the furniture of the deck of a ship of war to the company and occupation of a ball that is striking.

> The little warlike world within,
> The well-reeved guns and netted canopy,[70]

all dressed with evergreens and flowers, waving over the heads of gay girls and their smiling partners, furnish forth combinations in which poetry and romance delight, and which one must be stoical indeed to contemplate without emotion. I never loved dancing myself, perhaps because I never excelled in it; but yet, a ball-room is to me a delightful place. There are happy faces, and hearts not the less happy for the little anxious palpitations that arise now and then, and curiosity, and hope, and all the amiable feelings of youth and nature; and if among it a little elderly gaiety mingles, and excites a smile, I, for my part, rather reverence the youth of heart which lives through the cares and vexations of this life, and can mingle in, without disturbing, the hilarity of youth.

17th.—Nothing remarkable yesterday or to-day, but the perfect quiet of the town. The Prince goes on discharging the soldiers.

19th.—This day the new ministers arrived from St. Paul's; the chief of whom in station, as in talent, is Jose Bonifacio de Andrada e Silva. According to the opinion entertained of him by the people here, I should say that Cowper had described him, when he wrote

> Great offices will have

---

* This journey was very disastrous, as it caused the death of the infant Prince.

70. George Gordon, Lord Byron (1788-1824), *Childe Harold's Pilgrimage* (1812-18).

> Great talents. And God gives to every man
> The virtue, temper, understanding, taste,
> That lift him into life, and lets him fall
> Just in the niche he was ordained to fill.
> To the deliverer of an injured land
> He gives a tongue to enlarge upon, a heart
> To feel, and courage to redress her wrongs.[71]

He had been sent early from Brazil to study at Coimbra, where he lay sick at the time of the King's departure from Lisbon; and afterwards, during the time of the French, he could not find means to return to his native country; but upon the first rising of the people in the districts round Oporto and Coimbra, he put himself at the head of the students of the university, in their successful resistance to Junot, and afterwards served in the campaign against Soult.[72] When he returned to Lisbon, I believe, he there entered the regular army; for after bearing arms against Massena, I find that at the end of the war he had the rank of lieutenant-colonel, with which he returned to Brazil in 1819.[73] But his whole time in Europe was not spent in warfare: he had travelled, and had become acquainted with several among the most distinguished characters in England, France, and Italy, and had contracted a particular esteem for Alfieri.[74] The object of his travels was rather to see and learn what might be useful to his own country, than the mere pleasure of visiting different parts of the world; and I am told, that he has particularly attended to those branches of science which may improve the agriculture and the mining of Brazil.

71. William Cowper (1731-1800), another of Graham's favorite poets; here she quotes his musings on human life from the "Winter Evening" section of what some readers call his masterpiece, *The Task* (1785). Cowper's poems were so popular that he became a literary touchstone; for example, Marianne Dashwood uses his poem *The Castaway* to test Edward Ferrar's reading ability (and thus his sensibility) in Jane Austen's *Sense and Sensibility*.
72. Nicolas-Jean de Dieu Soult, duke de Dalmatie (1769-1851), French general.
73. Andre duc de Rivoli Massena (1758-1817), French general during the French Revolution and the Napoleonic Wars, was Napoleon Bonaparte's valued lieutenant during the Italian campaign, 1796-1797. However, in the end Massena disagreed with Napoleon's imperial regime and ultimately supported the restoration of the monarchy to France.
74. Count Alfieri Vittorio (1749-1803), Italian nationalist poet whose work emphasized rebellion against tyranny.

One of his brothers, Martin Francisco, is possessed of scarcely less talent than himself; and their family, their character, and the esteem in which they are held, add weight not only to their own interest, but to the government which employs them.

The guards and patroles were doubled along the road, by which they and the veteran General Corado arrived, as it was feared the Portuguese, who since the 12th have been completely distinct from the Brazilians, might have impeded their progress. However, every thing was perfectly tranquil.

20th.—The Aurora arrived from Pernambuco and Bahia, at both which places it appears that every thing is quiet. But as the meeting of the camara of Bahia is to take place early next month, for the purpose of choosing a new provisional government, the English are apprehensive of some disturbance, and therefore we are to return thither to protect our friends in case of need.

21st.—I went ashore to shop with Glennie. There are a good many English shops, such as saddlers, and stores, not unlike what we call in England an Italian warehouse, for eatables and drinkables; but the English here generally sell their goods wholesale to native or French retailers. The latter have a great many shops of mercery, haberdashery, and millinery. For tailors, I think, there are more English than French, and but few of either. There are bakers' shops of both nations, and plenty of English pot-houses, whose Union Jacks, Red Lions, Jolly Tars, with their English inscriptions, vie with those of Greenwich or Deptford. The goldsmiths all live in one street, called by their name *Rua dos Ourives,* and their goods are exposed in hanging frames at each side of the shop-door or window, in the fashion of two centuries back. The workmanship of their chains, crosses, buttons, and other ornaments, is exquisite, and the price of the labour, charged over the weight of the metal, moderate.

Most of the streets are lined with English goods: at every door the words *London superfine* meet the eye: printed cottons, broad cloths, crockery, but above all, hardware from Birmingham, are to be had little dearer than at home, in the Brazilian shops; besides silks, crapes, and other articles from China. But any thing bought by retail in an English or French shop is, usually speaking, very dear.

I am amused at the apparent apathy of the Brazilian shopkeepers. If they are engaged, as now is not unfrequently the case, in talking politics, or reading a newspaper, or perhaps only enjoying a cool seat in the back of their shop, they will often say they have not the article enquired for, rather than rise to fetch it; and if the customer persists and points it out in the shop, he is coolly desired to get it for himself, and lay down the money. This happened several times during the course of our search for some tools for turning to-day along the Rua Direita, where every second house is a hardware shop, furnished from Sheffield and Birmingham.

22d.—The Princess's birth-day was celebrated by firing of cannon, a review, and a drawing-room. Capt. Prescott, of the Aurora, and Capt. Graham, attended it.[75] It seems the Prince took little or no notice of them, or any of the English. I think it probable that the Brazilians are jealous of us, on account of our long alliance with Portugal; and besides, they may take the converse of the maxim, "those that are not against us are for us;" and think because we are not for them, we are against them.*

24th.—We sailed at daylight for Bahia. It was one of the finest mornings of this fine climate, and the remarkable land behind the Sugar-loaf was seen to its best advantage in the early light. The extreme beauty of this country is such, that it is impossible not to talk and think of it for ever; not a turn but presents some scene both beautiful and new; and if a mountainous and picturesque country have really the power of attaching its inhabitants, above all others, the *Fluminenses* ought to be as great patriots as any in the world.

February 8th, Bahia.—After a fortnight's sail, the two first days of which were calm, followed by a gale of wind, which lasted nearly three days, we anchored to-day in the bay of All Saints, which we found looking as gaily beautiful as ever. The election of the new provisional government took place yesterday, quite peaceably; and of the seven members of the junta, only one is a native of Portugal.

* I have since learned that some very warm expressions of personal regard and sympathy used by an English officer (not, however, belonging either to the Aurora or Doris) to a Portuguese, with whom he had but a slight acquaintance, on occasion of his embarking for Praya Grande, had led the Portuguese to believe that it meant something more, and that, in case of need, the English would join with the Portuguese. This at least was whispered in the town, and very naturally accounts for the jealousy entertained against us.

---

75. Sir Henry Prescott (1783-1874), captain of the frigate *Aurora* (1821-1825), protected the interests of British merchants in Brazil as well as along the west coast of South America during the wars of independence (*ODNB* 45: 246).

I remark, that the language of the writers of gazettes here is much bolder than at Rio; and I think that there is here a truly republican spirit among a very considerable number of persons: whether it extends throughout the province I cannot judge; but I am assured that a desire for independence, and a resolution to possess it, is universal.

10th.—We went ashore yesterday. The advance of the season has ripened the oranges and mangoes since we left Bahia, and has increased the number of insects, so that the nights are no longer silent. The hissing, chirping, and buzzing of crickets, beetles, and grasshoppers, continue from sunset to sunrise; and all day long the trees and flowers are surrounded by myriads of brilliant wings. The most destructive insects are the ants, and every variety of them that can hurt vegetable life is to be found here. Some form nests, like huge hanging cones, among the branches of the trees, to which a covered gallery of clay from the ground may be traced along the trunk: others surround the trunks and larger branches with their nests; many more live under ground. I have seen in a single night the most flourishing orange tree stripped of every leaf by this mischievous creature.

16th.—We sailed from Bahia, finding every thing, to all appearance, quiet;* and no apprehension being entertained by the English, a ball at the consul's, another at Mrs. N.'s, and a third at Mrs. R.'s, at each of which, as many of our young men as could get ashore were present, made them very happy, and we had some very pleasant rides into the country. I had intended, if possible, visiting a huge mass, said to be so similar to the meteoric stones that have fallen in different parts of the world as to induce a belief that it is also one of them, although it weighs many tons, and I hoped to get a piece of it; but I find it is near Nazareth de Farinha, on the other side of the bay, and too far off for this present visit to Bahia. The first time we were at Bahia, I could not even learn where it was, so incurious are my countrymen here about what brings no profit. [When a portion of the stone procured for Mr. Thornton was analyzed *here* (Bahia) the result was unfavorable—not near the proportion of Nickell.]

24th. Rio de Janeiro.—Nothing remarkable occurred on our passage here from Bahia. The school-room proceeds exceedingly well, both with the master and the scholars; and as we are all in tolerable

---

* Very shortly after we sailed, I believe within a day or two, those disturbances broke out at Bahia, which lasted until the 2d of July, 1823.

health, we look forward with no small pleasure to our voyage to Chile, for which we are preparing.

During our absence, the Prince Don Pedro has been very active, and has dismissed all the Portuguese troops. On the ships being provided to transport them to Europe, they refused to embark, on which His Royal Highness caused a heavy frigate to anchor opposite to their quarters, and went on board himself the night before the morning appointed by him for their sailing. The steam-vessel attended for the purpose of towing the transports, in case of necessity; and several gun-vessels were stationed so as to command the barracks of the refractory regiments, while a body of Brazilian soldiers was stationed in the neighbourhood. The Prince was, during the greater part of the night, in his barge, going from vessel to vessel, and disposing every thing to make good his threat, that if the Portuguese were not all on board by eight o'clock the next morning, he would give them such a breakfast of Brazilian balls as should make them glad to leave the country. This he had been provoked to say, by a message from the officers and men, insolently delivered that very night, desiring more time to prepare for their voyage. Seeing His Royal Highness in earnest, which they could hardly be brought to believe he was, they thought it most prudent to do as they were bid; and accordingly embarked, to the no small joy of the Brazilians, who had long cordially hated them.

Friday, March 1st.—The weather is now excessively hot, the thermometer being seldom under 88°, and we have had it on board at 92° Fahrenheit. Capt. Graham has had a slight attack of gout, for which reason I have not been ashore since our return from Bahia; but as he is a little better to-day he has insisted on my accompanying a party of our young men in an expedition up the harbour to see a country estate and factory.

At one o'clock, our friend, Mr. N. called for us, with a large boat of the country, which is better for the purpose than our ship's boats. These vessels have a standing awning, and two very large triangular sails: they are managed according to their size, by four, six, eight, or more negroes, besides the man at the helm: when rowing, the rowers rise at every stroke, and then throw themselves back on their seats. I think I have heard that within the memory of persons now in the navy it was the fashion to row the admiral's barges so in England. The boatmen are here universally negroes; some free, and owners of their boats; others slaves, who are obliged to take home a daily fixed sum to their masters, who often pass a life of total indolence, being fed in this way by their slaves.

The place we were going to is Nossa Senhora da Luz, about twelve miles from Rio, up the harbour, near the mouth of the river Guaxindiba, which river rises in the hills of Taypu; and though its straight course is only five miles, its windings would measure twenty or more: it is navigable, and its banks are astonishingly fertile.

The evening was charming, and we sailed past many a smiling island and gay wooded promontory, where gardens and country-houses are thickly scattered, and whence provisions in innumerable boats and canoes cross the bay every morning for the city. Our first view of N. S. da Luz presented such a high red bank, half covered with grass and trees, overhanging the water in the evening sun, as Cuyp would have chosen for a landscape; and just as I was wishing for something to animate it, the oxen belonging to the factory came down to drink and cool themselves in the bay, and completed the scene. The cattle here are large and well-shaped, something like our own Lancashire breed, and mottled in colour, though mostly red. On doubling the point of the bank, we came upon a small white church, with some venerable trees near it; beyond that was the house, with a long veranda, supported by white columns; and still farther on, the sugar-house, and the pottery and brick-work. We landed close to the house; but as the beach is shallow and muddy, we were carried ashore by negroes. Nothing can be finer than the scenery here. From the veranda, besides the picturesque and domestic fore-ground, we see the bay, dotted with rocky islands; one of these, called Itaoca, is remarkable as having, in the opinion of the Indians, been the residence of some divine person: it is connected with the traditions concerning their benefactor, Zome, who taught them the use of the mandioc, and whom the first missionaries here contrived to convert into St. Thomas the apostle. It consists of one immense stone cleft throughout, and a little earth and sand gathered round it, on which are trees and shrubs of the freshest verdure; some of the other islets are bare, and some again have houses and villages on them: the whole scene is terminated by the Organ Mountains, whose spiry and fantastic summits attracting the passing clouds, secure an everlasting variety to the eye.

We found, that owing to our neglect in not sending beforehand to announce our visit, neither the master of the house nor his housekeeper were at home: however, Mr. N. being an old friend, went into the poultry yard, and ordered thence an excellent supper; and while it was preparing, we went to look at the pottery, which is only for the coarsest red ware. The wheel used here is the clumsiest and rudest I ever saw, and the potter is obliged to sit sideways by it. The clay, both for the pottery and the bricks, is dug on the spot; it is coarse and red: it is tempered by the trampling of mules; but all that we use spades and shovels for is done by the bare hands of the negroes: the furnaces for baking the bricks and jars are partly scooped out of the hill, and faced with brick. Leaving the pottery, we climbed the hill that marks the first approach to N. S. da Luz; and on the way up its steep and rugged side, our dogs disturbed a flock of sheep, as picturesque and as ragged as Paul Potter himself could have desired: they had been lying round the root of a huge old acacia, decorated with innumerable parasite plants, some of which cling like ivy to the trunk, and others climbing to the topmost boughs, fall thence in grey silky garlands, or, like the tillandsia, adorn them with hundreds of pink and white flowers; among these, many an ant and bee had fixed his nest, and every thing was teeming with life and beauty.

The moon was up long before we returned from our ramble, and long before our host arrived. Had the Neapolitan ambassador, who told George the Third that the moon of his country was worth the sun of England, ever been in Brazil, I could almost forgive the hyperbole. The clear mild light playing on such scenery, and the cool refreshing breeze of evening, after a day of all but intolerable heat, render the night indeed the season of pleasure in this climate: nor were the rude songs of the negroes, as they loaded the boats to be ready to sail down the harbour with the morning's land-breeze, unpleasing.

As we were looking over the bay, a larger boat appeared: it neared the shore; and our host, Mr. Lewis P., who superintends the fazenda, landed, and kindly received our apology for coming without previous notice. The visit had long been talked of; but now our time at Rio was likely to be so short, that had we not come to-day, we might not have come at all. He led the way to the garden, where we passed the time till supper was ready. The midshipmen found more oranges, and better than they had yet met with, and did full justice to them. The fruit and vegetables of Europe and America, of the temperate and torrid zones, meet here; nor are their flowers forgotten: over against the little parterre, an orange and a tamarind tree shade a pleasant bench; close to which, in something of oriental taste, the white stucco wall of the well is raised and crowned with flower-pots, filled with roses and sweet herbs.

2d.—I rose at daylight, and rode with Mr. N. through the estate, while Mr. Dance, my cousin Glennie, and the two boys, went to shoot in the marsh by the river side.

Every turn in our ride brought a new and varied landscape into view: beneath, the sugar-cane in luxuriant growth; above, the ripening orange and the palm; around and scattered through the plain enlivened by the windings of the Guaxindiba, the lime, the guava, and a thousand odorous and splendid shrubs, beautified the path.—But all is new here. The long lines of fazenda houses, that now and then take from the solitariness of nature, suggest no association with any advance either of old or present time, in the arts that civilise or that ennoble man. The rudest manufactures, carried on by African slaves, one half of whom are newly imported, (that is, are still smarting under the separation from all that endears the home, even of a savage,) are all the approaches to improvement; and though nature is at least as fine as in India or in Italy, the want of some reference to man, as an intellectual and moral being, robs it of half its charms. However, I returned well pleased from my ride, and found my young sportsmen not less pleased with their morning's ramble. Not, indeed, that they had shot snipes, as they intended, but they had gotten a huge lizard (*Lacerta Marmorata*), of a kind they had not seen before. They had seen the large land-crab (*Ruricola*), and they had brought down a boatswain bird, a sort of pelican, (*Pelicanus Lencocephalus*), which they proposed to stuff. Accordingly after breakfast, as the weather was too hot to walk farther, the bird and the lizard were both skinned, the guns were cleaned, and I made a sketch of the landscape.

In the evening I took a long walk to a point of view whence the whole bay with the city in the distance is distinctly seen, and on the way stopped at a cottage, where Mr. P. who is, literally, here "king, priest, and prophet," had some enquiry to make, concerning the health of the indwellers: these were two negroes, who have grown old in the service of the estate, and are no longer useful. I have seen examples of such being *freed,* that is, turned out of doors to starve. Here they would be entitled, by the rules of the estate, if not by law, to come every day for the same allowance as the working negroes: but they do not choose it. They indeed live in a hut, and on the ground of their master; but they maintain themselves by rearing a few fowls, and making baskets: so dear is the feeling of independence, even in old age, sickness, and slavery.

Sunday, 3d.—I went out before breakfast, with a negro carpenter for my guide. This man, with little instruction, has learned his art so as to be not only a good carpenter and joiner, but also a very tolerable cabinet-maker, and in other respects displays a quickness of understanding which gives no countenance to the pretended inferiority of negro intellect. I was much pleased with the observations he made on many things which I remarked as new, and with the perfect understanding he seemed to have of all country works. After breakfast, I attended the weekly muster of all the negroes of the fazenda; clean shirts and trowsers were given the men, and shifts and skirts to the women, of very coarse white cotton. Each, as he or she came in, kissed a hand, and then bowed to Mr. P. saying, either "Father, give me blessing," or "The names of Jesus and Mary be praised!" and were answered accordingly, either "Bless you," or "Be they praised." This is the custom in old establishments: it is repeated morning and evening, and seems to acknowledge a kind of relationship between master and slave. It must diminish the evils of slavery to one, the tyranny of mastership in the other, to acknowledge thus a common superior Master on whom they both depend.

As each slave passed in review, some questions were asked concerning himself, his family, if he had one, or his work; and each received a portion of snuff or tobacco, according to his taste. Mr. P. is one of the few persons whom I have met conversant among slaves, who appears to have made them an object of rational and humane attention. He tells me that the creole negroes and mulattoes are far superior in industry to the Portuguese and Brazilians; who, from causes not difficult to be imagined, are for the most part indolent and ignorant. The negroes and mulattoes have strong motives to exertion of every kind, and succeed in what they undertake accordingly. They are the best artificers and artists. The orchestra of the opera-house is composed of at least one-third of mulattoes. All decorative painting, carving, and inlaying is done by them; in short, they excel in all ingenious mechanical arts.

In the afternoon I attended Mr. P. to see the negroes receive their daily allowance of food. It consisted of farinha, kidney-beans, and dried beef, a fixed measure of each to every person. One man asked for two portions, on account of the absence of his neighbour, whose wife had desired it might be sent to her to make ready for him by the time he returned. Some enquiries which Mr. P. made about this person, induced me to ask his history. It seems he is a mulatto boatman, the most trusty servant on the estate, and rich, because he is industrious enough to have earned a good deal of private property, besides doing his duty to his master. In his youth, and he is not now old, he had become attached to a creole negress, born, like him, on the estate; but he did not marry her till he had earned money enough to purchase her, in order that their children, if they had any, might be born free. Since that time, he has become rich enough to purchase himself, even at the high price which such a slave might fetch; but his master will not sell him his freedom, his services being too valuable to lose, notwithstanding his promise to remain on the estate and work. Unfortunately these people have no children; therefore on their death their property, now considerable, will revert to the master. Had they children, as the woman is free, they might inherit the mother's property; and there is nothing to prevent the father's making over all he earns to her. I wish I had the talent of novel writing, for the sake of this slave's story; but my writing, like my drawing, goes no farther than sketching from nature, and I make better artists welcome to use the subject.

The evening was very stormy: deep clouds had covered the Organ Mountains; and vivid lightning, sharp rain, and boisterous wind, had threatened the fazenda with a night of terror. But it passed away, leaving all the grand and gloomy beauty of a departed thunder-storm in a mountainous country; when the moon broke through the clouds, and the night seemed, from the contrast with the last few hours, even lovelier than the last. Then just as the

> Sable clouds
> Turned forth their silver lining on the night,
> And cast a gleam over the tufted grove,[76]

I heard the sounds of music; not such, indeed, as Milton's echo, with Henry Lawes's notes, would have made,—of which the night and the scene had made me dream;[77] but the voice of the slaves on this their night of holiday, beguiling their cares with uncouth airs, played on rude

---

76. Milton, *Comus* (1634).
77. Henry Lawes (1595-1662), musician and composer whose work includes *Ayres* and *Dialogues for One, Two, and Three Voices* (1653), was a good friend of Milton's and wrote the music to accompany the masque *Comus* in 1634. In return, Milton immortalized his friend in a sonnet praising his musical talents.

African instruments. Taking one of my ship-mates with me, I immediately went to the huts of the married slaves, where all merrymakings are held; and found parties playing, singing, and dancing to the moonlight. A superstitious veneration for that beautiful planet is said to be pretty general in savage Africa, as that for the Pleiades was among the Indians of Brazil; and probably the slaves, though baptized, dance to the moon in memory of their homes. As for the instruments, they are the most inartificial things that ever gave out musical sounds; yet they have not an unpleasing effect. One is simply composed of a crooked stick, a small hollow gourd, and a single string of brass wire. The mouth of the gourd must be placed on the naked skin of the side; so that the ribs of the player form the sounding board, and the string is struck with a short stick. A second has more the appearance of a guitar: the hollow gourd is covered with skin; it has a bridge, and there are two strings; it is played with the finger. Another of the same class is played with a bow; it has but one string, but is fretted with the fingers. All these are called gourmis. There were, besides, drums made of the hollow trunks of trees, four or five feet long, closed at one end with wood, and covered with skin at the other. In playing these, the drummer lays his instrument on the ground and gets astride on it, when he beats time with his hands to his own songs, or the tunes of the gourmis. The small marimba has a very sweet tone. On a flat piece of sonorous wood a little bridge is fastened; and to this small slips of iron, of different lengths, are attached, so as that both ends vibrate on the board, one end being broader and more elevated than the other. This broad end is played with the thumbs, the instrument being held with both hands. All these are tuned in a peculiar manner, and with great nicety, especially the marimba;* but, as I am no musician, I cannot explain their methods.

* The simplest of these stringed instruments, and two kinds of marimba, have found a place in the Jesuit Bonnanis' *Gabinetto Armonico*, printed at Rome, 1722, and dedicated to Holy King David. The great marimba consists of a large wooden frame; in which a number of hollow canes, about nine inches long, are placed, with the mouth upwards; across these open ends are laid pieces of sonorous wood, which being struck with another yield a pleasant sound, like the wooden armonicas of Malacca. The whole is suspended round the neck, like the old man's psaltery in the Dance of Death. Each nation of negroes has its own peculiar instrument, which its exiles have introduced here. A king of each tribe is annually elected, to whom his people are obedient, something in the way of the gipsy monarchy. Before 1806 the election took place with great ceremony and feasting, and sometimes fighting, in the Campo de Santa Anna; and the king of the whole was seated during the day in the centre of the square under a huge state umbrella. This festival is now abolished.

4th.—I was very sorry indeed this morning at sunrise, when I saw the boats ready to convey us from N. S. da Luz, where we had enjoyed our three days as much as possible; a cheerful party, a kind host, free disposal of our time, and no business but such as might beseem the individuals of this castle of indolence, "where every man strolled off his own glad way."

> There freedom reigned without the least alloy;
> Nor gossip's tale, nor ancient maiden's gall,
> Nor saintly spleen, durst murmur at our joy,
> And with envenomed tongue our pleasures pall.
> For why? There was but one great rule for all
> To wit, that each should work his own desire.[78]

We returned to the ship by a different way from that by which we went, through the archapelago of beautiful islands on the eastern side of the harbour; and I had the pleasure to find the Captain really better, though still with tender feet.

6th.—His Majesty's ship, Slaney, Capt. Stanhope, sailed from Rio.

7th.—The Superb arrived from Valparaiso, bringing no news of importance. Indeed, if she had, we are scarcely in a state to attend to it: we have sat up all night with B., one of our midshipmen, who is dangerously ill.[79]

8th.—Captain Graham not feeling well enough to leave the ship, I went with Captain Prescott of the Aurora, to visit the French Commodore Roussin on board the Amazone. I have seldom been better pleased. The captains of the other French ships were there, to receive us. All the urbanity of Frenchmen, joined with the delightful frankness of the profession, assured us we were welcome. The ship itself, every part of which we saw, is a model of all that can be done, either in the dock-yard at home, or by officers afloat, for comfort, health, and cleanliness, and is well as a man of war. Her captain, however, is a superior man; and many ships of every and any nation might be visited before his equal would be met with. I wish it were possible that we should in-

---

78. James Thomson (1700-1748), Scottish poet and playwright; this passage is from *The Castle of Indolence* (1748).

79. Most likely James Brisbane, the only midshipman listed in the 1821 muster book of the *Doris* whose name begins with B. The Grahams' nursing apparently succeeded, since Brisbane survived to transfer to the ship Blossom after Captain Graham's death on April 2, 1822; he was promoted in 1826 (Vale, *Frigate* 169).

troduce into our ships the oven on the lower deck, which gives fresh bread twice a week for the whole ship's company, not only for the sake of the bread, but the heating it must air and ventilate the ship.

9th.—The Portuguese squadron from Lisbon, with a reinforcement of troops, arrived off the harbour. Troops are sent to reinforce the garrisons in the forts, at the entrance; and the ships are forbidden to enter, but promised victuals and water to carry them to Lisbon. I was on shore all day on business, preparatory to our sailing for Valparaiso. Captain Graham being too unwell to venture out of the ship himself, he therefore undertook to nurse the invalid for me. I returned late. I found B. dangerously ill, and Captain Graham very uneasy.

I received many persons on board, and took leave of many.

10th.—We sailed at daylight from Rio, in full hope that the cool weather we shall find on going round Cape Horn, and the fine climate of Chile, will do us all good. I have not been in bed for three nights; my invalids are in that state, that night watching is necessary for them.

13th.—In addition to our other troubles, the first lieutenant is taken dangerously ill: but Captain Graham appears better, though not yet able to go on deck.

16th.—Yesterday afternoon the mercury in the barometer sunk in a very short space of time a whole inch, and we had a gale of wind. The cold is sensibly increased. Fahrenheit's thermometer often stood at 92° in Rio harbour; it is now 68°, and we have many sick. B. is getting better.

17th.—Wind and sea abated, and the barometer rising once more; the mercury stands at 30 inches and two-tenths. I have lain down at four o'clock these two mornings, Glennie having kindly relieved my watching at that hour. We have removed the dead-lights from the cabin windows.

18th.—Every thing better. The young people again at school. Some lunars taken. We are in 36° 55' S. latitude, and the thermometer is at 68°; barometer 30—2.

On the *19th* and *20th* the mercury in the barometer sunk gradually from 30 to 29—02, and rose again as before on the 21st. It blew hard; the thermometer fell to 58°, in latitude 42° S. There are many albatrosses and stormy petrels about the ship.

22d.—Latitude 46° 25' S., longitude 52° 40' W. The weather very cold, though the thermometer is at 56°, barometer 29—08; a very heavy swell. Great numbers of the Cape pigeon about the ship.

24th.—Latitude 50° 30'; thermometer 44° morning and evening, 47° at noon. Seeing two penguins to-day, we supposed some land must be near, but found no bottom with 100 fathoms line. The cold weather seems to have a good effect on our invalids. The barometer fell suddenly, and a strong S. W. wind succeeded, and we were glad to light a fire in the cabin.

I am sorry we have passed so far out of sight of the Falkland Islands, Sir John Hawkins's maiden land.[80] The idea of seeing a town left standing as it was, by all its inhabitants at once, and of the tame animals becoming wild, had something romantic. It seemed like a realisation of the Arabian tale of the half-marble prince, and in real interest comes near the discovery of the lost Greenland settlements. I do not know any thing that gratifies the imagination, more than the situations and incidents that by bringing distant periods of time together, places them, as it were, at once within our own reach. I remember some years ago spending a whole day with no companion but my guide at Pompeii, and becoming so intimate with the ancients, their ways, and manners, that I felt, when I went home to Naples, and its lazaroni, and its English travellers, as I suppose, that one of the seven sleepers to have done, who went to purchase bread with money five centuries old. As to the marble cities of Moorish Africa, when we consider their exposure to the sirocco, and read Dolomieu's Experiments on the Atmosphere, during the prevalence of that wind at Malta, we shall find but too probable a reason for their existence as reported.[81]

25th.—Latitude 51° 58' S., longitude 51° W., thermometer 41°. Strong south-westerly gales and heavy sea. Just as our friends in England are looking forward to spring, its gay light days and early flowers, we are sailing towards frozen regions, where avarice's self has been forced to give up half-formed settlements by the severity of the climate. We are in the midst of a dark boisterous sea; over us, a dense, grey, cold sky. The albatross, stormy petrel, and pintado are our companions; yet there is a pleasure in stemming the apparently irresistible waves,

---

80. Sir John Hawkins (1532-1595), English merchant and naval commander in Elizabeth I's service; Lacombe notes that Hawkins bears the sad distinction of founding the English slave trade with Africa (247).

81. Déodat de Dolomieu (1750-1801), French geologist and mineralogist after whom dolomite was named; he studied the natural sciences across Europe as well as in Africa, visiting Egypt as part of Napoleon's expedition in 1798.

Figure 13. The End of an Island in the Harbour of Rio de Janeiro, drawn for the sake of the variety of Vegetation. Courtesy of The Catholic University of America, Oliveira Lima Library, Washington, D.C.

and in wrestling thus with the elements. I forget what writer it is who observes, that the sublime and the ridiculous border on each other; I am sure they approach very nearly at sea. If I look abroad, I see the grandest and most sublime object in nature,—the ocean raging in its might, and man, in all his honour, and dignity, and powers of mind and body, wrestling with and commanding it: then I look within, round my little home in the cabin, and every roll of the ship causes accidents irresistibly ludicrous; and in spite of the inconveniences they bring with them, one cannot choose but laugh. Sometimes, in spite of all usual precautions, of cushions and clothes, the breakfast-table is suddenly stripped of half its load, which is lodged in the lee scuppers, whither the coal-scuttle and its contents had adjourned the instant before: then succeed the school-room distresses of *capsized* ink-stands, broken slates, torn books, and lost places; not to mention the loss of many a painful calculation, and other evils exquisite in their kind, but abundantly laughable, especially, as it happened just now, if the school-master is induced to measure his length on the deck, when in the act of reprimanding the carelessness which subjects the slates and books to these untoward chances.

28th.—Latitude 55° 26' S., longitude 56° 11' W. Captain Graham and the first lieutenant still both very ill. At one o'clock this morning the mercury in the barometer sunk to 28—09; at seven it rose again to 29—01. The thermometer is at 38° of Fahrenheit, and we have had squalls of snow and sleet, and a heavy sea. There are flocks of very small birds about the ship, and we have seen a great many whales.

30th.—Latitude 56° 51' S., longitude 59° W.; the thermometer at 30° this morning, and 32° at noon. A violent gale of wind from the south-west; the only thing like a hard gale since we left England. I had breakfast spread on the cabin deck, as it was not possible to secure any thing on a table. Clarke, one of the quarter-masters, had two ribs broken by a fall on deck;[82] and Sinclair, a very strong man, was taken ill after being an hour at the wheel. We have made gloves for the men at the wheel of canvass, lined with dreadnought; and for the people at night, waistbands of canvass, with dreadnought linings. The snow and hail squalls are very severe; ice forms in every fold of the sails. This is hard upon the men, so soon after leaving Rio in the hottest part of the year.

Yesterday morning, about an hour before sunrise, a bright meteor was seen in the south-west. It was first taken for the signal lanterns of a large ship; then the officer of the watch thought it was a blue light, and we made no doubt of its being Sir T. Hardy in the Creole.[83] It remained a long time stationary; then it was lost behind the clouds, and re-appeared between them about 10° high, when it disappeared.*

April 1st.—Latitude 57° 46'; the weather much more mild and moderate. Our young men have caught a number of birds, principally petrels; the P. Pelagica, or Mother Cary's chicken, is the least; the P. Pintado is gayest on the water; but the P. Glacialis, or fulmer, is most beautiful when brought on board: I cannot enough admire the delicate beauty of the snow-white plumage, unwet and unsoiled, amid the salt waves. The poets have scandalised both the arctic and antarctic regions as

---

* Frezier mentions seeing such a meteor in latitude 57° 30' S., and longitude 69° W., in 1712.

82. Thomas Clark, Quartermaster of the Doris (Vale, *Frigate* 60).
83. Sir Thomas Hardy (1769-1839), British naval officer who served under Nelson at Trafalgar, was created a baronet of the Navy in 1806, fought in the war of 1812, and became Commander in chief of the South American Squadron (1819-1824). Lacombe tells us that Hardy was the first foreigner to salute the new Brazilian flag (318).

> A bleak expanse,
> Shagg'd o'er with wavy rocks, cheerless and *void*
> Of *ev'ry life;*

yet, on Capt. Parry's approach to the north pole, he found the solitude teeming with *life;* and the farther south we have sailed, the more *life* we have found on the waters. Yesterday the sea was covered with albatrosses, and four kinds of petrel: the penguin comes near us; shoals of porpoises are constantly flitting by, and whales for ever rising to the surface and blowing alongside of the ship.

With the thermometer not lower than 30°, we feel the cold excessive. Yesterday morning the main rigging was cased in ice; and the ropes were so frozen after the sleet in the night, that it was difficult to work them. I never see these things but I think of Thomson's description of Sir Hugh Willoughby's attempt to discover the north-west passage, when

> He with his hapless crew,
> Each full exerted at his several task,
> Froze into statues; to the cordage glued
> The sailor, and the pilot to the helm.[84]

I was glad to-day, when the dead-lights were removed, to see the bright, blue, but still boisterous sea, spreading with ample waves curled with snowy tops, in the sunshine; it is many days since we have seen the sun, and the white birds flying and chattering, or wrestling on the water, while the ship, like them, sometimes bravely mounts the very top of the wave, and sometimes quietly subsides with it. These are the things we behold "who go down to the sea in ships, and occupy our business in the great waters."[85] No one can imagine, who has not felt, the exhilaration of spirits produced by a dry clear day of sunshine at sea, after a week of rain and snow.

April 2d.—A few minutes after noon, an iceberg was reported on the lee-bow. As I had never seen one, I went on deck for the first time

---

84. These lines, as well as those above beginning "A bleak expanse," are from James Thomson's "Winter," in *The Seasons* (1730); the passage recounts the death of the British explorer Sir Hugh Willoughby (?-1554) who set out in search of a northeastern passage to the artic in 1553 but died en route and was discovered frozen, years later, with his crew (*ODNB* 54: 516-523).

85. *King James Bible*, Psalms 107:23-30.

since we left Rio to see it.* It appeared like a moderately high conical hill, and looked very white upon the bleak grey sky; it might be about twelve miles from us. The temperature of the water was 36° of Fahrenheit's thermometer, that of the air 38°, when the ice was nearest.

For some few days the violent motion of the ship, occasioned by the heavy sea, has rendered writing and drawing irksome; for, as Lord Dorset's song has it,

> Our paper, pens, and ink, and we,
> Roll up and down our ships, at sea.[86]

Nevertheless we are not idle. As the cabin has always a good fire in it, it is the general rendezvous for invalids; and the midshipmen come in and out as they please, as it is the school-room. In one corner Glennie has his apparatus for skinning and dissecting the birds we take; and we have constantly occasion to admire the beautiful contrivances of nature in providing for her creatures. These huge sea-birds, that we find so far from any land, have on each side large air-vessels adapted for floating them in the air, or on the water; they are placed below the wings, and the liver, gizzard, and entrails rest on them. In each gizzard of those we have yet opened, there have been two small pebbles, of unequal size; and the gizzard is very rough within. We have found more vegetable than animal food in their stomachs.

20th April, 1822.—To-day we made the coast of Chile. I had continued to write my Journal regularly; but though nearly two years are past since I wrote it, I cannot bring myself to copy it: from the 3d of April it became a register of acute suffering; and, on my part, of alternate hopes and fears through days and nights of darkness and storms, which aggravated the wretchedness of those wretched hours. On the night of the ninth of April, I regularly undressed and went to bed for

* We passed another on the 8th, which Glennie calculated to be 410 feet high; it was near enough for us to see the waves break on it. In conversing on this subject with the officers since,—for at the time I was indeed unable to think of it,—I find there is reason to think that, instead of an iceberg, we saw land on the 8th. It was seen in the latitude and longitude of an island visited by Drake, marked in the old charts.

---

86. Charles Sackville, Earl of Dorset (1638–1706), wrote *Song Written at Sea*, in the First Dutch War, 1665, the night before an Engagement, from which this couplet comes. Graham quotes the same lines in a letter to John Murray written on board the *Doris* while still in Portsmouth (Sunday 22nd July, 1821).

the first time since I left Rio de Janeiro. All was then over, and I slept long and rested; but I awoke to the consciousness of being alone, and a widow, with half the globe between me and my kindred.

Many things very painful occurred. But I had comfort too. I found sympathy and brotherly help from some; and I was not insensible to the affectionate behaviour of *my boys,* as the midshipmen were called. And I had the comfort to feel that no stranger hand had closed his eyes, or smoothed his pillow.

Mr. Loudon and Mr. Kift, the surgeon and assistant surgeon, never left the bed-side; and, when my strength failed, my cousin Mr. Glennie, and Mr. Blatchly, two passed midshipmen, did all that friends could do.

Mr. Dance, the second lieutenant,—though, from the illness of the first lieutenant, the whole business of the ship devolved on him,—found time to be near his friend's death-bed; and, whether at noon or midnight, was never absent where kindness could be shown.

But what could any human kindness do for me? My comfort must come from him who in his own time will "wipe off all tears from our faces."[87]

Second Visit to Brazil

BEFORE I begin the Journal of my Second Visit to Brazil, from which I was absent a year and three days, it will be necessary to give a short account of the principal events which took place during that year, and which changed the government of the country.

The Prince Regent had in vain sent the most pressing representations in favour of Brazil to the Cortes. No notice whatever was taken of his despatches; and the government at Lisbon continued to legislate for Brazil as if it were a settlement on the coast of savage Africa. The ministers who had served Don John had seen enough of the country, during their residence in it, to be persuaded that Brazil, united, was at any time competent to throw off all subjection to the mother country; the object, therefore, became to divide it. Accordingly a scheme for the government of Brazil was framed, by which each captaincy should be ruled by a junta, whose acts were to be totally independent on each other, and only recognisable by the authorities in Portugal; and the Prince was ordered home in a peremptory and indecent manner. I have

---

87. *King James Bible,* Isaiah 25:8.

mentioned in my Journal the reception those orders had met with, and the resolution His Royal Highness had adopted of staying in Brazil. As soon as this resolution became known to the provinces, addresses and deputations poured in on all sides from every town and captaincy, excepting the city of Bahia and the province of Maranham, which had always had a government independent of the rest of Brazil.

In December, 1821, the King had appointed General Madeira governor of Bahia and commander of the troops. He entered on his office in February; and shortly afterwards the first actual warfare between the Portuguese and Brazilians began in the city of St. Salvador, on the 6th of the month, when the Brazilians were defeated with some loss.* Meantime, the province of St. Paul's had made every exertion to raise and arm troops; and early in February 1100 men marched towards Rio, to put themselves at the disposal of the Prince. Some recruits for the seamen and marine corps were raised, and a naval academy established, the object of all which was to prevent the carrying away the Prince by force. It was now thought advisable that the Prince should visit the two most important provinces, St. Paul's and the Mines; and on the 26th or 27th of March he left Rio for that purpose, leaving the executive government in the hands of the minister Jose Bonefacio. His Royal Highness was received every where with enthusiasm, until he arrived at the last stage, on his way to Villa Rica, the capital of the province of Minas Geraes; there he received intelligence of a party raised to oppose his entrance by the Juiz de Fora, supported by a cap-

* On the 25th of May following a solemn mass was performed for the souls of those who had fallen on both sides, at the expense of the Bahians resident at Rio, in the church of San Francesco de Paulo. The cenotaph raised in the church was surrounded by inscriptions, in Latin and Portuguese; one of the most striking is, "Eternal glory to those who give their blood for their country."

> (He quha dies for his cuntre
> Sal herbyrit intil hewyn be, says *Barbour*.)

The day was one of those Brazilian rainy days, when it should seem another deluge was coming: but the Prince and Princess were the first at the ceremony. [Because her Scottish roots clearly shape her attitude towards South American independence movements, it is interesting that Graham quotes John Barbour (1325?-1395), from Book II of his Scottish national epic *The Bruce*, in the context of Brazilian independence.—*Eds.*]

tain of one of the regiments of Caçadores. He immediately caused some troops to be assembled and joined with those which accompanied him, and then remained where he was, and sent to the camara of the town, to say he was able to enter by force, but had rather come among them as a friend and protector. Several messages passed: the conspirators discovered that the Prince was, indeed, sufficiently strong to overpower them; and besides, they met with no support, as they had hoped, from the magistrates or people. His Royal Highness, therefore, entered Villa Rica on the 9th of April, and on the magistrates and people attending to compliment him, he addressed them thus:—

> Brave Mineros! The shackles of despotism, which began to be loosened on the 24th of August in Porto, are now bursting in this province. Be free,—be constitutional! Unite with me, and proceed constitutionally. I rely entirely on you. Do you depend on me. Let not yourselves be deluded by those who seek the ruin of your province, and of the whole nation.
>
> Viva, The Constitutional King!
> Viva, Our Religion!
> Viva, All honest men!
> Viva, The Mineros!

The next day the Prince held a general court, and remained eleven days at Villa Rica. The only punishment inflicted on the conspirators, was suspension from their offices; and this royal visit attached this province to him, as firmly as those of St. Paul's and Rio.

He returned to Rio de Janiero on the 25th, where he was received in the most flattering manner, and where he became daily more popular; and on the 13th of May, King John's birth-day, the senate and people bestowed on him the title of Perpetual Defender of Brazil, and thenceforward his style was, CONSTITUTIONAL PRINCE REGENT, AND PERPETUAL DEFENDER OF THE KINGDOM OF BRAZIL.

The impossibility of continuing united to Portugal had become daily more apparent. All the southern provinces were eager to declare their independence. Pernambuco and its dependencies had long manifested a similar feeling, and the province of Bahia was equally inclined to freedom although the city was full of Portuguese troops under Madeira, and receiving constant reinforcements and supplies from Lisbon.

The Cortes seemed resolved on bringing matters to extremities; the language used in their sessions, with respect to the Prince, was highly indecent. Such commanders either by sea or land as obeyed him, unless by force, were declared traitors, and he was ordered home anew within four months, under pain of submitting to the future disposition of the Cortes; and they decreed that the whole means of government should be employed to enforce obedience. The Brazilian members did indeed remonstrate and protest formally against these proceedings; but they were over-ruled; and the spectators in the galleries, on one occasion, went so far as to cry, "Down with the Brazilian!"

In the months of June and July, Madeira began to make sallies into the country around Bahia, as if it had been possessed by an enemy; and, indeed, he quickly found one most formidable. The town of Cachoeira, large and populous, and intimately connected with the hardy inhabitants of the Certam, soon became the headquarters of crowds of patriots, who assembled there, and resolved to expel the Portuguese from their capital.

They began to form regular troops; but though they were abundantly supplied with beef and other provisions, they were in want of arms and ammunition, and sent to Rio de Janeiro to represent their situation to the Prince, and request assistance. They were also in great distress for salt to preserve their provisions; and as to accoutrements, raw hides supplied the place of almost every thing. An apothecary, in Cachoeira, shortly began to boil sea-water in sugar-coppers, to make salt, and soon reduced the price of that article, so that the quantity at first sold for ten pataccas (eighteen shillings) fell to seven vintems (seven pence). The same apothecary, collecting all the salt-petre in the neighbourhood, applied himself to making of gunpowder, and a fortunate discovery of some hundred barrels smuggled into Itaparica by some English, was of essential use to them. But they had no cannon, no lead for ball for their muskets and matchlocks; the lead, indeed, and a quantity of gun-locks, their friends within the city contrived to smuggle to them; and their guns were supplied in the following manner. In each engenho, there was an old gun or two for the purpose of balancing some part of the machinery; these were at once sent to Cachoeira, where, being cleaned and bushed by an ingenious blacksmith, they were rendered serviceable; and the patriots ventured to take the field against Madeira's parties, even before the arrival of any assistance from Rio.

Meantime, news of these transactions arrived at Rio, as well as notice of the decrees of the Cortes at Lisbon. The Prince and people no longer hesitated. His Royal Highness, together with the senate, issued proclamations on the 3d of June, calling together a representative and legislative assembly, to be composed of members from every province and town, to meet in the city of Rio; and on the first of August he published that noble manifesto, by which the independence of Brazil was openly asserted, the grounds of its claims clearly stated, and the people exhorted to let no voice but that of honour be heard among them, and to let the shores, from the Amazons to the Plata, resound with no cry but that of independence. On the same day, a decree was put forth to resist the hostilities of Portugal, containing the following articles:—1st, All troops sent by any country whatever, without leave obtained from the Prince, shall be accounted enemies: 2d, If they come in peace, they shall remain on board their ships, and shall not communicate with the shore; but, having received supplies, shall depart: 3d, That in case of disobedience, they shall be repulsed by force: 4th, If they force a landing in any weak point, the inhabitants shall retire to the interior, with all their moveables, and the militia shall make war as guerillas against the strangers: 5th, That all governors, etc. shall fortify their ports, etc.: 6th, Reports to be forthwith made of the state of the ports in Brazil, for that end.

This last decree had been anticipated by the Pernambucans, who had marched a body of troops to the assistance of the patriots of Cachoeira, and a most harassing warfare was commenced against the Portuguese in St. Salvador: these last had received a reinforcement of seven hundred men on the 8th of August; but they had hardly had time to exult in their arrival, when a squadron from Rio Janeiro disembarked at Alagoas 5000 guns, six field-pieces, 270,000 cartridges, 2000 pikes, 500 carbines, 500 pistols, 500 cutlasses, and 260 men, chiefly officers, under Brigadier-general Labatut,* who soon joined the patriots, and fixed his head-quarters at Cachoeira, having stretched a line of troops across the peninsula on which the town is placed, and

---

* This gentleman was an officer under Napoleon, in the Spanish war. For some military irregularity, he was dismissed; but pardoned on condition of living in Cayenne, and procuring information for the French government. He left that country, however, and settled in Brazil; where, with the exception of a short time spent in the service of Bolivar [Simón Bolívar (1783–1830), a leader in the Spanish American independence movements—*Eds*.], he had lived quietly and respectably till the present juncture.

thus cut it off from provisions on that side; but the sea being still open, supplies were abundant, not only from abroad, but from the opposite island of Itaparica. That fertile district, however, was soon occupied by the Brazilians; and Madeira had only his supplies from seaward, unless he could by force dislodge the Brazilians from their quarters on that island.

The cabinet of Rio became sensible that it was necessary to provide a naval force, if they wished to preserve the kingdom from the farther attacks of Portugal, or to dislodge the enemy from his strong-hold in Bahia. Accordingly, the agents of the government in England were employed to engage officers and men: some were collected on the spot; others, such as Captain David Jewet, from Buenos Ayres and America, were instantly employed; and all exertions were made to repair such of the ships left behind by King John as would bear the repairs.

[The Andradas, sensible that Brazil could not much longer under any circumstances continue under the dominion of Portugal, yet anxious to spare the effusion of blood and to prevent their country from civil war and from the atrocious scenes which had disgraced the struggle for liberty in the Spanish American colonies, eagerly fostered the ambition of the Prince to become the leader in the great revolution that was proceeding. They considered that his descent from the ancient monarchs of their forefathers would be acknowledged on all hands, and that his birth would give him that prior claim to all other adventurers in the struggle that would ensure regularity in their proceedings. On the 7th of September the Emperor, being at St. Pauls, declared the Independence of Brazil on the famous plain of Piranga, whither the party had induced him to go and shew himself to the Paulistas, the boldest of the inhabitants of Brazil and those whose habits had more of freedom than any other of the southern settlers. On that plain then, at the quinta of Amador Bereno, the Prince harangued the people, and set the example of adopting a peculiar badge and the Motto of Independencia o Morte. The rosette of green and yellow and the plate with those words engraven became the mark of patriotism and the Prince, pleased with himself and with his ministers whose energy and activity he had for the moment imbibed, returned to Rio to celebrate his birthday and to take a step which, as it would render him peculiarly guilty in the eyes of his father and of all the Legitimates, would as was fondly hoped rivet him to the cause of Brazil and attach him unalterably to the counsellors who had in effect placed him at the head of the nation.]

At length, on the 12th of October, the birth-day of the Prince, the troops being, as usual, assembled in the great square of Santa Anna, and a great concourse of people attending, the Prince was suddenly hailed Emperor of Brazil, and the kingdom changed in style and title, and all dependence on, or connection with Portugal, for ever abjured.

This event seemed to give new spirit to the war of Bahia: as it exasperated the Portuguese, so it encouraged the Brazilians, now assured of independence. Madeira, resolved, if possible, to gain a communication with Nazareth on one of the rivers of the Reconcave, which is most fertile, and furnishes abundance of farinha, sent one hundred men of the Caçadores, under Colonel Russel, to attempt to gain possession of the Ilha do Medo, which commands the Funil, or passage between the mainland and Itaparica leading to Nazareth; but their boats grounded, and they were obliged to wait for the tide, while the Brazilians, who are excellent marksmen, and were concealed among the bushes ashore, picked them off at leisure. Another expedition, equally unfortunate, was sent with a large gun-vessel to Cachoeira, and arrived off the public square, just as it was filled with people proclaiming the Emperor. The guns began to play on the mob; but the tide was low, and the shot, instead of reaching the people, only struck the quays, and did little damage. The Brazilian soldiers now crowded to the wharfs, and thence commenced so brisk a fire on the enemy, that the commander of the vessel retreated hastily without killing a man, though he lost many. In this action Dona Maria de Jesus[88] distinguished herself; for the spirit of patriotism had not confined itself to the men.*

The most considerable expedition sent by Madeira from Bahia was to the Punto de Itaparica, the possession of which was becoming daily more important, as the provisions in the town diminished. For this purpose 1500 men were embarked on board the Promtadao, and two other brigs of war; they were to land half on one side and half on the other of the little peninsula forming the Punto, on which there is a

---

* Of her, see more in the Journal.

88. Maria Quitéria de Jesus's (1792-1853) role as a female soldier fighting for Brazilian independence made her famous; her biographer Fernando Alves notes that most modern accounts of her are based on "the writings of the illustrious Englishwoman," i.e. Maria Graham (Lacombe 349).

small fort and town, which the troops were to attack while the brigs fired on the fort. The passage from Bahia to this point is usually of six or seven hours at most, allowing for a contrary wind; but these vessels were two days in reaching it, by which time the Brazilians had thrown up heaps of sand; behind which they lay concealed, and deliberately fired on the Lusitanians as they passed, and committed great slaughter, without the loss of a man, though they had several wounded. This action, if it may be called so, took place on the 2d of January, 1823, and lasted from noon till sunset.

Meantime the land side of the city had been harassed by continual attacks, and the troops worn out with constant watching; for the Brazilians were continually riding about in the woods, and beating marches, and causing their trumpets to sound to charge in the night, and by the time the enemy could reach the spot they were fled. On the 18th of November, 1822, however, Madeira made a sortie, and was met by the Brazilians at Piraja, between two and three leagues from the city, when a severe action took place, with some loss on both sides, and both claimed the victory; but as the Lusitanians retired to the town, and the Brazilians took up new positions close to the city gates, the advantage must undoubtedly have been on the side of the latter. Meantime the scarcity of fresh provisions was such, that all the foreign merchants who had families, and who could by any means remove, did so. All the country-houses were abandoned, and the people crowded into the town. The heaviest contributions were levied on all natives and foreigners, and the misery of a siege was coming upon the city.

Rio de Janeiro presented a very different spectacle. The inhabitants were decorating their town with triumphal arches for the coronation of their Emperor, who, on the 1st of December, was solemnly crowned in the chapel of the palace, which serves as the cathedral; and it is no exaggeration to say, that the whole of southern Brazil presented one scene of joy.

The ministers, no less than the monarch, were beloved. The finances began to assume a flourishing aspect: large subscriptions flowed in from all quarters for the equipment of a fleet; and an invitation had been sent to Lord Cochrane to command it. The Emperor had accepted the most moderate income that ever crowned head was contented withal,* in order to spare his people. He visited his dock-yards and arsenals himself; attended business of every kind; encouraged im-

---

* Less than twenty thousand pounds sterling a year.

provements in every department, and Brazil had begun to assume a most flourishing aspect. Such was the state of things when I arrived for the second time in Brazil, along with Lord Cochrane, on the 13th of March, 1823.

March 13th, 1823. On board the Col. Allen, at anchor in Rio de Janeiro.—One of the most windy and rainy days that I ever remember seeing in Brazil; so that the beautiful landscape of the harbour is entirely lost to the strangers from Chile, and I cannot get ashore either to provide lodgings for myself and my invalid,† or to assist my friends in any way. When the officer of the visiting boat came on board, the captain of the ship showed him into the cabin, and left him with me. I found he spoke English, and immediately began to enquire of him concerning the news of Rio. And first he mentioned the coronation of the Emperor, and then the war at Bahia; on which I questioned him very closely, on the ground of having formerly visited the place. It appears that last night only His Imperial Majesty's ships Unaõ, (now Piranga,) Nitherohy, and Liberal, with a fleet of transports, had returned from Alagoas, where they had landed reinforcements for General Labatut; whose head-quarters are at Cachoeira, and who is investing the city of Bahia closely.[89] General Madeira has a strong force of Portuguese soldiers, besides 2000 seamen which occasionally do duty ashore, and a considerable naval force.* But it appears, that the seamen are on the point of mutining for want of pay. Having told me so much, the officer began to question me in my turn,—Did I come from Chile? Did I know Lord Cochrane? was he coming to Rio? for all eyes were turned towards him. When he found that His Lordship was actually on board, he flew to his cabin door, and entreated to kiss his hands; then snatched his hat, and calling to the captain to do as he would, and anchor where he pleased without ceremony, jumped over the side to be the first, if possi-

* Don Joam Sesto, 80 guns.—Constituiçam, 56.—Corvette, 10 de Fevréiro, 29.—Active, 22.—Calypso, 22.—Regeneraçaõ, 22.—A store-ship, 28.—Brig Audaz, 18.—Promptidaõ, 16.—Smack Emilia, 8.—Conceiçam, 8. *Armed Merchant Vessels.*—San Domingo, 20 guns.—Restauraçam, 24.—San Gualter, 26.—Bisarra, 18.

† My cousin Mr. Glennie invalided, from the Doris, having broken a blood-vessel.

89. A general in Napoleon Bonaparte's army, Pierre Labatut later became a commander for the Brazilian army in Bahia, fighting against Royalist forces, and for a short period served with Simón Bolívar (Vale, *Independence* 10-11; Lacombe 303-04).

ble, to convey to the Emperor the joyful intelligence. Nearly the same scene was acted over when Perez, the port-captain, came on board; in a few minutes Captain Garçaõ of the Liberal [having heard from Perry who was on board] came to pay his respects, and shortly afterwards Captain Taylor of the Nitherohy, from whom we learned something more of the state of His Imperial Majesty's fleet. [Taylor of Portsmouth was a lieutenant in the British navy and being Lieutenant of the Doris, in full pay and in employment, he left his ship to enter the Brazilian services some time before our arrival, having made a bargain with the Emperor to make good to him the worth of his English commission for life. He is exceedingly cunning but not truly clever, very active and pretty well trained to service. He is mean, and jealous of all superior talent or character. November eighteenth he married into a rich and influential family in Brazil but can no longer serve, having been claimed by England as a deserter.] The Pedro Primeiro, formerly the Martim Freitas, had been left by the King in want of thorough repair; this she has had, and came out of dock yesterday; she is said to sail well. The Caroline is a fine frigate, but not commissioned, for want of men. The Unaõ is a very fine ship, wants copper, and is commanded by Captain Jewitt. The Nitherohy is a corvette, well found, and in good repair, but a heavy sailor; and the Maria da Gloria, a fine corvette, is commanded by a French officer, Captain Beaurepair. [1824 found her at Bahia with the Constituicaõ o morte as prisoner.] The great difficulty the navy here has to dread is the want of men.* Portuguese sailors are worse than none; few Brazilians are sailors at all, and French, English, and Americans are very scarce. The Emperor is fond of the navy, and very active in looking into every department. He is often in the dock-yards by daylight, and the Empress generally accompanies him.

Their Majesties appear by all accounts to be highly popular. Their youth, their spirit, the singular situation in which they are placed, are

---

* The pay of seamen is but scanty. The advertisement of February for seamen to man the Pedro Primeiro is as follows:—To able-bodied seamen 8 mil. bounty; 4 mil. 800 rees to ordinary seamen. Monthly pay, 8 mil. to able-bodied seamen, 6 mil. 500 rees to ordinary, 4 mil. 800 rees to others, and 3 mil. to landsmen.—This very day, 13th of March, the able seamen's monthly pay was raised to 10 mil.; that of ordinaries to 8 mil.

Shortly afterwards a farther advance was made, and petty officers received extra pay, which they had not hitherto done. The bounty was also increased.

The pay in Bellard's foreign regiment, 8 mil. bounty, 80 rees per day, 40 rees stranger money, (both together 6d. sterling,) 24 oz. bread, 1 lb. meat, and clothing.

all interesting. It is seldom that a hereditary prince, ventures to stand forth in the cause of freedom or independence; and a son of the house of Braganza, and a daughter of that of Austria, leading the way to the independence of this great empire, cannot but excite the love as well as the admiration of their fortunate subjects.[90]

The weather cleared up in the afternoon, and I went ashore to see if I could find any of my old friends, or hear any news; but all the English were gone to their country-houses, and the opera, the proper place for gossip, is shut, because it is Lent; so I returned to the brig, and found Lord Cochrane ready to go ashore to wait on the Emperor, who had come in from San Cristovaõ to meet him at the palace in town. [I believe all the ministers were present; I know José Bonifacio {de Andrada e Silva} was.] His Lordship and Captain Crosbie, who went with him, did not return till late, but then well pleased with their reception.[91]

March 14th.—Another day of such heavy rain, that I have no chance of landing my invalid. Mr. May came on board, and told me I might have Sir T. Hardy's house for a few days, till I can get one for myself. He also gives us good accounts of the government, its finances, etc.

An embargo has been laid on all vessels to-day, to prevent the news of Lord Cochrane's arrival from reaching Bahia.

15th.—I went early ashore to prepare for leaving the brig. I observed two of the arches, under which the Emperor had passed on the day of coronation, designed in extremely good taste, and well executed. They are of course only temporary. Some more solid works have been executed, since I last saw Rio; new fountains opened, aqueducts repaired, all the forts and other public works visibly improved, and the streets new paved. There is besides every where an air of business. I carried Glennie ashore in the afternoon, and was foolish enough to feel very sorry to leave my fellow-passengers, and still more foolish to

---

90. The Braganza dynasty ruled Portugal from 1640 to 1910, and after Brazil declared its independence in 1822, the dynasty ruled Brazil as well until the country became a republic in 1889. Maria Leopoldina, daughter of Francis I of Austria and his second wife, Maria Teresa of Naples, was of the Hapsburg dynasty. Neill Macaulay discusses the dramatic contrasts between the Braganza and Hapsburg families in his *Dom Pedro: The Struggle for Liberty in Brazil and Portugal, 1798-1834* (1986).

91. Thomas Sackville Crosbie (1793-?), Lieutenant in the Royal Navy, followed Cochrane first into the Chilean and then the Brazilian navy (Vale, *Frigate* 190).

Figure 14. Convicts carrying Water at Rio de Janeiro. Courtesy of The Catholic University of America, Oliveira Lima Library, Washington, D.C.

be vexed at the perfect indifference with which they saw me go: both perhaps natural enough. I, am once more without any one to lean to, and alone in the world with my melancholy charge; they, have business and pleasure before them.

It was a fine evening, and the little voyage in the boat to Botafogo seemed to do Glennie good; but we had the mortification to find that neither the provisions I had bought in the town had arrived, nor the servant one of my friends had promised to procure me. So we were alone and supperless,—but, thank God, not helpless. I have learned so much in my wanderings as not to be dependent; and so, after a time, I had from the huckster's shop in the neighbourhood a tolerable *tea* to give my invalid, and sent him to bed in pretty good spirits, and took time afterwards to be pretty miserable myself.

March 20th.—These past days I have employed in looking about for a house, and have succeeded, in receiving and returning the visits of my old acquaintance, and in being very unwell.

I hear there is nothing yet settled about Lord Cochrane's command. The world says that he was asked to serve under two Portuguese admirals and for Portuguese pay. Of course, these are terms he could

Figure 15. Corcovada, from Botafogo. Courtesy of The Catholic University of America, Oliveira Lima Library, Washington, D.C.

never accept. I have not seen him, so am not sure about this. I suppose, however, it is true; or he would not still be living on board that dirty little brig in which we arrived. [Then when they granted him and the officers brought with him equal pay to Chile they wanted to make dollars 800 reis.]

21st.—Whatever difficulties were in the way of Lord Cochrane's command, they are over. I have a note from him announcing that he hoists his flag at four o'clock this afternoon, on board the Pedro Primeiro.*

22d.—Captain Bourchier of His Majesty's ship Beaver kindly lent me his boat to-day, to convey me with my cousin and my goods to my cottage on the Gloria hill, close to Mr. May's, and not very far from the house the government has given as a temporary residence to Lord Cochrane. It is pleasant to me on many accounts: it is cool, and there is a shady walk for the sick. It is almost surrounded by the sea, which breaks against the wall; and not being near any road, we shall be perfectly quiet here.

Friday, 28th.—This has been a busy week, both to me and to my friends, who are hurrying every thing to get to sea as quickly as possible; as it is of the utmost consequence to free Bahia of the enemy.

Saturday, 29th.—His Majesty's ship Tartar, Captain Brown, arrived to-day from England, bringing no good news of any kind. In the first place, Lord Cochrane suffers extreme distress on learning that Lady Cochrane and her infant daughter are on their way to Chile, so that they will have to perform the rough passage round Cape Horn twice before he sees them;—and in the next, Captain Brown gives a most formidable account of a Portuguese fleet bound for Bahia, which he met on this side of the line. I trust he is mistaken in the last, and I try to comfort Lord Cochrane as to the first piece of intelligence, by suggestions, of the probability, if not certainty, that the ship Lady Cochrane will sail in, must touch in this port; however, his natural anxiety is not to be overcome.

Monday, March 31st.—Yesterday the Pedro Primeiro dropped down the harbour, as far as Boa Viage, and to-day I went with Lord Cochrane on board of her. We found that the Emperor and Empress had been on board at daylight. On some of the Portuguese officers complaining that the English sailors had been drunk the day before, the Empress said, "Oh, 'tis the custom of the North, where brave men come from. The sailors are under my protection; I spread my mantle over them." The Pedro Primeiro is a fine two-decker, without a poop. She has a most

---

* Much was said among the English as well as Brazilians of His Lordship's high terms. I have reason to think (not from his information) that his pay and that of the English officers is only equal to that of England, rank for rank.

beautiful gun-deck [Crosbie exercising great guns]; but I could not see her to advantage, as she was still taking in stores, and receiving men. Her cabins are beautifully fitted up with handsome wood and green morocco cushions, etc.; and I am told the Emperor takes great pride in her. Captain Crosbie commands her; and three lieutenants who came with us from Chile are appointed to her.

April 1st.—I had expected the Admiral to breakfast with me; but, to my great disappointment, I saw the ship get under weigh, and sail. I afterwards learned that the Emperor and Empress were on board, and accompanied him out of the harbour as far as the light-house, so that he could not leave them. The morning was dull and grey when the Pedro Primeiro, the Maria da Gloria, the Unaõ, and the Liberal got under weigh; but just as the little squadron came abreast of Santa Cruz, and the fort began to salute, the sun broke from behind a cloud, and a bright yellow flood of light descended behind the ships to the sea, where they seemed to swim in a sea of glory; and that was the last sight I had of my kind friend.

10th.—Nothing of any note or variety has taken place during these ten days. Glennie is gaining ground: I write and read, and attend to him. The Nitherohy sails to-morrow to join Lord Cochrane off Bahia, with three mortars on board, two 10, and one 13-inch. I find, with surprise, that the cartridges are still made up here in canvass, not flannel; and I fear that the ships are not so well found as I wish them: great part of the canvass and cordage have been seventeen years in store, and, I should fear, partly rotten. But all this is nothing to the evil attending the having Portuguese among the crews. 'Tis not natural they should fight against their countrymen.

I have had the pleasure of reading Peveril of the Peak within these few days.[92] 'Tis a sort of historical portrait, like Kenilworth, where the Duke of Buckingham, he who

> In one revolving moon
> Was hero, fiddler, statesman, and buffoon,[93]

---

92. An 1822 novel by Sir Walter Scott (1771-1832), set during the Civil War; Graham clearly has managed to obtain this relatively recent novel in Brazil or perhaps in Chile. Charles II, King of Great Britain and Ireland (1630-1685; reigned 1660-85), was restored to the throne in 1660 after years in exile.
93. Graham slightly misquotes John Dryden's (1631-1700) *Absalom and Achitophel*, I: 545-50; in place of her "hero," the original reads "chemist."

is the principal figure: Charles II. and the rest of the court serve for the black boy and parrot in costume; while the story of Peveril is nothing more than the carved-work frieze of the very pleasant apartment he has been placed in.

14th.—The Fly sloop of war, and the packet from England, came in and brought the news of the war between France and Spain. This news is, of course, interesting here, as Portugal is considered to be implicated in the disputes in Europe; and then, the part England may take, and how that may affect this country, is a subject of anxious speculation. The more domestic news is not quite agreeable. The Imperial General Lecor, in the south, has suffered some loss in an action with the Portuguese: however, it is not considerable enough to give any serious uneasiness. The same vessel that brought the news from Lecor, also gives intelligence that the head of the Buenos Ayrian government, Rodriguez, having taken the field against some Indian tribes, who have lately committed great ravages in his territories, an attempt was made by one of the ex-chiefs to subvert his government; happily, without success. I say happily, because I am convinced that every week and month passed without change, is of infinite consequence both to the present and future wellbeing of the Spanish colonies. While they had still to struggle for their independence, while they had to amend the abuses of their old government, frequent changes were unavoidable, but natural; but now that they are independent, and that they have constitutions, which, if not perfect, contain the principles of freedom and greatness, those principles should have time and peace to grow, and to suit themselves to the genius of the people.

15th.—Glennie has been gaining so much strength lately, that he has determined on joining the Commodore at Bahia; and this day he left me, to sail in His Majesty's ship Beaver.

After having had him to attend to for six months, and being used to constant intercourse with an intelligent inmate, I feel so very lonely, that I believe I must leave off some of my sedentary habits, and visit a little among my neighbours.

25th.—A French brig of war came in to-day from Bahia. We learn that the ships seen by the Tartar were only a frigate, with a convoy of transports, on board of which was a reinforcement for Madeira of 1500 men. They will but increase the distress of the garrison, which is represented as very great, as they have brought no provisions.

28th.—I spent the day with Miss Hayne, and accompanied her in the evening to compliment Dona Ana, the wife of Senhor Luis Jose de Carvalho e Melo, on her birth-day.[94] The family were at their country-house at Botafogo; and a most excellent house it is, very handsomely built and richly furnished. The walls are decorated with French papers in compartments, with gold mouldings, and every thing corresponds. But the best decoration, was this night, the presence of a number of the handsomest women I have seen in Brazil, most of them sisters, or cousins, or nieces of the lady of the house, whose mother, the Baronesa de Campos, may boast of one of the finest families in the world. The daughter of the house, Dona Carlota, is distinguished here by talent and cultivation beyond her fellows. She speaks and writes French well, and has made no small progress in English. She knows the literature of her own country, draws correctly, sings with taste, and dances gracefully. Several of her cousins and aunts speak French fluently; so that I had the pleasure of conversing freely with them, and received a good deal of information on subjects that only women attend to. Soon after all the company was assembled, the ladies sitting all together in a formal circle, the gentlemen walking about generally in other rooms, the ceremony of tea-drinking commenced, and was conducted pretty much as in England; the servants handing round tea, coffee, and cakes, on broad silver salvers. But we all sat and took our refreshments at leisure, instead of standing with cups in our hands, and elbowing our way through crowds of persons, who all look as if they were bound on some particular business, and could scarcely afford time to recognise their passing acquaintance. We then adjourned to the music-room, where the music-master* attended to accompany the ladies, many of whom sang extremely well; but when it came to Dona Rosa's turn, I was ready to exclaim with Comus—

> Can any mortal mixture of earth's mould
> Breathe such divine enchanting ravishment?[95]

* This man is brother to the instructor of Catalani.

---

94. This influential family included Luís José de Carvalho e Melo, a prominent politician; his mother Dona Ana Francisca Macel da Costa, widow of Brás Cameiro Leão, and baronesa de São Salvador dos Campos dos Goitacazes; and his sister Dona Carlota Carvalho e Melo. Graham became closest with Carlota, later the wife of Gustavo Adolfo de Melo Matos (Lacombe 270).

95. These lines are spoken by Comus in response to the Lady's song in Milton's masque *Comus*.

The music ended, and who was not sorry at its conclusion? the dancing commenced, and then those who like myself were not dancers sat by to gossip. An Englishman who has been in this country many years, seeing me full of admiration of the beautiful and gay creatures before me, began to give me such a picture of the private morals in Brazil, as was beginning to darken their countenances and to dim their eyes, when luckily he went a step too far, and offered to wager, (the true English way of affirming,) that there were in that room not less than ten ladies, each provided with her note to slip into the hand of her gallant, and that the married and unmarried were alike; and referred me to my friend M—, who has long been here, and knows the people well. He looked slowly round the room, and I began to fear,—but he said, "No, not here; though I do not deny that such things are done in Rio. But, Mrs. G., do not you know, as well as I, that in all great cities, in your country and in mine as well as in this, a certain portion of every class of society is less moral than the rest? In some countries immorality is more refined indeed; and when manners lose their grossness, they are stripped apparently of half their vice. But suppose the fact, that women, even the unmarried, are less pure here than in Europe, remember that with us, besides the mother, there is the nurse of the family, or the governess, or even the waiting-maid of every young woman, who is supposed to be well brought up, and of good character and morals. These are all checks on conduct, and form a guardianship only inferior to a mother's. But here the servants are *slaves;* therefore naturally the enemies of their masters, and ready and willing to deceive them, by assisting in the corruption of their families." Here then is another curse of slavery; and this view of the subject has opened my eyes on many points, on which I have hitherto been wondering ignorantly.

There were several very pleasant French naval officers here tonight, and a few, very few English. I conversed with some sensible and well-bred Brazilians, so that I was scarcely aware of the lateness of the hour, when I left my younger friends dancing at midnight.

While at the ball, the tragic story of two lovely girls was told me. When mere children, they had accompanied their mother to some gala, and on returning at night, just as the mother advanced from the carriage, she was shot from the veranda of her own house. All search for the murderer was vain: but conjecture points to two possible causes of the crime. One, the jealousy of a woman, who it seems had been injured, and who hoped to succeed her rival as the wife of the man she loved; but he has not married again. Another conjecture is, that she was acquainted with some political secrets, and that fear caused her death. However it was, the girls have ever since lived with their grandmother, who cannot sleep if they are not both in the room with her. The family attachments here are quite beautiful; they are as close and as intimate as those of clanship in Scotland: but they have their inconveniences, in the constant intermarriages between near relations, as uncles with their nieces, aunts with their nephews, etc.; so that marriages, instead of widening connections, diffusing property, and producing more general relations in the country, seems to narrow all these, to hoard wealth, and to withdraw all the affections into too close and selfish a circle.

30th.—I went early to town, and found that the English packet had arrived. She fell in with Lord Cochrane's squadron near Bahia, so that His Lordship must be there long ere this time; she brings reports that the royalist party are becoming too strong for the Cortes at Lisbon.

I spent the day with Madame do Rio Seco. Her house is really a magnificent one; it has its ball-room, and its music-room, its grotto and fountains, besides extremely handsome apartments of every kind, both for family and public use, with rather more china and French clocks than we should think of displaying, but which do not assort ill with the silken hangings and gilt mouldings of the rooms.

The dinner was small, as we were only three persons, but excellently dressed. Soup of wild-fowl, a variety of small birds, and sweetmeats of the country, were rarities to me: the rest of the dinner might have been English or French; it was served in plate. I heard a great many anecdotes to-day of a great many persons of all degrees, for which M. Dutems would have given any price to enrich the *souvenirs* of the *voyageur qui se repose* withal, but which I will not write, because I think it neither honest nor womanly to take the protection of the laws and the feelings of a foreign country, and record the foibles of its inhabitants so as to give others the opportunity of laughing at them.[96] We know well enough the weak parts of human nature: if they are treated tenderly, they may mend. Vice indeed may require the lash, but weakness and folly should meet with indulgence. In a society rising like this, I am persuaded that men may be flattered into virtue. If a general calls his

---

96. Louis Dutens (1730-1812), French tutor, diplomat and author who lived in England; his *Mémoires d'un voyageur qui se repose* included anecdotes exposing the British and French upper classes.

soldiers brave before the battle, it becomes a point of honour to prove so. And were it in my power, I had rather persuade the Brazilians that they have every virtue under heaven, than make them so familiar with the least of their failings, as to lose the shame of it.

May 1st.—I have this day seen the Val Longo; it is the slave-market of Rio. Almost every house in this very long street is a depôt for slaves. On passing by the doors this evening, I saw in most of them long benches placed near the walls, on which rows of young creatures were sitting, their heads shaved, their bodies emaciated, and the marks of recent itch upon their skins. In some places the poor creatures were lying on mats, evidently too sick to sit up. At one house the half-doors were shut, and a group of boys and girls, apparently not above fifteen years old, and some much under, were leaning over the hatches, and gazing into the street with wondering faces. They were evidently quite new negroes. As I approached them, it appears that something about me attracted their attention; they touched one another, to be sure that all saw me, and then chattered in their own African dialect with great eagerness. I went and stood near them, and though certainly more disposed to weep, I forced myself to smile to them, and look cheerfully, and kissed my hand to them, with all which they seemed delighted, and jumped about and danced, as if returning my civilities. Poor things! I would not, if I could, shorten their moments of glee, by awakening them to a sense of the sad things of slavery; but, if I could, I would appeal to their masters, to those who buy, and to those who sell, and implore them to think of the evils slavery brings, not only to the negroes but to themselves, not only to themselves but to their families and their posterity.

After all, slaves are the worst and most expensive servants; and one proof of it is this, I think. The small patch that each is allowed to cultivate for his own use on many estates generally yields at least twice as much in proportion as the land of the master, though fewer hours of labour are bestowed upon it.* I have hitherto endeavoured, without success, to procure a correct statement of the number of slaves im-

---

* Since I returned to England, I have seen the account of the proceedings of Joshua Steele in Barbadoes [Absentee owner of a large plantation in Barbados, Steele attempted to improve inhumane conditions when he visited in 1780 and, horrified at the working conditions of his slaves, instituted reforms (*ODNB* 52:357)—*Eds*.]. I need not add one word on this part of the subject; but I present the reader with the two following statements of custom-house entries at Rio for the years 1821 and 1822.

ported into all Brazil. I fear, indeed, it will be hardly possible for me to do so, on account of the distance of some of the ports; but I will not rest till I procure at least a statement of the number entered at the custom-house here during the last two years. The number of ships from Africa that I see constantly entering the harbour, and the multitudes that throng the slave-houses in this street, convince me that the importation must be very great. The ordinary proportion of deaths on the passage is, I am told, about one in five.

May 3d.—Early this morning the French naval captain, La Susse, called on me to take me in his boat to town, for the purpose of going to Senhor Luis Jose's house in the Rua do Ouvidor, to see the Emperor go in state to the opening of the Constituent and Legislative Assembly. All the great officers of state, all the gentlemen of the household, most of the nobility, and several regiments accompanied him. First marched the soldiers, then the carriages of the nobility and other persons having the *entrée*, nobody driving more than a pair, such being the express order of the Emperor, in order that the rich might not mortify the poor; then the royal carriages, containing the household, the ladies of honour, and the young Princess Dona Maria da Gloria; the Emperor and Empress followed in a state-coach with eight mules. The crown was on the front seat. The Emperor wore the great cape of state, of yellow feathers, over his green robes. The Empress, much wrapped up on account of a recent indisposition, was seated by him, and the procession was closed by more troops.

The carriages displayed to-day would form a curious collection for a museum in London or Paris. Some were the indescribable sort of caleche used here; and in the middle of these was a very gay pea-green and silver chariot, evidently built in Europe, very light, with silver ornaments, silver fellies to the wheels, silver where any kind of metal could be used, and beautiful embossed silver plates on the harness of the mules. Many other gala carriages seemed as if they had been built in the age of Louis XIV. Such things! mounted on horizontal leathern bands, and all other kind of savage hangings; besides paint and gilding, and, by-the-bye, some very handsome silver and silver gilt harnesses. Then there were splendid liveries, and all manner of gaudiness, not without some taste.

The houses were hung with all the damask and satin of every colour that they could supply; and the balconies stored with ladies, whose bright eyes rain influence, dressed in gala dresses, with feathers and diamonds in profusion; and as the royal carriages passed, we waved our handkerchiefs, and scattered flowers on their heads.

When the procession had passed, I found it was expected that we should await its return, which I was well pleased to do. My young friend Dona Carlota improves on acquaintance; and as I begin to venture to speak Portuguese, I am becoming intimate with the elder part of the family. I was taken into the study, and for the first time saw a Brazilian private gentleman's library. As he is a judge, of course the greater part is law; but there are history and general literature, chiefly French, and some English books. I was introduced to several Portuguese authors; and Dona Carlota, who reads remarkably well, did me the favour to read some of Diniz's fine verses to me, and to lend me his works. We then returned to our station at the window, and saw the procession return in the order in which it came, when our pleasant party dispersed.

Yesterday, the assembly having finished its preliminary sittings, sent a deputation, headed by Jose Bonifacio, to His Imperial Majesty, to entreat that he would honour the assembly with his presence at their first sitting as a legislative body, and he was pleased to name half past eleven o'clock to-day for that purpose.*

This morning, therefore, the people of Rio de Janeiro had strewed the way with evergreens, sweet herbs, and flowers, from the bridge without the town by the street of St. Peter's, the Campo de Santa Anna, now Praça da Acclamaçaõ, the Theatre Square, and the streets Do Ouvidor and Direita to the palace; troops lined the whole space; the houses were decorated, and the bands of the different regiments relieved each other as their Imperial Majesties passed. I observe the Brazilians never say *the* Emperor, but *our* Emperor, *our* Empress; and seldom name either, without some epithet of affection.

In the House of Assembly, a throne had been prepared for the Emperor, and on his right hand a tribune for the Empress, the Princess, and their ladies. As soon as it was known that the Imperial party had arrived, a deputation from the assembly went to the door of the house to meet them, and conducted the Emperor, with his crown on his

---

* The crown is of a purple velvet, enriched with diamonds. There was some mistake or misunderstanding about the fact of wearing the crown at the opening of the assembly. As the crown is only a ceremonial badge of dignity, it should have been worn during the ceremony; but owing to the mistake alluded to, it was not.

head,* to the throne; the Empress, Princess, and ladies, being at the same time placed in the tribune.

The Emperor having deposited the crown and sceptre with the proper officer, and received the oaths of several of the deputies, spoke as follows; and it was remarked, that so far from the speech having the air of a thing read from a paper or studied, that it was spoken as freely as if it was the spontaneous effusion of the moment, and excited a feeling as free in his favour.

> This is the greatest day that Brazil has ever seen; a day on which, for the first time, it may show that it is an empire, and a free empire. How great is my delight, to behold real representatives from almost every one of its provinces, consulting together on its true interests, and on these founding a just and liberal constitution to gov-

* Various ordinances of the 3d and 19th June and the 3d of August, 1822, and of the 20th and 22d February, 1823, had been published for the assembling or regulating the election of deputies from the provinces of Brazil, to form a constituent assembly. Early in April, 1823, the greater number of those who could be collected in the present state of the country had arrived in the capital. On the 14th of that month, the Emperor fixed their first meeting for the 17th. Accordingly on the 17th of April, 1823, the deputies, in number 52, entered their house of assembly at nine o'clock in the morning, and proceeded to elect a temporary president and secretary, when the Right Reverend Don Jose Caetano da Silva Coutinho, bishop and grand chaplain, was elected president, and Manoel Jose de Sousa França secretary.

The first act was to name two committees; one of five members, to hold a scrutiny on the election of the deputies generally; and the other of three, to examine those of the five. This necessary business, and some consequent discussion, occupied the whole of the first and greater part of the second session; towards the end of the latter, the form of the oath to be administered to the members, was decided:—

> I swear to fulfil, faithfully and truly, the obligations of deputy to the General Constituent and Legislative Assembly of Brazil, convoked in order to frame a political constitution for the empire of Brazil, and to make indispensable and urgent reforms. Maintaining always the Roman Catholic and Apostolic religion, and the integrity and independence of the empire; without admitting any other nation whatever to any bond of union or federation which might oppose that independence. Maintaining also the constitutional empire, and the dynasty of the Lord Don Peter, our first Emperor, and his issue. [cont.]

ern them! We ought long since to have enjoyed a national representation. But either the nation did not in time perceive its real interests, or, perceiving them, was unable to declare them, on account of the forces and ascendancy of the Portuguese party; which, perceiving clearly to what a degree of weakness, littleness, and poverty, Portugal was reduced, and to how low a state it had fallen, would never consent (notwithstanding their proclamation of liberty, fearing a separation,) that the people of Brazil should enjoy a representation equal to what they themselves then possessed. They had miscalculated their plans for conquest, and from that miscalculation arises our good fortune.

Brazil, which for upwards of three hundred years had borne the degrading name of a colony, and had suffered all the evils arising from the destructive system then pursued, exulted with pleasure when my Lord Don John VI., King of Portugal and Algarve, my august father, raised it to the dignity of a kingdom, by his decree of the 16th of December, 1815; but Portugal burned with rage, and trembled with fear. The delight which the inhabitants of this vast continent displayed on the occasion was unbounded; but the politic measure was not followed up, as it ought to have been, by

---

[* cont.]The third session was occupied in regulating the forms of the assembly. The throne to be placed at one end of the hall; on the first step on the right-hand side, the President shall have his chair when the Emperor presides, otherwise the chair to be in front of the throne, with a small table, separate from the table of the members, and on it the Gospel, a copy of the constitution, and a list of the members. When the Emperor opens the assembly, his great officers may accompany him, and the ministers may sit on his right; proper places are appointed for ambassadors, and a gallery is open to strangers. Some other forms as to the reception of the Emperor, or a regent, or a minister commissioned by him, were also settled; and then the 1st of May was fixed on for the whole body of the members to go to the chapel royal, and after hearing the mass of the Holy Ghost, to take their oaths. The 2d was appointed for a deputation to wait on the Emperor, and inform him that they were ready to proceed on the 3d, and with his assistance to open the important business on which they had met.

another, that is, by the convocation of an assembly to organise the new kingdom.

Brazil, always frank in her mode of proceeding, and mortified at having borne the yoke of iron so long, both before and after that measure echoed the cry for the constitution of Portugal, immediately on the proclamation of liberty in Portugal; expecting that after this proof of confidence given to her pseudo brethren, they would assist her to deliver herself from the vipers that were consuming her entrails, and little thinking she should be deceived.

The Brazilians, who truly loved their country, never intended, however, to subject themselves to a constitution in which all had not a voice, and whose views were to convert them at once from free men into vile slaves. Nevertheless, the obstacles which, before the 26th April, 1821, opposed the liberties of Brazil, and which continued to exist, being maintained by the European troops, caused the people, fearing that they should never enjoy a representative assembly of their own, even for the very love of liberty, to follow the infamous Cortes of Portugal, and they even made the sacrifice of submitting to be insulted by the demagogue party which predominated in this hemisphere.

Even this availed not. We were so oppressed by the European forces, that I was obliged to send them to the opposite shore of the Rio; to blockade them; to force them to embark and pass the bar, in order to save the honour of Brazil, and to procure that liberty which we desire and ought to enjoy: but in vain shall we labour to procure it, if we permit to exist among us a party inimical to our true cause.

Scarcely were we well free from these enemies, when in a few days arrived another expedition, which Lisbon had sent for our protection; but I took upon myself to protect this empire, and I refused to receive it. Pernambuco did the same. And Bahia, which was the first place to unite with Portugal, as a reward for her good faith, and because she perceived too late the track she ought to have followed, now suffers under a cruel war for those Vandals; and her chief city, occupied only by them, is on the point of being rased, for they cannot maintain themselves there.

Such is the freedom Portugal sought to bestow on Brazil: it was to be converted into slavery for us; and would have ruined us totally if we had continued to execute her commands; which we must have done, but for the heroic remonstrances conveyed by petitions, first from the junta of government of St. Paul's, then from the camara of this capital, and afterwards from all the other juntas of government and camaras, imploring me to remain here. It appeared to me that Brazil would be ruined, if I did not attend to the petitions; and I did attend to them. I know that this was my duty, though at the risk of my life; but as it was in defence of this empire, it was ready, as it is now, and ever, when it shall be requisite.

I had scarcely pronounced the words, *As it is for the good of all, and the general happiness of the nation, tell the people that I remain,* recommending to them at the same time *union* and *tranquillity,* when I began to take measures to put ourselves in a state to meet the attacks of our enemies, then concealed, since unmasked; one part among ourselves, the rest in the Portuguese democratic Cortes; providing for all the departments, especially those of the treasury and foreign affairs, by such means as prudence dictated, and which I shall not mention here, because they will be laid before you in proper time by the different officers of state.

The public treasury was in the very worst state, as the receipts had been much reduced; and, principally, because till within four or five months they had been solely those of this province. On this account it was not possible to raise money for all that was necessary, as we had already too little to pay the public creditors, or those employed in effective service, and to maintain my household, which cost one-fourth of that of the King, my august father. His disbursements exceeded four millions; mine did not amount to one. But although the diminution was so considerable, I could not be satisfied when I found that my expenses were so disproportioned to the reduced receipts of the treasury; and therefore I resolved to live as a private man, receiving only 110,000 milrees for the whole expenses of my household, excepting the allowance of the Empress, my much-beloved and valued wife, which was assigned to her by her marriage contract.

Not satisfied with these small savings in my household with which I commenced, I examined into every department, as was my duty, in order to regulate its expenditure, and to check its abuses. Yet, still the revenue did not suffice; but by changing some individuals not well affected to the cause of the empire, but only to that of the infamous Portuguese party, and who were continually betraying us, for others who loved Brazil with all their hearts,—some from birth and principle, others from the intimate conviction that the cause is that of reason,—I have caused, and I say it with pride, the bank, which was on the point of losing its credit, and threatened bankruptcy every moment,—as on the day of the departure of my august father, Don John VI., there only remained the sum of two hundred contos in money,—to discount its bills, to re-establish its credit so completely, that no one can imagine that it can ever fall again into the wretched state to which it had been reduced. The public treasury, which, on account of the extraordinary expenses which should have been borne in common by all the provinces, but which fell solely upon this, was totally exhausted, and without credit, has gained such credit, that it is already known in Europe; and so much cash, that the greater part of the creditors, and they were not few, or for trifling sums, have been so far satisfied, as that their houses have not suffered; that the public servants have no arrears due any more than the military on actual service; that the other provinces that have adhered to the holy cause,—not by force, but from conviction, for I love just liberty,—have been furnished for their defence with warlike stores, great part of which are newly purchased, besides those already in the arsenals; and, moreover, they have been assisted with money, because their funds did not cover their necessary expenses.

In a word, the province now yields from eleven to twelve millions; its produce, before the departure of my august father, having been at most from six to seven.

Among the extraordinary expenses are, the freights of the ships on board of which the different expeditions sent back to Lisbon were embarked; the purchase of several vessels; the repair of others; pay to civil and military officers who have arrived here on service, and to those expelled from the provinces for their private sufferings in the tumults there raised.

The expenditure has certainly been great: but hitherto, nevertheless, there remain untouched, the gratuitous contributions; the sequestrated property of the absentees on account of political opinions; the loan of 400,000 milrees for the purchase of ships of war indispensably necessary for the defence of the empire, and which exists entire; and the exchequer of the administration of diamonds.

In every department there was an urgent necessity for reform; but in this of finance still more, because it is the chief spring of the state.

The army had neither arms, men, nor discipline: with regard to arms, it is now perfectly ready; the men are increasing daily in proportion to the population; and in discipline it will soon be perfect, being already in obedience exemplary. I have twice sent assistance to Bahia: first 240 men, then 735, forming a battalion called the Emperor's Battalion; which in eight days was chosen, prepared, and sailed.

Besides these, a foreign regiment has been raised, and a battalion of artillery of freed men, which will shortly be completed.

In the military arsenal they have wrought diligently to prepare every thing necessary for the defence of the different provinces; and all, *from Paraiba of the North to Montevideo,* have received the assistance they have requested.

The walls of the fortifications of this city were totally ruined: they are now repaired; and important works necessary in the arsenal itself have been finished.

As to military works, the walls of all the fortresses have been repaired, and some entirely new-constructed. These are formed in the different points fittest to oppose any enemy's force approaching by sea; and in the defiles of the hills, to oppose the approach of an enemy already landed, (which would not be easy,) entrenchments, forts, redoubts, abatis, and batteries. The barracks of the Carioca are built, and the other barracks are prepared. That in the Praça da Acclamaçaõ is almost finished, and that ordered for the grenadiers will shortly be so.

The fleet consisted only of the frigate Piranga, then called the Union, not fitted; the corvette Liberal, only a hull; and of a few other small and insignificant vessels. Now we have the ship of the line, Pedro Primeiro; the frigates Piranga, Carolina, and Netherohy; the corvettes Maria da Gloria and Liberal, ready; a corvette, in Alagoas, which will soon be ready, named the Massaió: of the brigs of war, Guarani ready, and the Cacique and Caboclo under repair; besides several ships in ordinary, and various schooners.

I expect six frigates of fifty guns, manned and armed, and completely formed for action, for the purchase of which I have already given orders; and according to the information I have received, they will not cost above thirteen contos of rees.

In the dock-yard, the works are the following:—all the ships now actually employed have been repaired; gun-boats, and others of small size, which I need not name, have been built; and many others, which, altogether, are numerous and important.

I intend this year, in the same place, where for thirteen years back nothing has been done but caulking, rigging, and careening vessels,—swallowing immense sums, which might have been more usefully employed for the nation,—to lay down the keel of a forty-gun frigate; which, if the calculation I have made, the orders I have given, and the measures I have taken do not fail, I hope will be finished this year, or in the middle of the next, and will be called the *Campista*.

As to public works, much has been done. The police office in the Praça da Acclamaçaõ has been re-built: that large square has been drained of the marsh water, and has become an agreeable walk, with paved paths on all sides, and others across, and we are still continuing to embellish it. The greater part of the aqueduct of Carioca and Maracanaõ, have been repaired; besides the numerous bridges of wood and stone which have been renewed, several new ones have been made, and a great extent of roads has been mended.

Besides what I have mentioned, and much more which I have not touched on, the funds for these works, which in April, 1821, owed 60 contos of rees, now is not only out of debt, but possesses upwards of 600,000 crusadoes.

In different departments we have made the following progress. We have greatly increased the national typography; the public gardens have been put in order; the museum repaired, and enriched with minerals and a gallery of good pictures,—some of which were purchased, some were already in the public treasury, and others were my private property, which I have ordered to be placed there.

Every exertion has been made on the Caes da Praça de Commercio, so that it is nearly finished; the streets of the city have been new-paved; and in a very short time this house for the assembly, with all the rest adjoining, were properly fitted for their purpose.

Many works which are of less importance have been undertaken, begun, and finished; but I omit them, that I may not render my speech too long.

I have encouraged the public schools, as far as I could; but this will demand some peculiar provision of the legislature. What has been done is this:—In order to augment the public library I have bought a large collection of choice books; I have augmented the number of schools, and increased the salary of some of the masters, besides licensing innumerable private schools; and, aware of the benefits of the method of mutual instruction, I have opened a Lancasterian school.

I found the college of San Joaquim, which had been designed by its founders for the education of youth, employed as the hospital of the European troops. I caused it to be opened anew, for the purposes originally intended; and having granted to the *Casa de Misericordia*, and the foundling hospital, of which I will speak farther, a lottery for the better maintenance of those useful institutions, I assigned a certain portion of the said lottery to the college of San Joaquim, that it might the better answer the useful end which its worthy founders had in view. It is now full of students.

The first time I visited the foundling hospital, I found (and it seems incredible) seven infants with only two wet-nurses; no beds, no clothing: I called for the register, and found that in the last thirteen years nearly 12,000 children had been received, but scarcely 1000 were forthcoming, the Misericordia not knowing in fact what had become of them. Then by granting the lottery, a house proper for the establishment was built, where there are upwards of thirty beds, almost as many nurses as children, and on the whole, much better management. All these things of which I have now spoken merit your particular attention.—After this province was settled, and important provisions made for the rest, I felt it necessary to call together a council of state; and, therefore, by the degree of the 16th of February of last year, I convoked one, composed of procurators-general, chosen by the people, being desirous that they should have some persons near me to represent them, and who might at the same time advise me, and demand such things as should be conducive to the good of each of the respective provinces. Nor was this the only end and motive for which I called such a council together: I wished particularly that the Brazilians might know my constitutional feelings. How I delighted to govern to the satisfaction of the people, and how much my paternal heart desired (though at that time secretly, because circumstances did not then permit me to manifest such wishes,) that this loyal, grateful, brave, and heroic nation, should be represented in a general constituent and legislative assembly; which, thank God, has been brought about in consequence of the degree of the 3d of June of the last year, at the request of the people conveyed through their camaras, their procurators, and my councillors of state!

It has been very painful to me that, till now, Brazil should not have enjoyed a national representation, and to be forced by circumstances to take upon myself to legislate on some points: but my measures cannot appear to have arisen from ambition to legislate, arrogating to myself the whole power, of which I only could claim a part—for they were taken to save Brazil,—because when some of them were adopted the assembly had not been convoked, and when others were necessary it had not yet met; therefore, as Brazil was totally independent of Portugal, the three powers then existed in fact and by right in the person of the supreme chief of the nation, and much the more as he was its perpetual defender.

It is true that some measures appeared extremely strong; but as the peril was imminent, and the enemies who surrounded us were innumerable (and would to God they were not even now so many), it was necessary they should be proportionate.

I have not spared myself; nor will I ever spare toil, however great, if from it the smallest portion of happiness can be derived to the nation.

When the people of the rich and majestic province of *Minas* were suffering under the iron yoke of their mistaken governors, who disposed of it as they pleased, and obliged the pacific and gentle inhabitants to disobey me, I marched thither, only attended by my servants: I convicted the government and its creatures of the crime they had committed, and of the error in which they seemed desirous of persisting; I pardoned them, because the crime was more an offence against me, than against the nation, as we were then united to Portugal.

When a party of Portuguese and degenerate Brazilians attached to the Cortes of miserable, worn-out Portugal, arose among the brave people of the beautiful and delightful province of St. Paul's, I instantly repaired thither, and entered the province *fearlessly, because I knew the people loved me.* I took the measures that appeared to me to be necessary; and there, before any other place, our independence was declared, in the ever-memorable plain of Piranga.

It was at the country seat of the most faithful, and never-enough praised Amador Bueno de Rebeira, that I was first proclaimed Emperor.

My soul itself was grieved that I could not go to Bahia, as I had intended, but which I did not do on the remonstrance of my privy council, to mingle my blood with that of those warriors who have so bravely fought for their country.

At all hazards, at that of life itself, if necessary, I will maintain the title that the people of this rich and vast empire honoured me with on the 13th of May, of the past year—PERPETUAL DEFENDER OF BRAZIL. That title engaged my heart more, than all the splendour I acquired by their spontaneous and unanimous acclamation of me as Emperor of this desirable empire.

Thanks be to Providence, that we now see the nation represented by such worthy deputies! Would to God it could have been so earlier! But the circumstances preceding the decree of the 3d of June did not permit it; and since that time, the great distance, the want of public spirit in some, and the inconveniences of long journeys, especially in a country so new and extensive as Brazil, have retarded this much-wished and necessary meeting, notwithstanding all my repeated recommendations of speed.

At length the great day for this vast empire has arisen, which will be the grand epocha of its history. *The assembly is met to constitute the nation: what joy—what happiness for us all!*

As CONSTITUTIONAL EMPEROR, and most especially as PERPETUAL DEFENDER of this vast empire, I told the people on the 1st of December, the day when I was crowned and anointed, '*That with my sword I would defend the country, the nation, and the constitution, if it were worthy of Brazil and of me.*' I this day, in your presence, most solemnly ratify this promise, and I trust you will assist me in fulfilling it, by framing a wise, just, and practicable constitution, dictated by reason, not caprice; and having solely in view the general happiness, which can never be great if the constitution be not founded on solid grounds, grounds which the wisdom of ages has shown to be just, in order to give true liberty to the people, and sufficient strength to the executive power. A constitution in which the limits of the three powers shall be well defined, that they may never arrogate rights not their own; but shall be so organised and harmonised, that it shall be impossible for them, even in the lapse of time, to become inimical to each other, but shall every day jointly contribute to the general happiness of the state. In short, a constitution which shall oppose insuperable barriers to despotism, whether royal, aristocratic, or democratic; defeat anarchy; and plant that tree of liberty under whose shadow the honour, tranquillity, and independence of this empire, which will become the admiration of the Old and New World, must grow.

All the constitutions which have modelled themselves upon those of 1791 and 1792, have been shown by experience to be entirely theoretical and metaphysical, and therefore impracticable. Witness those of France, Spain, and Portugal: they have not, as they ought, produced public happiness; but after a licentious freedom, we see that in some countries there has already taken place, and in others there is on the point of doing so, a despotism of one, after that of many; and, by a necessary consequence, the people are reduced to the wretched state of registering and suffering all the horrors of anarchy.

But far from us be such melancholy reflections: they darken the joy and exultation of this happy day. You are not ignorant of them; and I am sure, that firmness in those true constitutional views, which have been sanctioned by experience, will characterise every one of the deputies who compose this illustrious assembly. I trust, that the constitution which you will frame will merit my Imperial assent; that it will be as wise and just as suited to the local situation and to the civilisation of the Brazilian people: also that it may be praised among the nations, so that even our enemies may imitate the sanctity and wisdom of its principles, and at length practise them.

So illustrious and patriotic an assembly will have in view no object but to cause the empire to prosper, and to fill it with happiness: it will wish its Emperor to be respected, not only at home but among foreign nations; and that its *Perpetual Defender* should exactly fulfil his promise of the first of last December, solemnly ratified to-day, in the presence of the nation legally represented.

When the Emperor had done speaking, the bishop of the diocese, acting as president of the assembly, made a short answer of thanks, praise, and promise; after which, the whole of the members, the spectators in the galleries, and the people without doors, cheered His Imperial Majesty enthusiastically, and the procession returned to San Cristovaõ in the order in which it came.

The theatre of course concluded the ceremonies of the day; and my friend, Madame do Rio Seco, having kindly offered me a seat in her box, I went thither, for the first time since my return to Brazil. She was in high spirits, because that day the Emperor had conferred on her husband the order of the Cruzeiro; and therefore she went really in grand gala to the opera. Her diamonds worn that night may be valued at 150,000*l.* sterling, and many splendid jewels remained behind in the strong box. For my part, I had gone to town in my morning dress; therefore I sent to a milliner's, and bought such a plain crape head-dress as the customs of the place warrant, in deep mourning; and wrapping myself in my shawl, accompanied my magnificent friend. The house appeared very splendid, being illuminated and dressed, and the ladies one and all in diamonds and feathers. Some decorations have been added since last year, and an allegorical drop-scene has been painted. The Empress did not come, on account of her recent illness; but the Emperor was there, looking pale, and a little fatigued. He was received with rapturous applause. The members of the assembly were seated one-half on his right, and one-half on his left, in boxes handsomely fitted up for them; and as soon as they had all taken their places, a poem on the occasion was recited by the Prima Donna, in which there were some good points, which called forth great applause. I think it is Gresset who, in one of his odes *Au Roi,* says,

> Le cri d'un peuple heureux est la seule éloquence
> Qui sait parler des rois.[97]

And indeed this night that eloquence was powerful. I cannot conceive a situation more full of interest to both prince and people.

There was nothing in the principal piece played to-night, for it was a clumsy translation of Lodoiska, without the songs.[98] But the after-piece excited much emotion: it was called "The Discovery of Brazil." Cabral and his officers were represented as just landed: they had discovered the natives of the country; and, according to the custom of the Portuguese discoverers, they had set up their white flag, with the red holy cross upon it, whence they had first named the land.[99] At

---

97. Jean-Baptise Gresset (1709-1777), French poet and playwright, *Ode IX Sur La Convalescence du Roi*. Graham may have come across this quotation in Thomas Gray's essay on Gresset, where he quotes precisely the same lines and concludes, "which is very true, and should have been a Hint to himself not to write Odes to the King at all" (Gray 157).

98. A heroic-comedic opera by Maria Luigi Carlo Zenobio Salvatore Cherubini (1760-1842), French composer. It was performed for the first time at the Théâtre Feydeau in Paris in 1791.

99. Pedro Alvarez Cabral, a Portuguese explorer sent by King Manuel I to establish trade relations with India in the wake of Vasco da Gama, sighted

the foot of this emblem they kneeled in worship, and endeavoured to induce the wild Brazilians to join them in their sacred rites. These, on their part, tried to persuade Cabral to reverence the heavenly bodies, and dissension seemed about to trouble the union of the new friends, when by a clumsy enough machine, a little genius came down from above, and leaping from its car, displayed the new Imperial standard, inscribed *Independencia o Morte*. This was totally unexpected in the house, which, for an instant, seemed electrified into silence. I believe I clapped my hands first, but the burst of feeling that came from every part of the house was long ere it subsided. Now I know nothing so overpowering, as that sort of unanimous expression of deep interest, from any large body of men. It overset me; and when I ought to have been waving my handkerchief decorously from the great chamberlain's box, I was hiding my face with it, and weeping heartily. When the house was quiet again, I looked at Don Pedro: he had become very pale, and had drawn a chair close to his own; on the back of which he leaned, and was very grave to the end of the piece, having his hand before his eyes for some time; and, indeed, his quick feelings could not have escaped what affected even strangers.

At the close of the piece there were loud cries of "Viva la Patria!" "Viva o Emperador!" "Viva a Emperatriz!" "Vivaõ os Deputados!" all originating in the body of the house; when Martim Francisco de Andrada stepped to the front of one of the boxes of the Deputies, and cried "Viva o povo leal e fiel do Rio de Janiero!" a cry that was extremely well seconded, especially by the Emperor, and kindly taken by the people; and so this important day ended.

May 6th.—To-day I rode to San Cristovaõ, through a very beautiful country. The palace, which once belonged to a convent, is placed upon a rising ground, and is built rather in the Moresco style, and coloured yellow with white mouldings. It has a beautiful screen, a gateway of Portland stone, and the court is planted with weeping willows; so that a group of great beauty is formed in the bosom of a valley, surrounded by high and picturesque mountains, the chief of which is the Beco do Perroquito.* The view from the palace opens to part of the bay, over an agreeable plain flanked by fertile hills, one of which is crowned by the very handsome barracks that were once a Jesuit estab-

---

* Nearly 2000 feet high.

---

land on April 22, 1500 (although he mistook the continent of Brazil for an island) and is often credited with "discovering" it (Tenenbaum I: 500-1).

lishment. I rode round by the back of the palace to the farm, which appears to be in good order; and the village of the slaves, with its little church, looks more comfortable than I could have believed it possible for a village of slaves to do. The Imperial family now live entirely here, and only go to town on formal business or occasions of state.

May 12th.—I have been too unwell to do any thing; and only write to-day to notice the arrival of the Jupiter frigate, with Lord Amherst on his way to India, and the rumour that he has some official character at this court.

16th.—Lord Amherst and suite went to court in such ceremony as induces people to believe he really has a diplomatic character here. The Alacrity has arrived from Valparaiso, and has brought me some old letters from England that have helped my sickness to depress my spirits. 'Tis after all a sad thing to be alone and sick in a foreign land! The Doris also is arrived from Bahia. She has had no direct communication with Lord Cochrane's little squadron; but it seems, that with his six ships, he keeps the enemy's fleet of fifteen sail in check. The town of Bahia is said to be in a dreadful state for want of provisions. The slaves are daily dying in the streets. Some houses, after appearing shut up for some days, have been opened by the police officers, who have found the masters escaped, and the slaves dead.—Twice a day the gates have been opened to allow the women and children to leave the town. Some of the officers of the Doris had the curiosity to attend on one of these occasions, and saw 500 persons, laden with as much furniture and clothes as in their weak hungry state they could carry, leave the city. The little fresh provision that finds its way into the town is exorbitantly dear. General Madeira has proclaimed martial-law in the place; he has seized some corn and flour out of a neutral ship, and has raised forced loans from all classes, both native and foreign.

The ship has brought two or three newspapers from Bahia. As might be expected, they breathe the most violent and inveterate spirit against the Imperial government, and every body employed by it; calling the Emperor a Turkish despot, a sultan, etc., and José Bonifacio a tyrannic vizier. Lord Cochrane, of course, does not escape; and to all old calumnies against him, they now add that he is a *coward,* for which agreeable compliments they are likely to pay dearly I should think. [This was repeated by the Cabal 1824—at the Rio!!!] The Supplement to the Idade d'Ouro of the 25th of April gives lists of the two squadrons, drawn up for the purpose of inspiring confidence in the Portuguese, under-rating the force of Lord Cochrane's ships, and representing them as so ill manned,—although, according to them, the most oppressive measures were adopted to man them,—as not to be able to face the Portuguese. However, they have thought fit to call in all their vessels from the Funil and other stations where they had their small ships placed, in order to reinforce their fleet.* They have published a circular letter, calling on all officers and crews to exert themselves, promising them the destruction of the Brazilian fleet. And, on the same day, the 24th of April, the Admiral Joaŏ Felix Pereira de Campos, under pretence of indisposition, turns over the command to another officer.

These measures were adopted, in consequence of the news of Lord Cochrane's arrival in Brazil having been conveyed to General Madeira by His Britannic Majesty's ship Tartar, the only vessel that sailed from Rio during the time of the embargo. We are becoming very anxious indeed for news from His Lordship: many rumours are afloat; but as there has been no direct communication from the squadron, they only increase the general anxiety.

May 17th.—Soon after I arrived here, in March, or rather as soon as my patient Glennie left me, I felt that, as a stranger here, and situated as I am, I was peculiarly unprotected, and therefore I spoke to the minister José Bonifacio, telling him my feelings; and saying, that from the amiable character of the Empress, I should wish to be allowed to wait on her, and to consider her as protecting me while I remain in the empire. She accordingly promised to fix a day for me to see her; but a severe indisposition has hitherto confined her to her room. Now, Lady Amherst having requested to see Her Imperial Majesty, the day after to-morrow is fixed on for the purpose; and I have an intimation that I shall be received on the same day, as the Empress wishes not to receive any other foreigner before me. This is polite, or rather it is more; it is really kind.

19th.—Though I was suffering exceedingly this morning, I resolved nevertheless to attend the Empress at noon, at San Cristovaŏ. I was obliged to take a quantity of opium, to enable me to do so. However, I arrived at the appointed time; and, as I had been desired to do, asked for the *camarista môr*,[100] Jose Bonifacio's sister, and was shown into the presence-chamber, where I found that lady and Lady

---

* [See Appendix 6. {Graham refers to her Appendix 6, not included in this edition. -- *Eds.*}]

100. Camareira-mor, or lady in waiting.

Amherst, Miss Amherst, and Mrs. Chamberlain. The Empress entered shortly after, in a handsome morning dress of purple satin, with white ornaments, and looking extremely well. Mrs. Chamberlain presented Lady and Miss Amherst; and Her Imperial Majesty spoke for some minutes with Her Ladyship. After which she motioned to me to go to her, which I did. She spoke to me most kindly; and said, in a very flattering way, that she had long known me by name, and several other things that persons in her rank can make so agreeable by voice and manner; and I left her with the most agreeable impressions. She is extremely like several persons whom I have seen of the Austrian Imperial family, and has a remarkably sweet expression.

The corridor through which I passed from the palace steps, and the presence-room, are both plain and handsome. As it might be called a private audience, there were neither guards, officers, nor attendants, excepting the camarista môr.

The Emperor is at present at his country-house of Santa Cruz; so that San Cristovaõ appeared like a private gentleman's seat, it was so still.

Saturday, June 7th.—Since the day I was at San Cristovaõ, I have been confined to my room, and totally unable to exert myself, either mind or body, from severe indisposition. The Creole is come in from Bahia, to get provisions, preparatory to going home. The Commodore has offered me a passage in her, and has written to that purpose; but I am in no state to embark for a long voyage. The accounts from Bahia are sadder than ever: as to the Bahians, though favourable to the Imperial cause the misery of the poor inhabitants is great indeed.

12th.—We have been for three days kept in a state of agitation, by reports that Bahia has fallen, and various rumours attending those reports: they all turn out to have arisen from a *russe de guerre* of Madeira, who contrived to despatch a small vessel to a port on the coast for flour, pretending that it was for Lord Cochrane, and spreading that report to cover its real purpose.

23d.—A brig, prize to the squadron, arrived, and also the Sesostris, a merchant ship bound to Valparaiso, on board of which were Lady Cochrane and her family going to Chile. Thank God, by putting in here, she has learned where Lord Cochrane is, and is thus spared the tedious voyage, and her excellent husband much anxiety on her account.

Figure 16. Palace of San Cristovaõ. Courtesy of The Catholic University of America, Oliveira Lima Library, Washington, D.C.

14th.—At length we have true news both from and of Lord Cochrane. I wrote to Lady Cochrane, excusing myself on account of illness from going to her, and she kindly called on me as she landed; and a few minutes afterwards I received letters from the Admiral, and from some others in the squadron.

As might have been expected, from the haste in which the squadron was equipped, the ships had to encounter some difficulties at first. Some of the sails and cordage, which had been seventeen years in store, were found almost unserviceable; the guns of some of the ships were without locks, as the Portuguese had not adopted them: the cartridges were mostly made up in canvass: but the real evil was the number of Portuguese, both men and officers, among the crews, which kept them in a continual state of discontent, if not mutiny.

Lord Cochrane had chosen as head-quarters for the squadron, the harbour behind the Moro of San Paulo, about thirty miles south of Bahia, and commanding the channel behind Itaparica; a country well watered and wooded, and in the neighbourhood of all supplies of fresh necessaries. There is good and sheltered anchorage in from seven to twenty fathoms water, and on the whole it was well adapted for its purpose. As soon as it was known that His Lordship was off Bahia, the Portuguese squadron came out, and spread itself along the shore north of the bay. Lord Cochrane, who had waited in vain at the place of rendezvous at sea for the two fire-ships, which he expected from Rio, had fitted one of his small vessels, the schooner Real, as a fire-ship, and had intended to run into Bahia on the 4th of May; when he fell in with the Portuguese fleet, in number thirteen,* he having with him five ships, a brig, and the fire vessel. He instantly ran through their line, cutting off the four sternmost ships; and had the men done their duty, nothing could have saved the ship they were first alongside of: but they fired too soon; and though the fire did great execution, wounding and killing many, both on board that ship and the Joam VI., which was immediately to the windward of the Pedro, yet the Admiral was disappointed. The slow sailing of the Piranga and Netherohy kept them farther behind the Pedro than their brave commanders wished; the others were forced to keep aloof, it is said, by the conviction that their crews could not be trusted against the Portuguese. As to the crew of the Admiral's ship, two of the Portuguese marines went into the magazine passage, and with their drawn swords impeded the handing up the powder. The squadrons separated after this. Lord Cochrane determined to attack the Portuguese again next day. Captain Crosbie, Lieutenant Shepherd, and eleven others were wounded; but no other damage was sustained by the Imperial squadron, while that of the Europeans had suffered much both in crews and rigging.

On the morning of the 5th, Lord Cochrane looked in vain for the enemy. He had apparently been satisfied with the skirmish of the 4th, and had taken refuge in the harbour; so that His Lordship returned to the Moro de San Paulo, with only the satisfaction of having driven the enemy from the open sea.

Meantime the Brazilian Imperial force that was posted behind the city, taking advantage of the absence of the fleet, and consequently of the two thousand seamen who served the artillery ashore, advanced from the sitio of Brotas, where their centre was quartered, towards the town. Madeira marched out to meet them, and an action took place entirely in favour of the Imperialists; and it is said that the King's fleet was recalled in consequence of this disaster.

Lord Cochrane had no sooner returned to San Paulo than he made such provisions with regard to his squadron, as he judged most pru-

* One ship of the line, five frigates, five corvettes, a brig, and a schooner.

dent for the public service. The vessel that has arrived here has brought down some of the ill-affected Portuguese. All, I believe, from the report of the officer who arrived in the prize, have been dismissed from the Pedro Primero.

Lord Cochrane has taken the officers and English seamen of the Piranga and Nitherohy on board the Pedro, so that now he has one ship he may depend on: he has exchanged the eighteen-pound guns of the main-deck, for the twenty-four pounders of the Piranga, and has placed guns along his gang-ways; and we trust the next news we have from him, we shall learn something favourable to the cause of independence.

As far as the government here could supply every thing to the squadron to insure its success, it was done in the most liberal manner; and the failures, where they occurred, were owing to the peculiar circumstances of the times and country, which admitted of no control. That some things should have been imperfect was to be expected: that so much should have been done, and well done, excites admiration. But the Emperor appreciates the brave man who commands his fleet; and while that is the case, a difficulty as soon as felt will be obviated.

19th.—My health grows worse and worse. The Creole sailed to-day. I have amused myself for two days with some English newspapers. If any thing can rouse me to health it surely ought to be news from England.

Lord Althorp has, I see, made a spirited but ineffectual effort for the repeal of the foreign enlistment bill; a most interesting subject in this country: and I see with pleasure a virtual acknowledgment from the English ministers of the independence of Spanish America.[101]

22d.—This is the eve of St. John's, whereon the maidens of Brazil practise some of the same rites as those of Scotland do at Hallowe'en, to ascertain the fate of their loves. They burn nuts together; they put

---

101. John Charles Spencer, Viscount Althorp and third Earl Spencer (1782-1845), politician and leader of the British House of Commons. Graham kept up with British political developments, apparently asking John Murray to send her reports; in 1824 she tells him, "I should like to see the proceedings in Parliament of 1809 – 1810 – and 1813-4" (April 28, 1824). The Foreign Enlistment Act of 1819 prevented British subjects from serving in foreign armies and ships from being prepared for war in British territory without the King's permission; Graham's interest in the repeal of this act obviously relates to Cochrane as well as other British officers and enlisted men fighting for South American countries in their wars of independence.

their hands, blindfold, on a table, with the letters of the alphabet; and practise many a simple conjuration. I think I recollect long ago, to have seen the maid-servants of a house in Berkshire place an herb, I think a kind of stone-crop, behind the door, calling it Midsummer men, that was to chain the favoured youth as he entered. For me I only wish for the *nucca* drop of the Arab to fall this night, so I might catch it, and be relieved from my weary sickness.

June 26th.—My friend, Dr. Dickson, who has attended me all this time with unvarying kindness, having advised change of air for me, he and Mr. May have pitched on a small house on Botafogo beach, having an upper story, which is considered as an advantage here, the ground-floor houses being often a little damp;[102] and to-day Captain Willis of the Brazen brought me in his boat to my new dwelling. My good neighbours, Colonel and Mrs. Cunningham, try by their hospitality to prevent my feeling so much the loss of my friends Mr. and Mrs. May, who were every thing kind to me while at the Gloria.

Botafogo bay is certainly one of the most beautiful scenes in the world; but, till of late years, its shores were little inhabited by the higher classes of society. At the farthest end there is a gorge between the Corcovado mountain and the rocks belonging to what may be called the Sugar-loaf group, which leads to the Lagoa of Rodrigo Freites, through which gorge a small rivulet of fine fresh water runs to the sea. Just at its mouth, there has long been a village inhabited by gipsies, who have found their way hither, and preserve much of their peculiarity of appearance and character in this their trans-atlantic home. They conform to the religion of the country in all outward things, and belong to the parish of which the curate of Nossa Senhora da Monte is pastor; but their conformity does not appear to have influenced their moral habits. They employ their slaves in fishing, and part of their families is generally resident at their settlements; but the men rove about the country, and are the great horse-jockies of this part of Brazil. Some of them engage in trade, and many are very rich, but still they are reputed thieves and cheats; and to call a man *Zingara* (gipsy) is as much as to call him knave. They retain their peculiar dialect; but I have not been able, personally, to get sufficiently acquainted with them to form any

---

102. Dr. John Dickson, a faithful friend of Maria Graham's; Cochrane wrote Dickson asking him to "restrain [Maria Graham's] enthusiasm" in advocating Cochrane's cause (Vale, *Independence* 94, 150-51).

judgment of the degree in which their change of country and climate may have affected their original habits.

His Majesty's ship Beaver arrived, two days since from Bahia. It seems that Madeira, unable to hold the place any longer, is resolved to leave it. He is pressed to the utmost by Lord Cochrane's squadron, which cuts off his provisions, and by continual alarms kept up on the coast, by His Lordship's own appearance from sea, and by the preparations he is making in the Reconcave for an attack with fire-ships and gun-boats on the town. It is expected, therefore, that Madeira will abandon the place as soon as he can get shipping together to embark the troops. It is asserted even that he has fixed the day, that of San Pedro, for evacuating the place. The following proclamation is certainly preparatory to his doing so; but as the time must depend on contingencies, it cannot be so certain:

> Inhabitants of Bahia!
>
> The crisis in which we find ourselves is perilous, because the means of subsistence fail us, and we cannot secure the entrance of any provisions. My duty as a soldier, and as governor, is to make every sacrifice in order to save the city; but it is equally my duty to prevent in an extreme case the sacrifice of the troops that I command, of the squadron, and of yourselves. I shall employ every means to fulfil both these duties. Do not suffer yourselves to be persuaded that measures of foresight are always followed by disasters. You have already seen me take such once before: they alarmed you; but you were afterwards convinced that they portended nothing extraordinary. Even in the midst of formidable armies, measures of precaution are daily used; because victory is not constant, and reverses should be provided against. You may assure yourselves, that the measures I am now taking are purely precautionary: but it is necessary to communicate them to you, because if it happens that we must abandon the city, many of you will leave it also; and I should be responsible to the nation and to the King, if I had not forewarned you.
>
> (Signed)

Ignacio Luiz Madeira de Mello.
Head-quarters, Bahia, May 28. 1823.

This proclamation increased the general alarm to the highest pitch. The editors of even the Portuguese newspapers use the strongest language. One of them says, "The few last days, we have witnessed in this city a most doleful spectacle, that must touch the heart even of the most insensible: a panic terror has seized on all men's minds," etc.* And then goes on to anticipate the horrors of a city left without protectors, and of families, whose fathers being obliged to fly, should be left like orphans, with their property, a prey to the invaders. These fears abated a little on the 2d of June, when a vessel entered Bahia, having on board 3000 alquieres of farinha; and the spirits of the troops were raised by a slight advantage obtained on the 3d over the patriots. But the relief was of short duration. On a rigorous search there were found in the city no more than six weeks' provisions besides those necessary for the ships, and the General proceeded in his preparations for quitting Brazil. He now allowed the magistrates to resume their functions suspended by the declaration of martial-law, and produced a letter from the King, naming five persons to form a provisional government; and though some of them were unwilling to accept of the office, he caused them to take the oaths, and enter directly on their functions.

Madeira's preparations for his departure were accelerated by an attack made by Lord Cochrane on the night of the 12th of June, with only the Pedro Primeiro. The Portuguese Admiral was ashore, dining with General Madeira; when, at ten o'clock at night, a shot was heard. "What is it?" exclaimed the latter to the messenger, who, in alarm, entered the room.— "'Tis Lord Cochrane's line-of-battle ship, in the very midst of our fleet."—"Impossible!" exclaimed the Admiral; "no large ship can have come up with the ebb tide." And there was as much consternation and as much bustle of preparation, as if the fleet of England had entered in a hostile manner. The Pedro Primeiro was indeed close alongside of the Constituiçaõ; but the Admiral disdained so small a prize, and pushed on to the Joam VI.; had he reached her, he might have carried the whole squadron out with him; but just as he seemed on the point of doing so, the breeze that had brought him in over the tide failed, and it fell a dead calm: by this time every ship was

---

* *Semanario Civico* of the 5th June.

in motion, the forts began to play, and, reluctantly, the Pedro dropped out of the harbour with the tide, untouched by the enemy.

The daring of this attempt has filled the Portuguese with astonishment and dismay, and they are now most willing to abandon Bahia. The church plate, and all the cash that can be collected, are believed to be on board the British ships of war.*

July 1st.—A good deal of sensation has been excited to-day of rather a painful nature: the Emperor has fallen from his horse, and has broken two of his ribs, and is otherwise much bruised; however, his youth and strength prevent any serious apprehension from the consequences of his accident. There is no public news, and I am much too ill to care for any other. A foreigner, and alone, and very sick, I have abundant leisure to see the worth to the world of riches, or the appearance of them, and show and parade; and to feel that if I had them all, they could neither relieve the head nor the heart of the suffering or the sorrowful.

I think I am grown selfish: I cannot interest myself in the little things of other people's lives as I used to do; I require the strong stimulus of public interest to rouse my attention. It is long since I have been able to go out among the beautiful scenery here, to enjoy the charms of nature.

11th.—Once more I begin to feel better, and to go out of doors a little. All sorts of people crowd daily to visit the Emperor, who is recovering, but is still confined to the house. For the first time for these many weeks, I took a drive to-day; and went, as far as San Cristovaõ, to enquire after His Imperial Majesty, and leave my name. The road, both as I went and returned, was crowded with carriages and horsemen, on the same errand. Besides that the people do love him, his life is of the utmost importance to the very existence of Brazil as an independent nation at present, at any rate in peace.

13th.—I have become acquainted with two or three pleasant Brazilians, and one or two of the better kind of Portuguese, who have

---

* This is reported only. I have never asked, nor should I, I imagine, receive an answer if I did ask, any English officer about such things. The general disposition among them is evidently towards the old government; but their conduct is, as it ought to be, strictly neutral.

adopted Brazil.* There are not above five Fidalgos of the number, and these ancient nobles are objects of jealousy to the new, in number about a dozen, who infinitely surpass them in riches; so that we have the usual gossip and scandal of courts and cities, in which, as the women are usually the most active, so they suffer most: nor are our English one whit behind them. There is not much formal visiting among the English, but a good deal of quiet tea-drinking, and now and then parties formed to dine out of doors in the cool weather.

In short, my countrywomen here are a discreet sober set of persons, with not more than a reasonable share of good or bad. They go pretty regularly to church on Sundays, for we have a very pretty protestant chapel in Rio, served by a respectable clergyman; meet after church to luncheon and gossip: some go afterwards to the opera, others play cards, and some few stay at home, or ride out with their husbands, and instruct themselves and families by reading; and all this much as it happens in Europe. However, they are all very civil to me; and why should I see faults, or be hurt at the absurd stories they tell of me, because they don't know me? Besides, 'tis no great affront to be called wiser than one is.

14th.—Several prizes have arrived from the Moro of San Paulo. One of these vessels has brought news from the Moro that I only half like. After Lord Cochrane's visit to Bahia on the night of the 12th of June, he had been employed for the eight ensuing days in maturing a plan for a farther attack, which seemed sure of success; when, on the 20th,† "some careless or malignant person set fire to a cask of spirits, which communicated to other casks, and created such terror, that more than a hundred persons jumped overboard; some of whom were drowned. [The spirit room was close to the great magazine—the people overboard and most of the officers sick or away on duty.] It is calculated that we should have been blown up if the fire had raged only three minutes longer; and its extinction is chiefly to be ascribed to the presence of mind and personal exertion of His Lordship himself; who,

---

* On the 9th of March, an Imperial edict was published, desiring all such as would not conform to the laws of the empire to quit it within two months, if they dwelt on the coast, and within four, if in-land, on pain of loss of property; and thenceforth all good subjects to wear on their arms the green rose and gold badge, with *Independencia o Morte*, engraved on it.

† Extracted from a letter written to me on the 21st by a friend on board.

I am grieved to add, was so overheated by the blaze and his own exertions, as to be too ill this morning to leave his bed."

17th.—At length Bahia has fallen. Madeira, in pursuance of the plans announced in his proclamation of the 28th, had prepared all his ships of war, and a great number of merchantmen, with provisions, and ammunition, and stores: the plate, money, and jewels, were transhipped from the English vessels to his own, and it was believed he was to sail on the 3d of July. Lord Cochrane, having intelligence to that effect, had come alone in the Pedro Primeiro to look into the harbour, on the morning of the 2d, when he saw the Portuguese squadron loose all their topsails and prepare to move. This manœuvre was not considered by the English within the bay as decisive, because it had been practised daily for some time. His Lordship, however, immediately made signals to the Maria de Gloria and Nitherohy to join him with all despatch. The Piranga, useless from her bad sailing, owing to the state of her copper, had been ordered to Rio; and she and the Liberal, who both arrived to-day, are the bearers of the official intelligence. Lord Cochrane, whose kindness is never-failing, writes to me as follows. I do not like to quote, even in my journal, private letters; but this is short, and tells in few words all that can be said:—

MY DEAR MADAM,

I have been grieved to learn your indisposition; but you must recover, now that I tell you we have starved the enemy out of Bahia. The forts were abandoned this morning; and the men of war, 13 in number, with about 32 sail of transports and merchant vessels, are under sail. We shall follow (*i.e.* the Maria da Gloria and Pedro Primeiro) to the world's end. I say again expect good news. Ever believe me your sincere and respectful friend,

COCHRANE.
2d July, 1823.
Eight miles north of Bahia.

I learn from the officers of the ships arrived, that the guns were all spiked, [and the magazines in Port Pedro blown up,] but otherwise every thing was left in good order in the town; and on the marching in of the Brazilian troops not the smallest disorder took place, nor was a life lost; a circumstance highly honourable to all parties.

Though the Admiral mentions only forty-five vessels, it appears that there were many more, amounting to at least eighty, who took the opportunity of getting out with the fleet. When the Piranga left the Moro, a reinforcement of men had arrived there for the Admiral; and the Nitherohy was manning herself, and preparing to follow him in a few hours. [The admiral went off the Moro and ordered the Nitherohy, the Colonel Allen, and a schooner to join him and the Maria da Gloria; Nitherohy without leave took double the number of the best men out of the Allen!!!]

This news is highly acceptable here, except among a class either secretly attached to, or interested in, Portugal. These are murmuring, and saying, "Is it not enough for Lord Cochrane to have driven the poor soldiers out of Bahia, without following to persecute them?" etc. And others are affecting to despise what they call an easy service. But the government knows that it was *not* an easy service to keep the sea with so small a squadron, so recently formed, against a fleet completely armed and manned,—vessels of the best class; far less to cut off the provisions of the enemy, so as to reduce him to the necessity of abandoning his city.

There are illuminations and a gala opera to-night; but as the Emperor is not yet able to go, his picture, and that of the Empress, will appear instead. It is an old Portuguese custom, I believe, to display the picture of the monarch in his absence on occasions of ceremony.

18th.—The city has been thrown into considerable agitation to-day, by the knowledge, that yesterday the ministry of the Andradas ceased. It appears that a few days ago, I believe on the 16th, an unknown person presented a letter at the palace-door, and told the servant who received it, that his life should not be safe if he did not deliver it into the Emperor's own hand. The letter was delivered accordingly, and read; upon which His Imperial Majesty sent for Jose Bonifacio: they remained closeted for a length of time, and the result of the conference was, that Jose Bonifacio resigned his employment; and Brazil has lost an able minister, and the Emperor a zealous servant. It is rumoured that the letter was written from St. Paul's, and contained at least 300 signatures of persons complaining of the Andradas' tyrannical conduct in that province; particularly imprisoning persons who had opposed the election of certain members of the assembly, and ordering others, on various pretexts, to repair to Rio, where they had been kept away from their families. [The story of the letter was a falsehood I believe. The real cause of Jose Bonifacio's disgrace was in the Emperor's mistress and in Placido—they concerted it—I suppose they are sold to the Portuguese faction being themselves Pes de Chumbo—the pretender paper from St. Pauls was I believe a complaint certainly signed by many—but which had come to Jose Bonifacio's hands and had never been out of them. When the Andradas were deported—it was an English lady, Mrs. C., that procured permission for their wives to accompany them.]

These things, however, are capable of a favourable interpretation; and, in such stormy times, some severity may have been necessary, or, indeed, the zeal of the minister may have carried him too far.*

However that may be, the resignation of Jose Bonifacio is certain; and not less so that of his brother, Martim Francisco, whose unimpeachable integrity at the head of the treasury it will not be easy to supply. The conjectures, reasonings, and reports, on these subjects, are, of course, very various. The most general idea is, that the Andradas are overpowered by a republican party in the assembly; which, though small, has a decided plan, and works accordingly; and, oddly enough, their fall is said to have been brought about by an attempt, on their part, to get rid of old monarchy men. Monis Tavares, a clever man, whose name will be remembered in the sittings of the Lisbon Cortes as an advocate for Brazil, proposed in an early sitting of the assembly, May 22, the absolute expulsion from Brazil of all persons born in Portugal. The proposal gave rise to a warm discussion, and was negatived. This defeat was the signal for all the Portuguese party, and they are not weak, to join with the republicans to overthrow the Andradas; and they have succeeded. [The Portuguese party had arisen to such influence in Sept. 1824 that the slightest appearance of intelligence in a Brazilian minister would have overthrown him; every officer in the palace, women and all, are Portuguese or Franco-Lusitanos!] Such is the view taken of this business by many intelligent persons. However the fact may be, the Emperor's feeling to disclaim all tyranny or connivance at tyranny, is praiseworthy; but a well-wisher to Brazil may be permitted to desire that such able men had proved their innocence to his satisfaction, and had retained their situations. This evening the Emperor has circulated the following address to his people:—

* The discussions in the assembly of the 9th of May throw much light on this transaction.

Inhabitants of Brazil,

The government which does not guide itself by public opinion, or which is ignorant of it, must become the scourge of humanity. The monarch who knows not this truth will precipitate his empire into a gulf of misfortunes, each more terrible than the preceding. Providence has granted to me the knowledge of this truth. I have founded my system on it, and to that system I will be faithful.

Despotism and arbitrary acts are detested by me. It is but a short time since that I gave you one among many other proofs of this. We may all be deceived; but monarchs rarely hear the truth: if they do not seek it, it seldom appears to them. When once they know it, they should follow it. I have known it, and I do act accordingly. Although we have not yet a fixed constitution to govern ourselves by, we have at least those foundations for one, built on reason, which ought to be inviolable. These are the sacred rights of personal security, property, and the inviolability of the home of every citizen. If these have hitherto been violated, it was because your Emperor knew not that such despotism and acts of arbitrary power, improper at all times, and contrary to the system we profess, were exercised. Be assured that henceforth they shall be religiously supported: you shall live happy and safe in the bosoms of your families, in the arms of your tender wives, and surrounded by your beloved children. In vain shall imprudent men try to belie my constitutional principles; they will always triumph, as the sun breaks through the darkest clouds. Rely upon me, as I on you, and you will see democracy and despotism annihilated by rational liberty.

The Emperor.

The address has been well received; and perhaps those incidents, which, in a time like the present, bring the monarch and people more together, are really conducive to the harmony and stability of the whole political system. Meantime, Jose Joaquin Carneiro de Campos is prime minister, and Manoel Jacintho Noguerra de Gama is at the head of the treasury; a man so rich as to be above temptation, and whose character for integrity is scarcely lower than that of his predecessor.

July 23d.—I had for some time promised to paint a sketch of San Cristovaŏ for the Empress, and to-day I resolved to carry it to her. So I went, and on my way breakfasted at my good friend the Viscondeça do Rio Seco's; I then proceeded to the palace, and went up first to enquire after the Emperor's health: while I was writing my name, he, having perceived me arrive from the window, politely sent to say he would see me, and accordingly I was ushered into the presence-chamber by the Viador Don Luiz da Ponte; there I saw ministers and generals all in state. The Emperor was in a small inner room, where were his piano, his shooting apparatus, etc.; he was in an undressed cotton jacket with his arm in a sling, but looking well, although thinner and paler than formerly: he sent for the little picture, with which he seemed much pleased; and after speaking for some time very politely in French, I made my courtesy and retired. I then went to the Empress's apartment: she was out, but I was asked to wait for her return from her walk; and in the meantime I saw the young Princesses, who are extremely fair, and like Her Imperial Majesty, especially the eldest, Dona Maria da Gloria, who has one of the most intelligent faces I have seen. The Empress came in soon, and talked to me a good while on a variety of subjects, and very kindly of my late illness. Setting aside the consideration of her high rank, it is not a little pleasing to me to meet so well-educated and well-bred a woman; and I felt quite sorry to leave her without telling her so: she is in all respects an amiable and respectable woman. No distressed person ever applies to her in vain; and her conduct, both public and private, justly commands the admiration and love of her family and subjects: her personal accomplishments would adorn the station of a private gentlewoman; her temper, prudence, and courage, fit her for her high situation. On my way back to town I stopped at a country-house belonging to M. do Rio Seco: it is called Rio Comprido, and is remarkable for its garden; the outer hedge of which is like a fairy bower, or rather might adorn the gardens of Armida. A fence, breast-high, of myrtle and other evergreens, is surmounted by arcades of ever-blowing roses; among which a Jessamine, or a scarlet or purple creeper, twines itself occasionally, enriching the flowery cornice of the pillars between which the paths of entrance lie. The inner part one might indeed wish less stiff; but then all is kept in such order, and filled with such rich flowers and shrubs, that one knows not how the change might be made with advantage. The house is low, and pleasant for the climate; the orchard, kitchen garden, and grass fields behind, delightful; and the whole is surrounded by beautiful views. The Padre Jose, who is the chaplain, is also the overseer of the estate; a combination of offices that I find is usual here.

After passing some hours there with my hospitable friends, I returned to town, and spent an hour with my friend Dona Carlota de Carvalho e Mello, and met a number of the ladies of her family; and among the rest, her aunt, the wife of Manoel Jacintho, the new minister of finance, one of the most pleasing women I have seen in Brazil. I had the pleasure of complementing Dona Carlota's father, on having just received his commission as member of the assembly for Bahia, now it is free: I might, with truth, have complimented Bahia on so judicious a choice. I returned home early, notwithstanding the entreaties of my young friend that I would stay, as she considered the evening scarcely begun: the family is so large, that, at the house of one or the other, there is always a pleasant evening society. The men converse apart till tea-time, after which music or dancing brings at least the younger part to join the ladies; and it is seldom that they separate before midnight.

July 25th.—Our society at Botafogo is enlivened by the arrival of Commodore Sir T. Hardy, who occupies the house of disembargador França, who is not only cheerful and sociable himself, but causes cheerfulness around him. The officers of his own ship, and those of the rest of the squadron, are of course great acquisitions to the parties at Rio; but I see little of them: my dull house, and duller self, offering nothing inviting except to the midshipmen of my old ship, who visit me very constantly. I have bought a small horse* for the sake of exercise, and sometimes accompany the boys on their evening rides. Last night I went with two of them to the Praya Vermelha; and finding the officer of the guard at the gate of the fort, we asked leave to go in, which being granted, we entered, and walked about admiring the views. It was the first time I had seen the little bay Vermelha from the land side, the fort being built quite along the isthmus that unites the Sugar-loaf with the mainland. We remained without thinking of the time till the sun was fairly set; and then, on returning to the gate, we

---

* For this beast, which is really fit for nothing but the riding of an invalid like myself, I gave 35 milrees; a price for which, in Chile, one might buy a very fine horse.

found it shut, and that the keys had been carried to the governor. So I had to go to the officer of the guard, who understanding what had happened, ordered the guard under arms, and went himself for the keys, and conducted us out of the fort with great politeness. Wherever I have met with Brazilians, from the greatest to the meanest, I must say I have always experienced the greatest politeness: from the fidalgo who calls on me in full court costume, to the peasant, or the common soldier, I have had occasion to admire, and be grateful for, their courtesy.

August 1st, 1823.—The English packet arrived to-day; and brings news that the royal party in Lisbon have overpowered that of the Cortes. This intelligence is looked on as very important here, because it is hoped that the court may be more easily induced to acknowledge the independence of Brazil; and it is said that the authorities in Madeira have already orders to receive, and treat amicably, ships under the Brazilian flag. The general tone of politics here is less pleasing than it has been. There have been some disagreeable discussions in the assembly: a vote has passed refusing the veto to the Emperor; and it is said that the republican party is so elated on the occasion, that they think of proposing to refuse him the command of the army. The Imperialists are of course indignant at all this. However, we shall see what will happen when the deputation of the assembly carries up the notice of the vote, as it is said will be done next week, when the Emperor will be strong enough to receive it. He is now so well that he intends in ten days to return thanks at the church of Santa Maria da Gloria, and means on the same day to review the troops at San Cristovaŏ. They are collecting there for that purpose; and I saw the artillery marching that way to-day while I was in town, whither I went to purchase some newspapers, particularly the Diario da Assemblea. I take it very ill that ladies may not attend the sittings of the assembly, not that I know there is any formal prohibition; but the thing is considered as so impossible, that I cannot go. It is provided with a gallery, scarcely larger in proportion than that of the English House of Commons, for strangers; and the proceedings are published. The members speak standing in their places: they are something more dressed than the Commons in England; but they have no peculiar costume. The President or Speaker is changed monthly.

3d.—I drank tea at the Baronesa de Campos'; and met a large family party, which always assembles on Sundays to pay their respects to the old lady. The tea was made by one of the young ladies, with the assistance of her sister, just as it would be in England. A large silver urn, silver tea-pots, milk-jugs, and sugar-dishes, with elegant china, were placed on a large table; round which several of the young people assembled, and sent round the tea to us, who sat at a distance. All sorts of bread, cakes, buttered toast, and rusks were handed with the tea; and after it was removed, sweetmeats of every description were presented, after which every body took a glass of water.

6th.—Sailed to-day, H. M. ship Beaver, with my friend Mr. Dance as acting captain; the world says she takes some very important despatches relating to the commerce of England with the independent provinces of La Plata; but as the world often tells what is not true, and as what is true is never confessed by those who know officially, I never trouble myself to ask about these things. I am sorry to see almost my last friend leave the station before me: but I am now so used to losing, one way or another, all who from any motive have ever acted or felt kindly to me, that I hope soon to grow callous to the pain such loss still gives. It is in vain that I flatter myself that I have recovered the tone of my mind. I am affected even to weakness by every little incident, and am obliged to take refuge from my private feelings, in the interest that I have lately forced myself to take in the affairs of this country; and surely, where the happiness of millions of its fellow-creatures is at stake, the human heart may unblamed busy itself.

This morning Sir T. Hardy, who is always anxious to do kind offices, carried me to call on Mrs. Chamberlain: I can truly say, if I had known her ideas on the subject of etiquette, I should have called on her before; and therefore I am glad to do what is expected.* She seems to be a well-informed woman, with pleasant manners.

After I returned, I joined a party in a pleasant ride to the *Copa Cabana,* a little fort that defends one of the small bays behind that of Vermelha, and whence there are to be seen some of the most beautiful views here. The woods in the neighbourhood are very fine, and produce a great deal of the excellent fruit called the Cambucáa; and among the hills the small opossum and the armadillo are frequently found.

---

* Notwithstanding the peculiar circumstances, both on my own account and that of the invalid I had with me, of my return to Rio, Mrs. C—, the wife of the British consul, took no notice of my arrival. I learnt afterwards, that it is expected that women, as well as men, should call on the consuls. I was not aware of this, having *formerly* received the first visits in such cases.

8th.—The discussions and vote concerning the Emperor's veto have excited a great commotion, of words at least; and the English fetchers and carriers of news have agreed that there will be some serious insurrection on the part of the soldiers, to defend the Emperor from some indefinite oppression of the Assembly. I believe it is true that the Assembly itself, being convinced that their vote concerning the veto is impolitic and unjust, have determined to cancel it; and it is equally true, that there have been some military clubs, whose language has been rather violent on the subject. But that there are the slightest grounds for expecting any serious disturbance, I cannot think. The Emperor appears too sincere in his desire to see the greatest possible prosperity in Brazil, to encourage any violent proceedings to overawe the Constituent Assembly; and at the same time he has too much spirit to submit to terms, from any quarter, derogatory to his dignity and rights. I have just received his proclamation on the occasion, which I doubt not will produce a good effect. These proclamations are agreeable to the taste of the people; and in fact are the only channels through which they can learn any thing of the disposition of the Emperor in the present state of the country. To-day's is as follows:—

Brazilians!

On not a few occasions have I laid open to you my mind and my heart: on the first you will always find engraven constitutional monarchy, on the last your happiness. I am now desirous of giving you a fresh assurance of my sentiments, and of my detestation of despotism, whether exercised by one or by many.

Some of the municipalities of the northern provinces have given instructions to their deputies, in which the spirit of democracy predominates. Democracy in Brazil, in this vast empire, is an absurdity; and not less absurd is the pretending to give laws to those who are to make them, threatening them with the loss or diminution of powers which the constituents neither have given nor have power to give.

In the city of Porto Alegre, the troops and the people, the junta of government and the civil and ecclesiastical authorities, have also just committed an error, which they have confirmed, or rather aggravated, by solemn oath. Troops which ought to obey the monarch holding a council; incompetent authorities defining an article of the constitution, which is the business of the General Constituent and Legislative Assembly (and such is the veto, whether absolute or suspensive);—are most scandalous absurdities, and crimes which would merit the severest punishment, but for the consideration that they were suggested by ignorance, or produced by base deceptions.

Listen not therefore to those who flatter the people, or to those who flatter the monarch: they are equally base, and moved by personal and low interests; and under the mask of liberality or that of servility, seek alike, only to rear their proud and precarious fortunes on the ruins of their country. The times in which we live are full of melancholy warnings. Let us use the catastrophes of foreign nations as beacons.

Brazilians! confide in your Emperor and Perpetual Defender, who seeks no legal powers; nor will he ever suffer those to be usurped which belong to him of right, and which are indispensable in order that you may be happy, and that this empire may fulfil the high destinies suited to its boundaries of the wide Atlantic, and the proud floods of the Plata and the Amazons. Let us await reverently the constitution of the empire, and let us hope that it may be worthy of us.

May the Supreme Disposer of the Universe grant us union and tranquillity, strength and constancy; and the great work of our liberty and independence will be accomplished.

The Emperor.

9th August.—The day on which the Pes de Chumbo predicted an insurrection has passed in perfect tranquillity, excepting for one melancholy accident. Their Imperial Majesties, as had been appointed, went to the Gloria church to return thanks for the Emperor's recovery. They were attended by the officers of state, and of the household, and as many officers of the different regiments as could attend. While the company were all on their knees, and just as the sacring-bell announced the elevation of the Host, the Chamberlain, Magalhaens, was struck with apoplexy, and died.

12th.—This day, as well as yesterday and the day before, there have been illuminations and dressed operas on account of the Emperor's recovery; and to-night a vessel, prize to the squadron, arrived, bringing news of their wellbeing, and of the arrival of many prizes at Bahia and Pernambuco. As officers and men from the Imperial ships cannot be spared in sufficient numbers to work the prizes into port, Lord Cochrane makes sure of their going thither by starting the water, excepting what is sufficient for a certain number of days, and cutting away the main and mizen masts, so that they must run for the ports to leeward. Seamen will appreciate this.

August 14th.—I went with M. Plasson, a very intelligent Frenchman, to whom I am indebted for a good deal of information about this country, to the museum, which I had seen in a hurried way, on my first visit to Rio. It is greatly improved since I was here, both externally and internally. The minerals of the country form the richest part of the collection. The diamonds, both colourless and black, surpass any thing I have seen; but I believe the crystals of gold to be the most precious articles here: there are several pieces of native gold, weighing three or four ounces; and some beautiful specimens of silver, as fine and as delicate as a lady's aigrette. I confess that the fine coloured copper, and the beautiful grained iron, pleased me as well as most things: some of the latter specimens yield 99 parts of iron. These are from the mines of St. Paul's, and I was shown some specimens of coal, as fine as Scotch coal, that has been recently discovered in the immediate neighbourhood of those very mines. The amethysts, topazes, quartzes of all colours, are innumerable: there are beautiful jaspers with veins of gold, and all manner of gorgeous works of nature, fit for Aladdin's cave, and the insects, especially the butterflies, fit to flit about in it. But the other branches of natural history are not rich here. Of birds there are few of note, beyond a splendid set of toucans; and of quadrupeds, a few monkies, two fawns like the roe-deer,* and some very curious armadillos, are all I remember. The collection of Indian weapons and dresses is incomplete, and wants arrangement: this is a pity; for by-and-by, as the wild natives adopt civilised habits, these will be unattainable. The African curiosities are scarcely better kept, but some of them are very curious in their kind. One very remarkable one is a king's dress made

* I have eaten of the venison, and it is like roe-deer.

of ox-gut, not in the state le Valliant describes, but carefully cleaned and dried, as we do bladders.[103] It is then split longitudinally, and the pieces sewed together, each seam being set with tufts or rather fringes of purple feathers; so that the vest is light, impervious to rain, and highly ornamental from its rich purple stripes. There is another entirely of rich Mazarine blue feathers; a sceptre most ingeniously wrought of scarlet feathers; and a cap of bark, with a long projecting beak in front, and a quantity of coloured feathers and hair behind, ornamented with beads. Besides all these things, there is the throne of an African prince of wood, beautifully carved. I could wish, since the situation of Brazil is so favourable for collecting African costume, that there were a room appropriated to these things, as they are curious in the history of man.

15th.—The feast of Our Lady of the Assumption, called here Nossa Senhora da Gloria, the patroness of the Emperor's eldest child, is celebrated to-day, and of course the whole of the royal family attended Mass in the morning and evening. I was spending the day with Mrs. May, at her pleasant house on the Gloria hill, and we agreed to go in the afternoon to see the ceremony. The church is situated on a platform, rather more than half way up a steep eminence overlooking the bay. The body is an octagon of thirty-two feet diameter; and the choir, of the same shape, is twenty-one feet in diameter. We entered among a great crowd of persons, and placed ourselves within the choir; and shortly afterwards the Imperial party entered, and I was not disagreeably surprised at being most pleasantly recognised. The salutation, as this evening's service is called, was well performed as to music, and very short: after it, for the first time, I heard a Portuguese sermon. It was of course occasional. The text, 1 Kings, chap. ii. ver. 19.—"And the king rose up to meet his mother, and bowed himself unto her, and sat down on his throne, and caused a seat to be set for the king's mother, and she sat on his right hand." The application of this text to the legend of the Assumption is obvious, and occupied the first division of the discourse. The second part consisted in an application of the history of the early part of Solomon's reign to the present circum-

---

103. François Le Vaillant (1753-1824), French explorer, was born in Dutch Guiana and, after studying natural history, traveled for the Dutch East India Company South Africa in 1781. His accounts of his travels, *Voyage dans l'intérieur de l'Afrique* (1790, 2 vols.), and *Second* [sic] *voyage dans l'intérieur de l'Afrique* (1796, 3 vols.), were translated into several languages, although Graham probably read them in the original French.

stances of Brazil; the restoration of the kingdom, the triumph over faction, and the institution of laws, forming the grounds of comparison. The whole people of Brazil were called upon to join in thanksgiving and prayers to the Virgin of Glory: thanksgiving that she had given to her people, as rulers, the descendants of the Emanuels, the Johns, and the Henrys of Portugal, and of the Maria Theresas of Austria; and prayers that she would continue her gracious protection, and that most especially to the eldest hope of Brazil, named after her and dedicated to her. The whole was gravely and properly done, with as little of the appearance of flattery to the illustrious persons present as possible, and did not last above fifteen minutes. On this occasion, the veadors, and other persons attendant on the Imperial family, wore white silk surplices, and bore torches in their hands.

I went in the evening to a ball and concert at the Baronesa de Campos: on entering, I was met by the young ladies of the family, and led up to their grandmother; and after paying my compliments to her, I was placed among the division of the family where I had most acquaintance. There were only two Englishwomen besides Lady Cochrane and myself, and these were the wives of the consul and the commissioner for the slave business. A foreign gentleman present remarked, that though we were but four, we hardly conversed together. This was perfectly true: I like, when I am in foreign society, to talk to foreigners; and think it neither wise nor civil to form coteries with those of one's own nation in such cases. Several rooms were open for cards; the stakes, I fancy, were high. The tea-room was no sooner full, than tea was handed round; and I perceived that some of the older servants, with great respect indeed, spoke to such of the guests as they were acquainted with. After tea, I had the pleasure of again hearing Dona Rosa sing, and almost grudged my gayer companions their ball, which broke in upon that "sober certainty of waking bliss,"[104] which music inspires into all, and especially to those who have known sorrow. I am no musician; but sweet sounds, especially those of the human voice, whether in speaking or singing, have a singular power over me.

After the first dance was over, we walked all about the house, and found a magnificent dining-room as to size, but scarcely furnished to correspond with the rest of the house; the bed-rooms and dressing-rooms of the ladies are neat and elegantly fitted up with English and

---

104. As she did above, Graham again quotes from Milton's *Comus* to praise Dona Rosa's singing.

French furniture; and all as different as possible from the houses I saw in Bahia. I am told that they are likewise as different from what they were here twenty years since, and can well believe it; even during the twelve months of my absence from Rio, I see a wonderful polishing has taken place, and every thing is gaining an European air.

I took the liberty of remarking to one of the ladies, the extreme youth of some of the children who accompanied their mothers this evening; and saying, that in England we should consider it injurious to them in all respects. She asked me what we did with them. I told her that some of them would be in bed, and others with their nurses and governesses. She said we were happy in that: but that here, there were no such persons, and that the children would be left to the care and example of the slaves, whose manners were so depraved, and practices so immoral, that it must be the destruction of the children; and that those who loved their children must keep them under their own eyes, where, if they were brought too forward in company, they at least could learn no ill. I love to collect these proofs of the evils of slavery—even here where it exists in a milder form than in most countries.—I left the dancers busily engaged at twelve o'clock, and I heard that they continued the ball until three. There is no peculiarity in the dancing here; the ladies of Rio being like ourselves, the pupils of the French, in that branch of the fine arts.

19th.—Sir T. Hardy gave a ball and supper to English, French, and Brazilians: where every thing was handsome, and well-ordered; and every body pleased.

20th.—I had long wished to see a little more of the neighbourhood of Rio than I have hitherto done; and had resolved on riding at least to Santa Cruz, about fourteen leagues from hence, and as the road is too well travelled to fear extraordinary accidents, and I am not timid as to common inconveniences, I had determined to hire a black attendant and go alone. This determination, however, was over-ruled by Mr. and Mrs. May, whose brother, Mr. Dampier, kindly offered to escort me. I confess I was very glad to be relieved of the absolute charge of myself, and not a little pleased to have the society of a well-bred, intelligent young man, whose taste for the picturesque beauties of nature agrees with my own.—I think that if there is one decided point in which fellow-travellers agree, however different in age, temper, or disposition, there may always be peace and pleasant conversation, more especially, if, as is our case, they travel on horseback. A difference of opinion is so easily evaded by a reference to one's horse, which may always go too fast or too slow, or exercise one's tongue or one's whip without any offence to one's two-legged companion.—We were well tried to-day. I had taken it into my head, that after having postponed our journey from week to week on one account or an other, if we did not begin it this day we never should go at all: and, therefore, though the afternoon was most unpromising, we left Mr. May's at half-past four o'clock, that we might reach Campinha, the first stage, to sleep; for, alas! these horses are not like my Chilian steeds, that would carry me twenty leagues a day without complaining. We mounted then, Mr. Dampier on a tall bay horse high in bone, with a brace of pistols buckled round him, in a huge straw hat, and a short jacket; I on a little grey horse, my boat-cloak over my saddle; otherwise dressed as usual, with a straw riding hat, and dark grey habit; and our attendant Antonio, the merriest of negroes, on a mule, with Mr. Dampier's portmanteau behind, and my bag before him.—We proceeded by the upper part of the town, and along the well-trodden road to San Cristovaõ, and after crossing the little hill to the left of the palace, entered on a country quite new to me. From the western side of the entrance to Rio Janeiro, a high mountainous ridge extends close to the sea, as far as the Bay of Angra dos Reyes, formed by Ilha Grande and Marambaya. On the northern side of this ridge there is a plain, here and there varied by low hills, extending quite to the most inland part of Rio de Janeiro, and reaching in a winding direction to the bay of Angra dos Reyes: itself having probably at no very remote period been covered with water, connecting these two bays, and insulating the mountains above mentioned. Along this plain our road lay between grand scenery on the one hand, and soft and beautiful landscape on the other; but to-night all was dark and louring; the tops of the mountains were wrapped in mists, that rushed impetuously down their sides, or through their clefts, and every now and then a hollow sound of wind came from out of them, though the blast did not quite reach us. Under this sort of cloud we passed the picturesque Pedragulha, and the little port of Benefica, formed by a creek of the Rio. By the time we reached Praya Pequena, where a good deal of produce is embarked for the city, the clouds had closed dully in, and the grand mountain mists had lost their character. Still we went on, leaving the bay entirely: and first we passed the Venda Grande, where every necessary for horse or man travelling, is to be sold; then the Capon do Bispo, a pretty village, which the rain clouds made me long to stop at; and then the stone bridge of Rio de Ferreira, where the rain at length began to fall in large cold drops; then tremendous gusts of wind came out of the mountain gaps, and long before we reached the Casca d'ouro, the protection of cloaks and umbrellas had ceased to avail. There we might have stopped; but having been told that the Venda of Campinha was the best resting-place, we resolved to proceed, and with some pains prevailed on my horse to go on: we reached the venda. But if it be delightful, after a long wet ride in a dark and boisterous night, to arrive at a place of rest, it is at least as wretched to be turned from the door where you hope to find shelter, with dripping clothes and shivering limbs; yet such was our fate. There was nothing at the venda to eat, no place for us, none for our horses, and so we set out again to brave the pitiless storm; a few yards, however, brought us to a low cottage on the road side, and there we knocked. A mulatto serving-man came round cautiously to reconnoitre from the back of the house, when having ascertained that we really were English travellers benighted and wet, the front door was opened, and we found within a middle-aged very kind-looking woman, and her little daughter; her name is Maria Rosa d'Acunha. Her husband and son were absent on business, and she and the little girl were alone. As soon as we had changed our wet clothes, and had provided for the horses, which our hostess put into an empty building, she gave us warm coffee, bread and cheese, and extended her hospitable care to the negro. She gave Mr. Dampier her son's bed, and made up a couch for me in the room where she and the child slept. These people are of the poorest class of farmers, not possessing above four or five slaves, and working hard themselves. They appear happy however, and I am sure are very hospitable.

21st.—This morning looked at least as threatening as yesterday, but we determined to go as far as the Engenho dos Affonsos, for whose owner, Senhor Joaõ Marcus Vieira, we had letters from a friend in town. Accordingly we took leave of our kind hostess, who had made coffee early for us, and proceeded along a league of very pretty road to the Affonsos. Where that estate joins Campinha there is a large tiled shed where we found a party of travellers, apparently from the mines, drying their clothes and baggage after the last night's storm. A priest, and two or three men apparently above the common, appeared to be the masters of the party; the baggage was piled up on one side of the shed, and the arms were stuck into the cordage which bound it. There was a great fire in the middle, where a negro was boiling coffee, and several persons round drying clothes. Generally speaking, the men we met on their way from the mines are a fine, handsome race, lightly and actively made. Their dress is very picturesque. It consists of an oval cloak, lined and bordered with some bright colour such as rose or apple green, worn as the Spanish Americans wear the poncho. The sides are often turned up over the shoulders, and display a bright coloured jacket below. The breeches are loose, and reach to the knee, and loose boots of brown leather are frequently seen on the better sort, though it is very common to see the spurs upon the naked heel, and no boot or shoe of any kind. The higher classes have generally handsome pistols or great knives, the others content themselves with a good cudgel. A short league from the last house of Campinha, brought us to Affonsos, where we presented our letter, and were most kindly welcomed.—The estate belongs in fact to the grandmother of Senhor Joaõ Marcus, who is a native of St. Catherine's, and a widow. His mother, and sister, and brother, and two dumb cousins also reside here, but he is only an occasional visitor, being married, and living near his wife's family. The dumb ladies, no longer young, are very interesting; they are extremely intelligent, understanding most things said in Portuguese by the motion of the lips, so that their cousin spoke in French, when he wished to say any thing of them; they make themselves understood by signs, many of which, I may say most, would be perfectly intelligible to the pupils of Sicard or Braidwood.[105] They are part of a family of eight children, four of whom are dumb, the dumb and the speakers being born alternately. One of them made breakfast for us, which consisted of coffee, and various kinds of bread and butter.

After breakfast, as the day continued cold and showery, we were easily prevailed on by our host to remain all day at Affonsos. I was indeed glad of the opportunity of spending a whole day with a country family. The first place we visited after breakfast was the sugar-mill, which is worked by mules. The machinery is rather coarse, but seems to answer its purpose.

The estate employs 200 oxen and 180 slaves as labourers, besides those for the service of the family. The produce is somewhere about

---

105. Thomas Braidwood (1715-1806), a Scotsman educated at Edinburgh University who specialized in education of the deaf. Roch-Ambroise Cucurron Sicard (1742-1822), a Frenchman who governed a school for the deaf in Bordeaux and later another in Paris; his theories on educating the deaf influenced international methods of education (*ODNB* 6).

3000 arobas of sugar, and 70 pipes of spirits. The lands extend from Tapera, the place where we met the travellers, and where 200 years ago there was an aldea of reclaimed Indians, about a league to Piraquara. There are about forty white tenants who keep vendas, and other useful shops on the borders of the estate near the roads, and exercise the more necessary handicrafts. But a small portion of the estate is in actual cultivation, the rest being covered with its native woods; but these are valuable as fuel for the sugar-furnaces, and timber for machinery, and occasionally for sale. The owners of estates prefer hiring either free blacks, or negroes let out by their masters,* to send into the woods, on account of the numerous accidents that happen in felling the trees, particularly in steep situations. The death of an estate negro is the loss of his value, of a hired negro, only that of a small fine; and of a free black, it is often the saving even of his wages, if he has no son to claim them.

Wheat does not grow in this part of Brazil, though in the southern and inland mountainous districts it thrives admirably. The luxury of wheaten bread is introduced every where, North America furnishing the flour. Wherever one travels in this neighbourhood, one is sure of excellent rusk at every venda, though soft bread is rare.

The sugar-canes are planted here during the months of March, April, May, and even June and July. In the ridges between them maize and kidney-beans are planted, the cultivation of which is favourable to the sugar-cane: first the beans are gathered in, when the ground is weeded, and cleared, and loosened around the roots of the canes; then the maize is pulled, when a second weeding and clearing takes place; after which the sugar is tall enough to shade the ground, and prevent the growth of weeds. The first canes are ripe about May. The Cayenne cane yields best, and thrives in low grounds, the soil a mixture of sand and loam. The Creole cane takes the hill, and, though less productive, is supposed to yield sugar of a better quality. The cool months from May to September are the properest for boiling sugar. After October, the canes yield less juice by one-eighth, sometimes by one-fourth, and nearly as much more is lost in claying by the lightness of the sugar, the pots of three arobas not returning after the operation more than two and a half at most. The clay used in refining the sugar is dug close to the mill; it feels soft and fat in the fingers. It is placed in a wooden trough, with a quantity of lie made by steeping the twigs of a small

* The wages from a patac and half to two patacs per day, besides food.

shrub, which has a taste of soda,* and worked up and down with a machine, something like a churn-staff, until it is of the consistence of thick cream, when it is ready for use. I suppose that the main business of expressing the juice, boiling it, and drying the sugars, as well as cleansing them, are carried on here as in every part of the world, though probably there may be some difference in every country, or even in every sugar-work; nor can the distilling the spirits be very different. Nothing is wasted in a sugar-house; the trash that remains after the canes are pressed, when dried, assists as fuel in heating the furnaces; the sweet refuse water that runs off from the still is eagerly drank by the oxen, who always seem to fatten on it.

By the time we had examined the sugar-work, and seen the garden, it was two o'clock, and we were summoned to dinner. Every thing was excellent in its kind, with only a little more garlic than is used in English cookery. On the side-table there was a large dish of dry farinha, which the elder part of the family called for and used instead of bread. I preferred the dish of farinha moistened with broth, not unlike brose, which was presented along with the bouillie and sliced sausage after the soup. The mutton was from the estate, small and very sweet. Every thing was served up on English blue and white ware. The table-cloths and napkins were of cotton diaper, and there was a good deal of plate used, but not displayed. After dinner some of the family retired to the siesta; others occupied themselves in embroidery, which is very beautiful, and the rest in the business of the house, and governing the female in-door slaves, who have been mostly born on the estate, and brought up in their mistress's house. I saw children of all ages and colours running about, who seemed to be as tenderly treated as if they had been of the family. Slavery under these circumstances is much alleviated, and more like that of the patriarchal times, where the purchased servant became to all intents one of the family. The great evil is, that though perhaps masters may not treat their slaves ill, they have the power of doing so; and the slave is subject to the worst of contingent evils, namely, the caprice of a half-educated, or it may be an ill-educated master. Were all slaves as well off as the house slaves of Affonsos, where the family is constantly resident, and nothing trusted to others, the state of the individuals might be compared with advantage to that of free servants. But the best is impossible, and the worst but too prob-

* This is brought to the Engenhos of the district from the lake of Jacarepagua. I had no opportunity of seeing the whole plant.

able; since the unchecked power of a fallible being may exercise itself without censure on its slaves.

One of the dumb ladies made tea, and afterwards we passed a couple of hours at a round game of cards, where the sisters felt themselves quite on an equality with the speakers, and enjoyed themselves accordingly. I remember an account given by Bishop Burnet in his Travels, of a dumb lady who had invented a way of communicating with her sister, even in the dark, before the instruction of such unfortunate persons had become an object of public attention. Some such method these ladies possess of discoursing together, and of making themselves understood by their young cousin, an intelligent girl, who is always at hand to interpret for them. They have also invented arbitrary signs for the names of the flowers and plants in their garden, which signs all the family know; and I was delighted with the quickness and precision with which they conversed on every subject within their knowledge.

The cards made way for the supper, a meal almost as ceremonious, and quite as constant, as the dinner. After it, toasted cheese was introduced, with girdle cakes of farinha freshly toasted, and spread with a very little Irish butter; they are the same as the Casava bread of the West Indies, but prepared here are more like Scotch oat-cakes.

On retiring to my room at night, a handsome young slave entered, with a large brass pan of tepid water, and a fringed towel over her arm, and offered to wash my feet. She seemed disappointed when I told her I never suffered any body to do that for me, or to assist me in undressing at any time. In the morning she returned, and removing the foot bath, brought fresh towels, and a large embossed silver basin and ewer, with plenty of tepid water; which she left without saying a word, and told her mistress I was a very quiet person, and, she supposed, liked nobody but my own people, so she would not disturb me.

Friday, August 22d.—The day as fine as possible; and after breakfast we pursued our journey to Santa Cruz, the road improving in beauty as we proceeded.

> Here lofty trees to ancient song unknown,
> The noble sons of potent heat, and floods
> Prone rushing from the clouds, rear'd high to heav'n
> Their thorny stems, and broad around them threw
> Meridian gloom.[106]

---

106. It is interesting that Graham chooses lines from Milton's *Paradise Lost*, Book II, to celebrate the landscape of the New World—particularly since she

And above all these the mountains rose in the distance, and lower hills more near, between which, long valleys stretched themselves till the eye could follow them no farther; and the foregrounds were filled up with gigantic aloes, streams, and pools, and groups of passing cattle and their picturesquely clad conductors. Near Campo Grande, the scenery is diversified by several little green plains, with only an insulated tree here and there, decorated with air plants in bloom, and scarlet creepers. Beyond this lies one of the most beautiful spots I ever saw, namely, Viaga; where the rocks, trees, plains, and buildings, seem all placed on purpose to be admired. Having loitered a little to admire it, we rode on to the New Freguezia of Sant Antonio, where we stopped at a very neat venda to rest and feed our horses. The church is on a little hill, overlooking a very pretty country and a neat village, but the greater part of the parish is very distant. While the horses were eating their maize, we procured for ourselves some rusk, cheese from the province of Minas exactly like Scotch kebbuck, and port wine from the cask of excellent quality. These provisions are always to be had, with beans, bacon, and dried beef. But the hospitality of a Brazilian inn does not extend to cooking food for travellers, who generally carry the utensils for that purpose with them, and who in some shed attached to the inn cook for themselves, and generally sleep in the same shed. At Sant Antonio there are decent sleeping-rooms provided with benches and mats, to which the guests add what bedding they please; but travellers commonly wrap themselves in their cloaks, and so rest. As soon as our horses were ready, we rode on to Mata Paciencia, the engenho of Dona Mariana, the eldest daughter of the Baroness de Campos, and to whom we had a letter of introduction. Here we met with a most polite reception from a handsome ladylike woman, whom we found attending to her engenho, which is indeed an interesting one. We were received at first by the chaplain, a polite and well-informed person; and with him was the chaplain of Santa Cruz, who having been formerly a professor in the college at Rio, is commonly known by the name of the Padre Mestre.

Dona Mariana led us into the engenho, where we had seats placed near the rollers, which are worked by an eight-horse power steam-engine, one of the first, if not the very first, erected in Brazil. There are here 200 slaves, and as many oxen, in constant employ. The steam-en-

---

drew lines from *Paradise Regained* to describe a thunderstorm at sea as the *Doris* approached the coast of Brazil for the first time.

gine, besides the rollers in the sugar-house, moves several saws; so that she has the advantage of having her timber prepared almost without expense. While we were sitting by the machine, Dona Mariana desired the women, who were supplying the canes, to sing and they began at first with some of their own wild African airs, with words adopted at the moment to suit the occasion. She then told them to sing their hymns to the Virgin; when, regularly in tune and time, and with some sweet voices, the evening and other hymns were sung; and we accompanied Dona Mariana into the house, where we found that while we had been occupied in looking at the machinery, the boilers, and the distillery, dinner had been prepared for us, though it was long after the family hour. On our departure, we were hospitably pressed to return on our way back to Rio, which we, "nothing loath," promised to do.

It was quite dark long before we reached Santa Cruz, and exceedingly cold: when there, we easily found the house of the gentleman to whom we had a letter of introduction, the Capitaõ de Fragata Joam da Cruz de Reis, who is the superintendant of the palace and estate. The Visconde do Rio Seco had kindly furnished us with this letter, and mentioned that the object of the journey was mere curiosity, so that the Capitaõ told us that he would next day do all he could to satisfy us. Soon after our arrival, several persons dropped in to converse half an hour; among the rest, a surgeon, who comes from Rio once a year to vaccinate the children born in the twelve months on the estate. The Padre Mestre and another friar also came in; and I soon found that Santa Cruz has its politics and gossip as well as the city, all the difference being in a little more or less refinement. Nothing can exceed the good-humoured hospitality of our host and hostess, who soon made us feel quite at home; and by the time tea was over, we were quite initiated into all the ways of the house and the village.

Saturday, 23d.—The morning was excessively cold but clear, and the view of the extensive plains of Santa Cruz, with the herds of cattle upon it, most magnificent. The pasture, which extends many leagues on each side of the little hill on which the palace and village are situated, is here and there varied by clumps of natural wood; the horizon extends to the sea in one direction, and every where else the view is bounded by mountains or woody hills. The palace itself occupies the site of the old Jesuits' college. Three sides are modern: the fourth contains the handsome chapel of the very reverend fathers, and a few tolerable apartments. The new part was built for King John VI., but the works were stopped on his departure. The apartments are handsome, and comfortably furnished. In this climate hangings, whether of paper or silk, are liable to speedy decay from damp and insects. The walls are therefore washed with a rich creamy white clay, called Taboa Tinga,* and cornices and borders painted on them in distemper. Some of these are exceedingly beautiful in design, and generally very well executed, the arabesques of the friezes being composed of the fruits, flowers, birds, and insects of the country. One of the rooms represents a pavilion; and between the open pilasters, the scenery round Santa Cruz is painted, not well indeed, but the room is pleasant and cheerful. The artists employed were chiefly mulattoes and creole negroes.

After breakfast, we rode along the causeway that crosses the plain of Santa Cruz, to the Indian aldea of San Francisco Xavier de Itaguahy, commonly called Taguahy, formed by the Jesuits not very long before their expulsion. The situation of the aldea and church is extremely fine; on the summit of a hill overlooking a rich plain, watered by a navigable river, and surrounded by mountains. We entered several of the huts of the Indians, whom I had understood to be of the Guaranee nation. I enquired of one of the women, in whose hut I sat down, if she knew whence her tribe came: she said no; she had been brought, when a mere child, from a great distance to Taguahy, by the fathers of the company; that her husband had died when she was young; that she and her daughters had always lived there; but her sons and grandsons, after the fathers of the company went, had returned to their fathers, by which she meant that they had resumed their savage life. This is not surprising. The Indians here must work for others, and become servants; a state they hardly distinguish from slavery. Besides, slaves are plentiful; and as the negro is hardier than the Indian, his labour is more profitable; therefore, a willing Indian does not always find a master. The produce of his little garden, or his fishing, is rarely sufficient for his family; and without the protection of the priest, whose chief favour was procuring constant occupation, the half-reclaimed savage droops, and flies again to the liberty of his forest, to his unrestrained hunting and fishing. The Chilian Indians rarely or never return to their forests when their villages are once formed; but that depends on circumstances, which have nothing in common with the

* Taboa tinga, a very fine white clay, proper for making porcelain, very abundant in Brazil, and, as far as I can judge, the same as is found in the valleys of Chile.

state of Brazil. Many of the Indian women have married the creole Portuguese; intermarriages between creole women and Indian men are more rare. The children of such couples are prettier, and appear to me to be more intelligent, than the pure race of either. The Indian huts at Taguahy are very poor; barely sufficient in walls and roof to keep out the weather, and furnished with little besides hammocks and cooking utensils; yet we were every where asked to go in and sit down: all the floors were cleanly swept, and a log of wood or a rude stool was generally to be found for a seat for the stranger, the people themselves squatting on the ground.

At the foot of the hill of Taguahy there is a very fine ingenho, sold by King Joam VI. to one de Barros; the rollers are worked by a horizontal water-wheel about twenty-two feet in diameter, turned by the little stream Taguahy. The quantity of sugar made in a given time is something more than that produced by the steam-engine at Mata Paciencia, the number of slaves employed being the same.

After we had admired the neatness of the engenho and the beauty of the situation sufficiently, we left Taguahy to return to Santa Cruz, and re-crossed the river Guandu, where there is a guard-house by the bridge, where passes from the police are required from ordinary travellers; but as we had a servant from Santa Cruz with us, we were not questioned. The Guandu rises in the mountain of Marapicu, in the barony of Itanhae; and having received the Tingui, it passes to the engenho of Palmares, occupied by the Visconde de Merendal; where there is a wharf where the produce of the neighbouring estates is embarked, and conveyed to Sepetiva, a little port in the bay of Angra dos Reyes, where it is shipped for Rio, the passage thither being generally of twenty-four hours.

In 1810 there was an intention of uniting the Guandu with the Itaipu by a short canal; by which means the produce, not only of this district, but of the Ilha Grande, would have been conveyed directly to Rio, without the risk of the navigation outside of the harbour: I know not why the project was abandoned.

Every time I pass through a grove in Brazil, I see new flowers and plants, and a richness of vegetation that seems inexhaustible. To-day I saw passion-flowers of colours I never observed before; green, pink, scarlet, and blue: wild pine apples, of beautiful crimson and purple: wild tea, even more beautiful than the elegant Chinese shrub: marsh-palms, and innumerable aquatic plants, new to me: and in every little pool, wild-ducks, water-hens, and varieties of storks, were wading about in graceful pride. At every step I am inclined to exclaim with the minstrel—

> Oh nature, how in every charm supreme!
> Whose votaries feast on raptures ever new:
> Oh, for the voice and fire of seraphim
> To paint thy glories with devotion due![107]

After dinner I walked about a little in the village of the negroes. There are, I believe, about fifteen hundred on the estate, the greater part of whom belong to the outlying farms or feitorias, of which there are, I believe, three; Bom Jardin, Piperi, and Serra: these yield coffee, feijoă, and maize. The immediate neighbourhood of Santa Cruz is appropriated to the rearing of cattle, of which there are this year about four thousand head; and a good deal of pasture land is annually let. The negroes of Santa Cruz are not fed and clothed by the Emperor, but they have their little portions of land; and they have half of Friday, all Saturday and Sunday, and every holiday, to labour for themselves; so that they at most work for their master four days, in return for their house and land; and some even of the external marks of slavery are removed, as the families feed and clothe themselves without the master's interference. The Emperor has appropriated great part of a very commodious building, erected by his father for the royal stud, to the purpose of an hospital. I visited it, and found a white surgeon and black assistant; decent beds, and well-ventilated apartments: the kitchen was clean, and the broth, which was all I found cooked at the time of night when I was there, good: there were about sixty patients, most of them merely for sores in their feet, some from giggers, others a sort of leprosy from working in damp grounds, and a few with elephantiasis; fevers are very rare, pulmonary complaints not uncommon. Several of the inmates of the hospital were there merely from old age; one was insane; and there was a large ward of women, with young children: so that, on the whole, I consider the hospital as affording a proof of the healthiness of the negroes of Santa Cruz.

Sunday, 24th, presented a very respectable congregation on its way to the chapel of Santa Cruz. There were all the officers belonging to the palace, with their wives and families; also the shopkeepers of the village and neighbourhood, besides a good many of the negro people;

---

107. From *The Minstrel*, by Scottish poet James Beattie (1735-1803).

all of them, I think, better dressed than persons of the same class elsewhere in this part of Brazil.

I walked up to the tea-gardens, which occupy many acres of a rocky hill, such as I suppose may be the favourite *habitat* of the plant in China. The introduction of the culture of tea into Brazil was a favourite project of the King Joam VI., who brought the plants and cultivators at great expense from China. The tea produced both here and at the botanic gardens is said to be of superior quality; but the quantity is so small, as never yet to have afforded the slightest promise of paying the expense of culture. Yet the plants are so thriving, that I have no doubt they will soon spread of themselves, and probably become as natives. His Majesty built Chinese gates and summer-houses to correspond with the destination of these gardens; and, placed where they are, among the beautiful tea-shrubs, whose dark shining leaves and myrtle-like flowers fit them for a parterre, they have no unpleasing effect. The walks are bordered on either hand with orange trees and roses, and the garden hedge is of a beautiful kind of mimosa; so that the *China* of Santa Cruz forms really a delightful walk. The Emperor, however, who perceives that it is more advantageous to sell coffee and buy tea, than to grow it at such expense, has discontinued the cultivation.

Our hospitable friends the Capitaŏ and his lady would not allow us to leave them till after dinner, having invited several persons to do honour to us, and to a sumptuous feast they had prepared, where every good thing that can be named was present. However, due honour having been done to the table, we took our leave; and at about four o'clock or a little earlier set off for Mata Paciencia, where we arrived a little before sunset.

On our arrival we went with Dona Mariana and the chaplain into the garden, which unites the flower, kitchen-garden, and orchard in one. Oranges and roses, cabbage and tobacco, melons and leeks, neighboured each other, as if they belonged to the same climate; and all were thriving among numbers of weeds, of which the wholesome calliloo and the splendid balsam attracted my eye most. A side-door in the garden let us into a beautiful field, whither chairs were brought, that we might sit and enjoy the freshness of the evening. Overhanging that field there is a steep hill, on whose side a great deal of wood has been cleared away, and the gardens and coffee plots of the negroes occupy the ground. This day—and blessed be the Sabbath!—is the negroes' own: after morning Mass they are free to do their own will; and then most of them run to the hill to gather their coffee or maize, or prepare the ground for these or other vegetables. They were just beginning to return from the wood, each with his little basket laden with something of his own, something in which the master had no share; and again and again as they passed me, and displayed with glistening eye the little treasure, I blessed the Sabbath, the day of freedom to the slave. Presently the last few stragglers dropped in. The sun by this time was only tinging the tops of the hills. The cattle flocked in from the pasture, and lowed impatiently at the gate of the corral: we opened it, and passed in with them, and crossed the court where the negroes live. All was bustle there: they were bargaining with a huckster, who, knowing the proper hour, had arrived to buy the fresh-picked coffee. Some sold it thus; others chose to keep it and dry it, and then to take the opportunity of one of the lady's messengers to town and send it thither, where it sells at a higher price. I do not know when I have passed so pleasant an evening.

After supper I had a great deal of conversation with Dona Mariana concerning the sugar-work, the cultivation of the cane, and the slaves, confirming what I had learnt at Affonsos. She also tells me, as I had heard before, that the creole negroes are less docile and less active than the new negroes. I think both facts may be accounted for without having recourse to the influence of climate. The new negro has the education of the slave-ship and the market, the lash being administered to drill him; so that when bought he is docile from fear, active from habit. The creole negro is a spoiled child, till he is strong enough to work; then, without previous habits of industry, he is expected to be industrious, and having eaten, drunk, and run about on terms of familiar equality, he is expected to be obedient; and where no moral feelings have been cultivated, he is expected to show his gratitude for early indulgence by future fidelity. Dona Mariana tells me, that not half the negroes born on her estate live to be ten years old. It would be worth while to enquire into the cause of this evil, and whether it is general.

I conversed also a good while with the chaplain on the general state of the country. He is a native of Pernambuco; of course a staunch independent. * * * It is needless to say that every thing in the manner of living at Mata Paciencia is not only agreeable but elegant. And if the stories of older travellers concerning the country life of the Brazilians be true, the change has been most rapid and complete.

25th August.—I was very sorry to leave Mata Paciencia this morning when it was time to return; however, the hour came, and we departed for Affonsos.

On the road we stopped to make some sketches, and at Campo Grande to refresh our horses; and were glad ourselves, as the day was pretty cool, to partake of a beef-steak which the good woman of the house cooked according to our directions, the first she had ever seen, regretting all the time that their own dinner was over, and that there was not time to boil or roast for us. But hospitality seems the temper of the country.

On our arrival at Affonsos we were received as old friends, and much pressed to stay a couple of days, in order to make excursions to some picturesque spots in the neighbourhood, which I would fain have done, but my young friend, Mr. Dampier, could not spare the time; so I was obliged to content myself with only hearing of the beauties of the lake of Jacarepagua, and N. S. da Pena, etc.

26th.—We left Affonsos by times this morning, and shortly afterwards met an original-looking group of travellers. First came rather a handsome woman, in a blue joseph and broad black hat, riding astride; then three gentlemen in Indian file, all natural Falstaffs, in enormous straw hats, and mounted on good well-groomed horses; next followed the lady's maid, also astride, with her mistress's portmanteau buckled behind her; and behind her the valet, with three leathern bags hanging to his saddle by long straps, so as to swing as low as the stirrups, and whose size and shape denoted the presence of at least a clean shirt; and, lastly, a bare-headed slave with two mules, one laden with baggage and provisions, and the other as a relay. They all saluted us gravely and courteously as they passed; and I thought I had gotten among some of Gil Blas' travellers in the neighbourhood of Oviedo or Astorga, so completely did they differ from any thing usual with us.

We stopped, of course, at Campinha, to call on our hospitable hostess, Senhora Maria Rosa, and found her at a neighbour's house; whither we followed her, and found her surrounded by four of the prettiest women I have seen in Brazil. From the veranda, where we sat talking with them for some time, we had leisure to admire the country about Campinha, which was totally obscured the first time we passed by rain. It is of the same beautiful character with the rest we have seen, being distinguished by a new mud fort, now building on a little insulated knoll, which commands the road through the hills, and by the plain to the capital. The want of some such point of defence was felt when Du Clerc landed in the bay of Angra dos Reyes, at the beginning of the last century, and marched without stop to the city.[108]

After feeding our horses at the very pretty station of Rio Ferreira, we proceeded homewards; and arrived at Mr. May's in good time to dinner, having had a very pleasant excursion, and, on my part, seeing more of Brazil and Brazilians in these few days, passed entirely out of English reach, than in all the time I had been here before.

On my arrival at home I found news from Lord Cochrane of the 9th July, in latitude 6° S., longitude 32° W.; when half the army, colours, ammunition, and stores of Madeira had fallen into his hands, and he was in pursuit of the rest, intending afterwards to follow the Joaõ VI. and frigates. Should he be able to separate them, no doubt he will capture them; but alone, under his circumstances, against them, so armed and manned, I fear it will be impossible.—He has already effected more than could have been expected, or perhaps than any commander besides himself could have done. He attributes much to the imprudence, or imbecility of the enemy, whose plan of saving an army he likens to Sterne's marble sheet.[109] However, others are just enough to him, to feel that no faults of the enemy's commander lessen his merit, or obscure the courage necessary to follow up, attack, and take half at least of a fleet of seventy sail,* well found and provisioned, and full of veteran troops.

There is a letter from Lord Cochrane to the magistrates of Pernambuco published in the gazette. His Lordship, after mentioning his success, and stating his want of seamen, says, "We must have sailors to end the war. If Your Excellencies will give 24 milrees bounty, as at Rio de Janeiro, drawing on government for the same, you will do a great service to the country. I do not say Portuguese sailors, who are enemies; but sailors of *any other nation*."

* It is now certain that Joaõ Felix had at least that number.

---

108. The notorious French pirate Jean-François Duclerc made the Southeastern coast of Brazil part of his territory.

109. Laurence Sterne (1713-1768), clergyman and author most famous for *Tristram Shandy* (1759-1767). One of Sterne's literary innovations was to juxtapose a marbled page of six colors, as well as an entirely black page, against his novel's text to highlight questions of textual interpretation. Graham here suggests, then, that according to Cochrane, his own military success as head of the Brazilian navy is as much due to the fanciful nature and flawed interpretation of the enemy's planning as it is to his own military genius.

His Lordship mentions farther in his letters to Pernambuco, that his reasons for rather following up the transports at first, instead of the ships of war, which were the objects he had most at heart, were, lest the troops should land, as they had threatened, in some other port of Brazil, and commit new hostilities in the empire. And he concludes with announcing that he sends several flags taken from the enemy.

August 29th.—To-day I received a visit from Dona Maria de Jesus, the young woman who has lately distinguished herself in the war of the Reconcave. Her dress is that of a soldier of one of the Emperor's battalions, with the addition of a tartan kilt, which she told me she had adopted from a picture representing a highlander, as the most feminine military dress. What would the Gordons and Mac Donalds say to this? The "garb of old Gaul," chosen as a womanish attire!—Her father is a Portuguese, named Gonsalvez de Almeida, and possesses a farm on the Rio do Pex, in the parish of San José, in the Certaỡ, about forty leagues in-land from Cachoeira. Her mother was also a Portuguese; yet the young woman's features, especially her eyes and forehead, have the strongest characteristics of the Indians. Her father has another daughter by the same wife; since whose death he has married again, and the new wife and the young children have made home not very comfortable to Dona Maria de Jesus. The farm of the Rio do Pex is chiefly a cattle farm, but the possessor seldom knows or counts his numbers. Senhor Gonsalvez, besides his cattle, raises some cotton; but as the Certaỡ is sometimes a whole year without rain, the quantity is uncertain. In wet years he may sell 400 arobas, at from four to five milrees; in dry seasons he can scarcely collect above sixty or seventy arobas, which may fetch from six to seven milrees. His farm employs twenty-six slaves.

The women of the interior spin and weave for their household, and they also embroider very beautifully. The young women learn the use of fire-arms, as their brothers do, either to shoot game or defend themselves from the wild Indians.

Dona Maria told me several particulars concerning the country, and more concerning her own adventures. It appears, that early in the late war of the Reconcave, emissaries had traversed the country in all directions, to raise patriot recruits; that one of these had arrived at her father's house one day about dinner time; that her father had invited him in, and that after their meal he began to talk on the subject of his visit. He represented the greatness and the riches of Brazil, and the happiness to which it might attain if independent. He set forth the long and oppressive tyranny of Portugal; and the meanness of submitting to be ruled by so poor and degraded a country. He talked long and eloquently of the services Don Pedro had rendered to Brazil; of his virtues, and those of the Empress: so that at the last, said the girl, "I felt my heart burning in my breast." Her father, however, had none of her enthusiasm of character. He is old, and said he neither could join the army himself; nor had he a son to send thither; and as to giving a slave for the ranks, what interest had a slave to fight for the independence of Brazil? He should wait in patience the result of the war, and be a peaceable subject to the winner. Dona Maria stole from home to the house of her own sister, who was married, and lived at a little distance. She recapitulated the whole of the stranger's discourse, and said she wished she was a man, that she might join the patriots. "Nay," said the sister, "if I had not a husband and children, for one half of what you say I would join the ranks for the Emperor." This was enough. Maria received some clothes belonging to her sister's husband to equip her; and as her father was then about to go to Cachoeira to dispose of some cottons, she resolved to take the opportunity of riding after him, near enough for protection in case of accident on the road, and far enough off to escape detection. At length being in sight of Cachoeira, she stopped; and going off the road, equipped herself in male attire, and entered the town. This was on Friday. By Sunday she had managed matters so well, that she had entered the regiment of artillery, and had mounted guard. She was too slight, however, for that service, and exchanged into the infantry, where she now is. She was sent hither, I believe, with despatches, and to be presented to the Emperor, who has given her an ensign's commission and the order of the cross, the decoration of which he himself fixed on her jacket.

She is illiterate, but clever. Her understanding is quick, and her perceptions keen. I think, with education she might have been a remarkable person. She is not particularly masculine in her appearance, and her manners are gentle and cheerful. She has not contracted any thing coarse or vulgar in her camp life, and I believe that no imputation has ever been substantiated against her modesty. One thing is certain, that her sex never was known until her father applied to her commanding officer to seek her.

There is nothing very peculiar in her manners at table, excepting that she eats farinha with her eggs at breakfast and her fish at dinner, instead of bread, and smokes a segar after each meal; but she is very temperate.

Sept. 8th, 1823.—I went with Mr. Hoste and Mr. Hately, of His Majesty's ship Briton, to Praya Grande, to see a party of Botocudo Indians, who are now there on a visit.[110] As it is desired to civilise these people by every possible means, whenever they manifest a wish to visit the neighbourhood of the city, they are always encouraged and received kindly, fed to their hearts' content, and given clothes, and such trinkets and ornaments as they value. We saw about six men, and ten women, with some young children. The faces are rather square, with very high cheek-bones, and low contracted foreheads. Some of the young women are really pretty, of a light copper-colour, which glows all over when they blush; and two of the young men were decidedly handsome, with very dark eyes, (the usual colour of the eyes is hazel,) and aquiline noses; the rest were so disfigured by the holes cut in their lower lips and their ears to receive their barbarous ornaments, that we could scarcely tell what they were like. I had understood that the privilege of thus beautifying the face was reserved for the men,* but the women of this party were equally disfigured. We purchased from one of the men a mouth-piece, measuring an inch and a half in diameter. The ornaments used by these people are pieces of wood perfectly circular, which are inserted into the slit of the lip or ear, like a button, and are extremely frightful, especially when they are eating. It gives the mouth the appearance of an ape's; and the peculiar mumping it occasions is so hideously unnatural, that it gives credit to, if it did not originally suggest, the stories of their cannibalism.† [The Bishop of Rio told me Nov. 1824 that in his many years travelling in the in-

* See Southy's Brazil, for the manners of the Tupayas. I am not sufficiently acquainted with the filiation of the Indian tribes, to know what relation the Botocudos bear to the Tupayas.

† Perhaps all the Indians may have been so far cannibals, as to taste of the flesh of prisoners taken in battle, or victims offered to the gods; but I cannot believe that any ever fed habitually on human flesh, for many reasons. But their traducers had their reasons for inventing and propagating the most atrocious falsehoods, as a sort of excuse for their own barbarity in hunting and making slaves of them. These practices, indeed, were so wicked, and so notorious, that in 1537, the Dominican Frey Domingos de Becançoo, provincial of the order in Mexico, sent Frey Domingos de Menaja to Rome to plead the cause of the Indians before Paul III.; who having heard *both sides*, pronounced that "The Indians of America are men of rational soul, of the same nature and species as all others, capable of the sacraments of the holy church, and consequently free by nature, and lords of their own actions."

---

110. Mr. Hoste may be Lieutenant Thomas Hoste, who served briefly on the Doris (in the spring of 1823) in exchange for invalided officers (Vale, *Frigate* 106); we are unable to identify Mr. Hately.

terior of the country he knew that most of the tribes would eat from revenge their enemies killed or taken in battle but in *no other instance* were they man eaters.] The mouth is still more ugly without the lip-piece, the teeth appearing, and saliva running through.

When we entered the room where the savages are lodged, most of them were lying in mats on the floor; some on their faces, and some on their backs. Three of the women were suckling their infants, and these were dressed only in coarse cotton petticoats; the rest of the females had cotton frocks, the men shirts and trowsers, given them on their arrival here. As they are usually naked in the woods, their garments seemed to sit uneasily on them: their usual motions seemed slow and lazy; but when roused, there was a springy activity hardly fitting a human being, in all they did. They begged for money; and when we took out a few vintems, the women crowded round me, and pinched me gently to attract my attention. They had learned a few words of Portuguese, which they addressed to us, but discoursed together in their own tongue, which seemed like a series of half-articulate sounds.

They had brought some of their bows and arrows with them of the rudest construction. The bow is of hard wood, with only two notches for the string. The arrows are of cane; some are pointed only with hard wood, others with a flat bit of cane tied with bark to the end of the hard wood: these arrows are five feet long; and I saw one of them penetrate several inches into the trunk of a tree, when shot by an Indian from his bow. I purchased one bow and two arrows. Most of these people had their hair closely clipped, excepting a tuft on the fore part of the head; and the men, who had slit their lips, had also pulled out their beards. The two handsome lads had cut their hair; but they had neither cut their lips nor pulled their beards. I tried to learn if this was a step towards civilisation, or if it was only that they had not reached the age when the ceremony of lip-slitting, etc. is practised, the interpreter attending them not being able to explain any thing but what concerns their commonest wants and actions.

September 9th.—I took two very fine Brazilian boys, who are about to enter the Imperial naval service, to spend the day at the botanical garden, which appears in much better order than when I saw it two years ago. The hedge-rows of the Bencoolen nut (*Vernilzia Montana*) are prodigiously grown: the Norfolk Island pine has shot up like a young giant, and I was glad to find many of the indigenous trees had been placed here; such as the *Andraguoa*, the nut of which is the stron-

Figure 17. Dona Maria de Jesus. Courtesy of The Catholic University of America, Oliveira Lima Library, Washington, D.C.

gest known purge; the *Cambucá,* whose fruit, as large as a russet apple, has the sub-acid taste of the gooseberry, to which its pulp bears a strong resemblance; the *Japatec-caba,* whose fruit is scarcely inferior to the damascene; and the *Grumaxama,* whence a liquor, as good as that from cherries, is made: these three last are like laurels, and as beautiful as they are useful. I took my young friends to see the powder-mills, which are not now at work, being under repair; but they learned the manner of making powder, from the first weighing of the ingredients to the filling cartridges: and then we had our table spread in a pleasant part of the garden, under the shade of a jumbu tree, and made the head gardener, a very ingenious Dutchman, partake of our luncheon; which being over, he showed us the cinnamon they have barked here, and the other specimens of spice: the cloves are very fine, and the cinnamon might be so; but the wood they have barked is generally too old, and they have not yet the method of stripping the twigs: this I endeavoured to explain, as I had seen it practised in Ceylon. The camphor tree grows very well here, but I do not know if the gum has ever been collected. The two boys were highly delighted with their jaunt, and I not less so. Poor things! they are entering on a hard service; and God knows whether the two cousins da Costa may not hereafter look back to this day passed with a stranger, as a bright "spot of azure in a stormy sky."[111]

Sept. 13th.—I rode again to the botanic gardens with Mr. Hoste and Mr. Hately. Our chief object this time was the powder-mills. After walking round the garden, we proceeded along the valley of the mills; and so beautiful and sequestered a place, in the bosom of the mountains, was surely never before chosen as a manufactory for so destructive an article: I suppose the great command of water for the machinery is the chief inducement to fix it here. The powder is mixed by pounding, the mortars being of rosewood, and the pestles of the same shod with copper; yet the mortar-hoops are iron, which seems to me to be a strange oversight. I do not understand these things, however; but the machinery interested me: it is extremely simple, and the timber used in the construction very beautiful. The principal mill blew up a few months since, and is now under repair; so that we had an opportunity of seeing the water-courses, dams, wheels, etc., which we could not otherwise have enjoyed. We could not learn the relative strength of the powder. I have heard, however, that it is good. What I have seen is about as fine in grain as what we call priming powder in the navy. While we were walking about we were invited into several houses, by the overseers and other persons employed in the works, and pressed to eat and drink with great hospitality. The greatest liberality to strangers, indeed, exists in all public establishments here. For instance, at the botanic garden there is a constant nursery of the rare and the useful plants, which are given away, on application, to strangers and natives alike; so that not

---

111. Graham slightly misquotes from John Scott (1730-1783), *Elegy Written at Amwell*; the line should read, "A spot of azure in a cloudy sky!"

only the gardens of Brazil are stocked with the rarer productions of the East, but they are carried to different countries in Europe, prepared by this cooler climate for their farther transplantation.

14th.—I observed on the beach to-day a line of red sandy-looking matter, extending all along the shore, and tinging the sea for several feet from the edge. At night this red edge became luminous; and I now recollect when on the passage to India in 1809, that on observing a peculiar luminous appearance of the sea, we took up a bucket of water, and on examining it next morning, we observed a similar red grainy substance floating in it. It is the first time I have seen it here, and I cannot find that any body has paid any attention to it. Perhaps it is not worth noticing; but I am so much alone, that I have grown more and more alive to all the appearances of inanimate nature. Besides, I must make much of the country, as in a few days I have to take up my abode in one of the narrow close streets of Rio; and this not from choice. It is the custom here, and a very natural and pleasant one it is, for every family that can, to live in the country all the summer: so that the houses of every kind, in the country, are in great request. The term for which that I live in was hired is expired, and I am therefore obliged to leave it. My going to town, perhaps, might be avoided, but there are some things I shall probably learn more perfectly by living there; and, besides, does not Lord Bacon advise that in order to profit much from travel, one should not only move from city to city, "but change his lodgings from one end and part of the city to another?"

The last fortnight has been extremely foggy, and rather cold; and we have had some fierce thunder-storms, that seem almost to rock the mountains, and threaten to bring them down upon us.

16th.—At length I am fixed in No. 79., Rua dos Pescadores, in the first floor of an excellent house, belonging to my kind friend Dr. Dickson, who himself inhabits a villa out of town; where he has a farm, a garden, a collection of minerals and insects, and all sorts of agreeable and profitable things, which he dispenses to others with the greatest good-nature. I am obliged to Sir Thomas Hardy for a pleasant passage to town from Botafogo, his carriage conveying me, and his boats my goods: so in a few hours I have changed my home, and have probably taken my leave of all English society, every body has such a dread of the heat of the town. However, as I look forward to going to England in a few months, perhaps in a few weeks, the more time I have for Brazil the better. My private affairs have so occupied me that I have scarcely had time to think of the public. Yet in the course of the last week the project of the constitution for Brazil, framed by the committee appointed, was sent from the Assembly to the Emperor; and yesterday the discussion of it, article by article, began in the full assembly.

17th.—One advantage has already arisen from my removal into town. I have received the very first news of the arrival of a ship from Lisbon with commissioners on the part of the King to the Emperor. I find, too, that at Lisbon they can publish false news, as well as in some other countries in Europe. That city had illuminated in consequence of news that Lord Cochrane had been beaten, and the Imperial navy destroyed by the Bahia squadron; and this illumination must have taken place just about the time that Madeira was evacuating the city, and flying before the Imperial Admiral's flag. As to the reception the commissioners are to meet with, it is doubtful. Some days since the brig 3° de Maio arrived here, having on board Luiz Paolino as successor to Madeira; who, finding he could not get into Bahia, came hither, to present, it is said, his commission as governor of Bahia to His Imperial Majesty as Prince Regent; and it is also said that he was the bearer of some letters. But as none of these acknowledged the title, or independence of the empire of Brazil, they were not received; and the vessel has already sailed on her return to Lisbon. It is believed that the same fate will attend the present commissioners, Vieira and his colleague, if indeed the ship should not be condemned as a prize. But hitherto of course nothing is known.

Another vessel also arrived with intelligence of some moment from Buenos Ayres. It appears that the captain of His Majesty's ship Brazen has been at variance with the authorities there concerning the old subject of the right of boarding vessels, the priority of which the Buenos Ayrians claim for their own health-boat. The Commodore means to go thither himself on the business, and I have no doubt all will be well and reasonably settled.

18th.—I went to-day to the public library to ask about some books, and am invited to go and use what I like there: the librarians are all extremely polite, and the library is open to all persons for six hours daily.

I have also walked a great deal about the town, and have again visited the arsenals; in which very great improvements have been made and are making, particularly building sheds for the workmen. After an English arsenal, to be sure, the want of machinery and all the luxuries of labour is conspicuous; but the work is well done, and reminds me of that I used to see under the old Parsee builder in Bombay. They are laying down new ships and repairing old ones. I only wish they could form a nursery for seamen, because Brazil must have ships to guard her coasts. Fisheries off the Abrolhos, and from St. Catherine's, might perhaps do something towards it. From the arsenal I climbed the hill immediately overlooking it, where there is the convent of San Bento; where, it is said, there is a good library, but it is not accessible to women. The situation of the convent is delightful, overlooking both divisions of the harbour and the whole town, and the hills many a mile beyond. I am not sure whether a cloister or a prison, commanding a fine view, be preferable to one without. Whether the gazing on a beautiful scene be in itself a pleasure great enough to alleviate confinement; or whether it does not increase the longing for liberty in a way analogous to that in which a well-remembered air creates a longing, even to death, for the home where that air was first heard;—it seems to me as if, once imprisoned, I would break every association with liberty, and keep my eyes from wandering where my limbs must no longer bear me. However, I do suppose, some may be, and some have been, happy in a cloister. I cannot envy them; I would fain not despise them.

[*September 19th.*—Our little English world at Rio is grieving in one common mourning for the death of one of the youngest, and certainly the loveliest, of our countrywomen here. Beautiful and gay, and the lately married and cherished wife of a most worthy man, Mrs. N. died a short time after the birth of her first child. She had appeared to be recovering well; she relapsed and died. It is one of those events that excites sympathy in the hardest, and commiseration in the coldest. {Graham deleted this material.}]

23d.—I have been unwell again—but I find that staying at home does not cure me; so I went both yesterday and to-day to the library, where a pleasant, cool, little cabinet has been assigned to me, where whatever book I ask for is brought to me, and where I have pen, ink, and paper always placed to make notes. This is a kindness and attention to a woman and a stranger that I was hardly prepared for. The library was brought hither from Lisbon in 1810, and placed in its present situation, which was once the hospital belonging to the Carmelites. That hospital was removed to a healthier and more commodious situation, and the rooms, admirably adapted to the purpose, received the books, of which there are between sixty and seventy thousand volumes. The greater number are books of theology and law. There is a great deal of ecclesiastical history, and particularly all the Jesuits' accounts of South America. General and civil history are not wanting;

and there are good editions of the classics. There are some fine works on natural history; but, excepting these, nothing modern; scarcely a book having been bought for sixty years. But a noble addition was made to the establishment by the purchase of the Conde de Barca's library; in which there are some valuable modern works, and a very fine collection of topographical prints of all parts of the world.[112]

I have begun to read diligently every scrap of Brazilian history I can find; and I have commenced by a collection of pamphlets, newspapers, some MS. letters and proclamations, from the year 1576 to 1757, bound up together;* some of these tracts Mr. Southey mentions, others he probably had not seen, but they contain nothing very material that he has not in his history.[113] [This morning's study of Brazilian

---

* To this collection is a printed and engraved title-page, as follows: "Noticias Historicas e Militares da America Collegidas por Diogo Barboso Machado Abbade da Igreja de Santo Adriano de Sever, e Academico da Academia Real. Comprehende do Anno de 1579 até 1757." It contains twenty-four pamphlets, etc. The Abbade Machado's name is in almost all the historical books I have yet seen in the library. I know not how the collection of the author of the Bibliotheca Lusitania became part of the royal library. [Father Diogo Barbosa Machado, abbot of the church of Santo Adrião de Sever, offered his impressive collection to the Portuguese Royal Family (1770–1773) and it traveled to Brazil with the transference of the site of government in 1808. Today this collection encompasses 4,300 items, including books, prints, maps, and a precious collection of rare brochures related to Brazilian and Portuguese history (Lacombe 360; Fundação Biblioteca Nacional de Brasil)—*Eds.*]

---

112. António de Araújo de Azevedo, Conde da Barca, Portuguese Foreign Minister and Dom João's chief minister. After the Conde's death in 1817, Dom João authorized his librarian to acquire da Barca's private library of over 74,000 volumes (according to Lacombe) and used it to help establish the Brazilian public library (Lacombe 359).

113. Robert Southey (1774-1843), English author of poetry and prose. After a trip to Portugal, where his uncle was the British chaplain at Lisbon, he planned to write a history of Portugal. He never completed this project, but his three-volume *History of Brazil* was published between 1810-1819. Although she draws heavily on his version of Brazilian history in her Introduction (see appendix), Graham mentions Southey only once in her travel narrative; in the Introduction, too, she corrects, amends, and revises his information based on her eye-witness experience of the country. Lacombe does not bother to correct either Graham or Southey's version of history in detail, noting that "nobody would consider using this book to study the formation of Brazil" (23, translation ours).

history in the original language is one great advantage I derive from my removal into town. Besides which, I speak now less English than Portuguese. {Graham deleted this material.}]

24th.—Having now received the portrait which Mr. Erle, an ingenious young English artist, has been painting of the Senhora Alerez Dona Maria de Jesus, I took it to show it to her friend and patron, Jose Bonifacio de Andrada e Silva.

I never spend half an hour any where with more pleasure and profit than with the ex-minister's family. His lady is of Irish parentage, an O'Leary, a most amiable and kind woman, and truly appreciating the worth and talent of her husband; and all the nephews and other relations I meet there appear superior in education and understanding to the generality of persons I see. But it is Jose Bonifacio himself who attracts and interests me most. He is a small man, with a thin lively countenance; and his manner and conversation at once impress the beholder with the idea of that restless activity of mind which

> O'er-informs its tenement of clay,[114]

and is but too likely to wear out the body that contains it. The first time I saw him in private was after he ceased to be minister, his occupations before that time leaving him little leisure for private society. I was curious to see the retreat of a public man. I found him surrounded by young people and children, some of whom he took on his knee and caressed; and I could easily see that he was very popular among the small people. To me, as a stranger, he was most ceremoniously yet kindly polite, and conversed on all subjects and of all countries. He has visited most of those of Europe.

His library is well stored with books in all languages. The collection on chemistry and on mining is particularly extensive, and rich in Swedish and German authors. These, indeed, are subjects peculiarly interesting to Brazil, and have naturally been of first-rate interest to him. But his delight is classical literature; and he is himself a poet of no mean order. Perhaps my knowledge of Portuguese does not entitle me to judge particularly on the vehicle or language of his poetry; but if lofty thoughts, new and beautiful combinations, keen sensibility, and a love of beauty and of nature, be essential to poetry, the poems

---

114. Graham again quotes from Dryden's *Absalom and Achitophel*: "A fiery soul, which working out its way,/Fretted the pigmy-body to decay:/And o'er inform'd the tenement of clay."

he read to me to-day have them all. There is one in particular, on the Creation of Woman, glowing as the sun under which it was written, and as pure as his light. Perhaps it derived some of its merit from his manner of reading it, which, though not what is called fine reading, is full of character and intelligence.

To-day, Jose Bonifacio gave me a translation from Meleager, which seems to me very beautiful. It was written at Lisbon in 1816, where two or three copies were printed by one of his friends; the last of these is now mine.*

Let no one say, that he is too miserable for any comfort to reach him. I am alone, and a widow, and in a foreign land; my health weak, my nerves irritable, and having neither wealth nor rank; forced to receive obligations painful and discordant with my former habits and prejudices, and often meeting with impertinence from those who take advantage of my solitary situation: but I am nevertheless sure that I have more *half-hours,* I dare not say *hours,* of true enjoyment, and fewer days of real misery, than half of those whom the world accounts happy. And I thank God, who gave me the temper to feel grief exquisitely, that he at the same time gave me an equal capacity for joy. And it is a joy to find minds that can understand and communicate with our own; to meet occasionally with persons of similar habits of thinking, and who, when the business of life rests a while, seek recreation in the same pursuits. This delight I do oftener enjoy than I could have hoped, so far from cultivated Europe. One or two of my friends are, indeed, like costly jewels, not to be worn every day; but there are several of sterling metal that even here disarm the ills of this "working-day world" of half their sting.[115]

* Traducção.

> Já do ether fugio ventosa inverno,
> E da florida primavera a hora
> Purpurea rio: de verde herva mimosa
> A Terra denegrida se corôa.
> Bebem os prados já liquido orvalho,
> Com que medraõ as plantas, e festejaõ
> Os abertos botões das novas rosas.
> Com as asperos sons da frauta rude
> Folga o Serrano, o Pegureiro folga   [cont.]

---

115. "Oh how full of briars is this working-day world!" exclaims Rosalind in Shakespeare's *As You Like It* I:iii.

[* cont.]

Com as alvos recentes cabritinhos.
Já sulcaŏ Nautas estendidas ondas;
   E Favonio innocente as velas boja.
As Menades, cubertas as cabeças
Da flor d'hera, tres vezes enrolada,
Do uvifero Baccho orgias celebraŏ:
A Geraçaŏ bovina das abelhas
Seus trabalhos completa; j'a produzem
Formoso mel; nos favos repousados
Candida cera multiplicaŏ. Cantaŏ
Por toda a parte as sonorosas aves:
Nas ondas o Alcyaŏ, em torna aos tectos
Canta a Andorinha; canta o branco Cysne
Na ribanceira, e o Rouxinol no bosque.
Se pois as plantas ledas reverdecem;
Florece a Terra; o Guardador a frauta
Tange, e folga co'as maçans folhudas;
Se aves gorgeiaŏ; se as abelhas criaŏ;
Navegaŏ Nautas; Baccho guia as choros:
Porque naŏ cantará tambem o Vate
   A risonha, a formosa Primavera?

English Translation (from *Fifty Poems of Meleager*, Walter Headlam, trans. London and New York: MacMillan and Company, 1890.)

XXXVIII
Spring

As soon as windy Winter was gone from the sky,
out smiled the sunny season of flower-bearing Spring:
the dark earth of green grass a coronal put on,
and sucking scions burgeoned with petals all anew.
And now the meadows drinking the tender dew of Dawn,
their foster-mother, laugh with the opening of the rose.
The shepherd in the mountains pipes gaily on his reed,
and in the white kids of the goats the goatherd takes delight.
Now on the ocean-billows the sailors are afloat,
outbosoming their canvas the Zephyr's harmless breath.
To clustered Dionysus men sing their praises now,
with berried ivy's blossom engarlanding their hair.
Now with their cunning duties the kine-engendered bees
are busy, and within the hive do seated labour out
the white, liquid treasures of the often-pierced comb. [cont.]

Sept. 26th, 1823.—A marriage in high life engages many of the talkers of Rio. A fidalgo, an officer distinguished under Beresford[116], Don Francisco—, whose other name I have forgotten, is fortunate enough to have obtained one of the loveliest granddaughters of the Baroness de Campos, *Maria de Loreto;* whose extraordinary likeness to our own Princess Charlotte of Wales is such, that I am sure no English person can have seen her without being struck with it.[117] Here, no unmarried women are allowed to be present at a marriage; but the ceremony is performed in the presence of the nearest relations, being married, on both sides. The mother of the bride sends notice to court, if she be of rank to do so, afterwards to other ladies, according to their degree, of the marriage of her daughter. The bride then goes to court; after which the ladies visit her, and proceed to congratulate the other members of the family. It is said this match is one in which the lawful lord of such things, *i.e.* Master Cupid, has had more to do than he is usually allowed to have in Brazil, even since it was independent; and truly a handsomer couple will not often be seen. I am glad of it. Surely free choice on such an important subject is as much to be desired as on any other. On this occasion,

> The god of love, who stood to spy them,

---

116. William Carr Beresford (1768-1854), British general and marshal in the Portuguese army.

117. Princess Charlotte Augusta of Wales (1796–1817), only child of the difficult marriage of George IV and Caroline of Brunswick, died young in childbirth. The nation mourned her with an extravagance only exceeded by its mourning for Princess Diana almost two hundred years later; given the national affection for her, it is interesting that Graham speaks of Charlotte as if she were still living.

[* cont.]

> The tribe of birds with voices clear are singing everywhere,
> the kingfisher about the wave, the swallow round the roof,
> the swan upon the river-banks, the nightingale in wood.
> Then if green leaves are merry, and earth is all in bloom,
> and if the shepherd pipeth, and fleecy flocks delight,
> if Dionysus danceth, and sailors are afloat,
> if chant the feathered creatures, and bees are travailing,
> how should not in the spring-time the poet sweetly sing?

> The god of love, who must be nigh them,
> Pleased and tickled at the sight,
> Sneezed aloud; and at his right
> The little loves that waited by,
> Bow'd and bless'd the augury;[118]

as my favourite Cowley says; and I hope we shall have more such free matches in our free Brazil, where, hitherto, the course of true love is apt not to run smooth, that is, if my informants on the subject are in the right. Seriously, perhaps there has not hitherto been refinement enough for the delicate metaphysical love of Europe; which, because it is more rational, more noble, than all others, is less easily turned aside into other channels. Grandison or Clarissa could not have been written here; but I think ere long we may look for the polish and prudent morals of Belinda.[119]

Sept. 29th.—I went to the orphan asylum, which is also the foundling hospital. The orphan boys are apprenticed at a proper age. The girls have a portion of 200 milrees; which, though little, assists in their establishment, and is often eked out from other funds. The house is exceedingly clean, and so are the beds for the foundling children, only three of whom are now in-door nurslings, the rest being placed out in the country. Till lately they have died in a proportion frightful compared with their numbers.* Within little more than nine years, 10,000 children have been received: these were placed out at nurse, and many were never accounted for. Not perhaps that they all died, because the

---
* See the Emperor's speech on the 3d May.

118. Slightly misquoted from Abraham Cowley's (1618-1667) *Septimnius and Acme.*

119. Graham's commentary uses popular novels as touchstones of particular character types as well as attitudes towards love and marriage. Samuel Richardson's (1689-1761) novel *The History of Sir Charles Grandison* (1753–54) features a gentlemanly, benevolent hero who must choose between an Englishwoman, Harriet Byron, and an Italian, Signora Clementina; he ultimately marries Harriet. In Richardson's tragic epistolary novel *Clarissa* (1747–48), the female protagonist seeks to preserve her virtue and her free choice in marriage, despite the pressures of her family and suitors. In Maria Edgeworth's (1767-1849) *Belinda* (1801), the heroine also marches towards marriage, but Edgeworth describes her as conducting herself "with prudence and integrity." Interestingly, the novel also featured an interracial marriage, though Edgeworth edited this out of the third (1810) edition.

temptation of retaining a mulatto child as a slave, would most likely secure care of its life; but the white ones had not even this chance of safety. Besides, the wages paid for the nursing of each was formerly so little, that the poor creatures who received them could hardly have afforded them the means of subsistence. A partial amendment has taken place, and still greater improvements are about to be made. There is a great want of medical treatment. Many of the foundlings are placed in the wheel* full of disease, fever, or more often a dreadful species of itch called sarna, and which is often fatal to them. Nay, dead children are also brought, that they may be decently interred.

From the asylum, I crossed the street to the great hospital of the Misericordia. It is a fine building, and has plenty of room; but it is not in so good a state as might be wished: there are usually four hundred patients, and the number of deaths very great; but I could not learn the exact proportion. The medical department is in great want of reform. The insane ward interested me most of all: it is on the ground floor, very cold and damp; and most of those placed in it die speedily of consumptive complaints. I found here a contradiction to the vulgar opinion, that hydrophobia is not known in Brazil. A poor negro had been bitten by a mad dog a month ago; he did not seem very ill till yesterday morning, when he was sent here. He was at the grate of his cell as we passed him, in a deplorable state: knowing the gentleman who was with me, he had hoped he would release him from confinement; this of course could not be: he expired a few hours after we saw him. The burial-ground of the Misericordia is so much too small as to be exceedingly disgusting, and, I should imagine, unwholesome for the neighbourhood. I had long wished to do what I have done to-day. I think the more persons that show an interest in such establishments the better: it fixes attention upon them; and that of itself must do good. Yet my courage had hitherto failed, and I owe the excursion of this morning to accident rather than design.

I rode this evening to the protestant burial-ground, at the Praya de Gamboa. I think it one of the loveliest spots I ever beheld, commanding beautiful views every way. It slopes gradually towards the road along the shore: at the highest point there is a pretty building, consisting of three chambers; one serves as a place of meeting or waiting for the clergyman occasionally; one as a repository for the mournful furniture of the grave; and the largest, which is between the other two, is

---

* A wheel or revolving box, like that at a convent, into which the infants are put.

generally occupied by the body of the dead for the few hours, it may be a day and a night, which can in this climate elapse between death and burial: in front of this are the various stones, and urns, and vain memorials we raise to relieve our own sorrow; and between these and the road, some magnificent trees. Three sides of this field are fenced by rock or wood. Even Crabbe's fanciful and delicate Jane might have thought without pain of sleeping here.*[120] In my illness I had often felt sorry that I had not seen this ground. I am satisfied now; and if my still lingering weakness should lay me here, the very very few who may come to see where their friend lies will feel no disgust at the prison-house.

30th.—I called at a very agreeable Brazilian lady's house to-day; and saw, for the first time in my life, a regular Brazilian *bas-blue* in the person of Dona Maria Clara: she reads a good deal, especially philosophy and politics; she is a tolerable botanist, and draws flowers exceedingly well; besides, she is what I think it is Miss Edgeworth calls "a fetcher and carrier of bays,"—a useful member of society, who, without harming herself or others, circulates the necessary literary news, and would be invaluable where new authors want puffing, and new poems should have the pretty passages pointed out for the advantage of literary misses.[121] Here, alas! such kindly offices are confined to comparing the rival passages in the Correiro and the Sentinela, or advocating the cause of the editor of the Sylpho or the Tamoyo. But, in sober earnest, I was delighted to find such a lady. Without arrogating much more than is due to the sex, it may claim some small influence over the occupations and amusements of home; and the woman who brings books instead of cards or private scandal into the domestic circle, is likely to promote a more general cultivation, and a more refined taste, in the society to which she belongs.

---

* See Tales of the Hall, "The Sisters".

120. George Crabbe (1754-1832), British poet known for his vivid descriptions of rural life in *The Village* (1770) and *The Parish Register* (1810). As Graham indicates in her note, "delicate Jane" is one of two sisters in George Crabbe's *Tales of the Hall* (1819), who spends her time reading and is particularly intrigued by spectacular, gothic texts. For example, "She was amused when sent to haunted rooms,/or some dark passage where the spirit comes/of one once murder'd" (Book VIII).

121. The phrase "fetcher and carrier of bays," used disparagingly to satirized a woman's literary affectation, appears in Chapter 10 of Edgeworth's 1809 novel *Ennui; Or, Memoirs Of The Earl Of Glenthorn*.

October 1st, 1823.—The court and city are in a state of rejoicing. Lord Cochrane has secured Maranham for the Emperor. Once more I break in on my own rule, and copy part of his letter to me:—

Maranham, August 12th, 1823.

My dear Madam,
 You would receive a few lines from me, dated from off Bahia, and also from the latitude of Pernambuco, saying briefly what we were about then. And now I have to add, that we followed the Portuguese squadron to the fifth degree of north latitude, and until only thirteen sail remained together out of seventy of their convoy; and then, judging it better for the interests of His Imperial Majesty, I hauled the wind for Maranham; and I have the pleasure to tell you, that my plan of adding it to the empire has had complete success. I ran in with this ship abreast of their forts; and having sent a notice of blockade, and intimated that the squadron of Bahia and Imperial forces were off the bar, the Portuguese flag was hauled down, and every thing went on without bloodshed, just as you could wish. We have found here a Portuguese brig of war, a schooner, and eight gun-boats; also sixteen merchant vessels, and a good deal of property belonging to Portuguese resident in Lisbon, deposited in the custom-house. The brig of war late the Infante Don Miguel, now the Imperatriz, is gone down with Grenfell to summon Para, where there is a beautiful newly-launched fifty-gun frigate, which I have no doubt but he has got before now.[122] Thus, my dear Madam, on my return I shall have the pleasure to acquaint His Imperial Majesty, that between the extremities of his empire there exists no enemy either on shore or afloat. This will probably be within the sixth month from

---

122. John Pascoe Grenfell (1800-1869), naval officer recruited for the Brazilian navy by Cochrane (with whom he had fought in Chile), lost an arm in action off Buenos Aires (1826). He ultimately became Commander of the Brazilian navy during its war against Argentina (1851), but then returned to England as Consul General in Liverpool (Vale, *Independence* 191).

our sailing from Rio, and at this moment is actually the case.

Together with this letter, His Lordship has sent me the public papers concerning the taking possession of the place for the Emperor, and the officer who brought the despatches has obligingly favoured me with further particulars; so that I believe the following to be a correct account, as far as it goes, of the whole.

As soon as it was perceived on board the Pedro Primeiro, by the orders given by Lord Cochrane for the course of the ship, that he had resolved on going to Maranham, the pilots became uneasy on account of the dangerous navigation of the coast, and, as they said, the impossibility of entering the harbour in so large a ship. I have often felt that there was something very captivating in the word *impossible*. The Admiral, however, had better motives, and had skill and knowledge to support his perseverance; and so on the 26th of July he entered the bay of San Luis de Maranham, under English colours. Seeing a vessel of war off the place, he sent a boat on board; and though some of the sailors recognised two of the boat's crew, the officer, Mr. Shepherd, performed his part so well, that he obtained all the necessary information; and the Admiral then went in with his ship, and anchored under fort San Francisco. Thence he sent in the following papers to the city.

Address to the Authorities.

The forces of His Imperial Majesty the Emperor of Brazil, having delivered the city and province of Bahia from the enemies of their independence, I, in conformity to the wishes of His Imperial Majesty, am desirous that the fruitful province of Maranham should enjoy a like freedom. I am now come to offer to the unfortunate inhabitants the protection and assistance necessary against the oppression of foreigners, wishing to accomplish their freedom, and to salute them as brethren and as friends. But should there be any who, from vexatious motives, oppose the liberation of this country, such persons may be assured that the naval and military forces which expelled the Portuguese from the South, are ready to draw the sword in the same just cause: and that sword once drawn, the consequences cannot be doubtful. I beg the principal authorities to make known to me their decisions, in order that, in case of opposition, the consequences may not be imputed to the hasty manner in which I set about the work which I must achieve. God keep Your Excellencies many years!—*On board the Pedro Primeiro, 26th July, 1823.*

Proclamation

By His Excellency Lord Cochrane, Admiral and Commander-in-Chief of the naval forces of His Imperial Majesty.

The port, river, and island of Maranham, the bay of San José, and roads adjacent, are declared to be in a state of blockade, as long as the Portuguese shall exercise the supreme authority there; and all entrance or departure is strictly prohibited, under those pains and penalties authorised by the law of nations against those who violate the rights of belligerents.—*On board the Pedro Primeiro, 26th July, 1823.*

These papers were received by the junta of Provisional Government, at whose head was the Bishop. There had previously been some movements in favour of independence, but they had been overruled by the Portuguese troops, of whom there were about 300 in the town. The junta of course accepted all Lord Cochrane's proposals; the 1st of August was appointed as the day for electing a new government under the empire, and the intermediate days for taking the oaths to the Emperor, and for embarking the Portuguese troops; a step the more necessary, as they had shown a disposition to oppose the Brazilians, and had even insulted Captain Crosbie and others as they were landing to settle affairs with the government. Besides, they were hourly in expectation of a reinforcement of 500 men from Lisbon. Meantime the anchorage under Fort Francisco was found inconvenient for so large a ship as the Pedro Primeiro, and the Admiral took her round the great shoal which forms the other side of the harbour, and anchored her between the Ilha do Medo and the main in fifteen fathoms water; where he left her, and returned to the town in the sloop of war Pambinha, in which vessel he could lie close to the city itself. One of his first steps was to substitute Brazilian for Portuguese troops, in all situations where soldiers were absolutely necessary to keep order; but he did not admit more than a very limited number within the walls. He caused all who had been imprisoned on account of their political opinions to be liberated; and he sent notices to the independent military commanders of Céara and Piauhy to desist from hostilities against Maranham.

On the 27th, Lord Cochrane published the following proclamation:—

The High Admiral of Brazil to the Inhabitants of Maranham.

The auspicious day is arrived on which the worthy inhabitants of Maranham have it in their power to declare at once the independence of their country, and their adhesion to, and satisfaction with, their patriot monarch, the Emperor Peter I. (son of the august Soverign Don John VI.); under whose protection they enjoy the glorious privileges of being free men, of choosing their own constitution, and of making their own laws by their representatives assembled to consult on their own interests, and in their own country.

That the glory of such a day should not be darkened by any excess, even though proceeding from enthusiasm in the cause we have embraced, must be the desire of every honest and thinking citizen. It is not necessary to advise such as to their conduct: but, should there be any individuals capable of interrupting the public tranquillity on any pretext, let them beware! The strictest orders are given for the chastisement of whoever shall cause any kind of disorder, according to the degree of the crime. To take the necessary oaths, to choose the members of the civil government, are acts that should be performed with deliberation: for which reason, the first of August is the earliest day which the preparation for such solemn ceremonies demands, will permit.—Citizens! let us go forward seriously and methodically, without tumult, hurry, or confusion; and accomplish the work we have in hand in such a manner as shall merit the approbation of His Imperial Majesty, and shall give us neither cause for repentance,

Figure 18. English Burial Ground. Courtesy of The Catholic University of America, Oliveira Lima Library, Washington, D.C.

nor room for amendment. Viva, our Emperor! Viva, the independence and constitution of Brazil!—*On board the Pedro Primeiro, 27th July, 1823.*

Cochrane

On the 28th, the junta of government, the camara of the town, the citizens and soldiers, with Captain Crosbie to represent Lord Cochrane, who was not well enough to attend, assembled to proclaim the independence of Brazil, and to swear allegiance to the Emperor, Don Pedro de Alcantara; after which there was a firing of the troops, and discharge of artillery, and ringing of bells, as is usual on such occasions. The public act of fealty was drawn up, and signed by as many as could conveniently do so, and the Brazilian flag was hoisted, a flag of truce having been flying from the arrival of the Pedro till then. [The Governor at arms did not appear and wrote to the Junta to excuse himself that very day.]

The next day the inhabitants proceeded to the choice of their new provisional government of the province, which was installed on the

8th of August, as had been appointed. The members are, Miguel Ignacio dos Santos Freire e Bruce, *President;* Lourenço de Castro Belford, *Secretary;* and José Joaquim Vieira Belford.

The first act of the new government was to issue a proclamation to the inhabitants of the province of Maranham, congratulating them on being no longer a nation of slaves to Portugal, but a free people of the empire of Brazil; [enjoying a national Independence which had formed the object of their wishes for three centuries and which they now owe to the prowess of Pedro Primeiro;] exhorting them to confidence, fidelity, tranquility, and harmony with their Portuguese brethren now denizens of Brazil; and concluding with *vivas* to the Roman Catholic religion; to our Constitutional Emperor and Perpetual Defender Don Pedro I., and his dynasty; to the Cortes of Brazil, and the people of Maranham.

The letter of the new government to His Imperial Majesty is dated the 12th of August, when every thing was finally settled. It begins by congratulating him on the happy state of things in general in Brazil, [congratulating Don Pedro in all manner of ways—as the favorite of Providence destined from the earliest of time to inherit the patrimonio do primogenito do Brazil—as fulfilling his destiny in becoming defensor perpetuo and Brazil as being one of the first empires in the world { . . . } and then a world of complements to his social virtues and military talents.] It then sets forth the wishes of the people of Maranham to have joined their brethren long since, but that these wishes had been thwarted by the Lisbon troops [and especially by a part of Madeira's army.—lately arrived in San Luis.]—

> But what was our joy and transport when unexpectedly we saw the ship Pedro Primeiro summoning our port!!! Oh, 26th of July, 1823! Thrice happy day! thou wilt be as conspicuous in the annals of our province, as the sentiments of gratitude and respect inspired by the virtues of the illustrious Admiral sent to our aid by the best and most amiable of Monarchs will be deeply engraven on our hearts and those of our posterity! Yes, august Sire! the wisdom, the prudence, and the gentle manners of Lord Cochrane, have contributed still more to the happy issue of our political difficulties, than even the fear of his forces, however respectable they might be. To anchor in our port; to proclaim in-

dependence; to administer the proper oaths of obedience to Your Imperial Majesty; to suspend hostilities throughout the province; to cause a new government to be elected; to bring the troops of the country into the town, and then only in sufficient numbers for the public order and tranquillity; to open communication between the interior and the capital; to provide it with necessaries; and to restore navigation and commerce to their pristine state: all this, SIRE, was the work of a few days. Grant, Heaven, that this noble Chief may end the glorious career of his political and military labours with the like felicity and success; and that Your Imperial Majesty being so well served, nothing more may be necessary to immortalise that admirable commander, not only in the annals of Brazil, but in those of the whole world!

And this, I think, is all of importance that I have learned with regard to the capture of Maranham to-day. It is true, the brig Maria, despatched by His Lordship on the 12th of August, only arrived to-day; so that much may be behind.

2d October.—A friend who was present at the Assembly to-day gives me the following account of the debate.—In the first place, the Emperor sent notice of Lord Cochrane's success at Maranham; and Martim Francisco Ribiero de Andrada rose and proposed a vote of thanks to His Lordship. The deputy Montezuma (of Bahia) opposed this, on the ground that he was the servant of the executive government, and the government ought to thank him. He felt as grateful to Lord Cochrane as any member of the Assembly could do, and would do as much to prove his gratitude; but he would not vote to thank him there. Dr. França (known by the nickname of Franzinho) seconded Montezuma, and said it derogated from the dignity of the legislative assembly of the vast, and noble, and rich empire of Brazil, to vote thanks to any individual.[123] On which Costa Barros, in a speech of eloquence and enthusiasm, maintained the propriety of thanking Lord Cochrane.[124] That the triumphal road, as in ancient Rome, did not

---

123. Dr. António Ferreira França (1771-1848), Bahian doctor and professor active in the fight for Independence (Grande XI: 761; Lacombe n. 374).
124. Pedro José da Costa Barros (1779-1839), military and political leader in newly independent Brazil and deputy to the Assembly for Ceará (Lacombe 374).

now exist; but the triumph might be granted by the voice of the national representatives. The gentleman who thought no thanks should be voted was a member for Bahia, and talked of his gratitude. He could tell him, that grateful as he (Costa Barros) now felt, were he, like that gentleman, a member for Bahia, his gratitude, and his eagerness to express it, would be tenfold. Who but Lord Cochrane had delivered Bahia from the Portuguese, that swarm of drones that threatened to devour the land? But he supposed the greatness of Sen. Montezuma's gratitude was such, that it smothered the expression. This produced a laugh, and that a challenge, and then a cry of "order, order" (*a ordem*).

Sen. Ribiero de Andrada then said, that as to the observation that had fallen from França, that His Lordship had only done his duty, was no man to be thanked for doing an important duty? Besides, though the blockade of Bahia was a duty, the reduction of Maranham was something more—it was undertaken on his own judgment, and at the risk of consequences to himself [and it was a voluntary service to the Nation and deserves public thanks]. Sen. Lisboa observed, that as to its being beneath the dignity of the Representative Assembly of Brazil to thank an individual, the English Parliament scrupled not to thank its naval and military chiefs; [The Roman Senate, that senate of kings gave thanks and praise to their Catos and Scipios]; and could what it did be beneath the Assembly of Brazil? Would to God the Assembly might one day emulate the British Parliament!

After this there was more sparring between Montezuma and Costa Barros: the former resuming the subject of the challenge; Barros bowing, and assuring him he did not refuse it: on which a member on the same side [Martino Francisco] observed sarcastically, only half rising as he spoke, that those who meant really to fight would hardly speak it aloud in the *General Assembly*. This ended the dispute; and the vote of thanks was carried with only the voices of Montezuma and França against it; and so passed this day's session. [Alencas was one opponent of Montezuma; I found afterwards by the printed report that several other members had spoken in this debate but these were the principle speakers and the chief arguments. The challenge led to a paper war between the two deputies as may be seen in the Gazette of Rio for the 13th of October, on which day the assembly decided that the vote of thanks should be signed by the president and secretary.]

I must say for the people here, that they do seem sensible that in Lord Cochrane they have obtained a treasure.* * * *

That there are some who find fault, and some who envy, is very true. But when was it otherwise? Sometimes I cry,

> O, what a world is this, where what is comely
> Envenoms him that bears it!

At others, I take it more easily, and say coolly with the Spaniard,

> Envy was honour's wife, the wise man said,
> Ne'er to be parted till the man was dead:[125]

and neither envy, nor any other injurious feeling, nor all the manifestations of them all together, can ever lessen the real merit of so great a man.

The acquisition of Maranham is exceedingly important to the empire: it is one of the provinces that, from the time of its first settlement, has carried on the greatest foreign trade.*

6th.—We had three days of public rejoicing, on account of the taking of Maranham; and on Friday, as I happened to be at the palace to show some drawings to the Empress, I perceived that the Emperor's levee was unusually crowded. During these few days, though I have been far from well, I have improved my acquaintance with my foreign friends; but of English I see, and wish to see, very little of any body but Mrs. May.

9th.—[I resolved to take a holiday: so went to spend it with Mrs. May, at the Gloria, only going first for half an hour to the library. That library is a great source of comfort to me: I every day find my cabinet quiet and cool, and provided with the means of study, and generally spend four hours there, reading Portuguese and Brazilian history; for which I shall not, probably, have so good an opportunity again. {Graham deleted this material.}]

This day the debate in the Assembly has been most interesting. It is some time since, in discussing that part of the proposed constitution, which treats of the persons who are to be considered as Brazilians, entitled to the protection of the laws of the empire, and amenable to those laws, the 8th paragraph of the 5th article was admitted without

---

* See the Appendix. {Graham refers to her appendix, not included in the edition. -- *Eds.*}

125. Graham first echoes the servant Adam in bemoaning evil in the world in Shakespeare's *As You Like It* II:iii, and then counters this despair with the cynicism of Lope de Vega (1562-1635) in *Polabio y Clarindo* (trans. Henry Holland).

a dissentient voice: it is this—"*All naturalised strangers, whatever be their religion.*" To-day the 3d paragraph of the 7th article came under discussion. This article treats of the individual rights of Brazilians; it runs thus—"The constitution guarantees to all Brazilians the following individual rights, with the explanations and limitations thereafter expressed:—"

      I. Personal Freedom.
      II. Trial by Jury.
      III. Religious Freedom.
      IV. Professional Freedom.
      V. Inviolability of Property.
      VI. Liberty of the Press.

The 14th article goes on to state, that all Christians may enjoy the political rights of the empire; 15th, "Other religions are hardly tolerated, and none but Christians shall enjoy political rights"; and the 16th declares the Roman Catholic religion to be that of the state, and the only one beneficed by the state.

Now this day's discussion was not merely one of form; but it has established toleration in all its extent. A man is at liberty to exercise his faith as he pleases, and even to change it: should he, indeed, have the folly to turn Turk, he must not vote at elections, nor be a member of the Assembly, nor enjoy an office in the state, civil or military; but he may sit under his vine and his fig-tree, and exercise an honest calling. All Christians are eligible to all offices and employments; and I only wish older countries would deign to take lessons from this new government in its noble liberality. The Diario of the Assembly is so far behind with the reports of the sessions, that I have not, of course, a correct account of the speeches; but I believe that I am not wrong in attributing to the Bishop the most benevolent and enlightened views on this momentous subject, together with that laudable attachment to the church of his fathers that belongs to good men of every creed.

October 12th.—This is the Emperor's birth-day, and the first anniversary of the coronation. I was curious to see the court of Brazil; so I rose early and dressed myself, and went to the royal chapel, where the Emperor and Empress, and the Imperial Princess were to be with the court before the drawing-room. I accordingly applied to the chaplain for a station, who showed me into what is called the *dip-*

lomatic tribune, but it is in fact for respectable foreigners: there I met all manner of consuls. However, the curiosity which led me to the chapel would not allow me to go home when the said consuls did; so I went to the drawing-room, which perhaps, after all, I should not have done, being quite alone, had not the gracious manner in which their Imperial Majesties saluted me, both in the Chapel and afterwards in the corridor leading to the royal apartments, induced me to proceed. I reached the inner room where the ladies were, just as the Emperor had, with a most pleasing compliment, announced to Lady Cochrane that she was Marchioness of Maranham; for that he had made her husband Marques, and had conferred on him the highest degree of the order of the Cruzeiro. [In the Section of the Assemblea October 10th, Montezuma made a handle of this creation for attacking the Imperial power, claiming for the Legislative body the exclusive privilege of conferring titles. Martino Francisco then questioned the Emperor's right to name a military chief! These questions {were} farther agitated on the 29th and 30th Oct. when Lord Cochrane's title was confirmed *because* the Emperor in conferring it, believed *Bonafide* that no law prevented him—but he must be desired not to do so again!!!!] I am sometimes absent; and now, when I ought to have been most attentive, I felt myself in the situation Sancho Pança so humourously describes, of sending my wits wool-gathering, and coming home shorn myself:[126] for I was so intent on the honour conferred on my friend and countryman; so charmed, that for once his services had been appreciated,—that when I found the Emperor in the middle of the room, and that his hand was extended towards me, and that all others had paid their compliments and passed to their places, I forgot I had my glove on, took his Imperial hand with that glove, and I suppose kissed it much in earnest, for I saw some of the ladies smile before I remembered any thing about it. Had this happened with regard to any other prince, I believe that I should have run away; but nobody is more good-natured than Don Pedro: I saw there was no harm done; and so determining to be on my guard when the Empress came in, and then to take an opportunity of telling her of my fault, I staid quietly, and began talking to two or three young ladies who were at court for the first time, and had just received their appointment as ladies of honour to the Empress.

126. Sancho Panza, Don Quixote's down-to-earth sidekick in Miguel de Cervantes Saavedra's 1602 novel *Don Quixote*, is full of proverbs, including one he repeats several times: one may "come for wool and go back shorn" or "go for wool and come back shorn."

Her Majesty, who had retired with the young Princess, now came in, and the ladies all paid their compliments while the Emperor was busy in the presence-chamber receiving the compliments of the Assembly and other public bodies. [There was a speech of some length made by the Speaker of the Assembly, Manoel Ferreira de Aranjo Guimares, congratulating the Emperor on the Independence of the land and on his being the guide and leader to that independence and the promulgation of a liberal constitution, titles still more illustrious than that derived from his noble house etc. etc., and concluding with the good wishes of the assembly. His Imperial Majesty made a very short speech of thanks.] There was little form and no stiffness. Her Imperial Majesty conversed easily with every body, only telling us all to speak Portuguese, which of course we did. She talked a good deal to me about English authors, and especially of the Scotch novels, and very kindly helped me in my Portuguese; which, though I now understand, I have few opportunities of speaking to cultivated persons. If I have been pleased with her before, I was charmed with her now. When the Emperor had received the public bodies, he came and led the Empress into the great receiving room, and there, both of them standing on the upper step of the throne, they had their hands kissed by naval, military, and civil officers, and private men; thousands, I should think, thus passed. It was curious, but it pleased me, to see some negro officers take the small white hand of the Empress in their clumsy black hands, and apply their pouting African lips to so delicate a skin; but they looked up to *Nosso Emperador,* and to her, with a reverence that seemed to me a promise of faith *from* them, a bond of kindness *to* them. The Emperor was dressed in a very rich military uniform, the Empress in a white dress embroidered with gold, a corresponding cap with feathers tipped with green; and her diamonds were superb, her head-tire and ear-rings having in them opals such as I suppose the world does not contain, and the brilliants surrounding the Emperor's picture, which she wears, the largest I have seen.

I should do wrong not to mention the ladies of the court. My partial eyes preferred my pretty countrywoman the new Marchioness; but there were the sweet young bride Maria de Loreto, and a number of others of most engaging appearance; and then there were the jewels of the Baronessa de Campos, and those of the Viscondeça do Rio Seco, only inferior to those of the Empress: but I cannot enumerate all the riches, or beauty; nor would it entertain my English friends, for whom this journal is written, if I could.

When their Imperial Majesties came out of the great room, I saw Madame do Rio Seco in earnest conversation with them; and soon I saw her and Lady Cochrane kissing hands, and found they had both been appointed honorary ladies of the Empress; and then the Viscountess told me she had been speaking to the Empress about me. This astonished me, for I had no thought of engaging in any thing away from England. Six months before, indeed, I had said that I was so pleased with the little Princess, that I should like to educate her. This, which I thought no more of at the time, was, like every thing in this gossiping place, told to Sir T. Hardy: he spoke of it to me, and said he had already mentioned it to a friend of mine. I said, that if the Emperor and Empress chose, as a warm climate agreed with me, I should not dislike it; that it required consideration; and that if I could render myself sufficiently agreeable to the Empress, I should ask the appointment of governess to the Princess; and so matters stood when Sir Thomas Hardy sailed for Buenos Ayres. I own that the more I saw of the Imperial family, the more I wished to belong to it; but I was frightened at the thoughts of Rio, by the impertinent behaviour of some of the English, so that I should probably not have proposed the thing myself. It was done, however: the Empress told me to apply to the Emperor. I observed he looked tired with the levee, and begged to be allowed to write to her another day. She said, "Write if you please, but come and see the Emperor at five o'clock to-morrow." And so they went out, and I remained marvelling at the chance that had brought me into a situation so unlike any thing I had ever contemplated; and came home to write a letter to Her Imperial Majesty, and to wonder what I should do next.

[*13th.*— It is decided in the assembly that the vote of thanks to Cochrane shall be signed by both the president and the secretary.]

Monday, October 13th.—I wrote my letter to the Empress, and was punctual to the time for seeing the Emperor. He received me very kindly, and sent me to speak to Her Imperial Majesty, who took my letter, and promised me an answer in two days, adding the most obliging expressions of personal kindness. And this was certainly the first letter I ever wrote on the subject; though my English *friends* tell me that I had a memorial in my hand yesterday, and that I went to court only to deliver it, for they saw it in my hand. Now I had a white pocket-handkerchief and a black fan in my hand, and thought as little of speaking about my own affairs to their Imperial Majesties, as of making a voyage to the moon. But people will always know each other's affairs best.

16th.—I have continued going regularly to the library, and have become acquainted with the principal librarian, who is also the Emperor's confessor. He is a polished and well-informed man. He showed me the Conde da Barca's library, which, as I knew before, had been purchased at the price of 15,530,900 rees, and added to the public collection. To-day, on returning from my study I received a letter from the Empress, written in English, full of kind expressions; and in the pleasantest manner accepting, in the Emperor's name and her own, my services as governess to her daughter; and giving me leave to go to England, before I entered on my employment, as the Princess is still so young.

I went to San Cristovaõ to return thanks.

19th.—I saw the Empress, who is pleased to allow me to sail for England in the packet, the day after to-morrow. I confess I am sorry to go before Lord Cochrane's return. I had set my heart on seeing my best friend in this country, after his exertions and triumph. But I have now put my hand to the plough, and I must not turn back.

[*20th.*— Sr Esteoan Ribeiro de Regendi presented the project of the Constitution drawn up by the assembly to the Emperor with a short speech—The Emperor accepted them in another—and anticipates the happiness of the new, the respect of the Old World.]

October 21st.—I embarked on board the packet for England. Mrs. May walked to the shore with me. Sir Murray Maxwell lent me his boats to bring myself and goods on board.[127] I had previously taken leave of every body I knew, English and foreign.

After I embarked, Mr. Anderson brought me the latest newspapers. The following are the principal ones published in Rio:—. The DIARIO DA ASSEMBLEA, which contains nothing but the proceedings of the Assembly; it appears as fast as the short-hand writers can publish it. The GOVERNMENT GAZETTE, which has all official articles, appointments, naval intelligence, and sometimes a few advertisements. The DIARIO DO RIO, which has nothing but advertisements, and ship

---

127. Sir Murray Maxwell (1775-1831), an officer in the Royal Navy, was appointed captain of the *Briton*, stationed in South America, in 1823 (*ODNB* 37: 525-26).

news, and prices current; it used to print a meteorological table. The CORREIRO, a democratic journal, which the editor wrote from prison, only occasionally for some time, but lately it has been a daily paper. The SENTINELA DA LIBERDAD E A BEIRA DO MAR DA PRAYA GRANDE is edited by a Genoese, assisted by one of the deputies, and is said to be pure *carbonarism*. The SYLPHO, also an occasional paper, moderately ministerial, and engaged in a war of words with several others. The ATALAIA, an advocate for limited monarchy, whose editor is a deputy of considerable reputation, is another occasional paper; as is also the TAMOYO, entirely devoted to the Andradas: it is, in my opinion, the best-written of all. The SENTINELA DA PAŎN D'ASUCAR is on the same side; its editor formerly published the *Regulador,* but this has ceased to appear since the change of ministry. The *Espelho* was a government paper; but the writer has discontinued it, having become a member of the Assembly. The *Malaguetta* was a paper whose first number attracted a great deal of attention; it fell off afterwards, and ceased on the declaration of the independence of Brazil. It was remarkable for its hostility to the Andradas. Indeed the war of words the author waged against the family was so virulent, that they were suspected of being the instigators of an attempt to assassinate him. This they indignantly denied, and satisfactorily disproved; and the man being almost maniacal with passion, accused any and every person of consequence in the state, and conceived himself, even wounded as he was, not safe. In vain did all persons, even the Emperor himself, visit him, to reassure him; his terrors continued, and he withdrew himself the moment he was sufficient recovered from his wounds. He was by birth a Portuguese, and his strong passions had probably rendered him an object of hatred or jealousy to some inferior person, the consequences of which his vanity made him attribute to a higher source.—I believe there are some other occasional papers, but I have not seen them.

Oct. 25th.—Happily for me there are no passengers in the packet, and still more happily, the captain's wife and daughter are on board; so that I feel as if lodging in a quiet English family, all is so decent, orderly, and, above all, clean. I am under no restraint, but walk, read, write, and draw, as if at home: every body, even to the monkey on board, looks kindly at me; and I receive all manner of friendly attention consistent with perfect liberty.

Nov. 1st.—"The longest way about is often the nearest way home," says the proverb; and, on that principle, ships bound for England from

Brazil at this time of the year stand far to the eastward. We are still in the latitude of Rio de Janeiro, though in long. 29° W., and shall probably stand still nearer to the coast of Africa, before we shall be able to look to the northward. To-day the thermometer is at 75°, the temperature of the sea 72°.

9th.—Lat. 14° 19' S., long. 24° W., thermometer 74°., sea 74 1/2°.

17th.—Lat. 5° N., long. 25° W. For several days the thermometer at 80°; the temperature of the sea at noon 82°. We spoke the Pambinha, 60 days from Maranham. She says Lord Cochrane had gone himself to Para, whence he meant to proceed directly for Rio; so that he would probably be there by this time, as the Pedro Primeiro sails well. I had no opportunity of learning more, as the vessel passed hastily.

We have, generally speaking, had hot winds from Africa, and there is a sultry feel in the air which the state of the thermometer hardly accounts for. I perceive that the sails are all tinged with a reddish colour; and wherever a rope has chafed upon them, they appear almost as if iron-moulded. This the captain and officers attribute to the wind from Africa. They were certainly perfectly white long after we left Rio; they have not been either furled or unbent. What may be the nature of the dust or sand that thus on the wings of the wind crosses so many miles of ocean, and stains the canvass? Can it be this minute dust affecting the lungs which makes us breathe as if in the sultry hours preceding a thunder-storm?

Dec. 3d.—We came in sight of St. Mary's, the eastern island of the Azores. I much wished to have touched at some of these isles; but this is not a good season for doing so, and the winds we have had have been unfavourable for the purpose. This afternoon, though near enough to have seen at least the face of the land, the weather was thick and rainy, so that we saw nothing.

18th.—After passing the Azores, a long succession of gales from the north-east kept us off the land. These were succeeded by three fine days; and the sea, which had been heavy, became smooth. Early the day before yesterday, however, it began to blow very hard from the north-west; and yesterday morning it changed to a gale from the south and south-west, and we lay-to under storm stay-sails, in a tremendous sea. About one o'clock the captain called to me, and desired me to come on deck and see what could not last ten minutes, and I might never see again. I ran up, as did Mrs. and Miss K—. A sudden shift of wind had taken place: we saw it before it came up, driving the sea

Figure 19. Stone Cart at Rio de Janeiro. Courtesy of The Catholic University of America, Oliveira Lima Library, Washington, D.C.

along furiously before it; and the meeting of the two winds broke the sea as high as any ship's mast-head in a long line, like the breakers on a reef of rocks. It was the most beautiful yet fearful sight I ever beheld; and the sea was surging over our little vessel so as to threaten to fill her: but the hatches were battened down; we were lying-to on a right tack, and a hawser had been passed round the bits in order to sustain the foremast, in case we lost our bowsprit, as we expected to do every instant. But in twenty minutes the gale moderated, and we bore up for Falmouth, which we reached this morning, having passed the cabin deck of a ship that doubtless had foundered in the storm of yesterday.—Once more I am in England; and, to use the words of a venerable though apocryphal writer, "Here will I make an end. And if I have done well, and as is fitting the story, it is that which I desired; but if slenderly and meanly, it is that which I could attain unto."*

M. G.

* 2 Maccabees, chap. xv. ver. 37, 38.

Appendix I: Maps of Brazil, 1818 and 1819

Brazil Map, 1818, from: *Historisch-Genealogischer Kalender Auf Das Gemein-Jarh* 1818 ([Berlin]: Herausgegeben Vaon Der Kön. Preusz. Kalender Deputation, [1818].) Courtesy of The Catholic University of America, Oliveira Lima Library, Washington, D.C.

Brazil Map, 1819, from: *Reports on the Present State of the United Provinces of South America* (London: Baldwin, Cradock and Joy, 1819). Courtesy of The Catholic University of America, Oliveira Lima Library, Washington, D.C.

Appendix II: Sketch of the History of Brazil

[Graham's Original Introduction to the 1824 Journal]

I JUDGED it necessary to prefix the following sketch of the history of Brazil to the journal of my voyage thither, in order that the political events to which I was an eye-witness might be the better understood.

The early part of the history is almost entirely taken from Mr. Southey. It would have been easy for me to have referred to the Portuguese authors, as I have read nearly all that are to be found in print of Mr. Southey's authorities, and some that he does not mention; but Mr. Southey had been so faithful as well as judicious in the use he has made of his authors, that it would have been absurd, if not impertinent, to have neglected his guidance. From the time of the King's arrival in Brazil, or rather of his leaving Lisbon, I am answerable for all I have stated: it is little, but I hope that little is correct.

The circumstances of Spanish and Portuguese America were very different in every stage. In Mexico, in Peru, in Chili, the conquerors encountered a people civilised and humane; acquainted with many of the arts of polished life; agriculturists and mechanics; knowing in the things belonging to the altar and the throne, and waging war for conquest and for glory. But the savages of Brazil were hunters and cannibals; they wandered, and they made war for food: few of the tribes knew even the cultivation of the mandioc; and fewer still had adopted any kind of covering, save paint and feathers for ornament. The Spanish conquests were more quickly made, and appeared more easily settled, because in states so far advanced in civilisation the defeat of an army decides the fate of a kingdom, and the land already cultivated, and the mines already known and worked, were entered upon at once by the conquerors.

In Brazil the land that was granted by leagues *was to be won by inches* from the hordes of savages who succeeded each other in incalculable multitudes, and whose migratory habits rendered it a matter of course for one tribe immediately to occupy the ground from which its predecessors had been driven. Hence the history of the early settlers in Brazil presents none of those splendid and chivalresque pictures that the chronicles of the Corteses, and Pizarros, and Almagros furnish. They are plain, and often pathetic scenes of human life, full of patience, and enterprise, and endurance; but the wickedness that stains even the best of them, is the more disgusting as it is more sordid.

But the very circumstances that facilitated the settling of the Spanish colonies were also likely to accelerate their liberation. A sense and a remembrance of national honour and freedom, remained among the polished Mexicans and Peruvians. Their numbers indeed had been thinned by the cruelties of the conquerors, but enough were left to perpetuate the memory of their fathers, to hand down the prophecies uttered in the phrenzy of their dying patriots; and the Peruvian, when he visited Lima, looked round the chamber of the viceroys, as he saw niche after niche filled up with their pictures, till the fated number should be accomplished, with no common emotion;* and many a dreamer on the Peruvian coast, when he saw the Admiral of the Chilian squadron, was ready to hail him as the golden-haired son of light who was to restore the kingdom of the Incas.*

But in Brazil, what was once gained was not likely to be lost by the efforts of the natives, or at least by any recollection of theirs, pointing to a better or more glorious time. They have been either exterminated, or wholly subdued. The slave hunting which had been systematic on the first occupation of the land, and more especially after the discovery of the mines, had diminished the wretched Indians, so that the introduction of the hardier Africans was deemed necessary: *they* now people the Brazilian fields; and if here and there an Indian aldea is to be found, the people are wretched, with less than Negro comforts, and much less than Negro spirit or industry. Hence, while the original Mexicans and Peruvians form a real and respectable part of the assertors of the independence of their country, along with the Creole Spaniards, the Indians are nothing in Brazil; even as a mixed race, they have

---

* This prophecy was recorded by Garcelaço de la Vega; and it is said, that the copies of his *Incas* were bought up, and an edition printed, omitting the prophecy.

less part among the different casts than in the Spanish colonies; and therefore jealousies among the Portuguese themselves could alone at this period have brought affairs to their present crisis. These jealousies have taken place, and though they did not arise principally out of the causes of the emigration and return of the Royal family, they were at least quickened and accelerated by them.

In 1499, Brazil was discovered by Vicente Yañez Pinçon, a native of Palos, and one of the companions of Columbus. He and his brothers were in search of new countries, and after touching at the Cape de Verde Islands, he steered to the south-west, till he came to the coast of Brazil, near Cape St. Augustine, and coasted along as far as the river Maranham, and thence to the mouth of the Oronoco. He carried home some valuable drugs, precious stones, and Brazil wood; but had lost two of his three ships on the voyage. He made no settlement, but had claimed the country for Spain.

Meantime Pedro Alvarez Cabral was appointed by Emanuel, King of Portugal, to the command of a large fleet, destined to follow the course of Vasco de Gama in the east. Adverse winds, however, drove the expedition so far to the westward, that it fell in with the coast of Brazil, and the ships anchored in Porto Seguro on Good Friday of the year 1500. On Easter-day the first Christian altar was raised in the new continent under a large tree, and mass was performed, at which the innocent natives assisted with pleased attention: the country was taken possession of for the crown of Portugal by the name of the land of the Holy Cross, and a stone cross was erected to commemorate the event. Cabral dispatched a small vessel to Lisbon to announce his discovery, and then, without making any settlement, proceeded to India.

On the arrival of the news in Europe, the King of Portugal invited Amerigo Vespucci from Seville, and sent him with three ships to explore the country. After a long and distressing voyage they arrived, and very early in their intercourse with the natives they discovered that they were cannibals, but nevertheless they established a friendly intercourse with some of the tribes; and after coasting along South America as far as lat. 52°, finding neither port nor inhabitants, and suffering from intolerable cold, they returned to Lisbon in 1502.

Early in the next year Amerigo sailed again with six ships; but having stood too near the coast of Africa, after passing the Cape de Verdes by the orders of the commander, four of the vessels were lost, but Amerigo with the other two reached a port which they called All

Saints.* There they remained five months, in friendship with the natives, with whom some of the party travelled forty leagues into the interior. They erected a small fort, and left twelve men with guns and provisions, and having loaded their two ships with Brazil wood, monkeys, and parrots, they returned to Lisbon early in 1504.

But as Brazil, as it now began to be called, did not promise that ample supply of gold which the Spaniards had discovered in their new countries, and which the Portuguese gained with less hazard from Africa, and from the East, the country ceased for a time to excite the attention of government, and the first actual settlements were made by private adventurers, who, on account of their trade, were desirous of having some kind of agents among the people. The first persons employed for this purpose were criminals, a sort of settlers that may do well in an unpeopled country, where there is nothing to do but to reclaim the land, but that must do ill where there are many and savage natives, because they either become degraded to the savage level themselves, if they continue friends, or, if not, they are apt to practise such cruelties and injustice as disgust the natives, render colonisation difficult, and if they teach any thing, it is all the worst part of the life of civilised nations.

But in 1508, Amerigo Vespucci having returned to the service of Spain, the King resolved to take possession of the new land which had been discovered; and founding his claims on the grant of Alexander VI., he sent Vincent Yañez Pinçon and Juan Diaz de Solis to assert them. They made Cape St. Augustine's, which Pinçon had discovered, and coasted along to lat. 40° south, erecting crosses as they went; but some disputes having arisen between them, they returned to Spain: and it appears that the remonstrances of Portugal against the voyage, as an interference with her discoveries, had some weight, for it was not until 1515 that Solis was dispatched on a second voyage, and then it was with the avowed purpose of seeking a passage to the Great Pacific Sea, which had been sought and seen by Balboa in 1513.

That extraordinary but unfortunate man was the first European whose eyes rested on the broad Pacific. He had heard from the Indians of its existence, and resolutely set out to discover it, well aware of the dangers and difficulties he had to encounter. After twenty-five

---

* This cannot be Bahia; for they say, that after coasting 260 leagues they were in 18° S.; now Bahia is in 12° 40', or nearly; the difference being 120 leagues; it must therefore be a port to the northward.

days of suffering and fatigue, he saw the South Sea; he heard of Peru, its mines, and its llamas, its cities and its aqueducts, and he received pearls† from the islands that lay in front of St. Miguel's bay, where he walked sword in hand up to his middle into the water and took possession for the King of Spain. No one in Europe now doubted that the western way to the East Indies was discovered.

Great hopes were therefore entertained from the expedition of Solis. That able navigator made the coast of Brazil far to the southward of Cape St. Augustine, where he had been with Pinçon; and on the 1st of January 1516 he discovered the harbour of Rio de Janeiro; thence he sailed still to the southward, and entered what he hoped at first would be a sea, or strait, by which he might communicate with the ocean; but it was the river La Plata, where Solis and several of his followers were murdered and devoured by the natives. The ships then put back to St. Augustines, loaded with Brazil wood, and returned to Spain.

But the King Don Emanuel claimed these cargoes, and again remonstrated against the interference of Spain so effectually, that three years afterwards, when Magelhaens touched at Rio de Janeiro, he purchased nothing but provisions.

Meantime several French adventurers had come to Brazil, and had taken in their cargoes of Brazil wood, monkies and parrots, and sometimes plundered some of the weaker Portuguese traders. In 1616, two of these adventurers entered the bay of All Saints, and had begun to trade with the Indians, when the Portuguese commander, Cristovam Jaques, sailing into the port, and examining all its coves, discovered them, and sunk the ships, crews, and cargoes. About the same time, a young Portuguese nobleman, who had been wrecked on the shoal off the entrance of the harbour,‡ and who had seen half his companions drowned, and half eaten by the Indians, had contrived to conciliate the natives. He had saved a musket and some powder from the wreck, and having taken an opportunity of shooting a bird in the presence of the inhabitants, they called him Caramuru, or the man of fire; and, as he accompanied them on an expedition against their enemies the Tapuyas, he became a favourite, married at least one Indian wife, and fixed his residence at the spot now called Villa Velha, near an excellent spring, and not far from the entrance to the bay.

---

† Pearl islands, in the bay of Panama. The sand of the beach of those islands is iron, and is as easily attracted by the loadstone as steel filings.
‡ I suppose that off St. Antonio da Barre.

Caramuru, however, felt some natural longing to see his native land, and accordingly seized the opportunity afforded by the arrival of a French vessel, and taking his favourite wife, he went with her to France, where they were well received by the court, the king and queen standing sponsors at the baptism of the Brazilian lady, whose marriage was now celebrated according to the Christian form. Caramuru, however, was not permitted to go to Portugal; but by means of a young Portuguese student at Paris,[*] he communicated his situation to the King Joam III., and pressed him to send an expedition to the bay of All Saints. Shortly afterwards, Caramuru returned to Bahia, having agreed to freight two ships with Brazil wood as the price of his passage, of the artillery of the ships, and of the articles necessary for trading with the natives.

Still, however, as Brazil furnished neither gold, nor that rich commerce which the Portuguese derived from their Indian trade, it was pretty much left to itself for the first thirty years after its discovery; and then the regulations adopted by the court were not, perhaps, the most advantageous for the country. The coast was divided by Joam III. into captaincies, many of which extended fifty leagues, and each captaincy was made hereditary, and granted to any one who was willing to embark with sufficient means in the adventure; and to these captains an unlimited jurisdiction, both criminal and civil, was granted.

The first person who took possession of one of these captaincies was Martim Affonso de Souza, in 1531, who sometimes claims the discovery of Rio de Janeiro as his, although it had been named by Solis fifteen years before. Souza was probably deterred from fixing on the shores of that beautiful bay, by the number and fierceness of the Indian tribes that occupied them. He therefore coasted towards the south, naming Ilha Grande dos Magos on twelfth-day, when

> Three kings, or what is more, three wise men went
> Westward to seek the world's true orient.

St. Sebastian's on the 20th, and St. Vincent's on the 22d; but having proceeded as far south as the La Plata, he returned to the neighbourhood of San Vincente, where he ultimately founded his colony, and whence he named the whole captaincy.

---

[*] Pedro Fernandez Sardinha, the first bishop of Brazil.

Sketch of the History of Brazil

Martim Affonso de Souza was no ordinary man: his cares for his colony did not relax even after he had been recalled, and sent as governor-general to India, where he had before highly distinguished himself. He introduced the sugar-cane from Madeira into his colony, and in it also the first cattle were bred. Thence they have spread all over the continent of South America, and have proved of more real value to it than its mines.

Pero Lopes de Souza, the brother of Martim Affonso, had his fifty leagues of coast in two allotments; one part, St. Amaro, was immediately to the north of San Vincente, and the other was Tamaraca, between Pernambuco and Paraiba.

About the same time the Fidalgo Pedro de Goes attempted a settlement at Paraiba do Sul; but after two years tolerable prosperity, he was attacked by the native tribe of Goaytacazes, and five years of warfare reduced him to the necessity of sending to Espirito Santo for vessels to remove his colonists.

Vasco Fernandez de Coutinho began to settle Espirito Santo in the same year (1531) in which the former colonies had been begun. He had amassed a great fortune in the East, and expended most of it in collecting volunteers for his new colony; sixty fidalgoes and men of the royal household accompanied him. The adventurers had a prosperous voyage. On their arrival they built a fort, which they called N. S. da Victoria, and established four sugar-works. Coutinho returned to Lisbon for recruits and implements for mining, the settlers having now obtained some indications of gold and jewels to be found in the country.

The adjoining captaincy of Porto Seguro was given to Pedro de Campo Tourinho, a nobleman and a navigator. He sold his possessions at home, and raised a large body of colonists, with which he established himself at Porto Seguro, the harbour where Cabral had first taken possession of Brazil. The history of the settlement of Porto Seguro, like that of all the others, is stained with the most atrocious cruelties; not such as soldiers in the heat of war commit, but cold calculated cruelties, exterminating men for the sake of growing canes, so waiting patiently for the *fruit* of crime.†

---

† I hope the following tale is not true, though my authority is good. In this very captaincy, within these twenty years, an Indian tribe had been so troublesome, that the Capitam Môr resolved to get rid of it. It was attacked, but defended itself so bravely, that the Portuguese resolved to desist from open warfare; but with unnatural ingenuity exposed ribands and toys infected with smallpox matter in the places where the poor savages were likely to find

Ilheos, so called from its principal river, which has three islands at the mouth, was settled by Jorge de Figueredo Correa, who had a place in the treasury, under Joam III., between 1531 and 1540, and speedily became flourishing, being remarkably favourable to the sugar cultivation.

Bahia de Todo os Santos was, with its adjacent territory, given to Francisco Pereira Coutinho, a fidalgo who had made himself a name in India. He fixed his abode at Villa Velha, where Caramuru had formed his little settlement, and two of his followers married the daughters of Caramuru.

The bay, or reconcave of All Saints, is a magnificent harbour: the entrance appears to be a league in breadth; but on the right hand, on entering, there is a shoal dangerous to large vessels, called that of St. Antonio da Barre; and on the left, coral reefs running off from Itaporica. The country that surrounds it is so fertile, that it must always have been an object of desire whether to savage or civilised inhabitants; and it is not surprising that three revolutions, that is, three changes of indwellers, driven out by each other, should have been, in the memory of the Indians, before the settlement of Coutinho.

That nobleman, whose early life had been passed in the East-Indian Portuguese wars, imprudently and cruelly disturbed the peace of the rising settlement, by the murder of a son of one of the chiefs. The consequence was, that after a most disastrous warfare, in the course of which the already flourishing sugar-works were burnt, he and Caramuru were both obliged to abandon the settlement and retire to Ilheos. Soon afterwards, however, he made peace with the Indians; but on his return to the Reconcave, he was wrecked on the reef off Itaporica, where the natives murdered him, but spared Caramuru, who returned to his old dwelling.

In the settlement of Pernambuco, the first donatory, Duarte Coelho Pereira, was opposed not only by the natives, but by numbers of French, who having carried on a desultory though profitable trade on the coast, now joined the Indians in retarding those regular settlements which were likely to put an end to their commerce. The colony, however, had been planted at Olinda,* a situation as strong as it is

---

them: the plan succeeded. The Indians were so thinned, that they were easily overcome!

* There is a note in the first volume of Southey's Brazil concerning the name of Marino given to Olinda by Hans Staade. The other Brazilians call the Pernambucans of Recife Marineros still. Is this from the town or their nautical

beautiful, and Pereira contrived to engage some of the Indian tribes in his favour. The war was but of short continuance, and nothing farther, except the seizure of the little settlement of Garussa, in the woods and near the creek which separates Itameraca from the main land, occurred to impede the prosperity of the captaincy.

The last colony which was founded during these ten eventful years was that of Maranham. Three adventurers undertook this settlement jointly. The most celebrated was Joam de Barros, the historian; the others were Fernam Alvares de Andrada, father of the writer of the Chronicle, and Aires da Cunha.

Aires da Cunha, Barros's two sons, and nine hundred men, sailed in ten ships for their new possession, but were wrecked on the shoals of Maranham; so that it was long before any success attended the undertaking. Da Cunha was drowned, the sons of Barros slain by the Indians, and the rest of the people with difficulty survived in a very wretched condition.

Meantime the passage through Magellan's Straits had been discovered, and the Spaniards, first under Sebastian Cabot, and afterwards under Don Pedro de Mendoza, who founded Buenos Ayres, had begun to settle on the shores of the Plata, not without opposition from the Portuguese, and a more obstinate and fatal resistance from the Indians. The tribes in this neighbourhood appear to have been more civilised than those of the coast of Brazil, and consequently more formidable enemies to the rising towns. Orellana had also made his daring voyage down the mighty river that is sometimes called by his name. He had afterwards perished in an attempt to make a settlement on its shores, and nearly the same fate had attended Luiz de Mello da Silva, who made a similar attempt on the part of Portugal.

[Within the same period] Cabeza de Vacca had also made his adventurous overland journey from St. Catherine's, and after settling himself in the government of Assumption, had conducted various expeditions of discovery, always in hopes of finding an easy way to the gold countries. In one of these he found traces of the adventurer Garcia, a Portuguese, who, under the orders of Martim Affonso de Souza, had, with five companions, undertaken to explore the interior of South America. This man had by some means so conciliated the Indians, that he was followed by a very considerable army, and is said

---

habits? or from the name of the Indian village Marim which existed in the neighbourhood?

to have penetrated even into Tarija. He is believed to have perished by the hand of one of his own followers, but no particulars were ever known of his fate.

During the next ten years, nothing remarkable occurred with regard to Brazil, except the founding of the city of St. Salvadors, by Thome de Souza, the first Captain General of Brazil, who carried out with him the first Jesuit missionaries. For the site of his new town De Souza fixed upon the hill immediately above the deepest part of the harbour of Bahia, which is defended at the back by a deep lake, and lies about half a league from the Villa Velha of Coutinho and Caramuru.

The temporal concerns of the new colony, derived inestimable advantage from the friendship and assistance of the patriarch Caramuru: as to the spiritual, it was indeed time that some rule of faith and morals should find its way to Brazil. The settlers had hitherto had no instructors but friars, whose manners were as dissolute as their own, and who encouraged in them a licentious depravity, scarcely less shocking than the cannibalism of the savages. These latter are said to have eaten the children born by their own daughters to their prisoners of war,—a thing so unnatural, that it only gains credit because the Portuguese sold as slaves even their own children by the native women. The apostle of Brazil, as he may in truth be called, and chief of the six Jesuits who accompanied Souza, was Nobrega, the cotemporary and rival in the race of disinterested services to his fellow creatures of St. Francis Xavier; and, with regard to his steady attempts to protect as well as to convert the Indians, another Las Casas.

Brazil was becoming an object of importance to the crown of Portugal. The new settlement of Bahia was established on the king's account, and at his expense 1000 persons had been sent out the first year, 1549. In four months there were 100 houses, six batteries, and a cathedral: a college for the Jesuits, a palace, and a custom house were begun; the whole was defended by a mud wall. The next year supplies of all kinds arrived from Lisbon, and the year after that several female orphans, of noble family, were sent out as wives for the officers, with dowries in negroes, kine, and brood-mares.

About this time, a Spanish expedition destined for the river Plata miscarried; one of the ships was wrecked off St. Vincent's, and to Hans Staade, one of the crew who survived and after various adventures fell into the power of the Indians, we are indebted for the most authentic and particular account of the Brazilian Savages.* It is curious that the Indians of the new world, should so very far exceed all the savage tribes of the old in barbarity. But it is certain that no authentic accounts of cannibals have ever been brought from Africa; whereas, none of the early writers on Brazil and its inhabitants have failed to dwell upon their love of human flesh, as characteristic of the people.

The year 1552 is distinguished by the arrival of the first bishop in Brazil. His see was fixed at St. Salvador's, or, as it is generally called, Bahia. In the next year, Thome de Souza retired from his government, and was succeeded by Don Duarte da Costa, who was accompanied by seven jesuits, among whom was the celebrated Anchieta.† The chief of the order, Loyola, was still alive, he erected Brazil into a new province, and appointed Nobrega and Luis de Gran, who had been principal at Coimbra, joint provincials. From that moment the labours of the fathers for the real good of the country commenced. And whatever may be the opinions entertained, as to their politics and ultimate views, there is not a doubt but that the means they employed to reclaim and civilise the Indians, were mild, and therefore successful; that while they wrought their own purposes, they made their people happy; and that centuries will not repair the evil done by their sudden expulsion,

---

* In the *Historia da Provincia Sancta Cruz*, by Pero de Magalhaens de Gandano, 1576, there is an account sufficiently tallying with that which Southey has compiled from Hans Staade and De Lery. But it is far from being so disgusting. There is a copper plate representing the dragging the prisoner with cords, and felling him with a club. The author gives a short account of the then known plants and animals of Brazil, and concludes with the hope that the mines believed to exist may speedily be found. — See the collection of tracts by Barbosa Machado.

† Anchieta was not only a man of extraordinary firmness of mind and real piety, but a politician of no common cast, and his civil services to the Portuguese government were equal to those of the greatest captains, while his labours as a missionary and teacher were beyond those of any individual of whom I have ever read. His merits as a christian apostle and a man of literature, have disarmed even Mr. Southey of his usual rancour against the Roman Catholic faith. That excellent writer's book on Brazil is spoilt by intemperate language on a subject on which human feeling is least patient of direct contradiction, so that the general circulation of it is rendered impossible, and the good it might otherwise do in the country for which it is written frustrated. Oh, that Mr. Southey would remember the quotation which he himself brings forward from Jeremy Taylor! "Zeal against an error is not always the best instrument to find out truth."

which broke up the bands of humanised society which were beginning to unite the Indians with their fellow creatures.

In 1553, the first school was established in Brazil, by Nobrega, in the high plains of Piratininga, about thirteen leagues from the colony of San Vicente. Anchieta was the school-master. The school was opened on the feast of the conversion of St. Paul, and the establishment, and the infant colony rising round it, received the name of the saint. St. Paul's has since grown to be one of the most important towns in Brazil. Its rich minerals, its iron-works, and other manufactures, but, above all, the high and free spirit of its inhabitants, who have taken the lead in every effort for the good of the country, distinguish it above all the southern towns of Brazil.

Anchieta, while he taught Latin to the Portuguese and Mamalucos,* and Portuguese to the Brazilians, learnt from these last their own tongue, and composed a grammar and dictionary for them. He had no books for his pupils, so that he wrote on separate leaves, in four different languages, the daily lesson for each. He served as physician, as well as priest and school-master, and practised and taught the most useful domestic arts. But the colony had, like all the others, to fight for its early existence; it was attacked by the Mamalucos of the neighbouring settlement of St. André, who regarded the instruction of the Indians as a step towards abolishing their slavery, and exclaimed against it as an infringement of what they called their right to the services of the natives. They engaged by other pretences some of the neighbouring tribes to assist them, but they were met and defeated by those of St. Paul's.

Meantime some disputes having arisen between the Governor and the Bishop, the latter resolved to return to Lisbon, but was wrecked on the coast at a place called the Baixos de San Francisco, and there seized, and with one hundred other white persons put to death by the Cahetes. The revenge of the Portuguese was horrible, the Cahetes were hunted, slaughtered, and all but exterminated.

In the year 1557, Joam III. died. His appointment of Mem de Sa, before his death, to the government of Brazil, prevented the country from immediately feeling the evils which a regency generally entails even in an established government, but which are sure to fall with tenfold weight upon a rising colony.

---

* Mamaluco. These were the Creole Portuguese, who had most of them intermarried with the natives.

Mem de Sa was a man of more enlightened mind, and more humane principles than most of those to whom the government of the Brazilian provinces had been intrusted. He arrived at Bahia in 1558, and earnestly applied himself to learn the relations in which the Portuguese, the Creoles, the Indians, and the mixed race stood to each other.

His first acts were directed towards reclaiming the allied Indians from some of their most brutal practices, and to induce them to form settlements near those of the Jesuits. The selfish planters, interested in keeping up the feuds of the Indians, in order to procure slaves, exclaimed against these proceedings as violations of the freedom of the natives, and they were equally displeased at the orders issued, to set at liberty all the Indians who had been wrongfully enslaved. One powerful colonist alone refused to obey: Mem de Sa ordered his house to be surrounded and instantly levelled with the ground. Such an act was certainly calculated to inspire the Indians with confidence in his good intentions towards them, at the same time that his vigorous measures to punish them for any infraction of their engagements kept them in awe.

Meantime an adventurer of no ordinary stamp, had formed a settlement in the finest harbour of Brazil, namely, that of Rio de Janeiro. Nicholas Durand de Villegagnon was a native of Provins en Brie, and a Knight of Malta. In 1648, he had been employed by Mary of Guise, at the entreaty of the French court, to convey her daughter the young Queen of Scots to France: in 1651 he was engaged in the defence of Malta, against the Pacha Sinan and the famous Dragut Reis, and two years afterwards published an account of that campaign. Having visited Brazil in 1558, Villegagnon could not be insensible to the advantages that must arise to France from having a settlement there; and, on his return to Europe, he made such representations at court of these advantages, that Henry II. gave him two vessels, each of 200 tons, and a store ship of 100 tons, to convey the adventurers who might wish to leave France, and who at that time were numerous. Villegagnon, wishing to make use of Coligny's interest, gave out that the new settlement was to be a refuge for the persecuted Hugonots, and this answered the double purpose of securing the Admiral's friendship, and gaining a number of respectable colonists. With these he reached Rio de Janiero, and made his first settlement in a low rock at the mouth of the harbour, where there is now a small fort called the Laje, but finding it not sufficiently elevated to resist the high tides, he pitched on an island within the harbour, where there is only one landing place, and whose form and situation is singularly adapted for safety, especially against such enemies as the Indians. Those, however, of the Rio had been long accustomed to trade with the French, who, if they had not taught them, had at least encouraged them, to hate the Portuguese, whom Villegagnon flattered himself that he should be able to keep aloof by the assistance of the Savages.

Meantime Coligny had exerted himself to send out assistance of every kind; provisions, recruits,* and Protestant ministers. But Villegagnon now imagined himself secure in his colony, and threw off the mask of toleration. He behaved so tyrannically that many of the Hugonots were obliged to return to France, and of them he made the most malicious complaints, and concluded by saying, that they were heretics worthy of the stake.

But nothing is so short-sighted as wickedness. Villegagnon's treachery was the cause of the ruin of his enterprise. Ten thousand Protestants were ready to embark for Coligny, as the island, now called Villegagnon, was then named: but the report of those who had returned, stopped them, and the colony was left in a defenceless state.

At length the attention of the court of Lisbon had been drawn towards the French settlement, and orders were sent to the Captain General to examine into its state first, and then, if possible, to take it.

Accordingly, Mem de Sa, accompanied by Nobrega and two other Jesuits, attacked it in January, 1560, while Villegagnon was absent in France, and demolished the works, but had not sufficient force to attempt forming a settlement; and had Villegagnon succeeded in returning with the recruits he expected, he would have found it easy to re-establish and perhaps revenge himself. But his bad faith deterred the Hugonots from joining him, the civil war prevented the government from assisting him, and the French colony was lost.

In 1564, Estacio de Sa, nephew of Mem, was sent out from Portugal to form a settlement in Rio, but finding his means inadequate to contend with the Indians, led on by the few remaining French, he went to San Vincente for reinforcements; these, however, only enabled him to keep up the war, and to maintain himself in a 'post he

---

* Among these was Jean de Lery.

had fortified,† not far from the entrance of the harbour, and near the Sugar-loaf mountain, a bare and inaccessible rock, which, from a base of about four hundred feet, shoots up to a thousand in perpendicular height, on the west side of the bar. He therefore applied to his uncle for succour, who, collecting what force he could, led them in person, and arrived in the harbour on the 18th of January, 1567. On the 20th, St. Sebastian's day, the Indians and French were attacked in their strongest hold, then called Uraçumiri, and having obtained a decisive victory, the French embarked in the four ships they still possessed, and fled to the coast of Pernambuco, where they attempted to form a settlement at Recife, but were dislodged by the Portuguese of Olinda.

Mem de Sa now founded the city of St. Sebastian, more commonly called the city of Rio; and for its security the Jesuits, with their Indians, fortified both sides of the entrance to the harbour, which is about four miles distant from the city across the bay. Before these works, however, or the walls of the town were completed, the French made a vigorous effort to disturb the rising colony; but it ended in their defeat, and their guns were made use of to fortify the mouth of the harbour.

Driven from Rio, the French attempted to form a settlement at Paraiba the next year; but the Indians, with the Jesuits at their head, and a very few troops, under the commander Martim Leytam, expelled them.

Under Mem de Sa the state had been so prosperous, that though he had been Captain-general far beyond the term of his original appointment, Don Sebastian, on assuming the crown, continued him in office for two years longer, and then named Luiz de Vasconcellos to succeed him. That nobleman never reached Brazil. With him sailed a fleet of seven ships, bearing, besides the governor, sixty-nine Jesuit missionaries, and a number of orphan girls, whose parents had died of the plague, and whom the government was sending out to settle in Brazil. The fleet, in different divisions, fell in with French and English ships, and the Jesuits, save one, to use their own expression, received the crown of martyrdom, and the new governor was killed in action off Tercera. As soon as his death was known at Lisbon, Luiz de Brito de Almeida was appointed to his vacant office; and Mem de Sa just

† Mr. Southey says this spot is called Villa Velha. But there is no place existing in the neighbourhood of that name, nor could I find any person at Rio de Janeiro who remembered such a place. It was, however, most probably on the site of the present St. Juan, or of the fort of Praya Vermelha, which answers exactly to the description.

lived long enough to witness the arrival of his successor. Nobrega, who had begun that system, on which the singular government of the Jesuits in Paraguay was conducted, had died a few months before, so that Brazil was deprived nearly at once of the two ablest men that had yet been concerned in its government.

But Luiz de Brito did not succeed to the government of all Brazil. It was judged proper to divide the colony into two captaincies, Rio de Janeiro being the capital of the southern division, which included Porto Seguro and every thing to the south of it; while Bahia remained the capital of the northern districts. There Luiz de Brito fixed his residence, and Doctor Antonio Salerna was appointed governor of the south. But this division was soon found inconvenient, and the two parts were re-united* about 1578, the year in which a new governor, Diego Laurenço da Viega, arrived.

This was the year when the loss of Don Sebastian in Africa threw Portugal into the hands of Spain. King Philip, eager to annex that kingdom for ever to his crown, offered Brazil, with the title of King, to Braganza if he would give tip his claim to the crown of Portugal. But it was reserved for his descendant to achieve the independence of Brazil, and he refused it.

The colony was at this period most flourishing, though not altogether able to do without occasional supplies from the mother country. But already the original mud-cottages, supported by framework and thatched with palm-leaves, of the first settlers, had given way to well built and handsome houses of stone and brick, covered with tiles as in Europe. The reconcave of Bahia had sixty-two churches, and upwards of seventy sugar-works: the land was well stocked with cattle, all the kinds of orange and lime trees introduced by Europeans had flourished. The country abounded in excellent native fruits, and the mandioc furnished never-failing stores of bread. Olinda partook of all these advantages, and was itself the best built and most populous town in Brazil. Rio de Janeiro had become a place only inferior in importance to the other two, its natural advantages being still greater, and the climate milder; nor were the other captaincies less prosperous.

But the transfer of the crown into foreign hands changed the aspect of affairs in Brazil. Inferior to the Spanish American countries

---

* When the *Historia da Provincia de Sancta Cruz*, by Pero Magalhaes de Gadano, was printed, 1575, they were still separate; but Southey's MS. of 1578 says they had been re-united.

in mines, it was considered only of consequence as being occupied by Spanish subjects, and so forming a barrier against the intrusion of other nations.

By this time the English had begun to trade on the coast of Brazil, and in 1577 Drake had passed through the Straits of Magellan in his memorable voyage round the world. His appearance in the southern seas alarmed Philip the Second, now King of Portugal as well as of Spain, and consequently Lord of Brazil. He attempted to form a colony and maintain a fort in the Straits, in order to prevent future navigators from passing; but of it nothing is left but the name, *Port Famine,* which attests the miserable fate of the colonists. The English commerce was also cut off in Brazil. Some vessels trading peaceably at San Vincente were attacked in the harbour by the Spaniards in superior force; one of the latter was sunk, and the English escaped next day. In 1586, the Earl of Cumberland fitted out an expedition, in which Raleigh served and Witherington was admiral, which entered the reconcave of Bahia and plundered it, remaining there six weeks, the city being only saved by the Indian archers. Baretto, the governor of Brazil, died the next year, and was succeeded by D. Antonio Barreiros the bishop, and Christovam de Barros as joint governors; and they were soon superseded by Francisco Giraldes: he, however, never arrived in the country, and Don Francisco de Souza was appointed in his stead.

During his captaincy some search was made after mines by a descendant of Caramuru, who offered to discover where he had found the silver of which he had services in his house and chapel, on condition of receiving the title of Marques. This Philip refused to grant, and the secret, if indeed the man had one, died with him.

Meantime the celebrated Cavendish had made one voyage round the world, and had committed such ravages on the coast of Spanish America, as not even the atrocious habits of naval warfare in those days can excuse. In 1591, he embarked in a second expedition, arrived in December on the coast of Brazil, and took Santos and burned San Vincente. The ships then sailed for the Straits, but were baffled in their attempt to pass, and returned to the coast of Brazil to obtain provisions. Cavendish, who had many great and good qualities, and who might certainly think it allowable to supply himself on an enemy's coast, made an attempt on Espiritu Santo, but by a mistake in executing his orders it failed, and he sailed for England, but died of a broken heart on the passage.

The most remarkable expedition of the English to the coast of Brazil was that of Sir James Lancaster to Pernambuco. He had the command of three small vessels of 240, 120, and 60 tons. At Cape Blanco he learned that a rich carrack from India had been wrecked near Olinda, and that her cargo was safely stowed at Recife. He therefore fitted five out of near thirty small prizes to accompany him, and built a galley frigate to land with. He was also reinforced by Captain Vernon with two ships, a pinnace, and a prize, and then sailed direct for Recife, where they arrived in March, 1595. On Good Friday of that year the town was taken with little resistance, and Lancaster permitted not the slightest disorder after the place was taken. He fortified the sandy isthmus which connects Recife with Olinda, and then proceeded at leisure to stow his ships with the goods found in the town, and hired the Dutch vessels lying in the port as store-ships. Some French privateers coming in, he also hired them with part of the booty to assist in the defence of the place, till the lading of the vessels should be completed. The Portuguese made several attempts to burn Lancaster's ships, which were all baffled by his prudence, and after remaining in possession of Recife twenty days he prepared to sail. However, on the very last day of his stay, some of his people, both English and French, having advanced too far in a sally against the Portuguese, were killed, and the enemy claimed a victory, which Lancaster being now ready for sea had no inclination to dispute. And this was the last attack made by the English on the coast of Brazil.

But the French had renewed their attempts, and under Rifault and his successor De Vaux had succeeded in forming a settlement in the island of Maranham, 1611. And shortly afterwards Henry IV. sent Daniel de la Touche, Lord of La Rivardière,* to examine the country, in order to form a permanent colony. His report was favourable; and though on his return to France Henry was dead, an expedition of three ships, containing 500 men, was fitted out, and in 1612 they arrived on the island, speedily conciliated the natives, and the colony promised to thrive. But the court of Madrid quickly sent out orders to the governor of Brazil to attack the intruders. Various accidents prolonged

* In Barbosa Machado's curious collection of pamphlets, in the library of Rio de Janeiro, is one by the Capt. Symam Estacio da Sylveira, printed in 1624. He had been at the taking of Maranham from the French, and his paper is evidently a decoy for colonists. He says, that Daniel de la Touche was induced to go thither by Itayuba of the *Iron arm*, a Frenchman who had been brought up among the Tupinambas. Is this Mr. Southey's Rifault?

Sketch of the History of Brazil

the warfare, and it was not until 1618 that they were dislodged, and a permanent Portuguese colony formed. Its distance from the seat of government determined the court of Madrid to erect Maranham and Para into a separate state, of which the capital was fixed at San Luiz, a town and fort built by the French on the island.

Meantime the Dutch had formed a West Indian Company, trusting that they would thereby be able to annoy the court of Spain in their American possessions, as they had already done in the East Indies. In 1624, a fleet under Jacob Willekins and the famous Peter Heyne was fitted out for that purpose. The ships having been separated in a gale of wind, Willekins made the Morro de San Paulo, about forty miles south of Bahia, where he waited for the rest of the convoy. When it arrived he sailed boldly into the reconcave, and St. Salvador was taken almost without a struggle. Vandort, the Dutch general, immediately began to fortify the place, and proclamations being issued promising freedom and redress of wrongs to all who should submit, many Indians, negroes, and Jews instantly joined him. But the Portuguese, who had hoped that the Dutch had only come to plunder the city, seeing that they were sitting quietly down as in a permanent establishment, roused themselves, and after some little disagreement as to who should command them, pitched on the Bishop Don Marcos Texeira. He fixed his head-quarters on the Rio Vermelho. The Dutch were weakened by the departure of Willekins for Holland, and of Peter Heyne for Angola, the plan of the West India Company being to secure that settlement, in order to have a certain supply of slaves for their new conquests in Brazil. Dort had been killed, and there was no competent commander. The Bishop's troops harassed those of the city in every direction, and the Dutch were prepared to become an easy prey to Don Fadrique de Toledo, who had been sent from Spain with a strong force to recover the capital of Brazil. They capitulated, therefore, in May, 1625, and conditioned for being sent to Holland with sufficient arms and their personal baggage, leaving the city and forts as they were.

The next year, however, Peter Heyne returned to the reconcave. Every precaution was taken against him by the governor. Four large ships with men and artillery were placed to intercept him; but in his single ship, the rest of his squadron not being able to come up with him, ran in between two of them, sunk one, and compelled several others to strike: his own ship, however, grounded, and he burnt her. He added four ships to his own fleet, loaded four others with prize-goods, and burnt the rest. Nor was this his only success; for although the Dutch had been baffled in several attempts on the coast, they sent home prizes enough to be of national importance.

But a conquest of infinitely more consequence was shortly made; that of Olinda, which, in 1630, was taken after a feeble resistance on the part of Matthias de Albuquerque. The Dutch general-in-chief was Henrik Loncq, the admiral was Peter Ardian, and Wardenburg commanded the troops. The latter landed at Pao Amarello, three leagues to the north, while the ships kept up a regular fire opposite to the place; consequently the Portuguese were surprised, and the towns and forts easily taken.

But the country around continued to be the theatre of a most cruel predatory war, during which atrocious cruelties were committed by both parties, but chiefly by the Dutch; and while these things were going on, a number of negroes had escaped from time to time into the great palm-forests, about thirty leagues inland, and had multiplied so that they are said to have amounted to upwards of thirty thousand. These men were governed by a chief whom they called Zombi: they had some laws, a shadow of the Christian religion, and were agriculturists. They harassed the Portuguese, and added by their depredations to the general misery.

At length the Dutch government sent out Count Maurice of Nassau, to take the command at Pernambuco. He arrived in 1637, and carried on the war so vigorously that the Portuguese retired out of the province. He also set about reforming the abuses which existed among the Dutch, themselves at Recife, and having established himself firmly there, he sent one of his officers, Jan Koin, over to the coast of Africa, who took possession of St. Jorge da Mina, by which a supply of slaves was secured, and leaving a garrison there, returned to Recife. The next year, Maurice made an unsuccessful attack on St. Salvador. His fleet anchored in the bay of Tapagipe; but though he obtained at first some important posts, he was finally repulsed and returned with loss to Pernambuco. There he occupied himself in building a new town, and making the two first bridges that had yet been built in Portuguese America, besides planting trees, and improving the fortifications. In 1640 he sent the famous sea-warrior Jol into the reconcave, to lay it waste; and he accordingly burnt the whole of the sugar-works in the bay, while the Indians who were friendly to the Dutch, fell on the land-side of the captaincy, and harassed the unhappy settlers in an equal degree.

At length the court of Madrid began to be alarmed for the safety of Brazil, and fitted out a large armament for its relief. Storms and sickness diminished it, ere it arrived, to nearly one half. That half arrived at Bahia, in 1640, under D. Jorge de Mascasentras, Marques de Monte Alvam. Before he had time either to make open war, or to negociate, the revolution in Portugal, which placed Braganza on the throne of his ancestors, took place. The viceroy, unjustly suspected of adhering to Spain, was sent home, and a commission, composed of Barbalho, Correa, and the bishop, appointed in his stead.

One of the first acts of the restored Portuguese government was to make a ten years' truce with the Seven United States. But this did not prevent the continuance of hostilities in Brazil, and the other foreign possessions of Portugal. Serigipe was surprised, Maranham conquered, and Loanda in Angola and St. Thomas's taken.

Notwithstanding these successes, the Dutch government disapproved of Count Maurice's administration. Instead of sending home either to the States or the Company, all the money and produce which he had gained in Brazil, he had laid out great part of it, as well as of his private fortune, in fortifying the mouths of rivers and harbours, particularly Recife, in repairing and beautifying the towns, and in other public works, which, looking forward to the permanent establishment of the Dutch in the country, he considered as absolutely necessary. He was accordingly recalled, and returned to Holland in 1644.

After the departure of Maurice the tyranny of the Dutch became so intolerable, that the Portuguese began to rise against it almost universally.

Maranham had already been wrested from their hands at the time of his returning, and that event seemed to be the signal for the long and calamitous struggle that ensued in Pernambuco and the neighbouring Captaincies. Joam Fernandes Vieyra, a native of Madeira, had, at a very early age, left his native island in hopes of bettering his fortune in Brazil. He had succeeded, and at the time we speak of; he was one of the richest Portuguese of Pernambuco, and highly esteemed by both his countrymen and the Dutch. Against the latter, however, he was animated both by patrotism and superstition. They oppressed his people, and they were heretics. After waiting for years for a proper opportunity to attempt their destruction, he seized the first months of Nassau's absence, and communicating his plans to none but to two friends, one of whom he commissioned to apply to the government of Bahia in person for succour, he waited patiently for an answer. This man, André Vidal de Negreiros, executed his commission exactly, and shortly afterwards Antonio Diaz Cardozo, and sixty soldiers, were sent to Vieyra. He concealed them in the woods in the neighbourhood of his dwelling, called the Varzea, which was on the plain to the westward of the city, and then summoned the Indian chief Camaram and the Negro chief Henrique Diaz[*], to his assistance, and communicated his designs to his neighbours.

Early in 1645 the war began in earnest. The most shocking atrocities were committed by both parties, especially towards the Indians, who themselves as they were the most faithful allies, were, also the most inveterate and cruel enemies. In the course of the struggle, which lasted until 1654, several leaders on both sides were slain, but none so remarkable as the Indian Camaram. He had been educated by the Jesuits; he understood Latin, wrote, read, and spoke Portuguese perfectly, but on all occasions of ceremony used an interpreter, that he might not in public do any thing imperfectly, and thereby derogate from the dignity of his chieftainship. When a number of Indians were taken along the Dutch, at one of the strong posts of the latter, a relation of Camaram's was found among them. These men had all been condemned to death. Camaram did not intercede for the life of his kinsman, but he saved his honour: he slew him with his own hand, and buried him decently. The rest were hanged by the common executioner, and left for the fowls of the air.

At length this horrible warfare was ended. The two battles of the Gararapes[†], had decided the fate of the Dutch in Brazil: but it was the co-operation of the fleet of the new Brazilian company that enabled

---

[*] The following is an extract from one of the letters of this Creole Negro: "Faltamos a obediença que nos occupava no certain de Bahia, por naõ faltarémos as obrigaçoens da patria; respeitando primeiro as leys da naturenza, que as do imperio." —*Castrioto Lusitano.*

[†] Ves Agros Gararapes, entre a negra,
   Nuvem de Marte horrendo
   Qual Jupiter em flegra,
   Hollanda o vistes fulminar tremendo. — DINIZ.

The Portuguese reader will do well to read the whole of Diniz's fine ode to Vieyra, as well as that to Mem de Sa, on his conquests at Rio de Janeiro. This writer is one of the best of the Arcadian school. — But he wrote on subjects of

Vieyra, who was the real commander in this war, although several military men of reputation had, from time to time, had the nominal chieftainship, to reduce Recife, and on the 23d of January 1654, to present the keys of the city to the Royal Commander Francisco Beretto, and to restore to the crown of Portugal the empire of Brazil, after nine years of the most cruel war, during which the private fortune, and the determined spirit of individuals had sustained the conflict, generally without the aid, and often in direct opposition to the commands of the court. But men once determined on freedom, or on national independence, must in the end overcome all obstacles and vanquish every difficulty.

While these things were going on in the northern provinces, the Jesuits had formed their singular establishments in Paraguay, and endeavoured to stop, or at least limit the slave hunting of the Portuguese in the interior, though without effect. The best part of the colony of St. Vincent's had been removed to St. Paul's, a settlement on the plain of Piratininga, and had flourished surprisingly. The people had become hardy, if not fierce. They had distinguished themselves by the courage and perseverance with which they had explored the country in search of mines, and the activity with which they had brought in slaves for the new settlements. The consciousness of their strength begot in them a longing for independence, and seizing the opportunity of the accession of the House of Braganza to the throne of Portugal, they attempted to set up a king for themselves. Their attempt was baffled by Amador Bueno de Ribiero, the very person they intended for their monarch, who, when the people shouted "Long live king Amador," cried out "Long live Joam IV." and, being swift of foot, ran and took refuge in the Benedictine convent; and the same day, as there was no alternative, Joam IV. was proclaimed by all the people.

The low state to which Portugal was now reduced, was seen in its effects on the government of Brazil. When the appointed governors, either on their own judgement, or in obedience to the orders of the court of Lisbon, attempted to carry any new measure into execution which the people disliked, it was seldom in their power to enforce it, and they could expect little assistance from home. The Jesuits had undertaken the defence of the Indians, and endeavoured by every means to restrain the practice of making slaves of them and to mitigate the lot

---

a minor interest, while Guidi wrote to the "d'Arcadia fortunate Genti" — of the Eternal city, where every civilised being feels he has an interest.

of such as were already enslaved. But the Franciscans and some other orders derived equal pecuniary benefit with the hunters from the sale of slaves, and therefore they opposed them with vehemence. Interest was on the side of the Friars, and the most disgraceful scenes took place in various captaincies between the parties, the Governors being either not able or not willing to interfere with effect.

Meantime, however, the people became accustomed to canvass and to understand public questions; their government began to respect them as a real part of the estate; and a value for independence, and a feeling that to attain it was in their own power, grew out of these disorders.

Had it been possible to have purified their religion from some of its most superstitious observances, and to reform the moral habits of the people, the prosperity of the country would soon have been equal to its means; but wherever slavery is established it brings a twofold curse with it. It degrades both parties even where the slaves are imported. How much more then, as was the case here, when they were hunted on their own grounds, where all the details, disgusting and iniquitous as they are, of the seeking, capturing, and bending to the yoke, pass under the eye till the heart grows callous to the cry of the orphan, the grief of the widow, and the despair of the parent in being torn from whatever has been dear to them?

The history of the Jesuit Vieyra's mission to Maranham is as humiliating to human nature, as his sincere exertions in the cause of the suffering Indians is creditable to himself; but neither his exertions, nor the royal authority, could baffle the selfish cruelty and avarice of the people of that captaincy; they broke out into open rebellion in defence of their detestable practices, and even when they returned to obedience, there was a compromise between humanity and avarice, to which the Indians were again sacrificed.

Rio de Janeiro had enjoyed a greater degree of tranquillity during the eighty years since its foundation than any other settlement, and its trade had increased together with its population; but the southern part of its jurisdiction was little more peaceable than Maranham, and not at all more inclined to listen to the remonstrances of the friends of the Indians. The Paulistas were the most difficult of all to manage; they had been the most active and daring of all that hunted either for slaves or for mines, and they were not willing to participate with others, far less to resign the advantages they had gained by unwearied labour and great sacrifices. Their conduct on the restoration of Portugal had evinced a desire of more than the freedom of a colony, and their neighbours were little less disposed for independence than themselves. Santos, and even Rio, had joined them, and had shewn a disposition to depose the governor appointed by the crown; and nothing but the unimpeachable character and firm conduct of Salvador Correa de Sa e Benevides (1658) prevented him from falling a sacrifice to that disposition. Bahia continued to be the capital of the Brazilian states, and its inhabitants proceeded to beautify it with churches, and convents, and nunneries, while they defied the spirit of Christianity by the importation of African, as well as the kidnapping Indian slaves. Pernambuco was still undergoing the miserable effects of the long and desultory war it had sustained; all the bands of government had been loosed during that disastrous period; law and justice had fallen into disuse; and had there not been a redeeming virtue in the free spirit that lived on in spite of the evils among which it had sprung, its very emancipation from a foreign power might have been regretted. The negroes who had escaped to the Palmares, and whose depredations had been disregarded in comparison with the evils of a foreign government, had become a real source of ill to the Pernambucans. Although they cultivated maize, and mandioc, and plaintains, they wanted every other supply. They therefore robbed the Creoles of their cattle, their sugar, their manufactured goods, and even of their Mulatto daughters and female slaves; till at length the government resolved to free the country of them, and called in the aid of a Paulista regiment for the purpose. Ten thousand of the negroes bearing arms had assembled in their chief city, which was surrounded by wooden walls, leaving the lesser ones uninhabited. But their enemies had the advantage of cannon against them, and of supplies of every kind; yet once the negroes beat off their assailants. But numbers overpowered them, and being weakened by famine, their city was forced, and the inmates seized as slaves. Zombi, however, and the most resolute of his followers, threw themselves from a high rock when they perceived their condition desperate. The Portuguese abused their victory, and murdered the rest.

But there was an evil that affected Brazil generally—the too much and the too little power of the governors. They had too much power, if any appeal lay from them—too little, if they were absolute for the term of their government. They were also virtually free from responsibility; their opportunities, nay, their temptations to extortion were almost irresistible; and, to crown all, the corrupt administration of the laws kept pace with the vices and the irregularity of the government. In vain had the wisest regulations been made, and the most just decrees issued. The judges were in many cases parties concerned; they were so in all cases where Indians and negroes were the objects of their judgment, for they were possessors of both. Their salaries were insufficient, their fees arbitrary. What wonder then if the administration was corrupt!

The cultivation of sugar and cotton had proceeded silently amidst all this confusion. The discovery of the gold and diamond mines assisted the government, both in Brazil and in the mother country, to make a stand in the midst of the eminent peril which threatened, in consequence of the hopes sustained in the east, while at home there was a scanty and impoverished population, ruined manufactures, and, above all, a neglect of agriculture, that rendered Portugal dependent on foreigners for corn. Every thing was wanted; there was nothing to return; and at the beginning of the eighteenth century, Brazil may be truly said to have saved Portugal, by covering with her precious metals the excessive balance that was against her in every branch of commerce, in every department of government.

Yet, though absolute ruin was averted, the weakness of the crown rendered it impossible to defend its foreign possessions from the attacks of a daring enemy. In 1710, a French squadron, under Duclerc, appeared off Rio de Janeiro, but not daring to pass the forts, sailed on, and after making several attempts to land a force at the different inlets, where he was deterred by the appearance of the militia of the country, succeeded at Guaratiba, between thirty and forty miles from the city, and thence he marched upon it with about one thousand marines. The governor, Francisco Castro de Moraes, made no attempt to stop him until his arrival at the city. There the first check the enemy met was from F. Francisco de Menezes, a Trinitarian friar, who appeared every where, and did what the governor, who remained quietly intrenched in a flat space, where the place of the Rosario now is, between two hills, ought to have done. The French having divided, one party attacked the palace, but the students of the college defended it successfully; and after a short, but desperate struggle, the French were overpowered, and the victory disgraced by the inhuman conduct of the Portuguese. Duclerc and his people were imprisoned and harshly treated. Duclerc himself is said to have been murdered in his bed.

The next year drew on Rio de Janeiro a signal punishment for these proceedings. The famous Duguay Trouin undertook to inflict it; and accordingly, in August, 1711, one year after Duclerc's adventure, he arrived off the coast, and taking advantage of a fog, entered the bay, notwithstanding the fire of the forts.

The Portuguese government had notice of his design, and had sent out stores and ammunition to meet the attack, and had appointed Gasper da Costa commander of the troops. But the sudden appearance of the French actually within the harbour, seems to have palsied the understanding of every person on shore, whose business it should have been to oppose them, and the forts and the city were given up almost without a struggle.

It would, however, have been impossible for the French to maintain themselves in Rio; therefore Duguay Trouin, after refreshing his people, ransomed the city for 600,000 cruzadoes. Bad weather alone prevented him from laying waste the reconcave of Bahia, as he had done Rio: but he had fulfilled the ostensible purpose of his voyage by avenging the treatment of Duclerc and his people, and returned to France early in 1712.

These circumstances had awakened the greatest anxiety on account of Brazil in the cabinet of Lisbon: and at the peace of Utrecht, 1713, every precaution was adopted by the Portuguese ministers to avoid any expression that might seem to admit of a free trade by any power whatever to Brazil, notwithstanding the agreements to that effect actually existing at the time. Disputes without end arose between Portugal and Spain concerning the colonies adjoining to the Rio de la Plata, and it was especially stipulated that no other power, particularly England, should be allowed to form settlements there on account of the facilities such settlements might afford for smuggling the precious metals out of the country. These had now become the first object in Brazil. St. Paul's had been erected into a city, and the district of the mines had been formed into a captaincy: the inhabitants of the coast flocked to the interior, where new towns were daily springing up; all were desirous of a share in that lottery where the prizes were so enormous, that the great preponderance of blanks was overlooked. Great inconvenience must have been felt by the early adventurers to the mines: for so many hands were employed in searching for gold, that few remained to cultivate the soil, and provide the necessaries of life. Yet that insatiable thirst of gold is a stimulus which has led to useful and to hourable things: it is not the love of the metal, but the possession of it gives power, and that is the real object of most men's ambition: it is certainly that of the ambition of all nations, and this object is held legitimate: we account those base or wicked who seek the means; we admire those who attain the end. The philosophic historian and the poet are alike ready to condemn the man who first dug the ore from the mine: the panegyric in prose and in verse is lavished on the hero and the patron. But gold furnished the means for the hero's conquests and the patron's liberality, and gold, or the worth of gold, is the object of both; whether in the form of continued power, or of that fame which patronage can bring. Sad indeed has been the waste of human life in searching for gold: but have all the mines together consumed more men than the single revolutionary war? And have not the religious contests among Christians, and their persecutions and mutilations and burnings cost many more? I would not justify the gold finders; their actions were horrible, their oppressions atrocious; but let them have justice: the stimulus was great; urged on by it, they performed great things, they braved cold, and hunger, and fatigue, and persecution, and death; they persevered, they opened the way to unknown lands, they laid the foundations for future civilisation in countries which will have reason to bless their discoveries, when the effect of their evil deeds, as well as the memory of the brutal customs of the savages they so unjustly oppressed, shall have passed away.

But I have neither space nor inclination to follow their adventures, and must refer to Mr. Southey's elaborate and excellent account of them. Daniel Defoe alone could have so handled the subject as to make delightful so dull and so sad a tale. I am but a looker on to whom the actions of the present are more interesting than the past, but yet am not insensible to the influence that the elder days have had upon us.

Pernambuco had during the half century which had elapsed since the expulsion of the Dutch had time to recruit. The sugar plantations had reappeared, and the commerce of Recife had become extremely important. The merchants, and especially those from Europe, had settled there, and the town had increased till it became the second of Brazil; while Olinda gradually declined, having few inhabitants besides priests and the representatives of the old families of the province, who might be called its nobility: still Recife was but a village until, in 1710, it solicited and obtained the royal assent to its becoming a town, and having a camera or municipal council to govern its internal affairs. The jealousy of the people of Olinda and the other old Brazilians was violently excited by this concession, which they conceived would raise the plebeian traders and foreigners to an equality with themselves. After several tumultuous meetings on the subject, three of the ten parishes belonging to Olinda were assigned to Recife, and the governor, fearing to set up the pillar which marks a township openly, had it erected in the night. Fresh disturbances ensued, in which some of the magistrates were concerned, and there were not wanting voices to exclaim that the Pernambucans had shown they could shake off the strong chains of the Dutch, and that they could as easily shake off others and govern themselves. The seditious magistrates were arrested and thrown into prison. The soldiers were employed to disarm the people; but they had now advanced too far to be easily reduced. The governor was fired at and dangerously wounded, and proofs were not wanting that the judge and the bishop had at least consented to the attempt on his life. The most serious disturbances followed: the inhabitants of the whole district took up arms, some blood was shed in the course of their contentions with the soldiers, and Sebastian de Castro, the governor, weakened both in body and mind, was induced to fly to Bahia for safety. Six of the chief Pernambucans were now appointed to exercise the functions of a provisional government till orders should be received from Lisbon, and all Europeans were deprived of their offices and commissions.

But the bishop, who had been at Paraiba since the time when de Castro was wounded, now returned to claim his office as governor on the removal of the former one. He began to exercise his authority in the king's name, and his first act was to declare a general pardon. But he, however appears to have been a timid man: willing yet not daring to join the party who wished to shake off the yoke of Portugal, and by his vacillating conduct betraying both his friends in that party, and the trust reposed in him by the crown. At length, in 1711, these disturbances were quieted by a new governor, Felix Jose Machado de Mendonça. Brazil was not yet ripe for independence; nor indeed could so small and ill-peopled a state as Pernambuco have maintained its freedom even for a year unconnected with the other captaincies. While these things were going on in the captaincies of Brazil, the Jesuits were labouring in the interior to reclaim the Indians, with success far beyond the apparent means, and some towns, which have since become of importance, were built on the coast and on the shores of the Plata, particularly Monte Video, in 1733; but the border war, between the Spaniards and Portuguese, which was waged on account of these settlements, disquieted the neighbourhood for a time. Its importance, however, was soon forgotten in the disturbances caused by the treaty of division between Spain and Portugal, which forcing the Indians who had been reclaimed to emigrate, roused them to a vigorous but short and useless resistance, which only began the evils that the Jesuit missions were destined to perish under.

The Portuguese government, under the administration of Carvalho, afterwards Marquis of Pombal, had begun to attend to, and attempt to reform the abuses which existed throughout Brazil, but particularly in the newly founded captaincies and settlements, when the war with France and Spain broke out in 1762. For a time defence against a foreign enemy superseded every other consideration. The first act of hostility in the western world was the seizing of the Portuguese settlement of Columbia, in the Plata, by the governor of Buenos Ayres, before the squadron despatched by the governor of Brazil, Gomez Freyre, could arrive to protect it. That squadron consisted of the Lord Clive, of 64 guns, an English ship commanded by Capt. Macnamara; the Ambuscade, of 40 guns, in which Penrose, the poet, served as lieutenant; and the Gloria, of 38 guns. The Spanish ships retired before Macnamara, and he ran under the guns of the forts of Colonia, in order to retake the place. He had nearly succeeded in silencing the batteries, when, by accident or negligence, the ship took fire; the enemy renewed their fire; three-fourths of the crew of the Lord Clive, among which was the captain, were drowned. The other ships were nearly destroyed and obliged to retreat; but owing to the neglect of the Spaniards, they were able to refit and return to Rio. And this was the most remarkable action of the war beyond the Atlantic, and the first in which the English distinguished themselves in the defence of Brazil.

Pombal, meantime, having resolved on the suppression of the order of Jesuits, overlooked, in the ardour with which he pursued that measure, the important services they had rendered, and were daily rendering, to one of his favourite objects, namely, the improvement of the condition of the Indians. Their plan of discipline, indeed, hitherto had kept their pupils rather in a state of childish innocence than of manly improvement. Their fault was, that in order to secure obedience, they had stopped short of what they might have effected. Their dominion was an Utopia; and had it been possible to shut out every European and every wild Indian, it might have lasted. But such artificial polities can never be of long duration. Some convulsions either from without or from within must end them, and that with a more complete ruin than could befal states less curiously framed. But the well-intentioned labours of the missionaries had produced one decided good effect,— the habits of savage life were abandoned, and the advantages of agriculture and manufactures had been felt. The rock on which the education of the Indians split, was the community of goods. When a man has no property, but depends for the supply of his daily wants upon the providence of others, he has no incitement to particular exertion. The stimulus to industry cannot exist where a man has no hope of growing richer, no fear of becoming poorer, no anxiety about the provision of his family. His judgment in the portioning and disposing of his property is never called forth; all the qualities and virtues that arise out of the practice of domestic economy lie dormant, and the man remains an infant. It would have been easy to remedy this, by allowing the Indians to possess private stock, and to provide for their own families after the first generation. The newly reclaimed did require to be provided for, but the children growing up in the Aldeas might have been intrusted with their own property. They would have become men; and when the removal of their spiritual fathers took place, that wide and deep desolation would not have overwhelmed them, nor would Paraguay have gone back as it has done towards a savage state.

The Jesuits of Brazil were expelled in 1760, in the most cruel and arbitrary manner. Those of the Spanish American colonies eight years later. Whatever might have been their faults, or even their crimes, in other countries, in these their conduct had been exemplary. They had been the protectors of a persecuted race, the advocates of mercy, the founders of civilisation; and their patience under their unmerited sufferings forms not the least honourable trait in their character.

The history of Brazil, for the next thirty years, is composed of the mismanagement and decay of the Jesuit establishments; the enlargement of the mining districts, particularly in the direction of Mato Grosso; some disputes with the French on the frontier of Cayenne; and the more peaceful occupations of opening roads, and the introduction of new branches of commerce, and the improvement of the old.

This tranquillity was for a moment interrupted by a conspiracy in the province of Minas Geraes, headed by an officer named Joaquim

Jose de Silva Xavier, commonly called Tiradentes. The project of the conspirators was to form an independent republic in Minas, and, if possible, to induce Rio de Janeiro to unite with it. But their measures were most inadequate for the end proposed, and their conduct so imprudent, that, although there was a pretty general feeling of discontent on account of the taxes and some other grievances, the conspirators were all seized before they had formed anything like a party capable of resistance, much less of beginning the meditated revolution.

The direct effects upon Brazil of the first thirteen years of the revolutionary war in Europe were confined to some slight disputes regarding the boundaries of the Portuguese and French Guiana, and concerning the limits of which, there was an article in Lord Cornwallis's negotiations with France, or rather the peace of Amiens in 1802.

The indirect effects were greater. Being a good deal left to themselves, the colonists had leisure to discover what sort of cultivation and crops suited best with the climate, and were fittest for the market; and some branches of industry were introduced, and others improved, to the great advantage of the province. Foreign ships, and even fleets, had also begun to resort thither:* so that, though the ports had as yet been closed against foreign traders, the entrance of men of war, and such merchant ships as could find no others to refit in, introduced a virtual freedom, which it would afterwards have been impossible not to have confirmed.

The court of Portugal meanwhile, as if infatuated by the negotiations of France, consented to buy a disgraceful neutrality at the price of 1,000,000 of livres or 40,000£. per month, besides granting free entrance to French woollens into the kingdom.

It was in vain that frequent representations were made to the ministry at Lisbon on the subject; that the armament at Bayonne, and the refusal of Spain to forbid the passage of French troops through her territories, were pointed out. The Portuguese forces were marched to the sea-coast, as if they apprehended an invasion from England; thus leaving the kingdom defenceless on the land side, and the ports were shut against English commerce, by a proclamation, dated 20th October, 1807. But the importance of Portugal to England, as neutral ground, or, in the event of a French government in Spain, as a point whence to

---

* That under Sir H. Popham, on Sir D. Baird's expedition to the Cape of Good Hope, for instance, in 1805, and that of the French admiral, Guillaumez, in 1806.

attack the great enemy, was such, that the resentment which at another time would certainly have been openly declared, was suppressed; but a strong squadron was always kept up off the coast, partly to watch the proceedings on shore, partly to prevent the Portuguese vessels from coming out of port, and joining the French and Spaniards.

While this system of watchfulness was kept up in Europe, the English ministry was not less attentive to the designs of France on the South American colonies. As long as Spain and Portugal continued to pay the enormous price in money for their neutrality, which France had demanded, the views of Napoleon were better answered than they could have been by the possession of all their territory and all their colonies. But the moment in which they should become unable or unwilling to pay that price, would of course be that of aggression and invasion. So early as 1796, Mr. Pitt had contemplated the advantages that must arise to Britain from the possession of a port in South America, and particularly in the Rio de la Plata, nor did he ever afterwards lose sight of it. Some circumstances occurred in December, 1804, to draw his attention, particularly towards the subject, inasmuch as he had intelligence that France was about to attempt to seize on one of the Spanish settlements on the first opportunity. But we were then at peace with Spain, and however willing to prevent such an aggression on the part of France, and to assist General Miranda in his intended expedition to South America, it was impossible to cooperate with him, as he earnestly pressed the ministry to do, although the advantage to England of securing such a market for her manufactures was clearly perceived. Among the officers who had been most confidentially consulted by Mr. Pitt, on the practicability of obtaining a settlement on the La Plata, was Sir Home Popham; and it was probably his knowledge of the views so long entertained by that minister, that induced him to take the hazardous step, of leaving the Cape of Good Hope so soon after it had been occupied by the English forces, in 1806, and taking Buenos Ayres without orders to that effect. His immediate motive was, the intelligence he had procured, that the squadron of the French admiral, Guillaumez, had intentions of touching on the coast of Brazil, entering the La Plata, and, if possible, seizing, or forming a settlement there; and some North Americans whom he had met, encouraged the undertaking, by observing, that to throw open the ports of South America would be a common benefit to all commercial nations, but particularly to England.*

In 1806, the demonstrations of hostilities against Portugal on the part of France were so evident, that Lord Rosslyn was dispatched thither on a special mission, in which Lord St. Vincent and General Simcoe were joined with him. His instructions from Mr. Fox, then prime minister, were to lay before the ministry of Lisbon, the imminent danger which threatened the country, and to offer assistance in men, money, and stores from England, to put Portugal in a state of defence, in case the government should decide on a vigorous and effective resistance. If, on the other hand, Portugal should think itself too weak to contend with France, the idea that had once occurred to King Don Alfonso of emigrating to Brazil, and there establishing the capital of the empire, was to be revived, and promises made of assistance and protection for that purpose. If, however, Portugal insisted on rejecting assistance in either case, the troops under General Simcoe were to be landed, the strong forts on the Tagus occupied by them, and the fleet was to enter the river and secure the Portuguese ships and vessels, taking care to impress the government and people with the feeling that this was done from regard to the nation, and by no means for the sake of selfish aggrandisement on the part of England. It appears, however, that the French preparations for the invasion were not at that time so far advanced as had been imagined, and at the earnest entreaty of the court of Lisbon, the troops and the fleet were withdrawn from the Tagus.

On the 8th of August, the next year, however, (1807) Mr. Rayneval, the French chargé d'affaires at Lisbon, received orders from his court to declare to the Prince Regent of Portugal, that if by the first of September he did not declare war against England, and send back the English minister, recalling the Portuguese ambassador from London, and did not seize all the English residents, confiscate their property, and shut the ports of the kingdom against the English; and lastly, if he did not, without delay, unite his armies and fleets with those of the rest of the continent against England, he had orders to demand his passports and to declare war.

---

* For the political and commercial views entertained with regard to the assisting Miranda, or obtaining for England a port in South America, see Lord Melville's evidence on the court martial on Sir Home Popham.

The Conde de Barca, then prime minister, was certainly aware of the preparations of the French government. But with that obstinate blindness which sometimes seems to possess men like a fate, he persisted in regarding them only as measures to intimidate and harass England. This nobleman had been ambassador at the court of St. Petersburg, and on his recall to take the first place in the cabinet at Lisbon, he was ordered to go by sea to London, and thence to Portugal, but he chose to perform the journey by way of Paris, where he saw and conversed both with Napoleon and Talleyrand. There cannot be the least doubt but that he was duped by those able men. Many considered him as a traitor. But the vanity of the Conde, who always said he had gone to judge of these men by his own eyes, though it makes him weaker, makes him less wicked, and was, perhaps, the true spring of his actions. He it was who carried the measures for the detention of the English, the confiscation of their property, and the shutting the ports against English commerce: adopting, in short, the whole of the continental system. The very day before Junot was to reach Lisbon, however, a Paris newspaper, written in anticipation of the event, announced that *"The House of Braganza no longer reigned,"* and that its members were reduced to the common herd of ex-princes, etc., giving no very favourable description of them, and holding out no very flattering expectations for the future. The Prince Regent's eyes were now opened, and he consented to that step, which D. John IV. and Don José had contemplated, namely, the transferring the seat of his empire to his Transatlantic possessions. {Graham writes "J.B.A.S." in the margin of this paragraph, perhaps indicating that the Prince Regent's eyes were opened by José Bonifácio de Andrada e Silva.}

This was in the month of November, 1807, but the events of that month, the most interesting that had occurred to Portugal since the revolution that had placed Braganza on the throne of his ancestors, will be best understood by the following extracts from the despatches received by the British ministry from Lord Strangford and from Sir Sydney Smith at the time. On the 29th November, 1807, His Lordship writes, after mentioning the Prince's departure for Brazil:—

> I had frequently and distinctly stated to the cabinet of Lisbon, that in agreeing not to resent the exclusion of British commerce from the ports of Portugal, His Majesty had exhausted the means of forbearance; that in making that concession to the peculiar circum-

stances of the Prince Regent's situation, His Majesty had done all that friendship and the remembrance of ancient alliance could justly require; but that a single step beyond the line of modified hostility, thus most reluctantly consented to, must necessarily lead to the extremity of actual war.

The Prince Regent, however, suffered himself for a moment to forget that, in the present state of Europe, no country could be permitted to be an enemy to England with impunity, and that however much His Majesty might be disposed to make allowance for the deficiency of means possessed by Portugal of resistance to the power of France, neither his own dignity nor the interests of his people would permit His Majesty to accept that excuse for a compliance with the full extent of her unprincipled demands. On the 8th inst. His Royal Highness was induced to sign an order for the detention of the few British subjects, and of the inconsiderable portion of British property which yet remained at Lisbon. On the publication of this order, I caused the arms of England to be removed from the gates of my residence, demanded my passports, presented a final remonstrance against the recent conduct of the court of Lisbon, and proceeded to the squadron commanded by Sir Sydney Smith, which arrived off the coast of Portugal some days after I had received my passports, and which I joined on the 17th inst.

I immediately suggested to Sir Sydney Smith the expediency of establishing the most rigorous blockade at the mouth of the Tagus; and I had the high satisfaction of afterwards finding that I had thus anticipated the intentions of His Majesty: for despatches (which I received on the 23d) directing me to authorise that measure, in case the Portuguese government should pass the bounds which His Majesty had thought fit to set to his forbearance, and attempt to take any further step injurious to the honour or interests of Great Britain.—

—I resolved, therefore, to proceed forthwith to ascertain the effect produced by the blockade of Lisbon, and to propose to the Portuguese government, as the only condition upon which that blockade should cease, the alternative (stated by you) either of surrendering the fleet to His Majesty, or of immediately employing it to remove the Prince Regent and his family to the Brazils.—

I accordingly requested an audience of the Prince Regent, together with due assurances of protection and security; and upon receiving His Royal Highness's answer, I proceeded to Lisbon on the 27th, in His Majesty's sloop Confiance, bearing a flag of truce. I had immediately most interesting communications with the court of Lisbon, the particulars of which shall be detailed in a future despatch. It suffices to mention in this place, that the Prince Regent wisely directed all his apprehensions to a French army, and all his hopes to a British fleet: that he received the most explicit assurances from me that His Majesty would generously overlook those acts of unwilling and momentary hostility to which His Royal Highness's consent had been extorted; and that I promised to His Royal Highness, on the faith of my sovereign, that the British squadron before the Tagus should be employed to protect his retreat from Lisbon, and his voyage to the Brazils.

A decree was published yesterday, in which the Prince Regent announced his intention of retiring to the city of Rio de Janeiro until the conclusion of a general peace, and of appointing a regency to transact the administration of government at Lisbon, during His Royal Highness's absence from Europe.

[This despatch was written in Nerot's hotel in London—before he had left Lisbon, his Lordship sent Lord Cochrane with despatches to the foreign office to inform ministers that the Prince Regent was adopting every part of the Continental policy but that he was still in hopes of bringing him to go to Brazil. In North there had been a show of equipping the Portuguese Squadron etc. Cabbages etc. had been hung from the sterns and quarters of the ships to appear as if the provisions of the Royal party had been laid in. However, the French Army approaching nearer and nearer, and the Prince continuing obstinate, Sir James Gambier was dispatched, but his journey to England was unaccountably slow. Lord Strangford on going on board the Hibernia wanted Sir Sidney to blockade Lisbon on his word—but Sir Sidney said no: "*You* on board under these circumstances are like every man in the Squadron under my command—but on shore as minister I will of course comply with a written requisition." Lord Sidney went as he says on shore but that day saw neither Prince nor minister, but called on a Madame de—{blank} and then was lost till next morning when he gave out that he had been with Madame {illegible} of the Oyenhausens afterwards kept by Junot then by {blank} and now I think by Beresford. Next day indeed he was seen by the Minister and was told the Prince was actually on board.

Lord Strangford arrived in London before Sir James Gambier—Consequently the despatches containing his account of having left Lisbon in despair of prevailing on the prince to move were not received—His credit was saved and the new despatches were written in Nerot's hotel.]

Sir Sydney Smith writes on the first of December the following letter to the admiralty:—

> His Majesty's Ship Hibernia, 22 leagues west of the Tagus, Dec. 1, 1807.
>
> SIR,
>
> In a former despatch, dated 22d November, with a postscript of the 26th, I conveyed to you, for the information of my Lords Commissioners of the Admiralty, the proofs contained in various documents of the Portuguese government, being so much influenced by terror of the French arms as to have acquiesced to certain demands of France operating against Great Britain. The distribution of the Portuguese force was made wholly on the coast, while the land side was left totally unguarded. British subjects of all descriptions were detained; and it therefore became necessary to inform the Portuguese government, that the case had arisen, which required, in obedience to my instructions, that I should declare the Tagus in a state of blockade.

(Sir Sydney then repeats part of Lord Strangford's despatch.)

> On the morning of the 29th, the Portuguese fleet came out of the Tagus with His Royal Highness the Prince of Brazil, and the whole of the royal family of Braganza on board, together with many of his faithful councillors and adherents, as well as other persons attached to his present fortunes.
>
> This fleet of eight sail of the line, four frigates, two brigs, and one schooner, with a crowd of large armed merchant ships arranged itself under the protection of that of His Majesty, while the firing of a reciprocal salute of twenty-one guns announced the friendly meeting of those, who but the day before were on terms of hostility, the scene impressing every beholder (except the French army on the hills) with the most lively emotions of gratitude to Providence, that there yet existed a power in the world able, as well as willing, to protect the oppressed.—I have, etc.
>
> W. Sydney Smith.

Such are the public accounts transmitted by foreigners to their court of one of the most singular transactions that has occurred in the history of kingdoms and of courts. Yet such was the state of Europe at that time, so momentous the struggle between the principals in the mighty warfare that was going on, that the ancient house of Braganza left the seat of its ancestors, to seek shelter and security beyond the Atlantic, almost without notice and with less ceremony than had formerly attended an excursion to its country palaces.

The French Government had waited to invade Portugal till that unhappy country had exhausted its treasury, in the payment of the enormous sums demanded as the price of its neutrality. French influence had removed the Portuguese troops from the mountain passes, where they might have opposed the entrance of French armies, and the Prince Regent only declared his adherence to the continental system, and arrested the English on the simultaneous entrance of three Imperial and Spanish armies.

Junot invaded Algarve and passed the Zezere, at the same moment when Solano threw himself upon Oporto, and Carafa occupied Alentejo and Algarve.—Under these circumstances, the conduct of the ministry, though not courageous, was natural, and it was as natural when Lord Strangford returned to Lisbon, which, perhaps, he ought not to have left, that the last council held in that capital should decide on the emigration of the court to Brazil. Had it remained, and Portugal had become a French province, the Prince and all his family were prisoners in the hands of one who had respected no crown; and besides, England had intimated that in that case she must occupy Brazil for her own security. By emigrating to Brazil the Prince retained in his hands the largest and richest portion of his domains, and secured at least, the personal freedom and safety of his family. At the end therefore of the last meeting of his councillors the Prince called his confidential servants,* and ordered them to prepare every thing *in secret* for the embarkation of the court on the next night but one. One of these had been actually ordered to provide quarters for Junot, and on the next morning to have a breakfast ready for him at a house half-way between Sacavem and Lisbon. This man had smuggled his family on board one of the ships, he had been night and day getting provisions, plate, books, jewels, whatever could be moved on board the fleet, and, remaining to the last, was again ordered to provide quarters for Junot: but he was fortunate enough to secure a boat to carry him off to the fleet, leaving papers, money, and even his hat behind him on the beach.

Such is the picture of the hasty embarkation, given by some of the attendants on the royal family.

The fleets had no sooner got off the land than they encountered a violent gale of wind, but by the 5th of December they were all collected again; on that day Sir Sidney Smith having supplied the ships with every thing necessary for their safety, and having convoyed them to lat. 37° 47' north, and long. 14° 17' west, left them to go on under the protection of the Marlborough, Capt. Moore, with a broad pennant, the London, Monarch and Bedford.† They proceeded without

---

* These were the Visconde de Rio Seco, who managed all; the Marquis de Vagos, gentleman of the bed-chamber; Conde de Redondo, who had the charge of the royal pantries; Manoel da Cuaha, admiral of the fleet; the Padre José Eloi, who had the care of the valuables belonging to the patriarchal church.

† On the removal of the family of Braganza to Brazil, Sir Samuel Hood and General Beresford took possession of Madeira, in trust for Portugal, till a restoration should take place.

farther accident to the coast of Brazil, and landed at Bahia on the 21st of January, 1808.[‡]

The Conde da Ponta was at that time governor of Bahia, and is said to have been very popular:[§] he had married a lady of high family who was not less so, and she possessed, besides the manners of the court, a considerable portion of both beauty and talent.

The reception of the royal party was rendered so agreeable to the Prince by the governor and his lady, that he remained at St. Salvador's a month, every day being a festival, and then left it with regret. In commemoration of the visit, a spot was cleared near the fortress of St. Peter's, and commanding a fine view over the whole of the beautiful bay, and there an obelisk was erected with an inscription, stating its purpose, and the surrounding ground was planted and converted into a public garden.

But, however agreeable a residence at Bahia might have been to His Royal Highness, the place is too insecure for the purposes for which he emigrated. If it is besieged by sea, and the smallest land force gets possession of the neck of land between the Cape and Rio Vermelha, it is actually without the means of subsistence. The entrance of the bay is so wide, that nothing can prevent ships from going in when they please. Whereas, the harbour of Rio is easily defended, it not being possible for ships to enter without being exposed to the fire of the forts. Besides, it has resources which Bahia has not, being at all times able to communicate with the rich province of the Minas, which, besides the metals, abounds in corn, mandioc, cotton, coffee, cattle, hogs, and even the coarse manufactures such as cotton, etc., for the use of the slaves and for ordinary purposes.

Rio was therefore the best adapted for the asylum of the illustrious house of Braganza, and, on the 26th February, His Royal Highness sailed from Bahia, and arrived in Rio de Janeiro on the 7th March.

Meantime the French troops had occupied Portugal, and Junot, who commanded in chief, and had fixed his head-quarters at Lisbon, began by disarming the inhabitants, and war between France and Portugal was formally announced, eight days before the signature of the

---

‡ The Rainha de Portugal, and Conde Henrique with Princess Dowager and the younger Princesses arrived straight at Rio on the 15th of January. The Martim de Freitas and Golfinho arrived on the 15th at Bahia for supplies, sailed for Rio on the 24th, and arrived on the 30th.

§ The Conde died in May, 1809, at the age of 35, leaving ten children and an embarrassed estate.

treaty of Fontainbleau, by which Portugal was divided into three great feoffs, which, under the King of Etruria, the Prince of Peace Godoy, and a Braganza, if he would submit to the conditions,* were to be subject to the crown of Spain.

Junot published a proclamation flattering the people in proportion to his oppressions and exactions, and nearly ruined them by a forced war contribution of nearly 3,000,000£.—In addition to this a conscription of 40,000 men was raised, and thus the means which Portugal possessed, and which, if timely used, might have saved her from invasion were turned against her.

The first ministry appointed on the arrival of the court at Rio, consisted of Don Rodriguez de Souza Continho, Don Juan d'Almeida, the Visconde d'Anadia, and the Marquez d'Aguiar.

The first measure of the court was to publish a manifesto, setting forth the conduct of France towards Portugal, from the beginning of the revolution; the efforts of the government to preserve its neutrality; and detailing all the events which had led immediately to the emigration of the royal family. The manifesto also denied having, as the French government alleged, given any succours to the English fleet or troops in their expedition to the River Plate; and it states, that the French government having broken faith with that of Portugal, His Royal Highness considered himself at war with France, and declared that he could only make peace by consent of, and in conjunction with, his old and faithful ally the king of England; and this was all the direct interference of the Prince in the affairs of his ancient European kingdom, where a junta of five persons was appointed to govern, and where, before the end of the year (1808), the battle of Vimiera had been fought, and the convention of Cintra had been signed.

The first sensible effect of the arrival of the royal family in Brazil was the opening of its numerous ports;† and in the very first year (1808) ninety foreign ships entered the single harbour of Rio, and a proportional number, those of Maranham, Pernambuco, and Bahia. The effect of the residence of the court was soon felt in the city of Rio de Janeiro. It was before 1808 confined to little more than the ground it occupied when attacked by the Duguay Trouen in 1712; and the

* Godoy was to have Alentejo and Algarve; Etruria, Entre Minho e Douro with the city of Oporto, the rest was to be sequestrated till a general peace, when a Braganza was to be placed at its head, on condition that England should restore Gibraltar, Trinidad, etcetera. to Spain.
† 28th January, 1808.

beautiful bays above and below it, formed by the harbour, were unoccupied, except by a few fishermen, while the swamps and morasses which surrounded it rendered it filthy in the extreme. A spot near the church of San Francisco de Paulo has been cleared for a square, but scarcely a dozen houses had risen round it, and a muddy pond filled up the centre, into which the negroes were in the habit of throwing all the impurities from the neighbourhood. This was now filled up. On one side of the square a theatre was begun, not inferior to those of Europe in size and accommodation, and placed under the patronage of St. John; several magnificent houses rose in the immediate neighbourhood, the square was finished, and another and much larger laid out beyond it, on one side of the city, while on the other, between the foot of the mountain of the Corcovado, with its surrounding hills, and the sea, every station was occupied by delightful country-houses, and the beautiful bay of Botafogo, where there were before only fishermen and gipsies, soon became a populous and wealthy suburb.

It is not in my power to give a detailed account of all the transactions of this important year. The trade had naturally rapidly increased; the money brought by the emigrants from Portugal, had called forth greater exertions and speculations in commerce; and in October a public bank was chartered in Rio, with a capital of from seventy to eighty thousand pounds sterling.

The establishment of a regular gazette naturally took place, for the speedier dissemination of whatever tidings might arrive from Portugal, where lay the possessions and the interest of the court and the new people of Brazil; and though the press, of course, did not boast of much freedom, nor indeed would its freedom at that time have been of any consequence, it formed the first step towards awakening rational curiosity and that desire for reading, which has become not only a luxury, but even a necessary, in some countries, and which makes a rapid and daily progress here.

On the arrival of the court many of the old Creole families hastened to the capital to greet their sovereigns. The sons and the daughters of these married into the noble houses of Portugal; the union of the two nations became intimate and permanent; and the manners and habits of the Brazilians more polished. With the artificial wants that sprung up, new industry was excited, especially near the capital; the woods and hills were cleared, the desert islands of the bay became thriving farms, gardens sprung up every where, and the delicate table vegetables of Europe and Africa were added to the native riches of the soil and climate.

The numbers of the royal family furnished birthdays for frequent galas, the foreigners vied with the Portuguese in their feasts, so that Rio presented a scene of almost continued festivity. On the 17th of December, the birthday of the queen, six counts were created, that is, Luiz de Vasconcellos e Souza was made Conde de Figuerio, Don Rodrigo de Souza Continho, Conde de Linhares, the Visconde d'Anadia, Conde d'Anadia, D. Joao d'Almeida de Mello e Castro, Conde das Galveas, D. Fernando Jose de Portugal, Conde d'Aguiar, and D. Jose de Souza Continho, Conde de Redondo. The Papal Nuncio, Sir Sidney Smith, and Lord Strangford,* were honoured with the order of the Tower and Sword; six English officers were named commanders of the order of the Cross, and five others were made knights of the same.

The beginning of 1809 was marked by an event of some importance. By the treaty of Amiens, Portuguese Guiana had been given up to France, and was now, together with French Guyana and Cayenne, governed by the infamous Victor Hughes. It was long since France had been able to send out succour to these colonies. The fleets of England impeded the navigation, and the demands at home were too urgent and too great to permit much to be hazarded for the sake of such a distant possession. The court of Rio, therefore, resolved to send a body of troops under Colonel Manoel Marquez, to the mouth of the Oyapok. The English ship of war, Confiance commanded by Captain Yeo, accompanied him, and their combined attack forced the enemy to surrender on the of 12th [sic] January. The terms were honourable to both parties and among the articles I observe the 14th, by which it is stipulated, that the botanic garden, called the Gabrielle, shall not only be spared, but kept up in the state of perfection in which it was given up. War is so horrible, that a trait like this, in the midst of its evils, is too pleasing to be over-looked.

The rest of the year passed in Brazil in quiet though important operations; many roads were opened through the still wild country in the interior; a naval academy was instituted; a school of anatomy was founded in the naval and military hospital; and the vaccine establishment formed in Brazil in 1804 having declined, it was renewed both

---

* Sir Sydney Smith had followed the Portuguese court to Rio, less as commander of the British naval force in those seas, than as the protector of the Braganzas. Lord Strangford had resumed his character of ambassador.

at Bahia and Rio, and immense numbers of persons of all colours were vaccinated.

Meanwhile the Portuguese arms were employed in another quarter of the world. The extensive dominions of Portugal in the east had fallen off one by one, as pearls from a broken thread. Yet Macao was still Portuguese. For twenty years past, it, in common with the coast of China, had been plagued with the pirates of the Yellow Sea; till, at length, the Chinese government found it necessary to take measures for suppressing them, and therefore made a treaty with the Portuguese government of Macao, signed by the following personages, on the 23d of November.

> Miguel de Arriga, Judge.
> Brun da Silva.
> Jose Joaquin Barros, General.
> Shin Kei Chi.
> Ches.
> Pom.

The Portuguese were by this treaty to furnish six vessels of from sixteen to twenty-six guns, but being in want of ball and other stores they were supplied liberally by the English East India Company's factory; and the result was, that after three months' resistance, the pirates surrendered their ships, and promised to become peaceable subjects, and the people of Macao performed a Te Deum in honour of their success; but twelve months elapsed ere the happy tidings reached Brazil.

The great European interests of Brazil and its sovereign might have been forgotten in the country itself, during the year 1810, so tranquil was it, but for the packets which brought across the Atlantic the details of those desperate battles, which the strength and the treasure of England were waging in defence of them in the Peninsula. On the 19th of February, Lord Strangford and the Conde de Linhares, in behalf of their respective governments, signed a commercial treaty at Rio, by which great and reciprocal advantages were obtained, and the English were allowed the free exercise of their own form of worship, provided they built no steeples to their churches, and that they used no bells.

This was followed in the month of May by a formal notice from Lord Strangford, that the British Parliament had voted 980,000£ for the carrying on of the war in Portugal. In fact, England had now taken the battle into her own hands, as she had decidedly the greatest interest in opposing France; and the royal house of Braganza was at leisure to devote its whole attention to its American dominions. Several well appointed detachments were sent into different parts of the country for the purpose of repelling the Indians, whose inroads had destroyed several of the Portuguese settlements, of forming roads to connect the different provinces with each other, and, above all, of furthering the gradual civilisation of the Indian tribes. Strict orders were given the commanders to proceed peaceably, especially among the friendly Indians; but such as were refractory were to be pursued even to extermination. To further the views with which these expeditions had been formed, a proclamation was issued in the month of September, holding out to such as should become proprietors and reclaimers of land in the province of the Minas Geraes and on the banks of the Rio Doce, all the advantages of original donatories and lords paramount; and promising that every settlement that should contain twelve huts of reclaimed Indians, and ten houses of white persons, should be erected into a villa, with all its privileges. The party that was sent up the Rio Doce discovered one hundred and forty-four farms that had been ruined by the Indians, and which they restored: they formed a friendly treaty with several tribes of Puri Indians, whom they found already settled in villages, to the number of nearly a thousand. These people were gentle, and not without some of the arts and habits of industry; but they were heathens and polygamists; not that a plurality of wives was general, or even common, for there were only one hundred and thirteen wives to ninety four husbands. They do not appear to have been cannibals, though it is strongly asserted that the neighbouring Botecudos were so, and that having gained a slight advantage over the Portuguese, they had eaten four of them who fell into their hands.* I confess I am sceptical about these anthropophagi. That savages may eat their enemies taken in battle I do not doubt; under the circumstances of savage life revenge and retaliation are sweet: but I doubt their eating the dead found after the battle, and I doubt their hunting

---

* I have in my possession a curious drawing, found in a Botecudo cottage and done by one of the Creole Brazilians, of mixed breed, who shows himself hidden in a cave, his white companions dead, and they, as well as the soldiers of the black regiment who accompanied them, have the flesh stripped from the bones, excepting the head, hands, and feet. The Botecudos are represented as carrying off this flesh in baskets. These savages appear quite naked, having their mouth pieces, and being armed with bows and arrows.

men, or devouring women and children. With the latter atrocities, indeed, they have not been charged in modern times; and as at the period the missionaries wrote the first histories of them, it was politic to exaggerate the difficulties these useful men had to encounter, in order to enhance their services, it is not uncharitable to believe that much exaggeration crept into the accounts of the savages, especially if we recollect the miracles ascribed in those very accounts to many of the missionaries themselves. Besides these measures concerning the Indians, other steps were taken for the good of the country of no less importance; several colonies, both of Europeans, and of islanders from the Açores, were invited and encouraged. The fisheries off the coast were attended to, and particularly that of the island of St. Catherine; and on the same island sufficient experiments were made upon the growth of hemp, to prove that time and industry only were wanting to furnish great quantities of that valuable article of a very good quality.

The year 1811 was the last of the life and ministry of the Conde de Linhares, whose views were all directed to the good of the country. Fully aware not only of its richness and fertility, he also perceived how poor and how backward it was, considering its natural advantages. In endeavouring to remedy the evils, he perhaps aimed at doing more than was possible in the short time, and under the circumstances, in which his active disposition could operate. He had formed roads and planned canals; he had invited colonies, which indeed afterwards sunk; but they left behind them some of their ingenious practice, and some seeds of improvement which have not utterly perished. The possibility of navigating both the St. Matthew's river and the Gequetinhonha had been ascertained; experiments in every kind of cultivation had been made; even the tea had been introduced from China. A botanical garden had been formed, in which the spices of the East were cultivated with success; and perhaps as the greatest possible good, a public library had been formed, and its regulations framed on the most liberal principles.

Towards the end of 1811 a royal decree was issued, assigning 120,000 crusadoes per annum to be taken from the customs of Bahia, Pernambuco, and Maranham, for forty years, to the Portuguese, who had suffered during the French war; a measure regarded even with jealousy by the northern captaincies. But they all continued tranquil for the present, and seemed to attend only domestic improvement. New buildings, both for use and ornament, arose in the cities. Maranham and Pernambuco improved their harbours. Bahia, besides the handsome theatre opened there in 1812, paved her streets; and at Rio, a subscription of 30,000 crusadoes was raised towards beautifying the palace square, completing the public gardens, and draining the campo de Santa Anna.

In 1813, some disputes arose between the court of Rio and England on account of the slave trade. Three ships had been captured by the British squadron off the coast of Africa, while certainly engaged in illegal *slaving;* remonstrances were made, and the matter continued suspended until after the congress of Vienna, when that illustrious meeting, though most of its highest and most powerful members had exclaimed loudly against the villanous practice, suffered it to be carried on. Then indeed England consented to pay 13,000£ to indemnify the Portuguese slave traders for their loss (July, 1815)!

In the same year there appears to have been some discontent manifested, or suspected in the provinces. Many of the salaries of officers, both civil and military, remained unpaid; yet there were exactions, the more grievous, because they were irregular, in every department; the administration of justice was notoriously corrupt; the clergy had fallen into disorder and disrepute; and though much that was useful had been done, yet that was forgotten, especially in the distant provinces, and such a portion of discontent existed, that various officers who had come to Rio either on private business or to remonstrate on public wrongs, were peremptorily ordered to return to their own provinces.

It was wisely done at this juncture, to take off the public attention from such vexations by a measure at once just and gratifying to the pride of the Brazilians: by an edict of the 16th of December, 1815, Brazil was raised to the dignity of a kingdom, and the style and title altered so as to place it on an equal footing with Portugal. For some months addresses of thanks and congratulation poured in to the king from various provinces, and the feasts and rejoicings on that happy occasion occupied the people to the exclusion of all other considerations.

Meantime the victories of the allies in Europe, having caused the exile of Napoleon to Elba, the necessity for an English guardian squadron at Rio had ceased; and accordingly the British establishment was broken up, and the stores sold, and the family of Braganza, again independent of foreign aid, began to renew its connections with the other courts of Europe.

These negotiations suffered some little interruption from an event which had long been expected, and which took place on the 20th of March, 1816, namely, the death of the queen, whose state, both of body and mind, had long precluded her from all share in public affairs. She was buried with great pomp in the church of the convent of the Ajuda; and, as is usual, dirges were sung for her in all the churches in the kingdom [after which succeeded the ceremonies of the coronation of Don Joam VI. Her bones were afterwards removed to Lisbon.]

In the month of June, the Marquis Marialva was received at Paris as ambassador of Portugal and Brazil, and shortly afterwards the way having been prepared by an inferior minister, he went to Vienna, to negotiate a marriage between Don Pedro de Alcantara, Prince of Portugal and Brazil, and the Archduchess Maria Leopoldina, which was happily effected. On the 28th of November, she was privately contracted at Vienna to the prince. On the 17th of February following, the contract was made public, and on the 18th of May she was married by proxy, the Marquis Marialva standing for Don Pedro; but it was not until the 11th of November that she arrived at Rio. The line of battle ship Joam VI. had been sent along with two frigates for her to Trieste, the voyage was performed without accident, and the person the most important to the hopes and happiness of Brazil, was welcomed with enthusiasm by all classes of people.

In the autumn preceding, two of the Infantas of Portugal had been married, [one] to Ferdinand the 7th of Spain, and [the other to] his brother the Infant Don Carlos.

But the frontier of Brazil to the southward now began to feel the effect of those disturbances which had long agitated Spanish South America. The chief Artigas showed a disposition to encroach on the Portuguese line, and, therefore, a corps of volunteers had been formed for the purposes of observation, and the Porte da Santa Theresa had been occupied in order to check the motions of that active leader: during the autumn of 1816, several skirmishes took place, but the arts of negotiation as well as of war were resorted to, and on the 19th of January, 1817, the keys of Montevideo were delivered up to the Portuguese general Lecor, by which the long-wished-for command of the eastern bank of the Plata was obtained.

Meantime the discontents in the northern provinces had broken out into open insurrection, in the captaincy of Pernambuco. The people of Recife, and its immediate neighbourhood, had imbibed some of the notions of democratical government from their former masters the Dutch. They remembered besides, that their own exertions, without any assistance from the government, had driven out those masters, and had restored to the crown the northern part of its richest domain. They were, therefore, disposed to be particularly jealous of the provinces of the south, especially of Rio, which they considered as more favoured than themselves, and they were disgusted at the payments of taxes and contributions, by which they never profited, and which only served to enrich the creatures of the court, while great abuses existed, especially in the judicial part of the government, which they despaired of ever seeing redressed. Such were the exciting causes of the insurrection of 1817, in Pernambuco, which threatened for many months the peace, if not the safety of Brazil. The example of the Spanish Americans had no doubt its weight, and a regular plan for obtaining independence was formed, troops were raised and disciplined, and Recife being secured, fortifications were begun at Alagoas and at Penedo.

The insurgents, however, had probably miscalculated the degree of concurrence or assistance they should meet with from their neighbours. The people of Serinhaem as soon as the insurrection was known, namely the middle of April, posted themselves on the Rio Formosa as a check on that quarter, and the king's troops under Lacerda, marched immediately from Bahia. The Pernambucan leader Victoriano, having attacked the Villa de Pedras, received a decided check from a body of royalists, under Major Gordilho, who had been sent forward by Lacerda, on the 21st and by the 29th Gordilho had occupied that post, as well as Tamandré, where he was not long afterwards joined by Colonel Mello, with a strong reinforcement.

Meantime the Pernambucan chief, Domingos Jose Martins, was actively employed in collecting troops, and forming guerilla parties, in order to harass the marches of the enemy. These parties were headed by Cavalcante, a man of wealth and family, aided by a priest, Souto, a bold and enterprising man, who was far from being the only ecclesiastical partisan. On the 2d of May, a vigorous attack was made on Serinhaem, by the famous Pernambucan division of the south, which had hitherto received no check; but the assailants were repulsed with the loss of their artillery and baggage, and a column under Martins coming up met with the same fate, on which he drew off his people with those of the south to the ingenio of Trapiche. On the 6th of May they left that position, and meeting the royalists under Mello suffered a complete defeat. Their chiefs were either killed or taken; and of the latter some were exiled, others imprisoned, and three, Jose Luiz Mendonça, Domingos Jose Martins, and the priest, Miguel Joaquim de Alameida, were hanged in Bahia.

At this juncture Luiz do Rego Barreto was appointed by the government at Rio to the office of captain-general of Pernambuco. He was a native of Portugal, and had served with distinction under Lord Wellington. Of a firm and vigorous mind, and jealous of the honour of a soldier, he was perhaps too little yielding to the people and the temper of the times. The severe military punishments inflicted on this occasion certainly produced irritation, which though it did not break out immediately, was the cause of much evil afterwards, and brought an odium upon that gallant soldier himself, from which his high character in other situations could not shield him.

This year the ministry underwent a complete change. The Marquis d'Aguiar, who had succeeded to the Conde de Linhares, died in January, and the Conde da Barca in June; when the Conde de Palmela became prime minister, Bezerra became president of the treasury, the Conde dos Arcos secretary for transmarine and naval affairs, the Conde de Funchal councillor of state, and Don Tomas Antonio de Portugal secretary to the house of Braganza.

I cannot pretend to speak of the character or measures of these or any other Portuguese or Brazilian ministers. My opportunities of information were too few; my habits as a woman and a foreigner never led me into situations where I could acquire the necessary knowledge. I wish only to mark the course of events, and in as far as they are linked with each other, the causes of those effects which took place under my own eyes.

In the early part of 1818, some additional restrictions concerning the slave trade, which had been agreed to by Conde de Palmela during the last year at London, were published at Rio, and a commission of English and Portuguese jointly was formed for the examining into and deciding on causes arising out of the treaties on that most important subject, a certain number of commissioners being appointed to reside in the different ports in Africa and Brazil, where the trade was still considered lawful. That year opened at Rio with unusual festivity. On the 22d of January, a great bull-feast was given at San Cristovaõ, the royal country house, in honour of the young princess's birth-day; it was followed by a military dance, in which the costume of the natives of every part of the Portuguese dominions in the east and west were displayed. Portugal and Algarve, Africa and India, China and Brazil, all appeared to do homage to the illustrious stranger. Music, in which the taste of the king was unrivalled, formed a great part of the entertainment, and never perhaps had Brazil witnessed so magnificent a festival.

On the 6th of February the coronation of his majesty, John VI., took place, and these peaceful festivities gave a character to the year, which was remarkably quiet, the only public acts of note being the farther prosecution of the plans for civilising the interior, by facilitating the communications from place to place, and reclaiming the border tribes of Indians.

The following year was not less tranquil. The birth of the young princess, Dona Maria da Gloria, was an event to gratify both the court and the people of Brazil. They had now the heir of their kingdom born among them, a circumstance which they were disposed to hail as a pledge that the seat of government would not be removed from among them.

The early part of 1820 was disturbed by some irruptions of the Spanish Americans under Artigas, on the eastern side of the Plata. The Portuguese troops, however, soon repulsed him, and strengthened their line by the occupation of Taquarembo, Simar, and the Arroyo Grande.

Meantime the peace in Europe had not brought back all the tranquillity that was expected from it. In vain did the old governments expect to step back into exactly the same places they had occupied before the revolutionary war. The Cortes had assembled in Spain. Naples had been convulsed by an attempt to obtain a constitution similar to that promulgated by the Spanish Cortes; and now Portugal began to feel the universal impulse. Lisbon and Oporto were both the seats of juntas of provisional government, and both assembled Cortes to take into consideration the framing of a new constitution, and the reformation of ancient abuses. On the 21st of August the Cortes of Lisbon had sworn to adopt in part the constitution of the Spanish Cortes, but it was not until the month of November that the government of Brazil made public the recent occurrences in the mother country. Indeed it was not to be expected that Brazil should remain unconscious of the proceedings of Europe. The provinces were all more or less agitated. Pernambuco was as usual foremost in feeling, and in the expression of feeling. A considerable party had assembled at about thirty-six leagues from Olinda. They declared their grievances to be intolerable, and that nothing but a total reform in the government should reconcile them to longer subjection to the government of Rio. The royalist troops were sent out against them and were victorious, after an action of six hours, in which they lost six officers and 19 men killed, and 134 wounded. The loss on the other side was much greater, and as usual severe military executions increased the evils of the civil war, at the same time that they farther exasperated the people, and prepared them for a future and more obstinate resistance.

Bahia was far from tranquil. The old jealousy which had subsisted from the time the seat of government had been transferred from the city of St. Salvador to Rio, combined with other causes, tended to increase the desire of a constitutional government, from which all good was to be expected, and under which, it was hoped, that all abuses would be reformed. Rio itself began to manifest the same feelings. The provinces of St. Paul's and the Minas were always ready to unite in any cause that promised an increase of freedom; and the whole country seemed on the brink of revolution, if not civil war.

The court party, however, still flattered themselves that the determination of the King to remain in Brazil, instead of returning to Lisbon to put himself into the power of the Cortes, would be so grateful to the Brazilians, that they would be contented to forego the probable advantages of a constitution, for the sake of the positive good of having the seat of government fixed among themselves. But it was too late; the wish for improvement had been excited. The administration had been too corrupt, the exactions too heavy to be longer borne, when reform appeared to be within reach. The very soldiers became possessed with the same spirit, and though highly repugnant to the King's feelings, it soon became evident that a compliance with the wishes of the people and with the constitution, as declared by the Cortes at Lisbon, was inevitable.

It is said, that some of the wisest ministers had long pressed His Majesty to a compliance with the wishes of his people, but in vain. His reluctance was unconquerable, until at length, perceiving that force would certainly be resorted to, he adopted a half measure which probably accelerated the very event he was anxious to avoid.* On the 18th

---

* Some have imagined that a paper published at Rio, written by a Frenchman, and supposed to have been in the pay of the then ministry, desirous of

of February, 1821, the King accepted as a junta, to take into consideration such parts of the constitution as might be applicable to the state of Brazil, the following persons:—

> Marquez de Alegrete—*President*
> Baron de St. Amaro.
> Luiz José de Carvalho e Melo.
> Antonio Luiz Pereiro da Cunha.
> Antonio Rodriguez Velloso de Oliviera.
> Joaõ Severiano Maciel da Costa.
> Camillo Maria Tonelet.
> Joaõ de Souza de Mendonça Costa Real.
> José da Silva Lisboa.
> Mariano José Pereira da Fonseca.
> Joaõ Rodriguez Pereira de Almeida.
> Francisco Xavier Pires.
> José Caetano Gomes.
> *Procurador da Casa.*
> José de Oliviera Botelho Pinto Masquiera.
> *Secretarios.*
> Manoel Jacinto Noguerra de Gama.
> Manoel Moreira de Figueiredo.
> *Secretaries Substituti.*
> O Coronel Francisco Saraiva da Costa Refoios.
> O Desembargador Joaõ José de Mendonça.

These persons were all anxious to retain the King in Brazil. Most of them Brazilians, they had felt the advantage of having the seat of government fixed among themselves, and though the King's foreign allies and his Portuguese subjects had pressed him to return to Europe, his own dread of the Cortes of Lisbon, together with their natural desire to detain him in Brazil, produced on the 21st a manifesto, describing His Majesty's affection and reliance on his Brazilian subjects, and stating, that he was resolved to send the Prince Don Pedro to Lisbon, with

keeping the king in Brazil, had great effect on the subsequent events; and that greater still had been produced by the revolution of the 10th of February, at Bahia; but the motives of action were the same in all Brazil; the event must have been the same at Rio, whether Bahia had stirred or not, though, perhaps, it might be accelerated by that circumstance. [Mess^r Plancher and ——]

full powers to treat on his behalf with the Cortes, whom he seems to have considered as subjects in rebellion.

The Prince was also to consult with the Cortes concerning the drawing up of a constitution, and the King promised to adopt such parts of it as might be found applicable to existing circumstances and to the peculiar situation of Brazil. This manifesto appears to have produced an effect very different from what was intended. At four o'clock in the morning of the 26th, all the streets and squares of the city were found full of troops. Six pieces of artillery were planted at the heads of the principal streets, and the most lively sensation agitated every part of the city of Rio. As soon as this circumstance could be known at San Cristovaõ, the Prince Don Pedro, and the Infant Don Miguel, came into the city. The Camara* was assembled in the great saloon of the theatre.† The Prince, after conferring for a short time with the members of that body, appeared upon the balcony of the saloon, and read to the people and the troops, a royal proclamation, antedated the 24th, securing to them the Constitution, such as it should be framed by the Cortes of Lisbon. This was received with loud cries of Viva el Rei, Viva a Religiaõ, Viva a constituicaõ. The Prince then returned to the saloon, and ordered the secretary of the Camara to draw up the form of the oath to be taken to observe the constitution, and also a list of a new ministry, to be submitted to the people for their approbation. The list of ministers was first read, and each individually approved.‡

---

* The whole municipal body.
† The square in front of the theatre, from its size and situation, was most fit for the assembly of the people and troops on such an occasion.
‡ *New Ministers.*
 Vice-admiral and Commander-in-chief Quintella, secretary of state.
 Joaquin Jose Monteiro Torres, minister of marine, and secretary for transmarine affairs.
 Silvestre Pinhero Fereiro, secretary for foreign affairs.
 Conde de Louça, head of the treasury.
 Bishop of Rio, president of the board of conscience.
 Antonio Luis Pereiro da Cunha, head of police.
 José Caetano Gomes, grand treasurer.
 Joao Fereiro da Costa Sanpaio, second treasurer.
 Sebastian Luis Terioco, fiscal.
 José da Silva Lisboa, literary department.
 Joao Rodrigues Pereira de Almeida, director of the bank.
 Barboza, police.
 Conde de Aseca, head of the board of trade.
 Brigadier Carlos Frederico da Cunha, commander-in-chief, etcetera.

His Royal Highness then proceeded to take the oath for his father, in the following form:—

"I swear, in the name of the King, my father and lord, veneration and respect for our holy religion; to observe, keep, and maintain for ever the constitution such as established by the cortes in Portugal." The bishop then presented to him the holy Gospels, on which he laid his right hand, and solemnly vowed, promised, and signed the same.

The Prince then took the oath in like manner for himself, and was immediately followed by his brother, the Infant Don Miguel, after whom the ministers and a multitude of other persons crowded to follow his example. Meantime the Prince rode to the King at his country seat of Boa Vista, at San Cristovaõ, to inform him of all that had passed, and to entreat his presence in the city, as the best means of securing order and confidence. His Majesty accordingly set off immediately, and arrived at the great square at about eleven o'clock, when the people took the horses from his carriage and dragged him to the palace, the troops following as on a day of gala, and forming in the square before the doors. At one of the centre windows the King presently appeared, and confirmed all that the Prince had promised in his name, declaring at the same time his perfect approbation of every thing that had been done. The troops then dispersed, and the King held a court, which was most numerously attended; and the day ended at the opera, the people again assembling to drag the King's carriage thither.

It would be curious to investigate the feelings of princes on occasions so momentous to themselves and to their people. Joam VI., passionately fond of music, was dragged by a people, grateful for a boon granted that very day, to a theatre built by himself, where all the music vocal and instrumental was selected with exquisite taste, and where the piece presented was a decided favourite.* Yet it may be questioned whether there existed in his wide dominions one heart less at ease than his own. All his feelings and prejudices were in favour of the ancient order of things, and this day those feelings and prejudices had been obliged to bend to the spirit of the times, to a wide-spread desire for freedom, to every thing, in short, most contrary to the ancient system of continental Europe.

The next day,† there was nothing but joy in the city, the great saloon was again crowded with persons eager to sign the oath to the constitu-

---

* Rossini's Cenerentola.
† The 27th, on which day Messrs. Thornton, Grimaldi, and Maler, ministers from England and France, waited on His Majesty. The different motions or interferences of the members of the diplomatic body scarcely concern this

tion, illuminations, feux de joie, and fire-works succeeded; and at the opera, Puccito's Henrique IV. was ordered in compliment to the King. But he was too much fatigued with the events of the last two days to go, and when the curtain of the royal box was drawn up, the pictures only of the king and queen appeared; but they were received with loud acclamations, as if the royal personages themselves had been present.

Thus was a most important revolution brought about without bloodshed, and almost without disturbance. The junta occupied itself seriously on the business of the constitution, and began by publishing some edicts highly favourable to the people, and, among others, one insuring the liberty of the press.

Meantime Bahia, actuated by the same spirit as Rio, had anticipated the revolution at that place. On the 10th of February the troops and people assembled in the city, the magistrates were called on to take an oath to adhere to the constitution, a provisional government was formed, and troops were raised in order to maintain the constitution, in case the court at Rio should be adverse to its adoption. Among these the most forward was a small body of artillery, formed of the students at the different colleges and schools of the city. The new government early began to manifest a determination to be no longer subordinate to Rio, and to acknowledge no other authority than that of the Cortes at Lisbon. An intimation of what had taken place at Bahia was immediately forwarded to Luiz do Rego at Pernambuco, who assembled the magistrates, the troops, and the people, on the 3d of March, in Recife, and there, along with them, solemnly took the oath to adhere to the constitution; a measure which gave universal satisfaction. About the same time, several of the towns in the Comarca of Ilheos also took the oaths to maintain the constitution; and it appeared evidently that the whole country was equally desirous of a change, in hopes of relief from the vexations it had so long suffered under.

But the agitation of the capital was by no means at an end. Disputes arose concerning the election of deputies to the cortes, which, however, ended in adopting the method laid down in the Spanish constitution. The troops found it necessary to publish a declaration, denying that they had any factious views when they assembled on the 26th of February, and alleging that they appeared as citizens anxious for

---

period. There is no doubt but that they were busy. But circumstances which they could not control, though they might disturb, brought about the revolution of the 26th, the visible facts alone of which I pretend to give.

the rights of the whole community. The people assembled in different places, and are said to have insulted several persons, particularly the members of the council which existed immediately before the revolution; and in order to save three of them from the fury of the mob, they were placed in confinement for three days, and then liberated, with a proclamation tending to exculpate them from all criminal charges, and explaining the motives of their arrest.

The King meanwhile had resolved on returning to Lisbon, and on the 7th of March he published a proclamation announcing his resolution, together with an order for such deputies as should be elected by the time of his departure, to go with him to attend the Cortes, and promising to find means of conveying the rest when they should be ready.

Every thing now appeared to proceed in quiet. The preparations for His Majesty's departure went on, and he resolved to take the opportunity of the assembling of the electors on the 21st of April, to choose the deputies to the Cortes, to submit to them the plan for the government of Brazil which he had laid down, in order to receive their sanction. These electors were assembled in the exchange, a handsome new building on the shore, and thither a great concourse of people had flocked, some purely from curiosity, some from a desire, imagining they had a right, to express their opinion on so important a subject. The result of that meeting was a deputation sent to the king, insisting on the adoption of the entire Spanish constitution. The decree of the assembly received the signature of the King. But the members of that assembly met again on the 22d, many of whom had no legal title to be present, and proceeded to propose to stop the ships prepared for the King's return to Portugal. Some went so far as to propose an examination of the vessels, in order to stop the exportation of the quantity of wealth known to be on board of them, and the meeting at length assumed so alarming an aspect, that His Majesty revoked his royal consent to the act passed on the 21st, and sent a body of soldiers to intimidate the assembly. Unhappily, an order proceeding from some quarter, never known or never acknowledged, caused the soldiers to fire into the exchange, where the unarmed and innocent electors, as well as the others who had crowded thither, it might be, with less pure motives, were assembled, but all were there on the faith of the royal invitation given through the judge of the district.

Sketch of the History of Brazil　　　　　　　　　　　　　　　　　　311

About thirty persons were killed, many more were wounded: and the whole city was filled with an indescribable consternation. The sudden stop that was put to this strange, unwise and cruel attack, has always been attributed to the Prince Don Pedro, who, on this as on other occasions, has well merited the title of perpetual defender of Brazil. The attack itself, perhaps unjustly, was imputed to the Conde dos Arcos by some, to other individuals by others, according as passion or party directed the suspicion: the truth is, that it seems to have been the result of ill-understood orders, given hastily in a moment of alarm, for it is impossible to think, for an instant, that any man could wantonly have so cruelly irritated the people at the very time when so much depended on their tranquillity. This shocking event, however, seems to have quickened the King's resolution to leave Brazil. That very day he made over the government of that country to the Prince, with a council to be composed of

>   The Conde dos Arcos, Prime Minister.
>   Conda da Louça, Minister of Interior.
>   Brigadier Cauler, Minister of War.

And in case of the prince's death, the regency to remain in the hands of the Princess Maria Leopoldina.

The next day the King publicly addressed the troops, recommending to them fidelity to the crown and constitution, and obedience to the Prince Regent, and as a royal boon on leaving the army, promising a great increase of pay to all, and that the Brazilian officers should be put on the same footing as those of the Portuguese army. The ministers who advised this step, acted cruelly towards the government they left behind. The treasury was left empty at the King's departure, yet increase of pay beyond all precedent was promised, as well as other burdens on the prince's revenue. His Majesty published on the same day, a farewell to the inhabitants of Rio; and it cannot be imagined that he could leave the place which to him had been a haven of safety, during the storm in which most of his brother monarchs had suffered, without feelings of regret, if not affection.

The Prince also addressed the Brazilians on assuming the government by a proclamation, which, as it sets forth his intentions, I shall give literally:

Inhabitants of Brazil;

The necessity of paying attention to the general interests of the nation before every other, forces my august father to leave you, and to intrust me with the care of the public happiness of Brazil, until Portugal shall form a constitution, and confirm it.

And, as I judge it right, in the present circumstances, that all should from this time understand what are the objects of public administration which I have principally in view, I lose no time in declaring, that strict respect for the laws, constant vigilance over the administration of the same, opposition to the quibbles by which they are discredited and weakened, will be the objects of my first attention.

It will be highly agreeable to me to anticipate all such benefits of the constitution as shall be compatible with obedience to the laws.

Public education, which now demands the most especial attention of the government, will be provided for by every means in my power.

And in order that the commerce and agriculture of Brazil may be in a prosperous state, I shall not cease to encourage whatever may favour these copious sources of national riches.

I shall pay equal attention to the interesting subject of reform, without which it will be impossible to use liberal means for the public good.

Inhabitants of Brazil! all these intentions will be frustrated if certain evil-minded persons should accomplish their fatal views, and persuade you to adopt antisocial principles, destructive of all order, and diametrically opposed to the system of liberality, which from this moment it is my intention to follow.

The ceremonies of taking leave, occupied the following day. On the 24th, the royal family embarked, and with it many of the Portuguese nobles who had followed their king into exile, and many others whose fortunes were entirely attached to the court.

But this great re-emigration produced evils of no common magnitude in Brazil. It is computed that fifty millions of crusadoes, at least, were carried out of the country by the Portuguese returning to Lisbon. A great proportion of specie had been taken up in exchange for government bills on the treasuries of Bahia, Pernambuco, and Maranham. But these provinces, from the revolution in February, had disclaimed the superiority of the government at Rio, and had owned no other than that of the Cortes at Lisbon, and above all the ministry well knew, even at the time of granting the bills, that they had refused to remit any portion of the revenue to Rio. Hence arose commercial distress of every description, and as long-standing government debts had been also paid by these bills which were all dishonoured, the evil spread far and wide, not only among the natives but the foreign merchants. It was of little avail that the Prince acknowledged the debts;* the treasury was left so poor, that he was obliged to delay or modify the increase of military pay promised on the King's departure, a circumstance that occasioned much disquiet in several provinces. The funds for carrying on several branches of industry, and several works of public utility were destroyed by this great and sudden drain; and thereby much that had been begun after the arrival of the court, and which it was hoped would have been of the greatest benefit to the country, was stopped. Colonies that had been invited to settle with the most liberal promises perished for want of the necessary support in the beginning of their career, and the wonder is, not that disturbances in various quarters took place after the departure of the King, but that they were not of a more fierce and fatal tendency.

The Prince who remained at the head of the government was deservedly popular among the Brazilians. His first care was to examine into and redress causes of grievances; particularly those arising from arbitrary imprisonment and vexatious methods of collecting taxes. The great duties on salt conveyed into the interior, were remitted. Something was done towards improving the condition of the barracks, hospitals, and schools. Books were allowed to be imported duty free, and every thing that could be effected under the circumstances, was done by the Prince for the advantage of the people, and to preserve or promote public tranquillity.

---

* It was of little avail at the time. But as soon as it was possible, his royal highness's government began payments by installment, which are still going on, notwithstanding the toal change of government. This is highly honourable.

But the question of the independence of Brazil had now come to be publicly agitated, and out of it arose several others. Was it to be still part of the Portuguese monarchy, with a separate supreme jurisdiction civil and criminal under the Prince? or was it to return to the abject state in which it had been since its discovery, subject to all the vexatious delays occasioned by distant tribunals, by appeals beyond sea, and all that renders the state of a colony, irksome or degrading? Then if independent so far, was it to form one kingdom whose capital should be at Rio, or were there to be several unconnected provinces, each with its supreme government, accountable only to the king and cortes at Lisbon? Those who had republican views, and who looked forward to a federal state, favoured the latter views, and so did those who dreaded the final separation of Brazil from the mother country; for they argued that the separate provinces might be easily controlled, but that Brazil united would overmatch any force that Portugal could send against it, should a hostile struggle between them ever take place.

The people, jealous of all, but particularly of the ministers, accused the Conde dos Arcos of treachery, and of a wish to reduce Brazil once more to the state in which it had been before 1808. They insisted on his dismissal, and on the appointment of a provisional junta, which should deliberate on the best measures of government to be adopted, until the constitution of the cortes should arrive from Lisbon, and the fifth of June, the day of his dismissal, was held as a festival.*

Yet, distressed as the government was by an empty treasury, and by demands increasing daily on all sides, it was impossible to remove at once all causes of discontent; and the new junta was so well aware of this, that, on the 16th of June, on publishing an invitation to all persons to send in plans and projects for improvements, and statistical notices concerning the country, they also published an exhortation to tranquillity and obedience, and patient waiting till the event of the deliberation of the cortes, now to be joined by their own deputies, should be known. That same night both the Portuguese and Brazilian troops were under arms in the city, violent jealousies had arisen

---

* When he touched at Bahia on his way home, the junta of government there, prejudiced by letters from Rio, refused him permission to land; and he had the mortification of being treated as a criminal, in that very city where he had governed with honour, and where he had been beloved. On his arrival at Lisbon, he suffered a short imprisonment in the tower of Belem. Yet his misconduct, if it amounted to all he was charged with, seems to have been an error in judgment.

between them, and it required all the authority and all the popularity of the Prince to restore order. On the morning of the 17th His Royal Highness called together the officers of both nations, and in a short speech he ordered them as soldiers, and recommended to them as citizens, to preserve the subordination of the troops they commanded, and union among those troops, bidding them remember that they had sworn to support the constitution, and that they were to trust to that for the redress of their grievances.

Meanwhile the more distant provinces had acknowledged the authority of the cortes, and had sworn to support the constitution. But Maranham in its public acts took no notice whatever of the Prince, professing only to recognise the government of Lisbon. At Villa Rica, when the constitution was proclaimed, the troops refused to acknowledge the Prince, accusing him of withholding the pay promised by the King. At St. Catherine's, though the measures were less violent, yet the refusing to admit a new governor who had been sent, was decidedly an act of insubordination; but the political agitations at St. Paul's were not only of a more serious nature, but had more important results than those of any other province.

The ostensible cause of the first public ferment in that city was the discontent of the Caçadores at not receiving the promised augmentation of pay, which, indeed, it was not then in the power of the Prince to bestow on them.

The regiment, however, took up arms on the 3d of June, and declared they would not lay them down until they received the pay demanded, and were proceeding to threaten the municipal government of the city, when they were stopped by the good sense, and presence of mind of their captain, José Joaquim dos Santos. But though the ferment was soothed for the time, it continued to agitate not only the troops, but the people, to such a degree, that the magistrates and principal inhabitants thought it necessary to take some steps at once, to rule and to satisfy them. They took advantage of the occasion furnished by the assembling of the militia, on account of a festival on the 21st, and, keeping them together, they placed them on the morning of the 23d, in the square before the town-house, where the camara held its sittings. The great bell of the camara then tolled out, the people flocked to the square, with shouts of: "Viva el Re, Viva o Constituiçao, Viva o Principe Regente." They then demanded a provisional junta to be appointed for the government of the province, and that José Bonifacio de Andrada e Silva should be appointed president. This truly patriotic citizen and accomplished scholar, was a native of the country, and had now been residing in it some years, after having studied, travelled, and fought in Europe. As soon as he was named, a deputation was sent to his own dwelling, to bring him to the townhouse.

Meantime the standard of the camara had been displayed at one of the windows, and there the magistrates were placed in sight of the people. José Bonifacio appeared at another window, and addressed the people in a short, but energetic speech, calculated to give them courage, and at the same time to inspire peace and all good and orderly feeling. He then named, one by one, the members proposed by the chief citizens, to form the provisional junta, beginning with Joaõ Carlos Augusto de Oyenhausen, to continue general of arms in the province. Each name was received with cheers.* The troops and people then marched in an orderly manner to the house of José Bonifacio, to install him formally as president, and thence to the cathedral where a Te Deum was sung. At night the theatre was illuminated as for a gala, the national hymn was sung repeatedly; and from that moment all remained quiet in the city, and resolved to maintain the constitution, and the Prince Regent, for whom they expressed unbounded attachment.

Nothing could have been so important to the interest of the Prince at that time. The Paulistas are among the most hardy, generous, and enlightened of the Brazilians. Their country is in the happiest climate. The mines of St. Paul's are rich, not only in the precious, but in the useful metals. Iron, so rich as to yield 93 per cent. and coal abound.

---

* Provisional government of St. Paul's.
    The Archpriest Felisberto Gomes Jardin.
    The Rev. Joaõ Ferreiro da Oliviero Bueno.
    Antonio Lecto Perreiro da Gama Lobo.
    Daniel Pedro Muller.
    Francisco Ignacio.
    Manoel Rodriguez Jordaõ.
    Andre da Sylva Gomez.
    Francisco de Paulo Oliviera.
    Dr. Nicolaõ Perreira de Campos Noguerros.
    Antonio Maria Quertim.
    Martin Francisco de Andrada.
    Lazaro José Gonçalez.
    Miguel José de Oliviero Pinto.

The manufactures of that province are far before any others in Brazil. Corn and cattle are plenty there, as well as every other species of Brazilian produce. Agriculture is attended to, and the city by its distance from the sea, is safe from the attacks of any foreign power, while it is totally independent of external supplies.

Unfortunately, the port of Santos presented a different scene during the first days of June. The first battalion of the Caçadores assembled before the government house, and, accusing the governor and the camara of withholding their pay, seized and imprisoned them, in order to force them to give the money they demanded. Several murders were committed during the insurrection, and various robberies, both in the houses and the ships in the harbour. Some armed vessels were, however, speedily despatched from Rio, and a detachment of militia from St. Paul's. Fifty of the insurgents were killed, and two hundred and forty taken prisoners; after which every thing returned to a state of tranquillity; and as the most conciliatory measures were adopted towards the people, the peace continued.

The next three months were spent almost entirely in establishing provisional juntas in the different capitals. Many of the captaincies had, upon swearing to maintain the constitution, spontaneously adopted that measure. Others, such as Pernambuco, had been restrained by their governors from doing so, until the Prince's edicts of the 21st of August, to that effect, reached them. These edicts were followed by another of the 19th of September, directing the juntas to communicate directly with the cortes at Lisbon; and the whole attention of the government was now directed to preserve tranquillity until the arrival of instructions from the cortes concerning the form of government to be adopted.

It was fondly hoped, that the presence of Brazilian deputies, the importance of the country, and the consideration that it had been the asylum of the government during the stormy days of the revolutionary war, would have induced the cortes to have considered it no longer as a colony, but as an equal part of the nation, and that it might have retained its separate courts, civil and criminal, and all the consequent advantages of a prompt administration of the laws.

Such was the state of Brazil, generally speaking, on our arrival in that country, on the 21st of September, 1821. Much that might be interesting I have omitted, partly because I have not so correct a knowledge of it, as to venture to write it; much, because we are too near the time of action to know the motives and springs that guided the actors; and much, because neither my sex nor situation permitted me to inform myself more especially concerning the political events in a country where the periodical publications are few, recent, and though by law free, yet, in fact, owing to the circumstances of the times, imperfect, timorous, and uncertain. What I have ventured to write is, I trust, correct as to facts and dates; it is merely intended as an introduction, without which, the journal of what passed while I was in Brazil would be scarcely intelligible.

Appendix III: *The Quarterly Review*

April 1824

Art. I.-1, *Journal of a Voyage to Brazil, and Residence there during Part of the Years 1821, 1822, and 1823.* By Maria Graham. 1 vol. 4to.

2. *Travels in Brazil in the Years 1817–1820, undertaken by Command of His Majesty the King of Bavaria.* By Dr. John Bapt. Von Spix and Dr. C. F. Phil. Von Marius, etc. etc. 2 vols. 8vo.

The people who emigrated from Europe two or three centuries ago, and who have continued, generally speaking, in the spots first occupied by them, have undergone revolutions as various in their character and circumstances as the periods and countries from which they sprung.

The colonies planted by England in the western hemisphere, though the latest founded, were the first to separate from the parent state. There were peculiar circumstances in their establishment and growth which favored the assumption of independence, and adapted them for the exercise of it. The first settlers left Europe at a period when a mental excitement of the most stirring kind was universally felt. Topics were then discussed which created an intensity of interest very far beyond what the cold and calculating desire for wealth alone has ever been found to inspire; and eager and anxious inquiries into the present condition of man, and the foundations on which to build his hopes of future felicity, agitated every bosom and called into exercise faculties of the highest order. Though with the vulgar this produced much fanaticism which naturally and perhaps necessarily degenerated into hypocrisy; yet it called forth the master spirits of the age, who assumed their due stations as the leaders of mankind, and retained an influence in human affairs which endured long after the enthusiastic excitement amidst which it was generated had ceased to operate.

* * *

[The review proceeds to contrast the methods and results of British and Spanish colonial rule.]

The great difference between the effects of war as exhibited between the colonies planted by England and those settled by Spain, may arise in some measure from the comparative ignorance of the population of the latter, and from the long duration which civil wars commonly maintain; but the moral character of the actual combatants seems the principal cause. In North America the forces for the most part were composed of a local militia, of which every individual had a home and some comforts to return to when the short period for which he was called out had expired; but in Spanish America, the forces were composed of the coloured and mixed nations, the cowardly Indians, the artful Mulattos, the ferocious Zambos, and the patient Negroes. These descriptions of beings, forced into the service for an indefinite period, cut off from all excitement but of plunder, had never any other home than a cage, no utensils to preserve, no accumulation of food to rely upon, and scarcely a rag to cover them. They had no sympathy with the more civilized classes, and whilst they could obtain a bare subsistence from the spontaneous products of the earth, recked little of the destruction of houses and farms, which to them must have appeared not worth preservation, or at least as things in whose preservation they could feel no interest. We have drawn this contrast between the circumstances of British and Spanish America at the time of the separation from their respective parent states with feelings of regret. We had indulged the hope and even the expectation that the establishment of independent, free, and practically good governments in the western hemisphere, would be an augmentation of the sum of human felicity. We had overlooked the materials of which it was to be composed, for the sake of the beauty of the edifice which our imaginations had pictured. Those materials have been drawn from their quarries, have been tried and found utterly unfitted for either foundation or superstructure. In South America we see no termination to the contests that we can contemplate without pain. Whether the communities of Spanish origin in that division of America shall be reduced to the savage condition of the settlements of Paraguay since the abolition of the Jesuits, or to that the negro population of St. Domingo; or whether, after still further exhaustion and depression, they may have been induced in despair to throw themselves again at the feet of Spain; in any case we see nothing to console humanity for the tremendous evils to which the conflict has given birth. We would wish to indulge the hope of a better fate for Mexico, but with regret we feel those hopes gradually become fainter and fainter. We cannot conceal from ourselves that the elements of society there are too nearly similar to those whose failure in South America we bitterly lament, to admit of any but hesitating apprehensions amidst our ardent good wishes.

The circumstances which have given rise to the establishment of an independent government in Brazil are so singular in the history of mankind, and especially so very different from those which gave rise to the independence of the English and Spanish colonists, that whilst they invite examination they excite hope for the future.

The first establishments in Brazil differed but little from those formed by the Spaniards. The two nations, who were indeed under the same monarch for a long period, were similar in their habits, their laws, their religion, and especially in the progress which they had made towards civilization; their colonial settlement necessarily therefore resembled each other. Brazil, however, enjoys a much more fruitful soil upon the whole than the Spanish territories; and, if the vicinity of the great river Orinoco, and internal plains which are in some seasons extensively flooded by it, be excepted, is more salubrious: its extent is nearly equal to that of Spanish South America, as was its population before the inhabitants of the latter countries had been thinned by the destructive civil dissensions of the last fourteen years. As far as regards the adaptation to the purposes of human life and human enjoyment, Brazil is the largest country; as that stupendous range of mountains, the Andes, within the Spanish boundaries, covers nearly one-third of its surface, is incapable of cultivation and is scarcely fitted for the residence of mankind.

* * *

The advancement of Brazil was favored by the convulsions which ravaged the other countries in the western world, whose productions were of a similar kind. As cultivation was ruined in St. Domingo, the sugars of Brazil supplied the deficiency thereby created. The settlements of Spain were too much convulsed to attend to cultivation, and Brazil reaped advantages from their distresses. When the United States chose to quarrel with England, the cotton wool of Brazil supplied the space which that of Georgia, Carolina, and Louisiana had before occupied. Their tobacco and rice found an increased demand and advanced price as long as Virginia and South Carolina were precluded by the war from transmitting their productions with safety to Europe.

* * *

We must now briefly notice the two works whose title-pages are placed at the head of this Article.

Mrs. Graham, who has conveyed to the public her account of Brazil during two visits to that country, has thought proper to introduce it with a hasty and ill-arranged abridgement of Mr. Southey's valuable history of that country. As she boasts to have performed the Herculean task of having 'read nearly all that are to be found in print of his authorities, and some that he does not mention,' it would have been as well to take care to be correct in her quotations. We can assure her that Villegagnon did not convey the young queen of Scotland to France in 1648, for both he and that unfortunate female happen to have been dead many years before. Henry II., King of France, was killed in July, 1558, the year in which Villegagnon went to Brazil, and could not therefore, 'on his return to Europe,' have given him the command of two ships. Henry IV., King of France, was assassinated in May, 1610, and therefore could not 'send Daniel de la Touche, shortly after 1611, to examine Brazil in order to form a permanent colony.' The Earl of Cumberland died on his passage from Brazil in 1593, and therefore could not have equipped the expedition in which she states that Witherington and Raleigh sailed to Bahia in 1686. The trouble of correcting the press is undoubtedly great, but we would suggest to this lady that in dates it is of importance to the reader. Thus, from page 16, it must be supposed that Mary of Guise retained her activity when 140 years old; and, from page 6, that Christian Jaques was an able commander at a more advanced age.

If Mrs. Graham had copied nothing from the newspapers, and had been sensible that, with her slight knowledge of the characters with whom she mixed, her ignorance of the language in which they conversed, and her imperfect acquaintance with the customs and manners of the people, she was unqualified to write *political* disquisitions of Brazil, she might have presented to the public a small volume that would have been read with a considerable degree of interest. Her descriptions of the parties to which she was introduced are probably accurate, and in general characteristic. One of the most interesting events, however unusual with female adventurers, was an excursion from the city of Pernambuco, then in a state of siege, to the camp of the insurgents who had invested it; and is extremely well told.

> About two miles from Do Rego's last outpost, we came to the first post of the patriots, at a country-house on a rising ground, where arms piled at the door, and a sort of ragged guard, consisting of a merry-looking negro with a fowling-piece, a Brazilian with a blunderbuss, and two or three of doubtful colour with sticks, swords, pistols, etc., told us an officer was to be found. After a few minutes parley, we found he was not authorised to receive our letter, so we rode on under the direction of the old Brazilian with his blunderbuss, who, being on foot, threatened to shoot us if we attempted to ride faster than he walked. The slow pace at which we advanced gave us leisure to remark the beauties of a Brazilian spring. Gay plants, with birds still gayer hovering over them, sweet smelling flowers, and ripe oranges and citrons, formed a beautiful fore-ground to the very fine forest-trees that cover the plains, and clothe the sides of the low hills in the neighbourhood of Pernambuco. Here and there a little space is cleared for the growth of mandioc, which at this season is perfectly green: the wooden huts of the cultivators are generally on the road-side, and, for the most part, each has its little grove of mango and orange trees. At one of these little homesteads, we found a pretty large guard-house, established where four roads meet, and there our foot guide left us, and a gentlemanlike young officer, of the Brazilian Caçadores, rode with us, and entertained us by calling Luis do Rego a tyrant, and attributing the siege of Pernambuco entirely to the governor's obstinacy, in not joining the people of the province in throwing off the dominion of his master. Round the guard-house a number of negro girls, with broad flat baskets on their heads, were selling fruit and cold water: they had decked their woolly hair, and the edges of their baskets, with garlands of the scarlet althæa; their light blue or white cloaks were

thrown gracefully across their dusky shoulders, and white jackets, so that it was such a picture as the early Spaniards might have drawn of their Eldorado.

After riding a few miles, we came suddenly to the foot of an abrupt hill, on whose sides there were scattered groups of the most magnificent trees I ever beheld. There we were met by a small military party, which, after a parley with our guide, rather ordered, than invited us to ride up. In a few seconds, we came to a steep yellow sandstone bank, shaded on one side by tall trees, and open on the other to a lake surrounded by woody hills, on the most distant of which, the white buildings of Olinda sparkled like snow. On the top of the bank, and in the act of descending, was a group of forty horsemen, one of the foremost of whom bore a white banner; several were dressed in splendid military habits, others in the plain costume of the landed proprietors. These were deputies from Paraiba on their way to propose terms to Luis do Rego; they had just left the head-quarters of the besieging army, where the provisional government of Goyana is stationed, and were accompanied by a guard of honour: after exchanging civilities, part of the guard turned back with us, and the deputies went on their way. Having reached the top of the hill, we found about a hundred men, tolerably well armed, but strangely dressed, awaiting us; and there we were detained till our guide rode forward to ask leave to bring us to head-quarters.

* * *

Our guide soon returned with eighteen or twenty mounted soldiers, whose appearance was rather wild than military: the guard presented arms as we parted from them, and we soon cantered down the hill towards the main body of the troops. Not above two hundred had the arms or accoutrements of soldiers; but there were dresses and weapons of every kind, leather, cloth, and linen; short jackets and long Scotch plaids, and every tint of colour in their faces, from the sallow European to the ebony African. Military honours were paid us by these ragged regiments, and we were conducted to the palace square, where Mr. Dance and Mr. Caumont dismounted, and I determined to await the issue of their conference, with my cousin in the court.

This, however, was not permitted. In a few minutes, a smart little man, speaking tolerable French, came and told me the *government* desired my company. I suspected a mistake of the word government for governor, and endeavoured to decline the honour; but no denial could be taken, and the little man, who told me he was secretary to government, accordingly assisted me to dismount, and showed me the way to the palace. The hall was filled with men and horses, like a barrack stable, excepting a corner which served as an hospital for those wounded in the late skirmishes, the groans of the latter mingling uncouthly with the soldiers' cheerful noisy voices. The stairs were so crowded, that we got up with difficulty, and then I found that I was indeed to be confronted with the whole strength of the provisional government. At the end of a long dirty room, that had once been handsome, as the form of the windows and carving of the panels on which there were traces of colour and gilding, indicated, there was an old black hair sofa, on the centre of which I was placed, with Mr. Dance on one side, and Mr. Glennie on the other; by Mr. Dance sat the little secretary, and next to him our interpreter, in old-fashioned high-backed chairs; the rest of the furniture of the room consisted of nine seats of different sizes and forms, placed in a semicircle fronting the sofa, and on each of these sat one of the members of the junta of the provisional government, who act the part of senators or generals, as the occasion may require. To each of these I was introduced; the names of Albuquerque, Cavalcante, and Broderod, struck me, but I heard imperfectly, and forget most of them: some wore handsome military coats, others the humbler dress of farmers. They politely told me they would not read the letter while I was waiting below, but as soon as we were seated, the secretary read it aloud. Instead of taking any notice of its contents, the secretary began a long discourse, setting forth the injustice of the Portuguese governor and government towards Brazil in general, and the Pernambucans in particular; that in order to resist that injustice, they had formed the present respectable government, pointing to the junta, without intending the least detriment to the rights of the king.

* * *

The junta was extremely anxious to learn if there was a probability of England's acknowledging the independence of Brazil, or if she took part at all in the struggle; and many were the questions, and very variously were they shaped, which the secretary addressed to us on that head. They are of course violent in their language concerning Luis do Rego, in proportion as he has done his military duty, in keeping them at bay with his handful of men: and like all oppositions they can afford to reason upon general principles, because they have not to feel the hindrances of action, and the jarring of private interests in the disposal and fulfilment of office.

I was sitting opposite to one of the windows of the council-room, and had been remarking for some time, that the sun was getting very low, and, therefore, rose to go, having received a note from the secretary, ordering the officers at their advanced posts to offer no hindrance to the passing of any thing belonging to His British Majesty's frigate, Doris. But we were not suffered to depart without a hearty invitation to sup and spend the night: and a stirrup-cup (a huge glass) was brought, and a bottle of wine, with about half as much water, poured into it; it was then handed to me to begin, and all fourteen received it in turn. By this time the guard was drawn out, the band played the national hymn, to which we all listened bare-headed, and so we mounted among those wild-looking men, in that strange, yet lovely landscape, just as the evening mist began to veil the lower land, and the bright red evening sun to gild the topmost branches of the forest.

Our journey home was much more rapid than our journey out. The evening was cool, and the horses eager to return; but we did not reach Mr. S.'s till two hours after sunset.

The description of the residences, their internal appearance, and that of the inhabitants of Bahia, is sketched in a manner that only a lady seeing them without the parade which usually accompanies the public exhibitions of the females, could have successfuly executed.

Friday, 19th—I accompanied Miss Pennell in a tour of visits to her Portuguese friends. As it is not their custom to visit or be visited in the forenoon, it was hardly fair to take a stranger to see them. However, my curiosity, at least, was gratified. In the first place, the houses, for the most part, are disgustingly dirty: the lower story usually consists of cells for the slaves, stabling etc.; the staircases are narrow and dark; and, at more than one house, we waited in a passage while the servants ran to open the doors and windows of the sitting-rooms, and to call their mistresses, who were enjoying their undress in their own apartments. When they appeared, I could scarcely believe that one half were gentlewomen. As they wear neither stay nor bodice, the figure becomes almost indecently slovenly, after very early youth; and this is the more disgusting, as they are very thinly clad, wear no neck-handkerchiefs, and scarcely any sleeves. Then, in this hot climate, it is unpleasant to see dark cottons and stuffs, without any white linen, near the skin. Hair black, ill combed, and dishevelled, or knotted unbecomingly, or still worse, *en papillote,* and the whole person having an unwashed appearance. When at any of the houses the bustle of opening the cobwebbed windows, and assembling the family was over, in two or three instances, the servants had to remove dishes of sugar, mandioc, and other provisions, which had been left in the best rooms to dry. There is usually a sofa at each end of the room, and to the right and left a long file of chairs, which look as if they never could be moved out of their place. Between the two sets of seats is a space, which, I am told, is often used for dancing; and, in every house, I saw either a guitar or piano, and generally both. Prints and pictures, the latter the worst daubs I ever saw, decorate the walls pretty generally; and there are, besides, crucifixes and other things of the kind. Some houses, however, are more neatly arranged; one, I think belonging to a captain of the navy, was papered, the floors laid with mat, and the tables ornamented with pretty porcelain, Indian and French: the lady too was neatly dressed in a French wrapper. Another house belonging to one of the judges was also clean, and of a more stately appearance than the rest, though the inhabitant was neither richer nor of higher rank. Glass chandeliers were suspended from the roof; handsome mirrors were intermixed with the prints and pictures. A good deal of handsome china was displayed round the room; but the jars, as well as the chairs and tables, seemed to form an inseparable part of the walls. We were every where invited, after sitting a few moments on the sofa, to go to the balconies of the windows and enjoy the view and the breeze, or at least amuse ourselves with what was passing in the street. And yet they did not lack conversation: the principal topic, however, was praise of the beauty of Bahia; dress, children, and diseases, I think, made up the rest; and, to say the truth, their manner of talking on the latter subject is as disgusting as their dress, that is, in a morning: I am told they are different after dinner. They marry very early, and soon lose their bloom. I did not see one tolerably pretty woman to-day. But then who is there that can bear so total a disguise as filth and untidiness spread over a woman?

The contrast between the private and public appearance of the parties is well described.

> This evening there was a large party, both Portuguese and English, at the consul's. In the well-dressed women I saw to-night, I had great difficulty in recognising the slatterns of the other morning. The senhoras were all dressed after the French fashion: corset, fichu, garniture, all was proper, and even elegant, and there was a great display of jewels. Our English ladies, though quite of the second rate of even colonial gentility, however, bore away the prize of beauty and grace; for after all, the clothes, however elegant, that are not worn habitually, can only embarrass and cramp the native movements; and, as Mademoiselle Clairon remarks, "she who would *act* a gentlewoman in public, must *be* one in private life."
>
> The Portuguese men have all a mean look; none appear to have any education beyond counting-house forms, and their whole time is, I believe, spent between trade and gambling: in the latter, the ladies partake largely after they are married. Before that happy period, when there is no evening dance, they surround the card tables, and with eager eyes follow the game, and long for the time when they too may mingle in it. I scarcely wonder at this propensity. Without education, and consequently without the resources of mind, and in a climate where exercise out of doors is all but impossible, a stimulus must be had; and gambling, from the sage to the savage, has always been resorted to, to quicken the current of life.

The tables in the Appendix to this lady's volume, showing the state of the trade of the province of Maranham, are interesting as exhibiting the increase of the surplus productions furnished by that district in exchange for the commodities of other countries. The progress seems to be so regular that it can scarcely be considered as either accidental or transient; but to have arisen from that necessary accumulation of capital which must take place in a fertile soil where labour and economy prevail. We observe the pleasure as Englishmen that, of the imports, those from our country nearly equal in amount those from Portugal, and far exceed those from other parts of the world. The exports consist chiefly of cotton-wool, two-thirds of which is sent to this country. The trade with the United States appears to be very insignificant, and that of France to be scarcely worth mentioning. We should be glad to have seen similar reports of the other provinces which now form the empire of Brazil.

Among the other favorite circumstances arising from the intercourse opened with all the world as soon as the court had arrived from Lisbon, the visits of scientific travellers were not the least important. The Germans, especially, explored Brazil, and gave the public much valuable information concerning its natural history. Prince Maximilian of Neuweid, accompanied by Messrs. Freyrois and Sellow, spent a good deal of time in examining its botanical productions; and what he has published on the subject is equally creditable to his diligence and his science. Mr. Mawe went from Buenos Aires to Rio de Janeiro, by way of St. Paulo, and continued his route from thence to Tejuco, in the diamond district. Von Eschwege, setting out from Villa Rica, penetrated westward from Rio de San Francisco to Rio Abaité, where a lead mine is now working. Auguste de Saint Hilaire visited several parts of the province of Minas, the Indian settlements of Pasainha, Tejuco, and the Rio de San Francisco, at Salgado. To these may be added to our countrymen Koster and Luccock, the latter of whom was an accurate observer of the rural economy of the districts which he visited.

[The author praises the Bavarian travelers for their beautiful descriptions of the landscape, wildlife, industry, and agriculture of Brazil, including passages on their arrival to Rio, the effects of the removal of the court in Rio, the plants and land formations outside the city, the mule caravans at Porto de Estrella, and the dangerous plants, animals, and diseases of Brazil.]

* * *

We cannot conclude this article without a remark on one great source of apprehension, for countries so extensive in proportion to their population, and with only a few large cities in vast distances from one another, and equally distant in interests and feelings. We allude to that provincial spirit which must, with more or less force, be generated in such circumstances. Such rivalry is so natural as to appear inevitable, and it requires the greatest skill and coolest judgment in those who govern, to counteract its bad effects and to direct its spirit to the general advantage. North America has, for the present, been successful, by the establishment of a federal city and district, in suppressing the rivalry for power, which existed between the capitals of the several provinces up to the period of the general acquiescence in the present constitution. What effect may be produced, for good or for evil, when the western territory shall exceed in population that on the coast of the Atlantic, a period, probably, not so long as that which has passed since the recognition of their independence, when the wealth and the intelligence of the country shall be to the east, and the physical force to the west of the Allegany mountains, it is difficult to calculate; but a confederated republic of such vast extent would be a phenomenon in politics.

Appendix IV: Maria Graham's Unpublished "Life of Don Pedro"

[Maria Graham—now Lady Callcott—dictated these memoirs to her good friend Caroline Fox while confined to her room due to her worsening tuberculosis, 1834–1835.]

The following pages were written soon after the death of Don Pedro I, late Emperor of Brazil, Duke of Braganza, etc. I would rather say, they were begun at that time, in consequence of my having mentioned some of the circumstances related in them to Miss Fox, who undertook to write down whatever I would relate. I accordingly engaged to tell, not only what I know of my personal knowledge of Don Pedro, but what I had learned, on what I thought good authority, of his early life. Of course, as the narration proceeds, much that concerns the country becomes mixed with it. His little Daughter and his first most amiable Wife are also named often, and to me, what concerns the latter is the most interesting part of the narrative. To the few into whose hands this manuscript is likely to fall, perhaps the passage concerning myself may not be quite valueless.

Maria Callcott.

Kensington Gravel Pits,
Begun 1834—ended Feby. 1835.
This copy made by James Allen, Esq.[r]

[The memoir opens with a 5,800-word biography of Don Pedro, treating of his childhood, inadequate education, closest advisors, bad influences, and marriage to Maria Leopoldina. At this point, with the birth of their children and Graham's visit to Brazil just as Independence was declared, she appears on the scene. The selections to follow are all from chapter 3, the final chapter of Graham's manuscript.]

It is strange and it is true that I never knew how or when the idea arose of making me Governess to the young Princess. I was first asked whether I should like the office by Sir Thomas Hardy, then commanding the English Squadron on the South American Station. Not dreaming that he was in earnest, I answered "to be sure," and added what a delightful thing, to rescue that fine child from the hands of such creatures as surround her, to bring her up like a European gentlewoman— to teach her, since she is to govern this wide country, that the people are less made for Kings, than Kings for the people. Whether this discourse was repeated to any of the Andradas as a serious scheme on my part, I do not know; it is certain that from that time, I received a good deal of attention from them, and finally through some of their connections, a direct intimation, that the Emperor and Empress waited till I should have asked in form for the office they were predetermined to bestow on me in order to appoint me, without delay, Governess to the Imperial Princesses. I confess that I was carried away by the notion of bringing up a person, on whose education and personal qualities, the happiness of a whole Empire was to depend. I fancied what Brazil might be under a better Government than any country but my own had ever enjoyed. I never had much faith in new Constitutions, made to slip on like garments, whenever men fancy themselves tired of the old, and I knew that the best of our own institutions had grown with the Nation's Growth, and like the bark of our own Oak, had accommodated itself, in size and shape, as the tree itself increased its trunk, its branches and its root.

[Graham goes on to speak of the Constitution, the possibility of abolition, and the influence of the Andradas over the Brazil of her time; her plans to return to England at the Empress's urging to prepare her books for publication, gather educational materials, and then return to Brazil within six months to a year to take up her position; her time in England; changes in the Brazilian government during her absence; and particularly the waning influence of José Bonifacio de Andrada, her supporter.]

On reaching Bahia, though I found the place nominally settled under the Emperor's Government, it was impossible not to perceive that a great deal of discontent existed; and a strong desire to form a Federative Republic in imitation of the United States. Our stay here, however, was only a few hours and we, very speedily, reached Rio Janeiro, and there, when the Harbour Master came on board, I learnt that, during my twelve months' absence, two events most personally disastrous to myself had occurred; the first and greatest was the expulsion of the Andradas, not only from the Ministry, but the Country, and the other was the death of Don John de Souza, my best friend in the Palace, and the person to whom the Empress had desired that on my return I should address myself.

I had, however, the satisfaction of hearing by the Pilot that the Emperor himself had given orders that a signal should be made to the Palace as soon as I arrived, and accordingly the Captain of the Packet made the signal, but instead of waiting for the Imperial boat, which probably would not have appeared before sunset, I went on shore with an English friend, who had come off to the packet to tell me the news disagreeable as it was and to offer me his house in the city till I should be established in the palace, and to take charge of my Baggage and do whatever else might be of use to me. I proceeded immediately to San Cristovaõ, to wait on the Empress, but how was I surprised on arriving at the Gate, to find the Emperor loitering about by himself, evidently for the purpose of seeing me first, though at first he turned away, shyly, as if he did not mean to speak. He appeared as if just risen from his siesta, he had on slippers but no stockings, and a light gingham jacket and trousers, and a straw hat bound and tied with green; he was leaning with one hand on the iron rail leading to the principal door and the other hand stretched out to shake hands with me, as he said, "*a mode Ingreza.*" I was very well satisfied with his reception of me; I congratulated him on his apparent *good health,* to which he replied by making enquiries about seasickness. He then told me to go up into the Veranda, where I should find such a one, the Empress's Equerry for the day, who would conduct me to her private apartments, while he himself went through the house by a back way to prepare her for my visit. My ceremonious journey through the Palace took up much more time than His Imperial Majesty's underground course, for I found the Empress seated in an ante-room, where she told me she had been several minutes waiting for me. She immediately asked me if I had not received her letter in London; on finding that I had not, she told me that the object of it was to delay my coming out, that since the new Ministry had been established, the Emperor had been inclined to listen to a marriage between Donna Maria de Gloria and her Uncle Don Miguel; that she herself did not like the proposal, chiefly on account of the near relationship between the parties, though I must be aware that among Portuguese and Brazilians that is not thought an obstacle. She hinted that the time that must necessarily pass before this negotiation could be brought to a conclusion, had induced her to wish to delay my voyage; she thought that perhaps in another year, Donna Maria might be going to Portugal, that if my arrival had been delayed till near that time, she would have gladly put her daughter under my care, as I was accustomed to the sea and should be able to attend to her health during the voyage, which she could not look forward to without some dread. She seemed to doubt the practicability of sending me to Europe if I once took office as Governess to the four Princesses. The Empress then told me that my apartment was not ready, although the Emperor himself had given particular orders about it, as soon as he thought the packet in which I was to come was likely to arrive. She then took leave of me, or rather, gave me leave, and desired to see me again next day. Just before I left her, the Emperor came in, dressed for his afternoon's ride, and good naturedly offered to go up stairs with me to show me the rooms, an honour I of course declined, but not to seem ungrateful for his attentions, I said in answer to his enquiries as to my particular taste that I hoped there would be a good many bookshelves. I saw no more of Don Pedro till I became an inmate of the Palace; the day I went thither, I was conducted to my rooms by the favourite Barber, and attended by my own black woman; no servant being appointed for me, but a sort of Water Carrier, a slave whose business it was to bring water twice a day, to carry messages generally, but especially to communicate with a kind of Settlers who have formed a Colony round the Palace, to supply its inmates (especially the Ladies) with all the delicacies which the Royal Pantry did not afford.

I found my apartment at the very top of the wing occupied by the Empress and her oldest daughter; they lived in the highest story not an attic; mine was there, the attic over Donna Maria's own room; the Ladies of the Wardrobe occupying those over the Empress's. In that climate, it is a great pleasure to be lodged upstairs, and I never shall forget the pleasantness of the first morning, when on opening my window, instead of the noise and filth of the city, I looked upon the beautiful Gardens of the Palace and the Coffee Grounds which clothe the Mountains of Tijuoa and smelt the perfume of the orange blossoms that came with every breath of the morning breeze. I had seven small rooms, three on one side of a long passage and four on the other. On one side were sleeping rooms for myself and my servant and our kitchen. On the other side, I found the emperor had fulfilled his promise and furnished the walls of my room with bookshelves from top to bottom; there was besides a little waiting room and two small sitting rooms, quite sufficient for all our wants.

I received a message through the Barber, to be waiting in the Empress's apartments when she and the Emperor should return from their evening ride; and meanwhile the Ladies of the Wardrobe and the Barber himself, under pretence of offering me assistance, remained crowding round me, watching every article that Black Anna and I unpacked. Many were the criticisms on certain articles of English tidiness, of which the Portuguese and Brazilian Ladies had no notion, and which, had the Barber been an Englishman, even Black Anna, who knew the manners of the English, would not have ventured to expose. His observations on the smallness of my bed amused me; it happened to be a camp bedstead, which folded into a portmanteau. The smallness and modesty of my wardrobe was another thing that astonished them, for though as according to their notions, as a widow, I could only wear black out of doors, and white for an underdress within, they did expect new fashions, or laces or satins instead of my plain silk and cambric muslin. I redeemed my character a little, however, by the shape of a hat, which was copied in fifty different colours before the end of the week. They were also not a little pleased with several prints, which I had time to frame at Rio and which I hung up in different rooms; they actually screamed with delight at seeing an Assumption of the Virgin and which they declared was an omen of good luck, for that it was from her, my eldest pupil Donna Maria da Gloria received her name. As to their mistaking the Portrait of Raffaelle for the Arch-Angel, it was much too favourable a mistake for me to correct. The last chest I was able to open before them, as the return of the Empress drew nearer, and I confess I selected the case, maliciously, was a package containing a pair of Carey's two foot Globes, handsomely mounted, and in a corner of the chest, a few instruments for making observations on the weather and the climate, such as Leslie's Hygrometer, Gynometer, etc., and their cries of Marvellous! Marvellous! were only interrupted by the sound of the Emperor's horse's feet, and I was a little glad that the opening of my books was reserved for the quiet hours of the night or early morning, when I had resolved that Black Anna and myself would arrange them upon the shelves, before they could be seen by any of my afternoon's companions.

I went down, as appointed, to the Empress's apartments, where I found both their Imperial Majesties and Donna Maria, who was formally introduced to me as her Governess, though I had seen her before. Several of the attendants were present, but especially those belonging to Donna Maria. The Empress, in the very kindest manner, and speaking in a rather loud voice, hoped I liked my apartments and that the Barber had given all necessary assistance in unpacking, etc. He then gave me a letter which he said he was determined I should receive from no hand but his own, at the same time announcing its contents aloud for the benefit of the bystanders, and certainly, if words could have conveyed Power, I should from that moment have had the absolute direction of everything concerning the Princesses (to use His Majesty's words), *intellectual* and *physical*. Had my state and comfort depended on the good words and kind expressions and intentions of His Majesty or on the expressions of perfect confidence from the Empress, or the order directed to everyone in the Palace, contained in the written document which the Emperor placed in my hand, I should have been a Great Lady indeed, and if this greatness and authority could have insured comfort—a most comfortable one—but alas, the Barber was behind the scenes, as shall shortly appear.

Meantime I was extremely pleased with my Master and Mistress and little pupil, who, at her Mother's desire, showed me all her rooms and said she should expect me at 7 o'clock next morning, and when I would have kissed her hand, as I was instructed to do, she jump'd up and put her arms round my neck and kissing me, asked me to love her very much. On returning to my room I read the Emperor's letter. It was very complimentary and if he or any body had taken means to ensure compliance with either my wishes or the conditions laid down in the Order, which was in his own handwriting, all would have been well, but the very next morning our trouble began. In the first place, when I went to the Princess's apartments, I found the women washing her, not in the bath room but in the open apartment, where the slaves, male and female, were passing, and through which the Empress's Guard always paraded, and I could not think it right that she should be thus exposed, entirely naked, to all comers. The Dressers refused to alter their unseemly practice, till I obtained a written order from the Emperor, as they said it was too much trouble to use the bathroom; in fact, they had put it to a different use. The next most disgusting thing was the breakfast; they gave her the thigh of a fowl stewed in oil with garlick, and she picked the garlick out of the dish with her fingers and ate it. A glass of strong wine and water followed, and then, to my amazement, Coffee, Toast, and Sweetmeat. I said nothing at the moment, but resolved to speak, privately and seriously, to the Empress, on the probable consequences of such feeding to her child's health.

The lesson hours were more satisfactory; and she had been taught to speak French by the Abbé Boiret, and she repeated some of La Fontaine's Fables (Le Renard and Le Corbeau) with great spirit, but I never shall forget her rapture, when she discovered that the same letters that had enabled her to read French, would serve her for Portuguese, and when I put Mrs. Berbould's "Little Charles" translated for her use, into her hands and read with her, as she said "all these Portuguese words," she suddenly jumped from her chair, seized the book and ran to her Mother's room to shew her what a delightful new thing she had got, and scarcely stopping for a remark, she ran towards her Father's quarters of the Palace and it required the utmost speed of a long-legged Aide de Camp to catch her before she had broken into the Council Chamber. After this, the reading of Portuguese went on of itself, and the Abbé was, I thought, a little jealous of the preference my pupil gave to "Little Charles" over his French fable book; nor was he quite pleased that she herself said, she learnt the fable I chose for her, in half the time she had acquired his.

She was extremely delighted in the afternoons to go into my book room and to be allowed to search for Prints, and after she had once seen upon the Globe, the size of Brazil compared to Portugal, we could hardly get her away, so eager was she to show this wonderful difference to all the Ladies who lodged upon my floor and whom she caused to be assembled for the purpose.

I mention these little circumstances, to show that the child, though young, had a lively intelligent mind, such as with a European Education might have been turn'd to everything useful and noble, and when I saw that she was extremely affectionate, yet capable of great self-control, I hope I was not too sanguine in forming the highest expectations of the future. Of the latter quality I must give an instance. She had always been accustomed, not only to have little black slaves to play with and beat and tyrannise over, but a little White Girl, the daughter of one of the Ladies. I observed that in her rough play, she not only kicked and beat the little blacks, but slap't her white playmate (a small timid child) with the energy and spirit of a reckless little tyrant. I had spoken privately to the mother of this child, hoping that she would cooperate with me in correcting this improper practice, but she answered that she would put a child of hers to death, who did not think it an honour to receive a blow from the Princess! Seeing it was hopeless, therefore, to expect any help from that quarter, I tried what I could do with the Princess herself, and so, on the first occasion, I called her to me and said that I did not like her to give blows to her companions, asking her, at the same time, if she did not admire her Mother's gentle manners better than those of any lady she had ever seen, and whether she would not rather wish to resemble her. "Oh but," she said, "everybody says I am like Papa—very lively." "Yes," I replied, "but women do not show their feelings as men are allowed to do, and I assure you, your Mamma was taught to be gentle whenever she was a little Princess like yourself, and in our Country, none of the great people are permitted to beat the common folks, besides women are expected to be gentle, and especially Princesses, who, if they are not so, may perhaps make a great number of people unhappy, therefore I must not have you beat your Companions anymore—it is not like a Lady or a Princess." I trusted to time for the effect of my little lecture, but I had not long to wait before I saw the first fruit at least, for the very next time the Princess had her playmates, I heard her, according to custom, very loud and eager in talk with them; I immediately went to them and looked at her, seeing her face had become exceedingly red and that she was on the point of letting her passion get the better of her—she suddenly checked herself, dropped her little outstretched hands, and running to me, said to me, quite joyously, "Now was that not behaving like a Lady and a Princess?"

[Graham describes the everyday habits of the Emperor.]

After dinner His Imperial Majesty regularly retired to rest and it was while his siesta lasted, that I had, usually, the pleasure of conversing with the Empress. At first she used to send for me to her own apartments, but as there we could not be without some attendants, whose reports of the familiarity with which I was treated excited violent jealousies amongst the Ladies, she desired me, after the first three or four weeks, to remain after the dinner in my own room till she should come to me; of course I asked her in which of my little parlours I should receive her; she named the book-room and accordingly I made Anna prepare it to the best advantage and place only one chair in it. She came even earlier than I expected on the first day of our new arrangements. When she saw the one chair she hastily asked me if I did not mean Her to sit down in my House? My answer was, of course, that there was her chair, but that it was my duty to stand; but nothing could prevail on her to sit, till I had fetched another chair for myself. I mention this trait of good-nature, as one out of hundreds that I might quote of the kind and pleasant disposition of this most amiable woman. Perhaps with a view to my staying a long time in the Palace, it might have been more prudent if our hours of intercourse had been less frequent and less long but I could not if I would have done otherwise than obey, and it may be imagined that as Maria Leopoldina had no Ladies of her own station about her, not so much as the wife of an Ambassador nor Chargé d'affaires to speak occasionally with her, and that all her attendants were Portuguese who spoke no language but their own and whose whole education amounted to the Rule of Court etiquette, with just knowledge enough of reading and writing to conduct an intrigue either domestic or political, it is not very wonderful that she should have availed herself, eagerly, of the power of conversing in a more familiar language, with one, who could at least converse on European topics of interest, who had seen her father and most of her other relations since she had left them and who was familiar with the very places that she had frequented herself. These considerations, even had they occurred to our Ladies, would not have made them a whit more charitable; they had always complained of the policy which had married their young Master of the House of Braganza to a stranger instead of to an Aunt or a Cousin, as had been the invariable custom of the Royal Houses of Spain and Portugal.

They were now murmuring at the introduction of a *second stranger*, as they called me, into the Palace, as if no Portuguese lady were competent to instruct the Princess! Their murmurings produced their effect in time.

Our quiet little conversation lasted till the Empress went to prepare for her evening ride with the Emperor, which generally took place in about an hour after he awoke from his siesta; this was usually the best part of the day with him, provided, however, that his sleep had been undisturbed. It was seldom that his temper could stand being prematurely roused at this time of the day, and, in general, woe betide the unhappy wight, compelled by necessity or betrayed by accident, to break his slumbers. This the Barber and the rest of the Coterie well knew and they availed themselves of it accordingly.

The evening rides and drives were very much like those of the morning, and often lasted till very late, unless there was a Gala at the Opera House, in which case the rides were shortened as the Emperor made a point of attending the Opera and the Empress not unfrequently accompanied him. On Birth Nights or when any particular impression was to be made on the public, poor little Dona Maria was dressed out in a bandeau of diamonds, kept out of bed and accompanied her parents to the City where, placed in the front of the State Box in the Theatre, she had already been trained to play the little Queen with a grace and manner that perfectly astonished me the first time I saw them.

These occasional visits to the Theatre did not very often break in on our quiet hours at the Palace while I was an inmate. In general while their Majesties were riding, I took the children into the Garden with their Nurses, and to their great delight, not only allowed but encouraged them to run about in the shade; to pull flowers; look at insects without screaming, and even to dirty their frocks with the garden mould. Their mother, wishing to treat them like European children, had long ago ordered little sets of garden tools, of a proper size for the three eldest, but they had been kept scrupulously unsullied, because, as the Ladies said, it was not fit for a Princess to be turning up the dirty earth like the Blacks and that the tools were only a European fancy of the Empress, who neither knew what suited the climate of Brazil nor the dignity of the Braganzas.

That no time might be lost in feeding the Royal Children, the Merienda was generally taken into the garden, and notwithstanding the two very full meals of meat and poultry with which they had been crammed at Breakfast and Dinner, each child might be seen with the leg of a Capo or a Turkey in its hand to gnaw, after which some corner of sweet cake or fruit was administered. It was happy for the children that they had good strong constitutions, otherwise they must have been injured by their over-feeding. It may probably tell in after life and I should not wonder if the unhappy maladies, both bodily and mental, with which the wretched Braganza family has been afflicted, may have been caused by it.

It was necessary for the children to have returned home and to have supped (supper very like the dinner) before their Father and Mother returned from their ride. Then every Lady that could make out an excuse for being in attendance, rushed to the top of the private stairs to partake of the evening *Baja Mão*, the Children first kissing their father and mother's hands and the Ladies following with more or less fervour as they expected or not, some of those petty favours which the Barber had been instructed to ask for in the course of the day. Then everybody retired and our wing was locked up for the night.

The Empress, certainly, supped and retired to her own apartments all the time I was with her. The Emperor went to his part of the Palace; but before the return of the Old Court to Europe, Gaming and every other sort of vice was encouraged by the old Queen and her eldest daughter and the Infant of Spain, Don Sebastian.

[As she attempts to develop a new routine for the young princesses, Graham finds that servants do not respect her and that her orders are constantly countermanded; finally she receives a curt note from the Emperor, essentially demoting her from governess to English teacher. She speaks with the Empress, hoping to rectify the situation.]

I said that it was impossible, I perceived, for me to be of the use I had expected to be, unless some decided measures were taken to give me that support and countenance which the great importance of my situation as Governess to her Daughter required, and that were it not for my friendship for Her Majesty, nothing should tempt me to remain where my character was so little understood and my services so little appreciated; that she must be as sensible as I could be, that excepting the pleasant hours she had allowed me to pass in her company, my life had been that of a State prisoner, and one moreover subjected to all manner of impertinence and insolence from the persons of the lowest description, for as such I certainly looked on the Barber Placito and the female attendants in the Palace. She answered me very kindly and gently and told me that, as a friend, she should put her own wishes out of the way, that while she had a hope that Frey Antonio de Arrabida would have been permitted to superintend our studies and to give me his powerful support, she had encouraged me under all my little vexations, but that she was now convinced that he would not be allowed to do so, and that her enemies as well as mine were making use of some secret, but very powerful influence. That her support of me would do her no good and would make it more irksome than I must perceive it already was and that for both our sakes, she feared the best thing that could be done, was for me to leave the Palace. She did not mean to complain; she loved her husband and doated on her children and she hoped to have strength never to repine at what it was her duty to bear; that it had been her fate to be separated from all she loved best and in parting from me, whom she had looked on as the friend who was to keep her Daughters from the evil that the ignorance and grossness of all those around them threatened them with, she had only one trial the more, which she felt assured would not be the last. It was then agreed that I should write to the Emperor and ask for my dismissal. She then left me, promising to return in an hour and to take my letter.

I lost no time in sitting with half-a-dozen letters, none of them, I fear, breathing the sweetest spirit. She read them all aloud and after we had consulted together, we made the choice of the following:

> Sire,
>
> It is with feelings that I cannot express that I received the Order of today, signed by Your Imperial Majesty.
>
> I should never have quitted England nor a family which is honourable even in that distinguished country, to be a mere teacher of the English Language! If I am not the *Governess* of the Imperial Princess, I have nothing to do in this country. The person honoured with the title and employment of Governess in such a family, ought to have been secured from the impertinences I have met with since I have been here,—I will never submit to them. For my own sake I have no pride (amour proper) but for the sake of my Pupils there was an absolute necessity for my not being treated as a servant. I earnestly beg that Your Majesty will give me leave to retire.
>
> I shall quit Brazil, for ever, by the first ship that sails.
>
> Regretting my Pupils, regretting also that I have been unable to fulfil the wishes entertained by Your Majesty and the Empress when you invited me here as Governess.
>
> As to those Ladies who have invented so many falsehoods concerning me, I forgive them and I pray that Your Majesty may never find reason to have listened, too eagerly, to their complaints.

This was the body of the letter, which ended in a wish for the prosperity of his Family and for that of Brazil.

I sealed this letter in the presence of the Empress. She immediately took it to the Emperor, and shortly returned with a, not ungracious, permission for me to go where I pleased. The ink was not dry when she brought it. She said that she had been ordered to bring the document back and all former Letters, either of appointment to my situation, or promise as to salary, without delay.

If I had had a moment to reflect, I ought not to have given up those documents. But what could I do? The Empress, whom I really loved, was in tears and I plainly understood from her that she had to fear some unkindness if she did not carry back all that had been demanded. So I gave her everything and, after all, I believe I did well.

[Graham leaves the palace the next morning; she continues to exchange affectionate letters with Maria Leopoldina until the latter's death in 1826.]

Selected Bibliography

ABBREVIATIONS

CHLA: Bethel, Leslie, ed. *The Cambridge History of Latin America*. Vol. 3: *From Independence to c. 1870*. Cambridge: Cambridge UP, 1985.
ODNB: Harrison, Brian, and H.C.G. Matthew, eds. *Oxford Dictionary of National Biography*. Oxford: Oxford UP, 2004.
Fundação: Fundação Biblioteca Nacional de Brasil. "Por Dentro da BN: Histórico." 2006. Biblioteca Nacional de Brasil. 31 January 2008. http://www.bn.br/site/default.htm.
Grande: Grande Enciclopédia Portuguesa e Brasiliera. Rio de Janeiro: Editorial Enciclopédia, Limitada, 1936–60.

ARCHIVES

Biblioteca Nacional de Brasil, Rio de Janeiro

Letters between Maria Graham and Maria Leopoldina.

Bodleian Library

Special Collections and Western Manuscripts.
Papers, including journals, travel diaries, memoirs and other biographical materials (MSS.Eng.b.2020, 2025–2026; c.2730–2733; d.2273–2290; e.2428–2432).
typescript, n.d., made from a copy in the Brazilian Archives, of Lady Callcott's "Life of Don Pedro" and account of her life in Brazil, 1824–6, originally dictated to the Hon. Caroline Fox in 1834–5 and copied by James Allen, Lord Holland's librarian. iii. & 103 leaves. (MS. Eng. c. 2730).

British Library

MS Facs 512: facsimile of Maria Graham's "Life of Don Pedro" (original in Biblioteca Nacional de Brasil).

Holland House Papers: Add. MSS 51838–51839 (1834–36: correspondence of Maria Callcott with Lord Holland).
Holland House Papers: Unbound Mss. 51996.
Letters of George Dundas: Acc 10719 no 15.

National Library of Scotland

John Murray Archive: Acc.12604/1185–1186.
Lynedoch Collection: MSS 3610–3618.

Oliveira Lima Library, Catholic University of America

Transcript of Maria Graham's manuscript annotations contained in her personal copy of *Journal of a Voyage to Brazil*, now owned by the Oliveira Lima Library, and of an original letter from Adelia Bonpland bound therein. (Oliveira Lima Manuscript Collection, unnumbered manuscript).

Reading University Library

Longman archive.

Works of Maria Graham

Graham, Maria. *Journal of a Residence in India*. 1812; 2nd edition, 1813.
—. *Letters on India, with Etchings and a Map*. 1814.
—, trans. *Memoirs of the War of the French in Spain*. By Albert Jean Michel de Rocca. London: J. Murray, 1815.
—. *Memoir of the Life of Nicholas Poussin*. London: Longman, Hurst, Rees, Orme, Brown, and Green, and Edinburgh: Constable, 1820.
—. *Three Months Passed in the Mountains East of Rome, During the Year 1819*. 1820; 2nd edition 1821.
—. *A Short History of Spain*. London, J. Murray, 1828.
—. *Journal of a Voyage to Brazil, and Residence There, During Part of the Years 1821, 1822, 1823*. London: Longman et al. and John Murray, 1824; reprinted 1969.
Graham, Maria. *Diário de uma viagem ao Brasil e de uma estada nesse pais durante parte dos anos de 1821, 1822 e 1823*. Tradução e notas de Américo Jacobina Lacombe. 1956. São Paulo: Companhia Editora Nacional, 1990.
—. *Journal of a Residence in Chile during the Year 1822. And a Voyage from Chile to Brazil in 1823*. 1824; 2nd edition 1825; reprinted 1969; Spanish translation *Diario de su residencia en Chile, durante el año 1822*, trans. José Valenzuela Dooner. Santiago: 1902; reprinted 1916, 1956, 1988, 1992.

—. *Journal of a Residence in Chile during the Year 1822. And a Voyage from Chile to Brazil in 1823*. Ed. Jennifer Hayward. Charlottesville: UP of Virginia, 2003.
—. *Voyage of H.M.S. Blonde to the Sandwich Islands in the Years 1824[-]1825*, Captain *the Right Hon. Lord Byron, Commander*, 1826.
Callcott, Maria. *Letter to the President and Members of the Geological Society in Answer to Certain Observations Contained in Mr. Greenough's Anniversary Address of 1834*, 1834.
—. *Description of the Chapel of the Annunziata dell Aren in Padua, With Engravings from Drawings by A.W. Callcott, R.A.* 1835.
—. *Little Arthur's History of England.* 1835; reprinted and revised through 1947.
—. *Continuation of Essays towards the History of Painting*, 1838.
—. *The Seven Ages of Shakespeare: an Essay by Lady Callcott*, 1840.
—. *The Little Brackenburners and Little Mary's Four Saturdays*, 1841.
—. *A Scripture Herbal*, 1842.

Nineteenth Century Travel to Brazil

Agassiz, Louis. *A Journey in Brazil.* Boston: Ticknor & Fields, 1868.
Andrews, Joseph. *Journey from Buenos Ayres Through the Provinces of Cordova, Tucuman, and Salta, to Potosi, Thence by the Deserts of Caranja to Arica, and Subsequently, to Santiago de Chili and Coquimbo, Undertaken on Behalf of the Chilian and Peruvian Mining Association, in the Years 1825–26.* London: John Murray, 1827.
Armitage, John. *The History of Brazil, from the Period of the Arrival of the Braganza family in 1808, to the Abdication of Don Pedro the First ins 1831. Compiled from State Documents and Other Original Sources. Forming a Continuation to Southey's History of That Country.* 2 vols. London: Smith, Elder, and Co., 1836.
Ashe, Thomas. *A Commercial View and Geographical Sketch, on the Brasils in South America, and of the Island of Madeira.* London: Allen & Co, 1812.
Bingley, William. *Travels in South America from Modern Writers, with Remarks and Observations; Exhibiting a Connected View of the Geography and Present State of That Quarter of the Globe.* London: John Sharpe, Hailes's Juvenile Library, London Museum, 1820.
Caldcleugh, Alexander. *Travels in South America During the Years 1819, 1820, 1821.* London: John Murray, 1825.
Dundonald, Earl of Dent, Hastings Charles. *A Year in Brazil, with Notes on the Abolition of Slavery, the Finances of the Empire, Religion, Meteorology, Natural History, etc.* London: Kegan Paul, Trench & Co, 1886.
—. *Narrative of Services in the liberation of Chili, Peru, and Brazil from Spanish and Portuguese domination.* 2 vols. London, 1859.

Chamberlain, Henry. *Views and costumes of the city and neighbourhood of Rio de Janeiro Brazil.* London: Howlett and Brimmer, 1822.

Frézier, Amédée François. *Relation du voyage de la mer du Sud aux côtes du Chily et du Perou. Fait pendant les années 1712, 1713, & 1714.* Amsterdam: P. Humbert, 1717.

Grant, Andrew. *History of Brazil.* London: Henry Colburn, 1809.

Hakluyt, Richard. *The Principal Navigations, Voiages, Traffiques and Discoveries of the English Nation, Made by Sea or Over-Land,* etc. London: George Bishop, Ralph Newbery and Robert Barker, 1598.

Humboldt, Alexander von. *Histoire de la géographie du Nouveau continent et des progress de l'astronomie nautique au XV et XVI siècles comprenant l'histoire de la decouverte de l'Amerique.* Paris: Legrand, Pomey et Crouzet, [n.d.]

—. *Personal Narrative of Travels to the Equinoctial Regions of America during the Years 1799–1804.* Trans. Thomasina Ross. 3 Vols. London: Henry G. Bohn, 1852.

Keith, G. M. *A voyage to South America, and the Cape of Good Hope, in His Majesty's gun brig the Protector, commanded by Lieut. Sir G. M. Keith.* London: Richard Phillips, 1810.

Kidder, Daniel P. *Sketches of Residence and Travels in Brazil.* 2 vols. London: Wiley and Putman, 1845.

Kindersley, Jemima. *Briefe von der Insel Teneriffa, Brasilien, dem Vorgebirge der guten Hoffnung und Ostindien aus dem Englischen der Mistress Kindersley.* Leipzig: Weidmanns Erben und Reich, 1777.

Knight, E.F. *The Cruise of the 'Falcon': A Voyage to South America in a 30-Ton Yacht.* 4th ed. London: Sampson Low, Marston, Searle, & Rivington, 1887.

Koster, Henry. *Travels in Brazil.* London: Longman, Hurst, Rees, Orme, and Brown, 1816.

La Condamine, Charles Marie de. *Relation abrégée D'un voyage Fait Dans l'Interieur De l'Amerique Meridionale depuis la Côte de la Mer du Sud, jusqu'aux Côtes du Brésil & de la Guyane* etc. Paris: la veuve Pissot, 1745.

Langsdorff, G. H. von. *Bemerkungen auf einer Reise um die Welt in den Iahren 1803 bis 1807,* etc. Franfurt: Friedrich Wilmans, 1812.

Lévi-Strauss, Claude. *Tristes Tropiques.* Trans. John and Doreen Weightman. New York: Atheneum, 1974.

Lindley, Thomas. *Narrative of a Voyage to Brazil, Terminating in the Seizure of a British Vessel, and the Imprisonment of the Author and the Ship's Crew, by the Portuguese. with General Sketches of the Country, Its Natural Productions, Colonial Inhabitants, etc.* London: J. Johnson, 1805.

Lisle, J.G. Semple. *The Life of Major J.G. Semple Lisle: Containing a Faithful Narrative of His Alternate Vicissitude of Splendor and Misfortune, Written by Himself, the Whole Interspersed with Interesting Anecdotes, and Authentic Accounts of Important Public Transactions.* London: W. Steward, 1799.

Luccock, John. *Notes on Rio De Janeiro and the Southern Parts of Brazil; Taken During a Residence of Ten Years in That Country, from 1808 to 1818.* London: Samuel Leigh, 1820.

Mawe, John. *Travels in the Interior of Brazil, Particularly in the Gold and Diamond Districts of that Country, by Authority of the Prince Regent of Portugal: Including a Voyage to the Rio La Plata, and an Historical Sketch of the Revolution of Buenos Ayres.* Illustrated with engravings. London: Longman, Hurts, Rees, Orme, and Brown, 1812.

Mathison, Gilbert Farquhar. *Narrative of a Visit to Brazil, Chile, Peru, and the Sandwich Islands, during the years 1821–1822. With Miscellaneous Remarks on the Past and Present State, and Political Prospects of Those Countries.* London: Charles Knight, 1825.

Pfeiffer, Ida. *A Lady's Travels Round the World: travels from Vienna to Brazil, Chile, Otaheite [sic], China, the East Indies, Persia, & Asia Minor.* Trans. by Wm Hazlitt. London: Routledge, 1852.

Stevenson, William Bennett. *A Historical and Descriptive Narrative of Twenty Years' Residence in South America.* London: Hurst, Robinson, and Co, 1825.

Taunay, Hippolyte, and Ferdinand Denis. *Le Brésil, ou Histoire, Moeurs, usages et coutumes des habitans de ce royaume.* Paris: Nepveu, 1822.

Taylor, Rev. Isaac. *Scenes in America for the Amusement and Instruction of Little Tarry-at-Home Travellers.* London: John Harris, 1821.

Walsh, Rev. R. *Notices of Brazil in 1828 and 1829.* 2 vols. Boston: Richardson et al., 1831.

Secondary Sources

Almeida Camargo, Ana Maria de, and Rubens Borba de Moraes. *Bibliografia da Impressão Régia do Rio de Janeiro (1808–1822).* 2 vols. São Paulo: Libraria Kosmos Editora, 1993.

Amado, Janaína. "Mythic Origins: Caramuru and the Founding of Brazil." *Hispanic American Historical Review* 80.4 (2000): 783–811.

Bagno, Marcos. *O processo da independência do Brasil.* São Paulo: 2003.

Barman, Roderick J. *Citizen Emperor: Pedro II and the Making of Brazil, 1825–91.* Stanford UP, 1999.

Berger, Paulo. *Bibliografia Rio de Janeiro de viajantes e autores estrangeiros, 1531–1900.* Rio de Janeiro: Libraria São José, 1964.

Bethel, Leslie. *Brazil by British and Irish Authors.* Oxford: Centre for Brazilian Studies, University of Oxford, 2003.

—. "The British Contribution to the Study of Brazil." Working Paper CBS-37–2003 (http://www.brazil.ox.ac.uk/Bethell37.pdf). Oxford: Centre for Brazilian Studies, 2003.

—. *Brazil: Empire and Republic, 1822–1930*. Cambridge: Cambridge UP, 1989.

—. "Britain and Latin America in Historical Perspective." *Britain and Latin America: a Changing Relationship*. Ed. Victor Bulmer-Thomas. Cambridge: Cambridge UP, 1989. 1–24.

—. *The Abolition of the Brazilian Slave Trade: Britain, Brazil, and the Slave Trade Question, 1807–1869*. Cambridge: Cambridge UP, 1970.

—, ed. *The Cambridge History of Latin America. Volume III From Independence to c. 1870*. Cambridge: Cambridge UP, 1985. 197–228.

Biggins, Alan, and Valerie Cooper. *Latin American and Caribbean Library Resources in the British Isles: A Directory*. London: Institute of Latin American Studies and Advisory Council on Latin American and Iberian Information Resources, 2002.

Bohls, Elizabeth A. *Women Travel Writers and the Language of Aesthetics, 1716-1818*. Cambridge and New York: Cambridge UP, 1995.

Burman, Laura. *Os cadernos de viagem de Maria Graham: a visao de um novo imperio*. Sao Paulo, 1987. Dissertacao (mestrado). Pontificia Universidade Catolica de Sao Paulo. Autorias secundárias: Fraga, Estefania Knotz Cangucu.

Campos, Raymundo Carlos Bandeira. *Viagem ao nascimento de uma nação: o diário de Maria Graham*. São Paulo: Editora no Catálogo de Editores, 2002. Literatura infanto-juvenil.

Carvalho, Alfredo de. *Bibliotheca Exotico-Brasileira*. Vol 2. Rio de Janeiro: Empreza Graphica Editora, 1930.

Cavaliero, Roderick. *The Independence of Brazil*. London: British Academic Press, 1993.

Costa, Emilia Viotti da. "Politics and Society in Brazilian Independence." *Latin American Revolutions 1808–1826, Old and New World Origins*. Ed. John Lynch. Norman: Oklahoma UP, 1994.

—. *The Brazilian Empire: Myths and Histories*. Chicago: U of Chicago P, 1985.

Eastlake, Lady Elizabeth [as Anon]. "Lady Travellers." *Quarterly Review* LXXVI (June-September 1845): 98-137.

Edwards, Esther. *La miradora*. Santiago de Chile: Editorial Andrés Bello, 2005.

Fausto, Boris and Arthur Brakel. *A Concise History of Brazil*. Cambridge UP, 1999.

Freyre, Gilberto. *Social Life in Brazil in the Middle of the Nineteenth Century*. M.A. Thesis, Political Science, Columbia University, 1922.

Gotch, Rosamund Brunel. *Maria, Lady Calcott: The Creator of "Little Arthur."* London: John Murray, 1937.
Graham, G. S. and R. A. Humphries. *The Navy and South America, 1807–1823: Correspondence of the Commanders in Chief on the South American Station.* The Navy Records Society, 1962.
Gray, Thomas. "Gresset." *Essays and Criticism.* Ed. Clark Sutherland Northup. Boston and London: D. C. Heath & Co, 1911.
Guenther, Louise H. *British Merchants in Nineteenth-Century Brazil: Business, Culture, and Identity, 1808–50.* Oxford: Centre for Brazilian Studies, 2004.
Karasch, Mary C. *Slave Life in Rio de Janeiro, 1808-1850.* Princeton: Princeton UP, 1987.
Knecht, Susanne. *Flora Tristan und Maria Graham Lady Callcott: die zweite Entdeckung Lateinamerikas.* Hamburg: Europäische Verlagsanstalt, 2004.
Knight, Alan. "Britain and Latin America." *The Oxford History of the British Empire: Volume III 'The Nineteenth Century.'* Ed. Andrew Porter. Associate Ed. Alaine Low. 5 vols. Oxford: Oxford UP, 1999. 122–145.
Lacombe, Américo Jacobina, ed. and trans. Maria Graham: *Diário de uma viagem ao Brasil e de uma estada nesse pais durante parte dos anos de 1821, 1822 e 1823.* 1956. São Paulo: Companhia Editora Nacional, 1990.
Leask, Nigel. *Curiosity and the Aesthetics of Travel Writing, 1770-1840: 'from an antique land.'* Oxford and New York: Oxford UP, 2002.
Liss, Peggy K. *Atlantic Empires: The Network of Trade and Revolution, 1713-1826.* Baltimore & London: The Johns Hopkins UP, 1983.
Macaulay, Neill. *Dom Pedro: The Struggle for Liberty in Brazil and Portugal, 1798–1834.* Durham, N.C.: Duke UP, 1986.
Manchester, Alan K. *British Preeminence in Brazil Its Rise and Decline: A Study in European Expansion.* New York: Octagon Books, 1972.
Marques, Joaõ Pedro. *The Sounds of Silence: Nineteenth-Century Portugal and the Abolition of the Slave Trade.* Trans. Richard Wall. New York and Oxford: Berghahn Books, 2006.
Marshall, Oliver. *English, Irish and Irish-American Pioneer Settlers in Nineteenth-Century Brazil.* Oxford: Centre for Brazilian Studies, 2005.
—, ed. *English-Speaking Communities in Latin America.* London and New York: MacMillan and St. Martin's, 2000.
Mavor, Elizabeth. *The Captain's Wife: the South American Journals of Maria Graham 1821–1823.* London: Weildenfeld and Nicolson, 1993.
Mellor, Anne K. *Mothers of the Nation: Women's Political Writing in England, 1780-1830.* Bloomington: Indiana UP, 2000.
Mills, Sara. *Gender and Colonial Space.* Manchester and New York: Manchester UP, 2005.
Moraes, Rubens. *Borba De. Bibliographia Brasiliana: Rare Books About Brazil Published from 1504 to 1900 and Works by Brazilian Authors of the*

Colonial Period. Revised edition, 2 vols. Los Angeles and Rio de Janeiro: UCLA Latin American Center and Livraria Kosmos Editôra, 1958, 1983.

Morgan, Susan. *Place Matters: Gendered Geography in Victorian Women's Travel Books About Southeast Asia*. New Brunswick, N.J.: Rutgers UP, 1996.

Nemoianu, Virgil. *The Triumph of Imperfection: The Silver Age of Sociocultural Moderation in Europe, 1815-1848*. Columbia: U of South Carolina P, 2006.

Oliveira Lima, Manoel de. *Relação dos Manuscriptos portuguezes e estrangeiros, de interesse para o Brazil, existents no Museu Britannico de Londres*. Rio de Janeiro: Instituto Historico e Geographico Brazileiro, 1903.

Pratt, Mary Louise. *Imperial Eyes: Travel Writing and Transculturation*. London and New York: Routledge, 1992.

Russell-Wood, A. J. R., ed. *From Colony to Nation: Essays on the Independence of Brazil*. Baltimore and London: Johns Hopkins UP, 1975.

—. "Recognitions and Precipitants of the Independence Movement in Portuguese America." *From Colony to Nation: Essays on the Independence of Brazil*. Baltimore: Johns Hopkins UP, 1975. 3–40.

Schubert, Guilherme. *200 anos: Imperatriz Leopoldina*. Rio de Janeiro: Instituto Histórico e Geográfico Brasileiro, 1997.

Schwarcz, Lilia Moritz. *The Emperor's Beard: Dom Pedro II and the Tropical Monarchy of Brazil*. Trans. John Gledson. 1998. New York: Farrar, Straus and Giroux, 2004.

Springer, Haskell. "The Captain's Wife at Sea." *Iron Men and Wooden Women: Gender and Seafaring in the Atlantic World, 1700–1920*. Ed. Margaret S. Creighton and Lisa Norling. Baltimore: Johns Hopkins UP, 1996. 92–118.

Tenenbaum, Barbara. *Encyclopedia of Latin American Culture and History*. 3 vols. New York: Simon & Schuster Macmillan, 1996.

Vale, Brian. *A Frigate of King George: Life and Duty on a British Man-of-War*. London and New York: I.B. Tauris Publishers, 2001.

—. *Independence or Death! British Sailors and Brazilian Independence, 1822–1825*. London and New York: I. B Tauris, 1996.

Valente, Waldemar. *Antecipação de Pernambuco no movimento da independência ; testemunho de uma inglesa*. Recife: MEC, 1974.

—. *Maria Graham, uma inglêsa em Pernambuco nos começos do século XIX*. Recife: [s.n.], 1957.

Viotti da Costa, Emilia. *The Brazilian Empire: Myths and Histories*. Chicago: U of Chicago P, 1985.

Webster, Alison. "The Contribution of the Scottish Enlightenment to the Abandonment of the Institution of Slavery." *The European Legacy* I.4 (2003): 481-489.

Index

Albuquerque, Aires de Saldanha e, 100
Alves, Fernando, 145
Andrada, Martim Francisco Ribeiro de, 111, 122, 175, 189, 239, 316
Andrada, Viceroy Gomes Freire de, 100
Anson, George, xix
Austen, Jane, 100, 121; *Sense and Sensibility*, 121

Bacon, Sir Francis, 24–25, 222; Essay XVIII, *Of Travel*, 24; *Essays, Civil and Moral*, 24
Bahia, Brazil, xxii, xxv, xxxii, xxxv, 45, 62, 94, 140-57 and 176-97 *passim*, 234, 240; Graham's visits to, 65-90 and 123-24; compared with Rio, 100, 102, 200
Barros, Pedro José da Costa, 239-40
Belzoni, Giovanni Battista, 21
Blackstone, William: *Commentaries on the Laws of England*, 25
Bolívar, Simón, 143, 147
Bonaparte, Napoleon, xxviii, xxxiv, 121, 147
Braganza, xxv, 149, 268, 273, 275, 287, 291– 94, 298, 300, 303, 332, 340-41
British Museum, xxvii
Brooke, Frances Moore, 25

Broughty Ferry, Scotland, xv
Burns, Robert, 98
Byron, Commodore John, xix

Cabral, Pedro Alvarez, 30, 174-75, 255, 259
Caldcleugh, Alexander, xxi, xl-xli, xliv
Callcott, Augustus Wall, xvi
Camões, Luís Vaz de, 44-45; *Os Lusíadas*, 44
Canning, George, xxxvi, xxxviii
Carlyle, Thomas, xlv; *The French Revolution*, xlv
Carvalho, Bernardo, 112, 155, 192, 282, 306
Charles II, King of Great Britain and Ireland, 153-54
Cherubini, Maria Luigi Carlo Zenobio Salvatore, 174; *Lodoiska*, 174
Cochrane, Katherine (Lady Cochrane), 152, 178-79, 199, 243, 245
Cochrane, Thomas, xx-xxi, xxxvi, lvi-lvii, 5-6, 8, 30, 53-4, 56, 65, 146-47, 149-50, 152, 153, 157, 176-84, 186-88, 197, 199, 215, 223, 233-41, 243, 245-46, 248, 289; *Autobiography of a Seaman*, xx; *Narrative of Services in the Liberation of Chili, Peru and Brazil*, xx

Coligny, Gaspard II de, 91, 265-66
College of St Andrews, xv
Combe, George, 82; *Lectures on Phrenology*, 82
Cook, Captain James, xix
Cooke, Edward, xviii; *A voyage to the South Sea and round the world*, xviii
Correia, Diogo Álvares, 69
Cortes (of Brazil), 238, 315
Cortes (of Portugal), xxix, xxxiv-xxxv, xxxvii, 7, 13-14, 19, 36, 45, 47, 65, 73, 85, 106-07, 109-12, 114, 119, 139, 142-43, 157, 163-64, 171, 189, 193, 304-10, 313, 317
Cortes (of Spain), 304
Costa, Dona Ana Francisca Macel da, 155
Cowper, William, 120-21; *The Task*, 121
Crosbie, Thomas Sackville, 149, 153, 180, 235, 237

Dampier, William, xviii; *A Voyage to New Holland*, xviii
De Lolme (or Delolme), Jean Louis, 25
DeFoe, Daniel, 90, 280; *Robinson Crusoe*, 90
Dolomieu, Déodat de, 134
Dragon Tree, 11, 17-18, 21
Dryden, John, 153, 226
Dundas, Ann Thompson, xii
Dundas, Sir David, 3-4,
Dundas, George, xii, 52, 346
Dutch East India Company, 103, 198
Dutens, Louis, 157

Eastlake, Charles, xvi
Eastlake, Elizabeth, xviii
Edgeworth, Maria, xxiv, lviii, 230, 232

Edinburgh, Scotland, xiii, xlv, lvi, lxiv, 3, 203
Edinburgh University, xiii, 203
England, ix, xi, xii-xiii, xiv, xvi-xvii, xx, xxii-xxiii, xxxviii, xxxi-xxxii, xxxvi-xxxviii, xli, liv, 3, 14, 25, 40, 46, 52, 66, 72, 75, 84, 89, 105-06, 108-09, 121-22, 125, 127, 134, 136, 144, 148, 152, 154-55, 157-58, 176, 181, 184, 193-94, 200, 222, 233, 245-46, 248-49, 269, 279, 284-88, 290, 292, 294, 296-97, 300, 308, 319-21, 326, 333, 343
Enlightenment, Scottish, xlv

Finlayson, Captain John, 85, 87
Flecknoe, Richard, xviii; *A Relation of Ten Years Travells in Europe, Asia, Affrique and America*, xviii
Francis I of Austria, 149
Franqui, Marquis, 17-18
Frederick II of Prussia, 103

Glennie, William, 47-48, 50, 55, 58, 88, 122, 128, 133, 138-39, 147, 149, 150, 153-54, 177, 325
Goldsmith, Oliver, 69; *The Traveller*, 69
Gordon, George, Lord Byron, xiv, 15, 25, 120
Gotch, Rosamond Brunel, xii-xiii
Graham, Maria, *Journal of a Residence in Chile*, xvi, xvii, 100, 346, 347; *Journal of a Residence in India*, xiv, xviii, 346; *Journal of a Voyage to Brazil, and Residence There*, xvi, 346; letter to John Murray, 19 Dec. 1824, lvii; letter to John Murray, 23 Sept. 1821, xxvii, xl; letter to

Index   355

John Murray, 28 April 1824, lvi; letter to John Murray, 31 May 1821, liii; letter to John Murray, 5 Aug. 1823, liv; letter to John Murray, 9 Dec. 1815, xv; letter to John Murray, Jan. 1824, lv; letter to John Murray, Sunday 22nd July, 1821, 138; letter to Lord Lynedoch, 1813, xv; *Little Arthur's History of England* (as Lady Maria Callcott), xvii, 347; *Three Months passed in the Mountains East of Rome, during the year 1819*, xvi

Graham, Robert, 12th laird of Fintry, xiii, 52

Graham, Thomas, xiii, xix, 52; *Eclipse*, xiv; H.M.S. *Hecate*, xiv; H.M.S. *Russell*, xiv, 52

Gray, Thomas, 30, 174

Gresset, Jean-Baptise, 174; Ode IX *Sur La Convalescence du Roi*, 174

Guenther, Louise, xxiii

Guimaies, Francisco Ignacio de Souza, 111

Hakluyt, Richard, 12

Hapsburg dynasty, 149

Hardy, Sir Thomas, 136, 149, 192, 194, 200, 222, 245, 333

Hawkins, Sir John, 134

Hogendorp, Dirk van, 103-04

Holbein, Hans the Younger, 104; *Dance of Death*, 104

Hoock-Demarle, Marie-Claire, xxiv

Hooker, William, xxvii

Hope, Dr. Thomas, xiii

Humboldt, Alexander von, x, xviii, 16-17, 21

Hume, David, xlv, xlvii, 79; *Political Discourses*, 79

Hyslop, James, 24

Iberian Peninsula, xxviii

Jacob, William, lv

Jesus, Maria Quitéria de, 145

João VI, xxviii, xxix, xxx, xxxiii, xxxiv, 97, 162, 165, 141, 144, 208, 225, 236, 286, 304

Jordaen, Manoel Rodrigues, 111

Kindersley, Jemima, xix, xxi; *Letters from the island of Teneriffe, Brazil, the Cape of Good Hope, and the East Indies*, xix

Koster, Henry, xxii-xliii, xliv, 330

Labatut, Pierre, 143, 147

Lacombe, Américo Jacobina, lx, lxii, 36, 100, 134, 136, 145, 147, 155, 225, 239; *Diário de uma viagem ao Brasil*, lx

Latude, Claire Josèphe Hippolyte Legris de (stage name Mademoiselle Clairon), 77

Lawes, Henry, 130; *Ayres and Dialogues for One, Two, and Three Voices*, 130

Leão, Brás Cameiro, 155

Leslie, Sir John, xiii, xix, xxviii, xxx, 336

Liverpool, England, xii, 81, 233

Lobo, Antonio Leite Pereira de Gama, 111, 316

London, England, viii, xvi, xviii, xvi, xix, xxxi, xlii, liii-liv, lxiv, 3, 122, 159, 228, 252, 286-87, 289-90, 292, 304, 334

Longman, Hurst, Rees, Orme, Brown and Green, liii

Lorrain, Claude, 42

Luccock, John, xxii, xxiii, xl, xli, xliv, 330

Lynedoch, Lord, xiv-xv

Maria da Gloria, Maria II of

Portugal, ix-x, l, lviii, 159, 191, 304, 336
Maria Leopoldina, Empress of Brazil, ix-x, li, 3, 149, 301, 311, 332, 340, 344
Maria Teresa of Naples, 149
Massena, Andre duc de Rivoli, 121
Mathison, Gilbert, xxi, xli-xliv; *Narrative of a visit to Brazil*, xliii; *Notices respecting Jamaica 1808–1809–1810*, xliii
Matos, Gustavo Adolfo de Melo, 155
Maurice, John (of Nassau), 33-35, 43, 272-73
Mawe, John, xxi, xl, xliv, xlviii, 330; *Travels in the Interior of Brazil*, xlviii
Melo, Dona Carlota Carvalho e, xxiv, 155, 192
Melo, Luís José de Carvalho e, xxiv, 155, 306
Miliard, Dona Maria Carlota, 36
Milton, John, 29-30, 91, 130, 155, 199, 206; *Comus*, 130, 155-56, 199; *Paradise Regained*, 30, 206
Monteverde, Don Antonio de, 17
More, Hannah, xlvi
Muller, Daniel Pedro, 111, 316
Murray, John II, xiv-xv, xxvii, xxxix-xl, liii-lvii, lxiv, 16, 138, 181

Necker, Anne-Louise Germaine, Baronne de Staël-Holstein, 15; *Corinne*, 15
New World, the, x, xvii, xxvii, xxxviii, lii, lviii, 7, 172, 206, 263

Oeyenhausen, John Carlos Augusto de, 111
Oliveira, Francisco de Paulo e, 111

Oxford, England, xii, lxiv
Paes de Andrade, Manuel de Carvalho, 53-56, 65
Paine, Thomas, 15
Paley, William, 25; *A View of Evidences of Christianity*, 25; *Principles of Moral and Political Philosophy*, 25
Parkinson, Sydney, xix
Patriota Funchalense, 14
Patronhe, Colonel, xxvii, 31-32, 35
Pedro I, Emperor of Brazil (Graham's Don Pedro), ix, xxv, xxxiv, xxxv, xxxvi, xxxvii, li, 106, 115, 125, 145, 149, 175, 217, 234, 236-237, 243, 301, 306, 307, 311, 332, 335, 351-52
Pereira, Duarte Coelho, 33, 109, 111, 260
Pfeiffer, Ida, xxi, 349; *Eine Frau fährt um die Welt*, xxi
Pinto, Miguel José de Oliveria, 111, 316
Playfair, John, xiii
Poussin, Nicolas, 42
Pratt, Mary Louise, xvii, xviii, xxiv, xlix
Prescott, Sir Henry, 123, 132
Purchas, Samuel, 12

Quarterly Review, xiv, lvi, lvii, 6, 319, 321-31
Quartini, Antonio Maria, 111

Rêgo, Luís do, 31, 36, 46, 47, 49, 51-53, 55, 58, 64, 323-25
Rio de Janeiro, Brazil, x, xxiii, xxv, xxix, xxxiv, xxxvi-xxxvii, xlvi, 5, 7, 53, 73, 85, Graham residing in Rio, 91-123 and 147-200 (passim), 124-126, 135, 139, 142, 146; Graham leaves Rio for England, 246; 257-58, 265,

268, 276, 278-79
Rogers, Samuel, 10, 28; *Pleasures of Memory*, Part II., 10; *The Voyage of Columbus*, 28
Rogers, Woodes, xviii; *A cruising voyage round the world*, xviii
Rosquellas, Pablo Mariano, 106
Rossini, Gioachino Antonio, 106, 308
Royal Botanic Gardens at Kew, xxvii

Sackville, Charles, 138
Scott, Sir Walter, lvi, 153; *Peveril of the Peak*, 153
Selkirk, Alexander, 90
Shakespeare, William, xlv, 15, 41, 62, 227, 241; *Macbeth*, xlv; *Measure for Measure*, 62
Silva, António Dinis da Cruz e, 14
Silva, Jose Bonifacio de Andrada e, 111, 120, 226, 287, 333
Slavery, see editors' introduction beginning xxviii, 7, 38, 40, 57, 72, 79, 81, 85, 87, 89, 93, 96, 99, 103, 108, 129, 130, 156, 158, 159, 199, 200, 205-06, 209, 211, 213-14, 217, 231, 254, 264, 275, 276, 300, 303, 320, 333, 335
Smith, Adam, xiii, xlii, xlv; *The Wealth of Nations*, xiii
Soult, Nicolas-Jean de Dieu, 121

Sousa, Pedro Antonio de Noronha Albuquerque e, 100
Southey, Robert, xix, lvi, 225, 253, 260, 263, 267-68, 270, 280, 322
Stewart, Dugald, xiii

Tavares, General Jorge de Avilez Zuzarte de Souza, 115
Teneriffe, xix, 15-19, 20, 23
Thomson, James, 3, 132, 137; *The Castle of Indolence*, 132; *The Seasons*, 137
Titian, Pieve di Cadore, 63
Travel writing, xvii-xviii, xxvi, xlix, lvii, 12
Treaty of Alliance and Friendship, xxx-xxxii
Treaty of Navigation and Commerce, xxx
Tuberculosis, xiii, xvi-xvii, xxiii, 332

Vittorio, Count Alfieri, 121
Voltaire (pen name of François-Marie Arouet), 75, 82; *Mahomet*, 75

Walter, Richard, xviii; *A voyage round the world in 1741-4*, xviii
Wilberforce, William, xxxii
Willoughby, Sir Hugh, 137
Wolfe, Major General James, 15

About the Authors

Jennifer Hayward, professor and chair of English at The College of Wooster, received her PhD in English Literature from Princeton University. In addition to essays on nineteenth century British travelers in Latin America, she is author of *Consuming Fictions: Active Audiences and Serial Fictions from Dickens to Soaps* (University Press of Kentucky, 1997) and editor of *Maria Graham's 1824 Journal of a Residence in Chile* (University Press of Virginia, 2003). Hayward's academic awards include an NEH Summer Stipend (2006), and BSA and Huntington Library/British Academy Fellowships (2006). Her current research focuses on nineteenth century Scottish travellers in the Americas, with particular focus on gendered perspectives and issues of national identity.

M. Soledad Caballero is an associate professor of English at Allegheny College and received her PhD from Tufts University. Her teaching and research interests include British Romanticism, travel writing, women's literature, and Latino/a contemporary literatures. She has published articles about women travel writers Maria Dundas Graham and Frances Calderón de la Barca in scholarly journals as well as edited collections. She has also published a short memoir piece about bilingualism. Currently she is working on a longer project about the aesthetics of monstrosity in the nineteenth century, in particular how ideas of the monstrous map onto foreign bodies or alienated bodies in the body politics of late eighteenth and early nineteenth century England.

Photograph of Jennifer Hayward by Sarah Zimmerman. Photograph of M. Soledad Caballero by M. Soledad Caballero. Used by permission.